Management: Functions and Modern Concepts

**The Scott, Foresman Series
in Management and Organizations**

Charles E. Summer
University of Washington
Advisory Editor

Boddewyn, Comparative Management and Marketing
Elbing, Behavioral Decisions in Organizations
Filley and House, Managerial Process and Organizational Behavior
*Turner, Filley, and House, Studies in Managerial Process and
Organizational Behavior*
*Hampton, Summer, and Webber, Organizational Behavior and the
Practice of Management, Revised*
*Jun and Storm, Tomorrow's Organizations: Challenges and
Strategies*
Perrow, Complex Organizations
Reeser, Management: Functions and Modern Concepts
Wadia, The Nature and Scope of Management
Young, Management: A Systems Analysis

MANAGEMENT
FUNCTIONS AND MODERN CONCEPTS

Clayton Reeser
University of Hawaii

Scott, Foresman and Company
Glenview, Illinois   Brighton, England

Library of Congress Catalog Card No. 72–95750
ISBN: 0–673–07681–4

Regional offices of Scott, Foresman and Company are located in
Dallas, Texas; Glenview, Illinois; Oakland, New Jersey; Palo Alto, California;
Tucker, Georgia; and Brighton, England.

CONTENTS

Preface   xix

WHAT IS MANAGEMENT?   1

Technical Vs. Managerial · Commonality of
Managerial Functions · Purpose and Plan of the Book ·
Discussion Questions

SOME IMPORTANT CONTRIBUTIONS
TO MANAGEMENT THEORY   5

1. **Max Weber and Bureaucracy   6**
   Central Principles · Stipulated Rules · Hierarchy of
   Authority · Accountability · Written Documents ·
   Professional Managers · Significance of the Bureaucratic
   Model · Discussion Questions

2. **Frederick Taylor and Scientific Management   10**
   Job Design · Worker Selection and Training · Worker
   Motivation · Separation of Planning From Performance ·
   Immediate Effects · Lasting Effects · Discussion Questions

3. **Henri Fayol and Management Principles   15**
   Fayol's Definition of Management · Fayol's Management
   Principles · The Importance of Fayol's Contributions ·
   Discussion Questions

4. **The Hawthorne Studies and Human Relations   19**
   Original Objectives · Unforeseen Results · Revised
   Objectives · Explanation · Additional Findings ·
   Subsequent Effects · Discussion Questions

5. **Chester Barnard, Transitionalist**   23
    Barnard's Role As a Transitionalist · Organization:
    A Cooperative System · Inducement-Contribution Balance ·
    The Informal Organization · Strategic Factors · Acceptance
    Theory of Authority · Discussion Questions

6. **The Behavioral Sciences and Management**   26
    Change in Thinking · Basic Assumptions · Organization
    Development: The Application of Behavioral Theories ·
    The Performance of Organization Development Changes ·
    Discussion Questions

7. **Management and Mathematics**   31
    Optimization · Satisficing Vs. Optimizing · Modeling ·
    Example · Discussion Questions

8. **Systems Management**   35
    A Different Way of Thinking · The Black Box · Feedback ·
    People Problems · The Future of Systems Management ·
    Discussion Questions

Summary   38

Selected Bibliography   40

PLANNING   41

9. **Setting Objectives**   42
    Spelling Out Primary Objectives · Expressing Objectives in
    Numerical Terms · Specifying Profit Goals · Setting
    Objectives in Descending Order · Communicating Objectives ·
    The Case of the Many-Headed Monster ·
    Discussion Questions

10. **Forecasting Sales**   49
    Projecting the Past · Refining Forecasts With Judgment ·
    Making Grass-Roots Adjustments · Using Leading Economic
    Indicators · Predicting Changes in the Money Supply ·
    Using Econometric Models · Ensuring Reliability of
    Long-Range Forecasts · *The Case of the Unpredicted
    Variable* · Discussion Questions

11. Major Plans 56
From Sales Forecast to Sales Plan · Production Plan ·
Financial Plan · *The Case of the Impending Disaster* ·
Discussion Questions

12. Supporting Plans 64
Organization Plan · Manpower Plan · Management
Development Plan · Capital Investment Plan · Research and
Development Plan · Discussion Questions

13. Long-Term and Short-Term Plans 68
Priority · Current Practice · Length of Long-Term Plans ·
Alternate Actions · General Nature of Long-Term Plans ·
Short-Term Plans · *The Case of the Markets That Will
Fade Away* · Discussion Questions

14. Standing Plans and Single-Purpose Plans 75
Policies · Procedures · Rules · Single-Purpose Plans ·
The Case of the Newborn SPM · Discussion Questions

15. Human Factors in Planning 81
Differences in Perception · Communication Channels ·
Semantics · Conflicting Goals · Countering the Effect of
Goal Conflict · *The Case of the Clogged Filter* ·
Discussion Questions

16. Analytical Techniques for Planning 88
Evaluating and Choosing Alternatives · Decision Factors ·
Critical-Path Scheduling · Linear Programming · Simulation ·
Probability Decision Theory · Discussion Questions

Summary 95

Selected Bibliography 97

ORGANIZING 99

17. Determining Activities 100
Up or Down · One Pitfall · Central and Supporting
Activities · Find Out What Support Is Wanted · A Better
Way · *The Case of the Misguided Organization Study* ·
Discussion Questions

18. **Conventional Departmentation**   107
     Why Conventional? · Functional Organization · Product
     Organization · Geographical Organization · Organization of
     Supporting Activities · *The Case of the Function That
     Wouldn't Fit* · Discussion Questions

19. **Project Organization**   116
     How It Works · Project Personnel · Similarities With Other
     Organization Forms · Differences From Other
     Organization Forms · Advantages · Unique Problems ·
     Authority for the Project · Effect on People · Challenge to
     Managers · Criteria for Its Application · *The Case of the
     Mexican Crazy Quilt* · Discussion Questions

20. **Spans of Control Vs. Departmental Levels**   126
     No Arbitrary Number · Factors Affecting a Manager's
     Capacity · Arguments for a Wide Span of Control · *The Case
     of Piggyback Management* · Discussion Questions

21. **Vertical Relationships**   132
     What Is Authority? · Source of Authority · Responsibility for
     Using Authority · Managers' Roles in the Vertical Structure ·
     The Location of Decision Making · Discussion Questions

22. **Decentralization Vs. Centralization**   136
     Factors Involved in Decentralization · How Far to
     Decentralize? · Advantages of Decentralization ·
     The Present Trend · *The Case of the Chicken With Its
     Head Cut Off* · Discussion Questions

23. **Advisory Relationships**   143
     The Line-Staff Concept · Reasons for Advisory Relationships ·
     Change in Role—Advisory to Prescriptive · Adverse Impact
     on Authority · Reactions to Advisory Relationships ·
     The Case of the Subtle Takeover · Discussion Questions

24. **Service Relationships**   150
     Reasons for Service Departments · Characteristics of
     Service Relationships · Resolution of Problems ·
     Discussion Questions

25. Other Lateral Relationships 154
The Significance of Lateral Relationships ·
Functional-Sequence Relationships · Evaluative
Relationships · Plural Relationships · Nonvertical,
Unequal-Status Relationships · Discussion Questions

26. The Informal Organization 159
Distinguishing Features · Need Deprivation in the
Formal Organization · Roots of Informal Groups · Inner
Workings of Informal Groups · Grapevine ·
Discussion Questions

27. Power Politics in Organizations 163
Machiavelli's Prescription · Will for Power · Definitions ·
Steps in Organizational Politics · Realistic Appraisal ·
Discussion Questions

28. Organizational Conflict 167
The Development of Conflict · Likely Locations for Conflict ·
Disruptive Effects of Conflict · Reduction of Destructive
Conflict · Discussion Questions

29. The Individual in the Formal Organization 171
Indifference to Efficiency · Frustrations · Effect of the
Goal Divergence · *The Case of the Encroaching Rut* ·
Discussion Questions

30. Coordination 177
What Coordination Is · Achieving Coordination ·
Accomplishing Through People · Discussion Questions

Summary 181

Selected Bibliography 184

STAFFING 185

31. Job Design 187
Job and Position · The Composition of a Job · The Job
Designer · Job Descriptions and Specifications · *The Case of
Picking the Right Words* · Discussion Questions

32. Job Evaluation   196
Evaluation of Top-Level Jobs · Purpose and Kinds of
Job Evaluation Systems · Problems in Job Evaluation ·
The Case of the Heated Furnace Repairmen ·
Discussion Questions

33. Financial Compensation   204
Basis for Compensation · Using a Scatter Diagram ·
Factors That Necessitate Adjustments · Other Forms of
Financial Compensation · Discussion Questions

34. Indirect Compensation   208
Importance of Fringe Benefits · Classifications of Fringe
Benefits · Returns to the Company · Control of Fringe
Benefits · Discussion Questions

35. Manpower Planning   211
Prerequisite: Detailed Appraisal · Looking Into the Future ·
At What Level to Hire? · Plan for Change · Integrate With
Other Plans · *The Case of the Defensive Defense Contractor
and the Pitiful Pawn* · Discussion Questions

36. Recruitment of New Personnel   218
A Centralized Service · Sources of Applicants ·
Discussion Questions

37. Selection of New Personnel   222
Validity of the Selection Process · Preliminary Screening ·
Subsequent Screening · Interviewing Methods · Interviewing
Mistakes and Pitfalls · Other Techniques; Checking
References · *The Case of the Un-Merry Widow* · Discussion
Questions

38. Psychological Testing   231
Supplemental Value · Characteristics Measured · Problems
in the Use of Tests · Attitudes Toward Tests · Requirements
of the Testing Program · Discussion Questions

39. Employee Training   235
Getting Started · Prerequisite: Accomplishment Goals ·
Training Methods · As Essential Factor · Retraining ·
Discussion Questions

40. Management Development   239
Mistaken Belief · Development Vs. Training ·
Development Opportunities · Need for Criteria · *The Case
of Four Roads to the Top* · Discussion Questions

41. Performance Appraisal   246
Appraisal Techniques · Use of Performance Appraisals ·
Unsatisfactory Results · Methods Under Development ·
Discussion Questions

42. Managing Change of Status   251
Promotions · Demotions · Terminations · Lateral Changes ·
The Case of the Out-Moded Vice-President ·
Discussion Questions

43. Assurance of Justice   258
Meanings of Justice · Distributive Justice · Problems in
the Administration of Justice · Corrective Justice ·
Discussion Questions

Summary   262

Selected Bibliography   265

DIRECTING   267

44. Leadership   269
Charismatic Leadership · Natural Leaders · Trait Theory of
Leadership · Influence on Subordinates · Leadership
As an Acquired Ability · Assumptions About Human
Nature · *The Case of the Loyalty-Loving Ex-Colonel* ·
Discussion Questions

45. Leadership Styles   277
Meaning of the Descriptive Terms · Usefulness of the Models ·
Achieving a Balance · *The Case of the Leopard That
Couldn't Change Its Spots* · Discussion Questions

46. Management by Objectives   284
Advantages of MBO · Preparation for MBO · Results of
MBO · Tools for Appraisal · *The Case of Deciding Which
One Was Best* · Discussion Questions

47. Motivation Through Incentives   291
Definitions · Recognition · Money · Promotion ·
Competition · Security · Participation · Motivation by
Example · Discussion Questions

48. Human Needs   296
Hierarchical Arrangement of Needs · Application of Need
Theory · *The Case of Why Some Engineers May Join Unions* ·
Discussion Questions

49. Motivation Through Need for Achievement   303
Characteristics of n Ach People · How to Identify n Ach
People · What Makes an n Ach Person? · How to Train
People to Be n Ach Types · Is n Ach Training Valid? ·
Discussion Questions

50. The Work Group As a Motivating Force   307
Norms of Group Behavior · Group Cohesiveness ·
Behavior in a Cohesive Group · Levels of Cohesiveness ·
The Scanlon Plan · *The Case of the Invisible Hand* ·
Discussion Questions

51. Motivation Through Job Satisfaction   315
Definitions and Criteria for Measurement · Findings ·
Dual Emphases of Recent Research · Discussion Questions

52. Nonrational Influences on Motivation   318
Animal Ancestry · Ethical Teachings · Freudian Psychology ·
The Case of the Contrary Conscience · Discussion Questions

53. The Communication Process   323
The Communication Model · The Manager As Sender ·
Subordinates' Messages · Avoiding the Authority Chain ·
Additional Factors · Discussion Questions

54. Accomplishing Change   331
The Perceptor of Change Signals · Alternative Methods for
Inducing Change · Time to Accomplish Change ·
Discussion Questions

55. Sensitivity Training   336
The Sensitivity Concept · Application to the Business

Organization · Conduct of a Training Program ·
Effectiveness of the Technique · Negative Factors ·
Discussion Questions

56. Directing Engineering and Scientific Personnel   341
Uniqueness of Professional Employees · Their Preferences ·
What Can Be Done · Current Policies · Argument for
Change · Discussion Questions

Summary   345

Selected Bibliography   348

CONTROLLING   351

57. The General Nature of Control   352
Description of the Controlling Function · Standards of
Measurement · Bases for Constructing Standards ·
Comparison of Plans and Events · Corrective Action ·
The Case of the Slippery Siding Salesman ·
Discussion Questions

58. Budgetary Financial Control   362
An Example of the Budgeting Process · Investigating
Deviations · Taking Corrective Action · Further Tracking ·
What Comes Next? · Discussion Questions

59. Nonbudgetary Financial Control   370
Balance Sheet Analysis · Breakeven Analysis · Capital
Investment Evaluation · *The Case of the Salesman Who
Did His Homework* · Discussion Questions

60. Production Control   382
Aggregate Control · Differences in Demand · Costs of
Alternative Actions · Optimal Response Rate · Intermediate
Level of Control · Control at the Basic Performance Level ·
Gantt Charts · Discussion Questions

61. Inventory Control   389
Inventory Responsibility · A B C Analysis · Inventory
Control Systems · Discussion Questions

62. Statistical Quality Control   396
Alternatives for Quality Control · Terms Used in Statistical
Quality Control · Acceptance Sampling · Discussion
Questions

63. Marketing Control   401
Control of the Product Line · Control of Selling Effort per
Customer · Control of Marketing Territories · Control of
Advertising Effort · *The Case of the Greedy Tire Customer* ·
Discussion Questions

64. Control of Research and Development   411
The Nature and Extent of R & D · Budgeting the R & D
Program · Staffing the R & D Effort · R & D Facilities ·
Specific Control Techniques · *The Case of Taking Too Big a
Bite* · Discussion Questions

65. The Systems Approach to Control   420
Control Characteristics · The Feedback Loop ·
Problems in a Feedback Loop · *The Case of the Double
Standards* · Discussion Questions

66. Behavioral Criticism of Control Systems   428
Natural Resistance to Control · Inhibitive Standards ·
Problems Associated With Measurement · Damaging
Evaluations · Ineffective Adjustments · Multiplicity of
Controls · Perceived Illegitimacy of Control Agents ·
The Case of the Controlled Controller · Discussion Questions

Summary   438

Selected Bibliography   441

SIGNIFICANT FACTORS IN THE
FUTURE OF MANAGEMENT   443

67. The Impact of the Computer   444
Characteristics of the Computer · Applications of the
Computer · Effect of Automation on Employment and
Job Content · Human Consequences · Implications for
Organizing and Decision Making · *The Case of the Elusive
Cost Savings* · Discussion Questions

68. Corporate Bigness and Social Responsibility 459
The Power of Corporate Managers · Means for Controlling
Business Power · The Social Responsibility Concept ·
A Conflicting Viewpoint · Evaluating the Managerial Role ·
The Case of Who Gets the Slice of Pie · Discussion Questions

Summary 474

Selected Bibliography 475

Appendix A. Critical-Path Scheduling 479

Appendix B. Linear Programming 487

Appendix C. Monte Carlo Simulation 493

Appendix D. Probability Decision Theory 498

Glossary 502

Name Index 511

Subject Index 513

LIST OF CASES

The Many-Headed Monster   45
The Unpredicted Variable   52
The Impending Disaster   59
The Markets That Will Fade Away   71
The Newborn SPM   78
The Clogged Filter   84
The Misguided Organization Study   103
The Function That Wouldn't Fit   112
The Mexican Crazy Quilt   122
Piggyback Management   129
The Chicken With Its Head Cut Off   139
The Subtle Takeover   146
The Encroaching Rut   174
Picking the Right Words   191
The Heated Furnace Repairmen   200
The Defensive Defense Contractor and the Pitiful Pawn   214
The Un-Merry Widow   227
Four Roads to the Top   242
The Outmoded Vice-President   255
The Loyalty-Loving Ex-Colonel   273
The Leopard That Couldn't Change Its Spots   280
Deciding Which One Was Best   287
Why Some Engineers May Join Unions   299
The Invisible Hand   311
The Contrary Conscience   320
The Slippery Siding Salesman   358
The Salesman Who Did His Homework   377
The Greedy Tire Customer   407
Taking Too Big a Bite   416
The Double Standards   425
The Controlled Controller   434
The Elusive Cost Savings   455
Who Gets the Slice of Pie   470

LIST OF FIGURES AND TABLES

1–1. The Hierarchy of Authority in an Organization   8

16–1. A Precedence Diagram for Changing a Tire   89

17–1. Organization Chart of a City Maintenance Department   104

18–1. Functional Organization at the Primary Level   108

18–2. Product Organization at the Primary Level; Functional Organization at the Secondary Level   109

18–3. Geographical Organization at the Primary Level; Functional Organization at the Secondary Level   110

18–4. Organization Chart of a Hypothetical Company   115

19–1. Product Organization at the Primary Level; Functional Organization at the Secondary Level; Project Organization in a Matrix Relationship to Functional Organizations   118

33–1. Wage/Points Scatter Diagram   205

53–1. The Communication Process   323

54–1. Resistance to Change Vs. Time to Accomplish Change   334

58–1. Operating Statement   363

58–2. Direct Labor Analysis   364

58–3. Direct Materials Analysis   365

58–4. Overhead Analysis   365

58–5. Sales Analysis   366

59–1. Balance Sheet   371

59–2. Ratio Analysis   371

59–3. The Breakeven Point   373

59–4. Discounted Rate of Return   375

60–1. Forecast Demand and Aggregate Production Plan   383

60–2. Actual Demand and Alternative Production Responses   383

60–3. Counter Costs Affected by Response Rate   385

60–4. Gantt Chart—Part Process Flow   387

61–1. A B C Inventory Categories   390

61–2. Basic Concept of the Fixed-Order Quantity System   392

61–3. The Economic Order Quantity   393

62–1. Operating Characteristic Curve   398

62–2. Average Outgoing Quality   399

63–1. Typical Life Cycle of a Successful Product   402

64–1. R & D Project Costs Vs. Accomplishment   415

65–1. The Characteristics of a Control System   421

65–2. Control Via a Feedback Loop   422

A–1. The Sequence of Events and Estimated Times to Build a House   479

A–2. The Network of Events to Build a House, in Application of Critical-Path Scheduling   480

A–3. The Development of Earliest Starts and Earliest Finishes   482

A–4. The Development of Latest Starts and Latest Finishes   483

A–5. Total Slack and Free Slack in Each Event   484

A–6. The Critical Path Through the Network of Events to Build a House   485

B–1. First Simplex Table, in Application of Linear Programming   489

B–2. Second Simplex Table   490

B–3. Third Simplex Table   492

C–1. Cumulative Frequency Distribution, Lives of Novelty Items   494

C–2. Calculating Lives of Novelty Items, in Application of Monte Carlo Simulation   495

C–3. Simulated Combined Lives of Ten Original Novelty Items and Their Replacements   496

D–1. A Payoff Matrix of Various Strategy/State of Nature Combinations, in Application of Probability Decision Theory   500

PREFACE

The purpose of this book is to summarize and integrate the central concepts of management. It has been designed especially for students in college-level schools which offer one general course in management; but it is also suitable for use in survey courses for students who did not major in business as undergraduates and who are commencing a graduate program in business administration; and it can be used in supervisory training programs as well.

Within each of the major parts of the book, the individual sections are relatively short and self-contained, so as to ensure a ready grasp of essential concepts in a given topic area. At the same time, the pattern of organization and system of cross-referencing link the sections and provide the reader with a sense of continuity.

Questions to stimulate reflection and discussion follow each section. To supplement the insights of instructors and students, and also to provide explanatory data, answers to these questions are contained in the Instructor's Guide and Test Items, available for use with this book.

Many short cases are interspersed throughout the text, and their purpose is twofold. First, they are designed to highlight the salient points under discussion, and second, to provide an introduction to actual business situations and human behavior.

To improve readability, footnotes have been omitted. However, the bibliographies serve both to credit the sources of my information and to suggest references for those students and instructors who are interested in further reading.

I wish to acknowledge the help that many friends have given me during the writing of this book, and specifically to mention Professors Harold Koontz, University of California, Los Angeles; John Cox, California State University at Sacramento; and Robert Meier and Harry Knudson, University of Washington. I also am grateful to

Dale Gibson, Rochester Institute of Technology; and Burl Worley, Allan Hancock College.

Special credit is due Margaret Martin of Scott, Foresman for a really outstanding job of editing and pushing the book through print production. I also wish to thank Virginia Scheuler, at the University of Nevada, who typed the first draft. Finally, my wife, Eloise, certainly deserves credit for putting up with my disposition at home while I was writing the book.

Clayton Reeser

WHAT IS MANAGEMENT?

Imagine a situation where the physical and human resources necessary to get something done are available. There are money to pay the bills (capital), a place to work (plant), tools (equipment), and raw materials; and there are people to do the work—engineers, accountants, machinists, assemblers, and salesmen. Yet nothing will get done until a third element enters—managers. Managers are the people who

- set objectives for using the available resources.
- formulate plans for achieving these objectives.
- identify the activities to be performed.
- organize the activities into groups (departments).
- define the tasks to be done.
- group the tasks into jobs.
- establish compensation levels for the jobs.
- staff the jobs with people.
- initiate work activities.
- supply incentives to stimulate productivity.
- set up controls to measure the achievement of objectives.
- take remedial action if the objectives are not being met.

Thus, the purpose of managers is to coordinate the use of resources to some deliberate end, even though the relationship of managers to physical resources is indirect. Other people are the instruments through which managers utilize capital, materials, plant, and equipment. Therefore, management is the utilization of physical and human resources through coordinative efforts, and it is accomplished by performing the functions of *planning, organizing, staffing, directing, and controlling.*

Technical Vs. Managerial

The term *technical* is used here merely in the sense of *nonmanagerial;* it is not restricted to scientific or engineering work. Technical functions are the ones performed by people acting individually rather than as coordinators of the efforts of other people. These technical functions are thus specific to a task, such as selling, accounting, or data analysis. And they are related to the end product or service of the firm where they are performed, such as automobiles or soap (manufactured products), a title search in a bank's escrow department, or laboratory work in a hospital.

The work that most employed people do is entirely technical. And most people who manage do technical work in addition to managing. But a person is a manager only when he or she is performing a managerial function; a vice-president of engineering is not managing when solving a heat-transfer problem; an army colonel is not managing when teaching a course in military logistics, and a head nurse is not managing when taking a patient's temperature.

Commonality of Managerial Functions

At all levels within all kinds of organizations, people who act as managers perform the same functions—that is, they plan, organize, staff, direct, and control. Thus, business managers, military officers, church leaders, government administrators, and so on, all do the same managerial things—as do the shop foreman, the wage and salary administrator, and the director of marketing. Each plans, organizes, staffs, directs, and controls when acting as a manager.

The differences are in the technical functions they do, the time they spend doing them (which decreases as they move up the management ladder), and the generality of the management goals they have (which increase as they move up the management ladder). Thus, although planning is done at each level, the foreman's plans are very detailed and are derived from a hierarchy of preceding plans. The wage and salary administrator's plans, although of a specialized nature, implement basic organization policies. The director of marketing's plans reflect broad policy, and serve as a basis for many derivative plans. The same is true of the other management functions; they are performed at each managerial level, but to a varying degree and for purposes that are greater in importance the higher the level.

Purpose and Plan of the Book

The purpose of this book is to summarize modern management functions and concepts. The concepts have been expressed before in written form, but the intent here is to integrate them. Although management functions are the same in all kinds of organizations, this book is written from the standpoint of business organizations. It is easy enough to visualize the application of management concepts to other social institutions.

Modern management theory has evolved from the contributions of practicing managers and management theorists in diverse disciplines, including economics, mathematics, psychology, sociology, and anthropology. This book begins by summarizing some of the most important contributions. The body of the book analyzes the functions that managers perform. In the discussions of each of the functions, ideas from various approaches to management theory are brought to bear. The book concludes with a discussion of two central problems which will be of major concern to business managers of the future: the computer, and big business in relation to society.

Discussion Questions

1. What would happen in a situation where there were adequate physical resources and people with skills, but no managers? Assume that five salesmen have pooled their savings, found a marketable product, and would like to start a business.
2. Are there any management functions that you think should be added to the array of planning, organizing, staffing, directing, and controlling? If so, why?
3. Consider a company president whose activities on a particular day include briefing an agency's representative on the objectives of an advertising program, conducting a meeting attended by immediate subordinates, interviewing a prospective administrative assistant, phoning the president of another company to ask for an important order, presenting a new bonus system to the

firm's salesmen, and investigating why a department's budget is overrun. During what part of this time is he not performing managerial functions?

4. If managers of all kinds of organizations perform the same functions, does this mean that a Navy harbormaster could effectively manage a large retail store, or that an electronics firm's production manager could direct a social work agency, or that the mayor of a medium-size city could manage a military weapons system?

5. Does the experience gained in performing a managerial function, such as planning, at a lower organizational level qualify a manager to move up to performing the function at a higher level? For example, will a shop foreman's planning experience qualify him to do the planning required by a manufacturing manager?

SOME IMPORTANT CONTRIBUTIONS TO MANAGEMENT THEORY

What is now formally known about management has accumulated from the findings and concepts of a host of contributors. However, many potentially valuable contributions have no doubt been lost because they were not written down by the practicing managers who conceived ideas and tested them through use. To this extent, formal knowledge of management lags behind working knowledge.

The reverse is also true. That is, much useful insight into effective management practice has been developed and written down by thinkers and researchers, but these findings are not known by many practicing managers, or are misunderstood and misapplied by them, or are simply rejected by them. Although many past ideas about management have been misinterpreted, have become partially discredited, or now seem incomplete in the light of newer discoveries, much that is still valid can be gained from an understanding of what past thinkers have contributed to the development of management theory.

The sections that follow summarize some of the important and influential contributions that have been made to management theory since the turn of the century.

1. Max Weber and Bureaucracy

In the 1890's a German sociologist named Max Weber prescribed a system for organization which he called *bureaucracy*. In his description, Weber in effect ushered in the era of the professional manager and bade farewell to the age of *patrimony,* which, liberally interpreted, means owner-dominated management. The bureaucratic model is an impersonal, rational system for enabling professional managers to efficiently concentrate and control the human resources of an organization.

Although the concept of bureaucracy is now commonly associated with Weber, it is certain that it did not originate with him. Long before Weber's time, military organizations, churches, and local governments were structured along the lines that he proposed. Moreover, business organizations in the United States were taking on bureaucratic characteristics while Weber's writings were still waiting for translation into English. It may be that bureaucracy naturally evolves when efficiency in organization is the end objective. But Weber is credited with the model, and his description of its typical operation is the standard one.

Central Principles

Weber stated that a bureaucratic organization is characterized by the conduct of business in accord with stipulated rules, a hierarchy of authority levels, the accountability of managers at each authority level for the use of resources committed to them, and the conduct of business on the basis of written documents. To anyone with experience in modern organizations—either business, government, or military—these principles have a familiar ring.

Stipulated Rules

Rules, which may be broadened to include policies and procedures, have as their primary purpose reducing the frequency of decision making. In a bureaucracy, rules are formulated to cover every occasion. When a situation arises requiring action, it is only necessary to consult the rule applying to that type of situation to discover that the appropriate action is spelled out. (This is popularly known as "going by the book.") Weber expanded the stipulated-rules principle to include the duties of each managerial position, specifying how much authority is assigned to each position and placing specific restrictions on the personal discretion permitted a manager. Thus, the objective in a bureaucracy is to assure predictable conformity of action throughout the organization.

Hierarchy of Authority

Weber viewed the authority structure of a bureaucratic organization as an inverted pyramid. Positions at the top of the structure have extensive authority, even though the content of the assignments would be specific and limited. In Weber's terms, the top people are responsible for supervision. Positions lower in the structure have less authority. The lowest levels have only the right of appeal. In terms of the number of positions at the various organizational levels, the shape of the structure is a conventional pyramid. Thus, the effect of bureaucracy is a concentration of authority in a relatively few positions. (These pyramidal concepts are illustrated in Figure 1-1.)

Accountability

Managers in a bureaucracy do not own the resources they employ. However, they are still held accountable for the prudent use of them. Weber emphasized the necessity for professional managers to strictly separate official business from their private affairs, and official revenue from their private income. In modern terms it would be said that managers should act as trustees for the property rights of the owners, and scrupulously avoid conflicts between the organization's interests and their personal interests.

Written Documents

Weber urged that in a bureaucracy all business should be conducted on the basis of written documents, and that each transaction should be recorded for reference. This principle is a control device to assure that the stipulated rules are followed and to restrain individuals from acting beyond their specified authority.

Extent of authority   Number of positions

Figure 1–1. The Hierarchy of Authority in an Organization.

Professional Managers

Weber characterized professional managers as appointed to their position, rather than acquiring it through property rights. Managers carry out their duties by obedience to impersonal rules. Their appointments to the jobs and tenure depend on their technical qualifications. Their jobs are their full-time occupations. They have no right to the revenues of the organization, but are compensated for their work by a salary and by the prospects of advancement. For the most part, this is an accurate portrayal of most business managers in the United States today.

Significance of the Bureaucratic Model

The extent to which bureaucratic principles permeate all organizations makes the model perhaps the most significant of management theories. This does not mean that it is an ideal prescription. Its keynote is the depersonalization of work tasks at every organizational level. Weber used the term *specialized cogs* to describe individuals in a bureaucratic system. The model does not accommodate human differences.

Bureaucracy is a rational response to the quest for systematic efficiency. Because of the increasing importance of the computer and the compatibility of the computer with impersonal systems, today there appears to be a trend toward an expansion of bureaucracy.

Discussion Questions

1. Most people have at some time been frustrated by what they call the "red tape" in organizations. How is "red tape" associated with bureaucracy?
2. The bureaucratic model insists on assignments of authority being "specific." What does this mean?
3. Some critics have observed that modern organizations have literally become "paper mills." How can this condition be traced to Weber?
4. To Weber's contemporaries, what was significant about his description of the characteristics of the professional manager?
5. What evidences of bureaucracy have you observed in organizations with which you have been associated? Do you perceive any diminishing of bureaucratic tendencies?

2. Frederick Taylor and Scientific Management

The term *scientific management* has come to be associated more with the mechanics its practitioners employed (time and motion study, for example) than with the concept itself. It was really a philosophy dedicated to improving efficiency through the elimination of wasted effort. Its ideal was a constant growth in wealth achieved through productivity, a wealth which was to be shared by workers and management and reflected by continual rises in the nation's prosperity.

Many important names are connected with the scientific management movement, including those of Henry Gantt, Frank and Lillian Gilbreth, and Harrington Emerson. The name that now epitomizes scientific management, however, is that of Frederick W. Taylor. It is even common to speak of "Taylorism" rather than of "scientific management."

Taylor was a steel-company engineer who had also worked as a trade craftsman and later became a widely known industrial consultant. He was convinced that workers perceived available work to be of a fixed amount (the "ball of work" concept), and that they believed it to be in their best interests to perform their tasks slowly in order to make the work last. His thinking led him to conceive an ideal condition where workers and management would cooperate to increase productivity, with both sides sharing the resulting growth in wealth. Thus, the inhibiting notion of "the ball of work" would be dispelled, and workers would be so satisfied with the larger absolute value of their share that the traditional labor-management conflicts would disappear.

Taylor's prescription for bringing about increased productivity was expressed in four principles which are fundamental to scientific management. These principles relate to job design, worker selection and training, worker motivation, and the separation of planning from performing.

Job Design

Until Taylor's time (about 1910), not much thought was given by managers to how work should be done. Work practices were passed down through generations of workers in the respective trades, and managers simply assumed that machinists, foundrymen, and shoe-makers, for example, possessed the traditional skills that would enable them to produce an acceptable day's work. To Taylor, this approach was wrong. He believed that there was "one best way" to do any job, and that the primary responsibility of managers was to find it. The mass of knowledge related to every kind of work should be accumulated, studied, and recorded; superfluous elements should be discarded; then each job should be carefully redesigned via stopwatch time-and-motion study, among other techniques, to the point that no further improvements were possible. The ultimate method would be established as the standard way for performing the job.

Worker Selection and Training

By this principle of Taylor's, the physical and mental attributes required to satisfactorily perform each job should be identified, and then workers should be selected for jobs on the basis of their possessing these qualities. (Before this principle was spelled out, no deliberate attention had been given to matching workers with jobs.) After it is assured that the workers selected for jobs have the potential for performing them, they should be carefully trained to do the work by the standardized method. The methods for doing each job should be specific enough so that each sequential movement can be learned and consistently followed.

Worker Motivation

Taylor said that once a standard method was established for doing each job and workers trained in following it, management was responsible for making the workers conform to the standards. He quite bluntly asserted that workers who would not follow the instructions should be removed from the job. Today this is called "motivation by negative incentive": workers either do things the way they are told or they are fired (Section 47). On the opposite side, Taylor urged the offering of "plums" to workers who would follow the standard methods. One way he suggested was to offer financial incentives. Minimum production rates should be established for doing every job according to the standard, and a base wage set for these rates. When workers followed the standard method and produced above the minimum rates, their wages should be increased to yield shares of greater productivity.

Taylor is now identified solely with the promising of more money to workers as a way of motivating them to higher productivity. However, money was only one of the motivating "plums" that he suggested. Other motivators included better, more kindly treatment, more consideration for workers' wishes, and an opportunity for them to express their desires freely.

Separation of Planning From Performance

Taylor introduced the notion that extensive preparation should precede actual work, and that management was responsible for such planning. Thus, organizing work, getting it started, and assessing its accomplishment should be removed from the workers and set up as a separate activity. Presumably this division would lead to a spirit of team effort among workers and management. Taylor divided the planning phase into specialized segments, such as scheduling, employee selection, timekeeping, and training. Although not developing exactly as he had intended, this division did lead to the functional specialization that is characteristic of all organizations today.

Immediate Effects

Scientific management was enthusiastically accepted by industry, first in the United States, and eventually in all industrialized countries. It was a new and exciting way of viewing management and it unquestionably led to dramatic improvements in efficiency when properly applied. Bright young people gravitated to Taylor to learn his methods, and many became well-known authorities in their own right as they developed and expanded Taylor's basic ideas.

On the negative side, workers rejected scientific management from the beginning. This was unfortunate because Taylor was apparently sincere in his belief that it was the best possible thing that could happen to labor. What it did was widen the schism between labor and management. Workers resented the depersonalization of jobs, with all of the individuality and craftsmanship taken out of them. They despised the speedup practices that evolved from wage-incentive systems. Intrinsic satisfaction in work was removed when the thinking part of jobs was taken over by management.

Lasting Effects

Some twenty years after Taylor's time, there began to be a wave of interest in human relations. It seemed that scientific management might disappear as a conceptual approach, although in practice it had permeated industry, with every organization following Taylor's principles in varying degrees. Eventually the human relations vogue reached its zenith and declined, and the two theories, together with others, are now viewed as mutually exclusive models to be examined in the abstract.

Scientific management and bureaucracy are commonly viewed together as an impersonally efficient model, with financial incentive as the primary basis for motivating workers. As far as scientific management goes, this is a convenient interpretation of what Taylor and his followers stood for, as it provides a basis for comparative analysis. However, it is incomplete because Taylor himself—and Gantt and Lillian Gilbreth to an even greater extent—was definitely concerned with the role of the individual and the group in organizations. Scientific management was not nearly so devoid of consideration for people as it is usually made out to be, and any assessment of its defects ought to take note of the fact that at the time of its greatest popularity, psychology had just become accepted as a professional discipline.

Discussion Questions

1. What restrictive practices by trade unions provide evidence that the "ball of work" notion still persists?
2. What do you suppose the effect on efficiency has been of finding the "one best way" to do any job, and then standardizing this method? What effect on the satisfaction that workers get out of their job?
3. Financial incentives are justified on the assumption that people will work harder if they are paid more money as a result. Is the assumption valid?

4. How do you think speedup practices would evolve from the use of wage incentives?
5. What consideration will you give to scientific management when you become a manager, or do you now give if you are presently responsible for managing people?

3. Henri Fayol and Management Principles

The writings of the French industrialist Henri Fayol have a very important place in management literature. In fact, it is from Fayol that the framework of managerial functions has evolved as a basis for understanding management. He also originated the concept of the universality of management in his proposition that managers at all levels of business organization, whether they be senior executives, department heads, or foremen, perform the same functions. In addition, he suggested that there are certain guiding principles of management, which was a thought that greatly influenced management writers in this country. Unfortunately, although Fayol completed his writing in 1925, the first popular English translation of his work was not published until 1949.

Fayol's Definition of Management

Fayol perceived that certain activities are essential to any business organization. For instance, all firms must buy raw materials, produce and sell goods or services, raise capital and use it efficiently, protect resources, and accurately record transactions. However, he felt that another activity, that of management, was often overlooked. Management to him meant planning, organizing, commanding, coordinating, and controlling.

To Fayol, planning involved assessing the future and making provisions for it; it was the most difficult and important thing that managers do. He emphasized the necessity for primary plans and derivative plans. Fayol was using one-year and ten-year forecasts in his own organization fifty years before they became common among United States firms.

Fayol visualized organizing in a very broad sense. First, it involved providing a business with all of the necessary physical resources. Second, it concerned the human organization, in which category Fayol focused on the way the management levels increase in proportion to increases in the number of employees. He defined the general duties at each organizational level; he stressed the need for organization charts; and finally he included prescriptions for selecting and training employees and for developing managers, which are now customarily considered part of the staffing function.

Commanding was the element of "setting the organization going," the function now called "directing." It was the face-to-face interaction between managers and subordinates in accomplishing the goals of the organization. Fayol clearly saw the need for managers to be personally involved with their subordinates as individuals, and to lead by their own exemplary conduct.

What Fayol called "coordinating" is now usually identified as the purpose of all managerial functions, rather than a separate function. Fayol perceived it as harmonizing all the activities of a firm and achieving a balance between input and output factors. He urged conferences and liaison activities as methods of achieving coordination.

Controlling was seen by Fayol in very much the same way that it is now understood. To him controlling consisted of verifying whether everything occurs in conformity with the plan adopted, the instructions issued, and the principles established. He emphasized that controlling depended on plans. Also, he stressed that controlling can be effective only if it is done within a reasonable time after events, and that undesirable variations between plans and events must be corrected.

Fayol's Management Principles

In looking back over his long and successful career as a business manager, Fayol saw certain principles that he frequently applied. However, he stated that there is no limit to the number of principles; any rule or procedure qualifies as a principle if the results it generates confirm its usefulness. He made the point that the difficult part of principles is knowing how to use them. The principles that he emphasized were

- division of work—large tasks should be divided into small ones, with people specializing in performing them.
- authority and responsibility—managers must have the right to give orders and the power to exact obedience. Responsibility of managers for their actions is the corollary of authority, arising whenever authority is exercised.
- discipline—managers must respect agreements made with employees, and employees must honor their commitments to the company.
- unity of command—subordinates should not receive orders from more than one supervisor.

- unity of direction—only one plan should exist for the achievement of any objective, and all members of the organization should follow that plan.
- subordination of interest—the interest of the organization should come before individual interests.
- remuneration—wages should rise or fall with effort. Bonuses should be used to motivate extended effort.
- centralization—optimal centralization of decision making varies with the individual firm, but should be determined according to the best use of all of the abilities of personnel.
- chain of command—authority is linked by a scalar (ladderlike) chain of supervisors and subordinates extending down from the highest management position to the lowest organizational level. Communication ideally flows up and down this chain, but in practice a "gangplank" approach must be used to permit individuals in different chains to deal with each other.
- order—the qualifications of individuals and the requirements of jobs should be matched.
- equity—personnel should be dealt with on the basis of kindliness and justice.
- job stability—conditions should be provided to motivate employees to stay with their jobs.
- initiative—employees should be given the opportunity to think out and execute plans.
- team spirit—rapport among the personnel should be striven for, and the setting up of divisive factors avoided. More reliance should be put on oral than on written communications.

The Importance of Fayol's Contributions

The feature of Fayol's writings that is especially significant is that he looked at *the total job of managing,* which no one else really attempted until the management theorists of the early 1950's. Taylor and his followers were preoccupied with improving the efficiency of workers at the operating level. Between 1900 and about 1950, valuable additions to management knowledge were made, but they were fragmentary, dealing either with organizing, planning and controlling, or staffing. Fayol, on the other hand, left a framework upon which the whole of management could be studied and analyzed.

Discussion Questions

1. To study and understand management, why is it necessary to break it down into managerial functions, or elements, as Fayol called them?
2. Do you think that Fayol looked upon his "principles" in the same sense that the term is applied in the physical sciences?
3. Fayol knew of and admired Taylor's work, although Taylor was apparently not aware of Fayol. What similarities are there in Fayol's and Taylor's principles? What dissimilarities are there, as Taylor is now interpreted?
4. Are there any of Fayol's principles with which you disagree, or think would be difficult to apply? Generally, would following Fayol's principles be useful to you as a manager?
5. What is the significant difference between Fayol's approach to management theory and the prescriptions offered by Weber?

4. The Hawthorne Studies and Human Relations

The most extensive and significant research ever conducted with social science methods was performed at the Hawthorne Works of the Western Electric Company over the interval of a few years before and after 1930. The research was sponsored by the National Research Council, and made possible by the cooperation of Western Electric. Names that will always be remembered because of their association with the research are those of F. J. Roethlisberger, Elton Mayo, and T. N. Whitehead.

Original Objectives

In the beginning the research was designed to determine if there was a relationship between worker productivity and the lighting of the work area. We can see the influence of Taylorism in this objective. Most of the workers involved in the particular experiments were women who performed routine assembly operations. The testing amounted to changing the intensity of lights over work stations and measuring any corresponding changes in productivity. However, in this experiment the researchers invited the participation of the workers whose productivity was to be measured—carefully explaining to them the objectives of the experiment and asking for comments and suggestions while the investigation was taking place.

Unforeseen Results

The experiment was conducted as planned. Lighting was increased, and productivity went up. Lighting was increased again, and again productivity went up. This pattern was repeated several more times. All during this time, the researchers demonstrated sincere interest in the workers, rather than treating them as impersonal research objects.

At one point, the change in illumination was reversed. Although not telling workers of the change, the researchers maintained their friendly, cooperative relationship with them. While the illumination was gradually being decreased, productivity continued to rise until it finally reached a plateau.

The conclusion was that any importance that lighting might have as a variable was obscured by other factors present in the experiment. These factors were plainly psychological, and suggested that the motivational effects of treating people as responsive individuals in their work environment offered exciting possibilities.

Revised Objectives

The research went on for a number of years, but with a different purpose. The new objective was to learn more about how the treatment of workers would affect productivity. The typical approach was to select a group of women workers to participate in an experiment in which changes in productivity could be accurately compared with changes in working conditions and with different attitudes toward the workers themselves.

Variations in working conditions included more precise control of work output, as well as changes in height and shape of stools and benches, rest periods, hours of work, methods of payment, and so on. The workers were told what the purpose of the experiment was and were asked for their consent to take part. Traditional management attitudes toward workers also were altered; as in the lighting experiment, worker participation was conscientiously encouraged. There was no direct supervisor over the women. No attempt was made to limit conversation on the job, and the permissiveness extended to allowing birthday parties in the work area. Moreover, the women were invited in interviews to talk about their problems and what they wanted from their jobs.

Nothing that was done to change working conditions had any consistent effect on productivity. For example, productivity rose when rest periods were introduced but it continued to rise when the rest periods were taken away. The work output by the experimental group increased until it reached an unpredicted high level, at which point it was sustained independently of any modification of work conditions.

Explanation

The improved work performance by the experimental group could only be attributed to the workers' response to being personally involved in their jobs. The treatment they received made them like their work. They felt that what they were doing was important, and recognizing that the purpose of the research was to find out the effect of certain factors on productivity, they reacted by performing at a far higher level than they had ever done before.

Additional Findings

In addition to disclosing factors of individual behavior which were empirically supported for the first time, the research led to a greatly improved understanding of group behavior. In studying the various experimental groups, the researchers discovered that informal leaders always emerged. Although the groups were told by the researchers to work without strain, it was apparent that they set their own norms of effort, enforced by informal leaders. In these experiments, the group norms were set higher than the formal standards, apparently because the groups perceived a cause-and-effect relationship between productivity and the job satisfaction that came from being well treated. Other factors that became clear included the way a group worked harder to support individuals having an off-day, and the close identification that the members felt with their group.

Subsequent Effects

The Hawthorne studies led to what became known as "the human relations school" of management theory. The Great Depression, with its potential for causing social revolt, and the acute shortage of labor during World War II a decade later, made it necessary for business managers to view their employees from a new perspective. Application of the Hawthorne methods appeared to be the answer.

The human relations approach was misapplied, however, just as scientific management was distorted and misused by people other than those who really understood it. For example, one approach used by managers to practice human relations was through "benevolent paternalism." Some managers actually tried to act the father figure in dealing with subordinates and became so engrossed with this role that they lost sight of their work objectives. This misguided paternalism also was observed in the random granting of fringe benefits—a practice that gained momentum with the imposition of wage controls during World War II. An analysis of the Hawthorne studies would have revealed that, as motivators, fringe benefits miss the point completely.

A second way in which managers misused the human relations concept was in trying to dupe workers into thinking that their participation was invited when they were really being manipulated. By the 1950's many managers were so disillusioned by so-called human relations methods of management that the concept fell into some disrepute.

Discussion Questions

1. Did the research conducted in the Hawthorne studies find out anything about the original objective, which was the relationship between illumination and worker productivity?
2. Can it be deduced from the Hawthorne studies that successful innovations, such as permitting conversation between employees on the job, will necessarily lead to greater productivity when transferred to other work situations?
3. Why is it important that managers understand the behavior of informal groups?
4. Does the quickness with which managers tried to apply human relations methods suggest an unusual managerial response to something new?
5. What are some necessary objectives of managers that could be overlooked in a preoccupation with human relations?

5. Chester Barnard, Transitionalist

Although Chester I. Barnard, as president of New Jersey Bell Telephone Company, was a practical businessman, his contributions to management thought are academic and profound. His best-known writing is the book *The Functions of the Executive* (1938), and while it is difficult reading, it is universally recognized as a valuable source of fundamental managerial concepts.

Barnard's Role As a Transitionalist

Most lists of important contributors to management theory include Barnard's name, even though his managerial ideas are not a school of thought, as are those of Weber with bureaucracy, or of Taylor with scientific management, or of Mayo with human relations. He acted as a bridge between the classicists in management theory who preceded him, and the modern behavioral writers who followed him. In effect, Barnard provides a transition between two eras.

Organization: A Cooperative System

Before Barnard, organization was viewed only in the rigid structural sense, with a focus on levels of managerial authority. Earlier writers called *authority* the "cement" of an organization. Barnard introduced a different theory, that organizations are *cooperative* systems. He pointed out that only a small number of people in an organization identify their personal objectives with the objectives of the organization; thus, they must somehow be induced to contribute their individual cooperation. This common purpose is achieved by *communication,* which is the "cement" that connects members of the organization and serves to transfer information and establish common purpose.

Barnard's emphasis on organizational purpose has been followed up by most modern writers on management, who see the need for clearly established objectives (purposes) as prerequisites to organizational planning.

Inducement-Contribution Balance

According to Barnard, each member of an organization theoretically gets some inducements from the organization in return for what he contributes. As long as he perceives that the inducements are as great as, or greater (measured in terms of his values and the other options open to him) than the contributions he is asked to make, he will continue to cooperate. What communication does is provide each individual with enough information to evaluate whether the inducements and contributions are in balance. Writers in the 1970's are increasingly urging that managers extend the same or greater care in preserving the "human" assets of their organization as they do with their financial assets, and the derivation from Barnard can plainly be seen.

The Informal Organization

The informal organization is discussed later in this book (Section 26), so not too much needs to be said about it at this point. However, one way that Barnard can clearly be seen as a transitionalist is in the way he linked the findings on informal organization of the Hawthorne studies (Section 4) to the power of the informal organization now perceived by the behavioralists. Barnard apparently originated the idea that every formal organization necessarily overlies an informal one. It is when people realize that they cannot accomplish what they want to do individually that they get together to form a common purpose and set up a system of communication.

Strategic Factors

A significant feature of the modern concept of decision making is the search for the strategic factors in any decision situation. A strategic factor is one that most clearly obstructs the attaining of a desired objective. The manager must identify the strategic factors early in the decision process, and search for alternative solutions which will take care of them. Although Barnard admitted that he did not originate the concept, his insistent emphasis on it has done much to perpetuate it as one of the basic planning principles.

Acceptance Theory of Authority

Barnard's systematic approach to the study of organizations and the functions of executives was comprehensive. However, he is best remembered for his *acceptance* theory of authority. Briefly, Barnard awakened management thinkers to the possibility that authority may not come down from the top of the organization, but may in fact rise upward from the bottom of the organization.

He said that managers only have as much authority as is granted to them by the people working under them. This authority falls within what Barnard called the worker's *zone of indifference*. In other words, some orders given by a supervisor may be clearly unacceptable to the worker, and he will try to subvert or get around these orders in one way or another; some orders may be more or less neutrally accepted; and others are clearly acceptable. This last type of order lies within the worker's "zone of indifference" or acceptance.

According to Barnard, this zone of acceptance will be wider or narrower depending on how much the inducements offered by the organization exceed the contributions a worker is expected to make. That is, the more an employee thinks he is getting from the organization compared to what he is giving, the more he will be inclined to accept the authority of the organization to tell him what to do.

The discussions of relationships between superiors and subordinates in Sections 21 and 44 owe much to the ideas of Chester Barnard.

Discussion Questions

1. Why is Barnard viewed as a transitionalist?
2. How did Barnard's perception of organization differ from that of the management theorists who preceded him?
3. What is meant by "inducement-contribution" balance?
4. Taking some real-life situation, can you identify its strategic factors?
5. Explain the "acceptance theory of authority" in terms of the student-instructor relationship.

6. The Behavioral Sciences and Management

At the same time that *human relations* declined as a magic term, patient research by psychologists, sociologists, anthropologists, and others began to develop a substantial body of knowledge that could be applied in practice. *Behavioral science* is the term associated with this work.

The term *behavioral scientist,* or *behavioralist,* identifies professionally trained people from the foregoing disciplines who attempt to apply the scientific method in the understanding, explanation, prediction, and changing of human behavior in organizations. There is no uniformity or singularity about behavioral science, however. Although the three disciplines constituting behavioral science have a common interest in human behavior as a general subject, the principal preoccupation of the psychologists is with the individual; the sociologists, with groups; and the anthropologists, with culture. Each of the disciplines have different and distinctive methodologies for collecting data and verifying their hypotheses. At the present time the psychologists seem to dominate, in that their theories seem to apply best to the real-life human problems confronting practicing managers.

Change in Thinking

Although the behavioral approach has apparent similarities to the human relations approach, its objectives are considerably more practical. The behavioralists say that organizational structures and relationships generate tensions that have bad effects on all employees, regardless of their place in the organizational hierarchy. The energy they expend on coping with tensions reduces their productive effort. The behavioralists see their own role as that of making changes in organizations that will cause tensions to be minimized. As obstructing tensions are removed, the overall organization should become more productive.

Basic Assumptions

Behavioralists possess certain assumptions and attitudes about the relation of formal organization goals to human needs. Elton Mayo wrote in 1919 that workmen are considered by employers to be "items in the cost of production." He speculated that belonging to a work organization caused individuals to become so regimented as to lose all sense of autonomous social function. He proposed that organization structures be changed to permit individuals to see their work as socially necessary, and he asserted that it is consistent with human nature for workers to want to collaborate in the design of their jobs. His conclusion was that a social system "which deprives the great majority of mankind of every vestige of autonomy" cannot possibly be satisfactory and would not be compensated for in the eyes of the workers by any increase in wages or improvements in working conditions.

In 1943 the psychologist Abraham Maslow offered a theory (expanded upon in Section 48) that human motivation is a process of sequentially seeking satisfaction of certain basic needs. He suggested that a possible ordering of these needs would begin with the lowest level, or the physiological. The next need is for safety, which implies freedom from any kind of threat. Following safety comes the love need, or the need that humans have for affection and the feeling of belonging. Next is the need for esteem—to feel a sense of achievement and to have the respect of others. The final and ultimate need is for self-actualization—the need people have to utilize their full potential.

Maslow's theory has exercised a powerful influence on the behavioral science assumption that the majority of members of organizations are frustrated in satisfying their higher needs, particularly the need for self-actualization, by the demands and structure of formal organizations. Chris Argyris in 1957 stated the proposition that the lack of congruence between the needs of healthy individuals and the demands of formal organizations results in human frustration, failure, short-time perspective, and interpersonal and intergroup conflict.

Also in 1957, Douglas McGregor came out with his intriguing Theory X/Theory Y model. McGregor proposed that management's conventional view, which he called Theory X, is that workers must be motivated and controlled by pressures applied by management, because the typical worker is lazy, lacks ambition, dislikes responsibility, prefers to be led, and when uncontrolled will be passive or resistant to organizational goals. Under Theory X, the most effective way to motivate workers is through financial incentives.

As an alternative, McGregor offered Theory Y, which is that if given the opportunity people will become self-motivated—through the striving for their personal growth and development—to achieve the organizational goals. Theory Y holds that the natural traits of people are the opposite of those represented by Theory X; that if people appear to be Theory X types it is because stultifying experiences in organizations have made them so. Therefore, the essential task of management is to arrange conditions so that people can satisfy their need for self-actualization, and at the same time accomplish organizational objectives.

Another assumption of the behavioralists is that bureaucracy is obsolete and "will not survive as the organizational form of the future," an idea expressed by Warren Bennis in 1966. From Bennis we have again the assumption that there is "an inescapable tension between individual and organization goals." Bureaucracy is assumed to be responsible for this tension, and must be done away with because it (1) does not allow for personal growth; (2) develops conformity; (3) uses outdated control and authority systems; and (4) thwarts communication by hierarchical boundaries.

Organization Development: The Application of Behavioral Theories

Organization development involves a long-term commitment by the top managers to diagnose problems obstructing their organization and to effect changes that will correct those problems. The approach implies that the top managers of the organization, called "clients," will call in behavioral scientists to act as external change agents. The change agents share certain assumptions about organizations and human behavior (the assumptions discussed earlier in this section).

Organization development starts with various educational strategies to accomplish a planned organizational change. The strategies, which can range from questionnaires to sensitivity programs (see Section 55), emphasize the concept of learning through shared experience. And typically, organization development programs comprise cycles of diagnosis and data gathering by the change agents, feedback to the client group, data discussion and work by the client group, action planning, and action.

The Permanence of Organization
Development Changes

Assuming that change does take place as a result of formal organization development, the next question is "How long do the changes last?" There seem to be patterns characteristic of both success and failure in maintaining organization change.

Successful programs appear to have been started in organizations when human relations conditions were at a low ebb and there was common agreement that something dramatic had to be done to avert a complete erosion of morale. There also was a strong individual at the top management level who favored organization development, and who induced other top managers to give it a fair trial. They, in turn, closely collaborated with the external change agents. Problem solutions were tested on a small scale at top management levels before being expanded to the total organization. Change effects were maintained and reinforced by periodic follow-up programs.

Programs that have not been successful seem to have originated without a consensus commitment by top management to the need for change. Often, programs have been entered into because "it seemed to be the popular thing to do." Also, there are many behavioral scientists who sell themselves as experts in guiding organization development programs but who simply lack the experience or other qualifications to do the job. Programs entrusted to a firm's personnel manager to be instituted at lower management levels rarely accomplish much of lasting benefit. And finally, unless an organization development is constantly rejuvenated, it will run down because of its own inertia.

Discussion Questions

1. What does the modern behavioral approach have in common with the earlier scientific management movement? How do they differ?
2. How do you react to the assumptions of the behavioralists about the relationship between human needs and formal organizational goals?
3. How would you explain organization development to a "hard-headed, practical" businessman?

4. What advantages are there in people who are members of the same organization learning through shared experience?
5. Why would organization development programs run by a company's personnel manager have a low probability for success?

7. Management and Mathematics

What is now understood to be the mathematical approach to the study of management seems to have had its beginnings at about the time of World War II in efforts to improve military logistics. It attracted considerable attention during the 1950's, became entrenched in the business curriculum at the college level in the 1960's, and appears to be gradually but inevitably becoming an important tool for the business manager. Some prominent names and their central contributions include G. B. Dantzig, linear programming; Wassily W. Leontief, input/output analysis; Leon Walras, general equilibrium theory; John von Neumann and Oscar Morgenstern, game theory; and F. H. Knight, decision theory.

Some of the methods of the mathematical school are described in Section 16, and a more detailed treatment of them in example form is provided in the appendixes of this book. If the mathematical school's salient characteristics can be singled out, however, they are its focus on optimal decision making and its requirement for descriptive and predictive models.

Optimization

To the disciples of the mathematical school, management fundamentally consists of the process of decision making. Managers are constantly faced with problems for which solutions must be decided. It is held that there exist many alternative solutions for every problem. The challenge to the manager is to assemble every possible solution to a given problem, and from this array select the one that will be most effective in terms of accomplishment and most efficient in terms of the costs required relative to the results achieved. An optimal decision is the choice of the best way to solve the given problem.

Optimal decisions are classified as either *maximizing* or *minimizing* functions. A maximizing function is one that generates the greatest possible profit, the highest output, and the maximum return on investment relative to the resources committed to the effort. When the function is minimizing, the optimal decision produces the desired result at the lowest possible cost.

There are also decisions that managers must make over and over again; that is, the decision conditions recur. For these kinds of decisions, the optimal solution can be formulated into a decision rule, which prescribes how the decision is to be made under the stipulated set of conditions. For nonrecurring decisions, or those where the conditions are not consistent, original optimal solutions must be sought.

Satisficing Vs. Optimizing

Herbert Simon, a prominent management theorist, suggests that optimization cannot ever be more than a theoretical concept because making optimal decisions would require infinite time and perfect knowledge. He contends further that managers cannot identify and examine every alternative to solving a problem, but that they can only consider the most obvious ones and select the course of action that will lead to a satisfactory solution. This is what is known as *satisficing*. The fact that managers settle for a solution somewhat less than optimal does not mean, however, that they do not attempt to quantify the variables involved in the possible courses of action, and through model building try to develop an answer expressed in numerical terms.

Modeling

Consider a manager who must make a decision and who has identified three or four possible solutions. How can it be determined which one will lead to the most satisfactory results?

The manager has three options. The first is to implement each of the possible solutions and evaluate their effects. If conditions remained exactly the same throughout the experiment, presumably the manager would know the best alternative. However, in terms of time and money, this approach is rarely feasible.

The second option is to apply personal experience, plus the experience of others, in trying to determine the best course of action. Unfortunately, experience does not often perfectly match up with the current situation. Thus, experience is an incomplete and unreliable guide to future action.

The manager's third option is to construct a model. A model may take many forms, but for decision making it is always in some way an abstraction from real life. In addition, a model is predictive; that is, real-life conditions that a model describes can be assumed to constantly recur if conditions are unaltered.

One of the forms that a model may take is a physical replica, such as a scaled-down model of a turbine engine. A second form is graphic, such as a chart of the behavior of stock-market prices. A third form is schematic, such as an electrical wiring diagram.

The mathematical model uses symbols to represent the factors in a real-life situation. The symbols can be manipulated to study the interactions between the factors, or "variables," as they are usually called. The construction and use of a mathematical model consists of five steps. First, precisely define the system or problem. Second, determine some way of measuring effects. Third, construct the model by assembling the pertinent variables in their proper relationships. Fourth, examine various alternatives to the problem solution by plugging each one into the model. Finally, evaluate the results and choose the most promising course of action.

Example

Assume that a student wishes to maximize his measurable academic effort over four years of college. Let this define his problem, and let the notation ME represent the measurement of effects. Grades are the unknowns, or variables, so let them be represented by X's with appropriate subscripts. Let courses in alternative programs be represented by C's, also with subscripts. The student's model then becomes:

$$ME = X_1 C_1 + X_2 C_2 + \cdots + X_n C_n$$

The student may evaluate his probable ME by plugging in the courses required in alternative programs, such as engineering, business, and liberal arts, with the grades that his past record, aptitudes, and what he can learn about the courses and instructors suggest as likely.

Discussion Questions

1. Speculate as to why World War II marked the beginning of the mathematical approach to the study of management.
2. Is there any inconsistency between viewing management as decision making and viewing it as planning, organizing, staffing, directing, and controlling?

3. What conceptual similarity do you see between the decision rules of the mathematical school and the ideas that Weber and Taylor advocated? (Refer to Sections 1 and 2.)
4. How do you suppose the stockholders of a corporation would feel about managers "satisficing" instead of optimizing in their decision making?
5. What is the connection between optimizing and the construction of models?

8. Systems Management

In the last decade there were some new ideas about old theories, such as the rejuvenation of the rationally efficient approach to management by mathematical models and the computer, and the transformation of "human relations" through the empirical research of behavioral scientists. The only new theory developed in the 1960's, and one that generated quite a bit of attention, is systems management.

A Different Way of Thinking

Systems management is difficult to explain, mainly because a specialized vocabulary has been developed for talking about it. However, simply expressed, systems theory looks at every organization as a subpart of a larger whole. The traditional way of thinking of a business firm, for example, was as a complete entity within itself. In systems theory the firm is viewed as one subsystem, which relates to many other subsystems, such as customers, suppliers, employees, governments, and competitors, to make up the total system. Each subsystem is in constant interaction with all other subsystems, and adapts and responds as a result of these interactions.

Within the firm, the conventional view considers the various functional departments, such as production, sales, engineering, and purchasing, to be independent units. Efficiency of the total organization results from efficient management of each of these semi-autonomous departments. In systems theory, on the other hand, the functions that these departments perform are viewed as subsystems of the total system (the firm) and the boundaries between the departments either disappear or become exceedingly vague. The objective is to optimize the output of the total system, even at the expense of underoptimizing the outputs of the subsystems.

The Black Box

Input and *output* have specific meanings in systems theory. Inputs are the human and physical resources allocated to a subsystem, and outputs are results, measured in terms of performance. A condition known as the *black box* exists within a subsystem; it is what transforms the input into output. It is called the black box because systems theory is not concerned with what goes on inside the box, but rather with what goes into it and comes out. When it is desired to observe the effect of any one input, the amount can be varied while other inputs are held constant and the change in output is measured. In this way it can be learned how to regulate inputs to cause predictable changes in outputs.

Feedback

Another essential feature of systems theory is *feedback,* which means that the systems network is regulated by the information produced by it. A simple example is in the way a thermostat works. When the temperature in a room drops below a predetermined level, the thermostat communicates this information to the heating unit, which increases its heat output, and the temperature rises. In similar fashion, the process is reversed when the temperature becomes too high. An important aspect of systems theory is its emphasis on feedback channels through which outputs are evaluated and compared to established standards. When differences become apparent between outputs and standards, the measuring mechanism communicates this fact to the device that regulates the inputs. Inputs are then adjusted to change outputs, while the feedback process continues.

People Problems

Systems theory as it is currently developing seems to represent a highly impersonal view of the people in organizations. It has efficiency as its goal, and employs rational means of reaching it. In this respect it is very similar to the bureaucratic model, and may have the potential of generating comparable human problems. People appear to be perceived as anonymous mechanical producers. The deemphasis of people is implied by the omission of staffing and directing in the usual lists of managerial functions in systems texts.

Planning, organizing, and controlling are emphasized as managerial functions, although the prescriptions for their performance vary considerably from traditional ones. Communication is identified as a separate function. (Communicating is not omitted in alternative theories, but is implied as a necessary element in the performance of all managerial functions.)

The Future of Systems Management

There are actually two applications of systems theory. In one, its concepts are used for the purpose of analyzing such major social problems as urban planning, airport logistics, and pollution, which are adaptable to solution by systems models. The second application of systems theory is in the development of an operational form of management. Many managers in business and military organizations, as well as management theorists, are saying that *project management* —which is sometimes used as the popular term for *applied systems management*—may very well be the management form of the future. (A discussion of project management appears in Section 19, while pertinent factors are discussed in Sections 30, 53, and 66.)

Discussion Questions

1. Has it ever been realistic to view any organization as an entity within itself?
2. What is the cost to the total organization of attempting to optimize the performance of subsystems of it, such as production, sales, and finance?
3. Try to imagine the workings of the "black box" in some actual situation. For example, consider an educational system to be a black box, with entering students, money, deferred earning power (opportunity cost), curriculum, and instruction as inputs, and graduated students with enhanced earning potential as outputs. Describe what happens.
4. What are the essential characteristics of a feedback system?
5. Why should a social problem such as urban planning be adaptable to solution by systems models?

Summary

Bureaucracy is a theory of management that was proposed by the German sociologist Max Weber in the 1890's as the ideal model for organizing activities. The theory is characterized by sharply defined departmental levels within organizations, a strict hierarchy of authority descending down through the levels, written rules and regulations covering the performance of all activities, and the requirement of written documents for the recording of all official transactions.

Scientific management (about 1910) is generally credited to Frederick W. Taylor, although there were other important contributors to the concept. The focus of scientific management is on work performed at the basic operator level. All such jobs are to be studied and improved until the "one best way" of performing them is discovered. This method becomes the standard, and a minimum rate of production using this standard is established. Incentive systems are set up whereby workers are paid more than a base wage if the minimum production rate is exceeded. A main assumption identified with "Taylorism" is that workers are motivated to greater productivity primarily by the desire to make more money.

Henri Fayol, a manager of a large French corporation, looked back on his career and identified certain concepts that he had followed and found to be useful to him (about 1925). Among them was a format for classifying what a manager does and a set of principles which, if applied in appropriate situations, can simplify and standardize the managerial job.

The Hawthorne studies (1930) awakened managers to the importance of the human resource of organizations. For the first time there was significant recognition, based on empirical data, that people can be motivated to greater productivity by incentives other than financial ones. In addition, the importance of the informal group in setting productivity norms was discovered.

Chester Barnard served as a transitionalist (in the late 1930's) between the early management theorists and those of the present day, particularly in the behavioral area. Barnard's ideas on organization and communication, inducements vs. contributions, the strategic factor, and the source of managerial authority continue to exert a significant influence on management theory.

The behavioral approach to management (which was an outgrowth of the Hawthorne studies) is based on scientific research into human attitudes and behavior. It finds expression in organization development, where behavioral theories are applied to change worker attitudes that can hinder productivity.

The mathematical school of management (begun about 1950) stresses decision making as the fundamental management process. Mathematical methods have been developed which, in theory, will point to the optimal decision from an array of all possible solutions. In practice, managers probably "satisfice" rather than optimize in their decision making. Decision making requires the use of models, which describe and predict real-life conditions.

Systems management (1960's) is evolving as the suggested "modern" management theory. Essential features of this theory include looking at each organization as a subsystem of a much larger total system, subordinating the subsystem goals to the goals of the total system, and analyzing the feedback (control information) to bring the outputs of subsystems into desired equilibrium.

Selected Bibliography

Argyris, Chris, "The Individual and the Organization: Some Problems of Mutual Adjustment." *Administrative Science Quarterly,* June 1957.

Barnard, C. I., *The Functions of the Executive.* Harvard University, 1938.

Baumol, William J., *Economic Theory and Operations Analysis.* Prentice-Hall, 1961.

Bendix, R., *Max Weber: An Intellectual Portrait.* Doubleday, 1960.

Bennis, Warren G., "Organization Development and the Fate of Bureaucracy." *Industrial Management Review,* Spring 1966.

Boddewyn, J., "Frederick Winslow Taylor Revisited." In Paul M. Dauten, Jr. (ed.), *Current Issues and Emerging Concepts in Management.* Houghton Mifflin, 1962.

Davis, R. C., *The Fundamentals of Top Management.* Harper, 1951.

Fayol, Henri, *General and Industrial Management.* Pitman, 1949.

Goetz, B. E., *Management Planning and Control.* McGraw-Hill, 1949.

Johnson, Richard A., Fremont E. Kast, and James E. Rosenzweig, *The Theory and Management of Systems.* McGraw-Hill, 1963.

Koontz, Harold, and Cyril O'Donnell, *Principles of Management,* 5th ed. McGraw-Hill, 1972.

Maslow, A. H., "A Theory of Human Motivation." *Psychological Review,* Vol. 50, 1943.

Mayo, Elton, "Democracy and Freedom." Workers Education Series No. 1, Macmillan, 1919.

McGregor, Douglas M., *The Human Side of Enterprise.* McGraw-Hill, 1960.

Newman, W. H., *Business Policies and Management.* South-Western, 1949.

Petersen, E., and E. G. Plowman, *Business Organization and Management,* 4th ed. Irwin, 1958.

Roethlisberger, F. J., and W. J. Dickson, *Management and the Worker.* Harvard University, 1939.

Simon, Herbert A., *Administrative Behavior,* Macmillan, 1957.

Sloan, Alfred P., Jr., "General Motors Corporation Study of Organization." In Ernest Dale (ed.), *Readings in Management.* McGraw-Hill, 1965.

Taylor, Frederick Winslow, "The Principles of Scientific Management." In Schlender, Scott, Filley (eds.), *Management in Perspective.* Houghton Mifflin, 1965.

PLANNING

In the planning function, objectives are established, and the means are determined for achieving them. Determination of means involves choosing from among alternatives, which fundamentally is decision making. Thus, planning comprises a range of activities that must be performed in order to culminate in decisions. It is always forward-looking; if the efforts of the present are to be effective, they must result from plans made in the past.

It is difficult to imagine any organization existing for long without planning, for depending on random happenings to produce results is a very shaky prescription. In a very real sense, planning provides the manager with some power over the future; even incomplete power is far better than no power at all.

Planning is a function that managers would often like to avoid. For one thing, it is hard work; to be effective, planning requires a sustained high level of concentration. Second, planning is costly in terms of both time and money. And finally, planning is unglamorous compared to the more exciting challenge of meeting day-to-day crises. However, all managers must plan, and, to some extent, all managers do plan, even though planning is more extensive at higher management levels, and usually more sophisticated in larger organizations.

Some of the fundamental concepts of planning are discussed in the following sections, but discussions of planning are not confined to these sections. The pervasiveness of planning and the existence and use of various types of plans is evidenced throughout later sections of this book dealing with the functions of organizing, staffing, directing, and controlling.

9. Setting Objectives

Plans are predetermined ways for accomplishing certain results. Obviously, the first step in planning is to decide what results are desired. These results, which are the reason for any organization to exist, are called its *goals* or *objectives*. Having objectives is common to all organizations, regardless of their nature. Governments, churches, schools, military forces, and business firms have all been created for specific purposes. Clear identification of those objectives is a must if planning is to proceed systematically and effectively.

Spelling Out Primary Objectives

The primary objective of any business organization is, of course, to make more money than it spends. However, a definition of what profit really is and how it is accurately measured have bothered economists for years. For example, when we speak of profit as the surplus that is left after paying the expenses of a business enterprise, do we just consider out-of-pocket expenses, or do we include depreciation, which is a non-cash allowance to replace assets when they wear out? And, over what period of time is profit to be figured? By avoiding advertising and research and development a firm might show a handsome profit for a few years, then plunge into a high-loss situation when its loose methods of operation catch up with it. Thus, a statement such as "the objective of this firm is to make a profit" is too general to serve as a basis for planning. Objectives must be spelled out in considerable detail before realistic planning can be done.

The planning function should start with decisions on the primary objectives of the firm. This seems straightforward, but it is surprising the number of companies, both large and small, that avoid facing up to these decisions. A way of determining these objectives is for the senior managers to develop thoughtful answers to such questions as:

- Do we want to concentrate on a single product or service, or should we spread our efforts over diversified products or service?
- Should we focus on high quality and high prices but low volume, or should we concentrate on high volume at low prices and sacrifice quality?
- What should our market be? Should it be the general public

or some specialized group? Should our market cover a large area or should it be local?

- What are our size ambitions? Do we want to grow rapidly? Or do we want slow but steady growth? Do we want to stay the same size that we are now?

Expressing Objectives in Numerical Terms

As much as possible, answers to the questions above should be developed in numerical terms. Whatever a firm's objectives are—in prices, volume, markets, growth, etc.—should be described in terms that are measurable. For example, a firm might state as an objective that its "prices will never be undercut." Another firm might express its objectives in terms of volume, such as selling 300,000 units of product next year, 400,000 units the year after, and so on. A firm that traditionally has been in the defense industry could express an objective of having its markets equally divided between defense and consumer goods in the next five years. And many firms express objectives in terms of capturing an increasing share of a market over some specified period of time.

Objectives expressed in general terms are difficult to develop plans for, because there is no way of knowing whether they have been achieved or not. A failing of many companies is a tendency to express ideals in platitudes, and call them objectives; such "objectives" are meaningless so far as planning is concerned.

Specifying Profit Goals

Each firm's approach to stating its product, price, volume, market, and growth objectives is its way of defining how it will go about achieving the ultimate objective of profit. However, for profit to be an objective that can be planned for adequately, it must be expressed precisely. Expressing profit as a certain number of dollars is not enough; it must be expressed in proportion to the resources required to generate it. Thus, profit as a percentage of investment and as a percentage of sales are commonly used ratios. For example, one very large chemical company in the United States requires a 20-percent return on every investment, and chain supermarkets are very sensitive to keeping profits as a percentage of sales to at least 1 percent.

Moreover, profit-ratio objectives should be established for different products. For example, a new product or service just being introduced might have one set of profit ratios; an established product with wide demand might have another set; and a product nearing the end of its life cycle might have still another set. In addition, profit ratios for specific markets and for planned growth are objectives that can be established.

Setting Objectives in Descending Order

The objectives of a total organization are set in descending order. First comes the main objective of the company: What kind of an operation is it going to be? Next come the supporting objectives necessary to bring about the main objective. Following these central objectives come the implementing objectives of the primary operating departments. Then come the objectives of the lower level organizational units, and finally the objectives of individual jobs.

Communicating Objectives

Since a firm's primary objectives become bases for setting the goals of the component organizational units, it is essential to communicate them effectively down through the organizational levels. Managers of such operations as finance, production, marketing, and personnel should all know the overall results desired in order to fit them in with their departmental goals. If this communication is accomplished as it should be, the entire organization from top to bottom will be synchronized to plan in a common direction.

*On March 31, 1972, the end of Tredco's fiscal year, Harold Greely,
president, held a meeting of his senior managers. "The trouble with
this company," he said, "is that there are no definite objectives. We
always eventually seem to do all right, but we have never set standards by which we can judge our performance. Starting this coming
year, our objective is to increase profits annually by 10 percent." He
went on to say, "You are all experts in your fields. I expect each of
you to develop plans for implementing this objective in your own
divisions."*

*Tredco (Transmission Engineering and Development Company) de-
signs and manufactures a line of power transmission equipment such
as gears, gear reducers, sprockets, and drive chains. It had been
founded by two brothers, Otto and Ben Hilga, in 1937, and by 1972
served a national market. Upon the deaths of both of the founders in
1967, their families, who together owned 55-percent control of the
company, brought in Greely to head the firm's operations. Greely
had been Tredco's attorney for about ten years. Although he admitted to not knowing much about the company's product, he prided
himself on his good relationships with the local banking institutions.
He was extremely interested in civic affairs, which took a great deal
of his time.*

*The response of Tredco's division managers to Greely's announce-
ment was that he "meant business" about a consistent annual increase
in profits. Roy Johnson, manufacturing vice-president, called his staff
together to break the news. "Personally, I am glad Greely has taken
this stand," he stated. "One thing we are going to do here in manufacturing is stop catering to the customer's preferences. We are going
to reduce the different options that we have been offering on all of
our various products, and standardize on those items where we can get
long production runs. Efficiency is going to be the password in our
shops. When we get our schedules adjusted to mass production, I am
going to expand our industrial engineering staff, and invest in auto-
mated equipment."*

*Ned Bannister, cost analyst, spoke up, "One of our heaviest costs is
from parts that are rejected because of minor deviations from the*

quality standards set by engineering. Is there anything that we can do about that?"

"You bet there is," replied Johnson. "From now on if there is a good chance of a part working we are going to let it go through, even if it doesn't quite come up to specifications."

Don Hayes, marketing vice-president, left on an extended trip where he visited each of his nine regional sales managers. "Increasing sales is the name of the game as far as I am concerned," he told them. "Profits are a direct function of sales. In our line, in order to sell more we have to offer the customer more. That means if he wants 51 teeth in a gear instead of our standard 50 we give it to him. If he wants immediate delivery on a special order, we tell manufacturing to break into their schedule. If he wants extended credit terms, we authorize them. Doing these things might cost us a little more, but the added profit that we get from the increased sales will more than offset the expenses."

Elmer Richardson, engineering vice-president, thought about what Greely had said for a long time before he called his department managers together. "It is finally clear to me that the answer to higher profits ultimately lies in a better quality product than is offered by our competitors," he said. "We are considering a design as being finished too soon. In the future we are going to test and change, then test and change again until no more improvements are possible before we release production drawings. If I have my way, our product will be the Rolls Royce in the power transmission industry."

Tredco's controller, George Stearns, had been largely responsible for planting the profit objective idea in Greely's mind. In fact, he had a memorandum (Exhibit 9–1) already prepared which he distributed on April 4, 1972.

· · · · ·

On April 20, 1973, Carter Drusig of the firm Drusig, Hall, and Pierce, Certified Public Accountants, presented Greely with a comparative summary of Tredco's past year of operations (Exhibit 9–2). It tells a dismal story.

Exhibit 9–1.   Memorandum of Tredco's Controller.

Tredco

Confidential Memorandum

To: Division Vice-Presidents   Date: 4/4/72

From: G. Stearns, Controller

Subject: Implementation of the 10% annual profit improvement objective

1. A 10% reduction in all division personnel is to be accomplished within 90 days.
2. There will be a moratorium on all salary increases for the
   next fiscal year.
3. No capital equipment expenditures will be authorized in the
   next fiscal year.
4. Salesmen's traveling expenses are to be reduced 25%. Customer entertainment expenses are to be reduced 50%.
5. The maximum age for accounts receivable is 40 days before
   aggressive collection action is undertaken.
6. Expenditures for office supplies last year totaled $4719.63.
   Division vice-presidents are requested to give their personal
   attention to cutting this figure 50% next year.

                     Countersigned: Harold Greely, President

Exhibit 9–2.   Comparative Summary, Tredco's Sales and Profits.

	Period *4/1/71–6/30/71*	*Period* *7/1/71–9/30/71*	*Period* *10/1/71–12/31/71*	*Period* *1/1/72–3/31/72*
Net Sales	$2,167,956	$2,554,221	$1,983,348	$2,236,609
Net Profits	85,173	127,050	79,316	111,500

	Period *4/1/72–6/30/72*	*Period* *7/1/72–9/30/72*	*Period* *10/1/72–12/31/72*	*Period* *1/1/73–3/31/73*
Net Sales	$2,341,992	$2,156,712	$1,564,447	$1,317,371
Net Profits	70,040	64,500	25,618	(2,038)

Discussion Questions

1. Did Harold Greely take the appropriate first steps in planning?
2. Were there any defects in the implementing plans of each of Tredco's division managers in response to Greely's overall objective?
3. How would you integrate the plans in order to establish the kind of company Tredco should aspire to be?
4. Having decided on the kind of company, what might be some derivative objectives for Tredco?
5. What was the single most important reason for Tredco's decline in both sales and profits?

10. Forecasting Sales

Forecasting sales, after setting objectives, is the chief prerequisite for planning. Forecasting is, in general, any process attempting to make the future less uncertain. Because the future is unknown, it is threatening, and people have always been seeking ways of overcoming this threat. One traditional technique has been to assume that the future will be something like the past. Without anything else to go on, this assumption at least provides some basis for making plans.

Projecting the Past

When a forecast is made, its purpose is to predict the future environment. Factors in this environment include conditions external to the firm making the forecast, such as depression or prosperity, war or peace, government spending, unemployment, population, the political party in power, and so on. These conditions are crucial in determining the demand for the firm's product or service.

Over the short run, changes in external conditions that affect demand are minor. That is, tomorrow will be almost exactly like today, next month will not be much different than this month, and even next year will probably be more like this year than different. Therefore, firms wanting to develop a short-term forecast of their sales can do it with some reliability by determining present sales trends, adjusting the trends for known influences, and then projecting the trends for a period as far ahead as a year.

Refining Forecasts With Judgment

Experience in developing sales forecasts, plus knowledge gained from reading and from business contacts, provide insights which enable managers to make some predictions about the demand for their firm's products. In addition, they may be intending to take some deliberate action that may increase sales; or conversely, they may be aware of competitors' strategies that may reduce sales. Therefore, sales forecasts developed by projecting the past will almost always be tempered by managerial knowledge and judgment, often by a pooling of judgments by a group of managers.

Making Grass-Roots Adjustments

Any forecast of sales that can be arrived at by more than one fore-casting method has greater apparent reliability. Therefore, what is often called the "grass-roots" method is frequently used to check forecasts. By this method, salesmen in the field are requested to esti-mate the demand for the firm's products by customers in their respec-tive areas, and to estimate the share of this demand that they expect to obtain in sales for the firm. Often they consult with customers in detail before preparing these estimates. The total of all these estimates are compiled, and the result becomes an independently determined sales forecast that can be compared with forecasts prepared by other methods. A good assumption is that forecasts prepared in this way will be on the low side, because salesmen—whose performances are often measured by comparing these forecast figures with their actual sales figures—will probably build in protection for themselves.

Using Leading Economic Indicators

A method of making a reliable sales forecast, commonly used by firms large enough to afford economists, is to relate the sales of the industry (or the firm itself if it is big enough) to what are called "leading indicators." Examples of leading indicators include gross national product (GNP), independent sectors of GNP, the Federal Reserve Board Industrial Production Index, and such other factors as population trends, construction awards, and freight-car loadings. Annual changes in the so-called leading indicators can be predicted with usable accuracy over periods extending several years into the future.

What economists do is find indicators that move in the same direction as the industry's or firm's sales. That is, when the indicator goes up, sales go up; when the indicator goes down, sales go down. This is called *correlation*. When a strong correlation can be estab-lished between an indicator (or indicators) and the firm's sales, then sales can be predicted on the basis of indicator predictions.

Predicting Changes in the Money Supply

Another technique used by economists in developing sales forecasts is analyzing the rate of change of the national money supply. The supply of money in the United States is regulated by the central Federal Reserve Bank, and is expanded in times of business depression to stimulate buying of goods, and is contracted during inflationary periods to curtail spending. Cost of money (interest rates) tends to be a function of the money supply, and strongly influences sales trends in some industries (for example, housing). Therefore, if the supply of money can be predicted by economists, sales forecasts can be developed for firms in the housing industry and other industries that are sensitive to interest rates.

Using Econometric Models

The most sophisticated forecasting is done by using econometric models. An econometric model is a series of complex simultaneous equations which simulate the operation of the total national economy, or some segment of it. A computer is usually needed to apply such models to forecasting. (See Section 67.)

Ensuring Reliability of Long-Range Forecasts

As was mentioned, greater confidence is built into a forecast when more than one method of forecasting points to the same conclusion. Therefore, firms will try to forecast by as many feasible methods as they can afford. In addition, the farther into the future a forecast extends, the more necessary it is to use sophisticated and expensive methods. However, the longer the period of the forecast, the less reliable it will be, in spite of using varied and sophisticated methods. For this reason, it is important to use short-term forecasts to critically adjust the long-range forecasts.

*"Actually, our forecast wouldn't have been too bad except for one
thing," said Harry Moore to his brother, Dinty, as they looked over
the past year's sales figures of the Central Texas Welding Supply
Company. "We knew business was going to fall off in the last half of
1972 and the first half of 1973, but what we missed was what Weld
Gas was going to do. And nobody could have predicted that."*

*Harry and Dinty had started Central Texas Welding Supply just after
World War II. Both of them had been sales representatives for a national manufacturer of welding equipment before the war, and they
had the experience, personal drive, and capital to make their business
successful. They had experienced only two periods of anxiety about
their company, one in 1954 and the other in 1958. In retrospect, they
realized that on both occasions they had failed to detect signs of a
general decline in business, and as a result had been caught with
inventories and overhead expenses so large that if there had not been
a quick business recovery in each of the following years, their firm
might have been in serious trouble. After the 1958 incident, they felt
that they had learned a lesson, and from then on they had diligently
prepared an annual sales forecast, in which they tried to predict the
behavior of as many variables that would affect their sales as they
possibly could.*

*Characteristically, a welding supply company is franchised by one of
the large manufacturers of welding equipment and supplies to sell that
manufacturer's products in a specified marketing area. The bread-
and-butter items in the welding supply business are oxygen and acetylene, and electrodes and gas rods. Although these are low-profit items,
if a welding supply firm can generate enough sales volume for them,
they will come close to covering fixed costs. There is no quality differentiation between competing lines of oxygen and acetylene, and,
except for the personal preferences of welders, very little between
the various brands of welding rods. Despite the quality and performance similarity of these basic products, customers tend to remain
loyal to one manufacturer's make, primarily because of convenience.
Oxygen and acetylene are delivered in cylinders which are returned
to the supplier, and customers find it inconvenient to be responsible
for the property of more than one supplier.*

In addition to the security of the gas and rod business from a loyal customer, a welding supply company gains in another way. When a customer is considering the high-profit items in the welding line, such as welding machines, generators, and torches, the natural inclination is to favor the supplier of the staple items. Therefore, the thing that a welding supply company hates most is to lose a gas and rod customer. Next to keeping those customers happy, the second priority goes to capturing the customers of its competitors. The spectre that haunts the industry is that some supply firm will use price cutting to accomplish the latter objective.

In March 1972, Harry and Dinty had begun spending several nights each week preparing a sales forecast for the fiscal year starting July 1. Harry, being the firm's outside man, had focused on gathering data from existing customers and from prospective customers who were then being courted. Dinty, who watched over the inside operations of the office, shop, and warehouse, had concentrated on the trends of regional and national statistics. To assist him in this work, he had engaged Dr. Paul Hastings, an economics professor.

Central Texas Welding Supply employed twelve salesmen, who worked under two sales supervisors. Harry directed the sales supervisors, as well as personally handling the high-level contacts with the firm's ten largest accounts. These accounts were vital to Central Texas, as they accounted for close to 40 percent of the total sales volume. Harry had cultivated friendships with policy-making executives in each of these companies, which he nurtured with golf games, lunches, and evening entertainment. Two salesmen handled five of these accounts each, and their duties were to assure perfect service, as well as to entertain the respective buyers, engineers, and shop superintendents. The other salesmen and the sales supervisors serviced the bulk of the company's remaining accounts, over three hundred, which were arranged by geographical territories.

Harry had called a meeting of the supervisors and salesmen to explain how to gather information for the sales forecast. "First of all, we are going to assume that we are not going to lose any accounts," he began. "I have a card here for each customer with whom we have done business this year, showing by item and date what each one has purchased from us. What I want you to do is to talk with your contacts in the accounts that you handle, and learn what they think their own busi-

*ness will be like next year in comparison to this year. If they think
it will be better, or worse, try to find out how much as a percentage.
Enter this information on the cards. In addition, each one of you is
working on some new accounts. Make a strong effort to find out what
their annual gas and rod volume is and then estimate the probability
that you will capture the account. Make out a card for each one of
them. We can approximate their hardware purchases from their gas
and rod business. I will do the same thing for the accounts I call on."*

*The approach Dr. Hastings had used in working with Dinty was to
identify and project the key variables affecting the sale of welding
equipment in the local area. One variable was construction awards,
which showed a definite downward trend. Defense spending was another variable, and this one seemed headed downward even more
sharply than construction. Agricultural production, in which welding
supplies are involved because of repairs to farm machinery, appeared
to be stable for the next year. No important change was noticed for
expenditures by state and local governments. Capital spending by
transportation firms was estimated to fall off, but this suggested more
repair work on old equipment, which meant a possible increase in
welding supply purchases. The integration of all of the projections
had pointed to a potential decrease in the demand for welding supplies of as much as 12 percent.*

*A careful recapping of the figures collected from the company's cus-
tomers had showed a similar decline, which were projected to drop
off even more sharply in the last half of the year. "Well, at least we
know that we are headed for lean times," Harry had said to his
brother. "If you agree, let's expect that our sales will fall off by as
much as $200,000 next year. This means that we are shooting for a
$1,000,000 year, and with our overhead costs what they are, we had
sure better get it."*

*In the meantime, something important had been taking place at Weld
Gas, one of Central Texas' smaller and less bothersome competitors.
Marguerite Burke, who had been running the company since the
death of her husband, had sold Weld Gas to a syndicate of wealthy
investors headed by a former vice-president of the leading welding
equipment manufacturer in the country. He had said that, as he had
always wanted to manage his own business, he was going to build
Weld Gas into the strongest welding equipment supply house in*

Texas. With his powerful financial resources, and some disregard for industry ethics, he had begun picking off the big accounts one by one by installing free bulk-storage gas tanks in their plants, eliminating charges on overdue cylinders, and consigning inventories of rod that would not have to be paid for until used. In addition, his entertainment capacities for wooing important customers appeared unlimited.

Small wonder that at the end of the year Harry and Dinty were crestfallen.

"Just look at those figures," Harry said to his brother. "Sales just over $800,000 for last year, with most of the loss coming from my own pet accounts."

Discussion Questions

1. If the future is so difficult to predict, why should a business firm invest time and money trying to develop a sales forecast?
2. Did the Moore brothers do all that they could to develop a reliable sales forecast?
3. Was there any way that the entrance of a strong competitor in the local market could have been predicted?
4. Speculate on some external factors that would be particularly important in sales forecasting in the following industries:
   a) public utilities
   b) color television sets
   c) toys
   d) aerospace
   e) ethical drugs
5. Who should be made aware of the assumptions about the future upon which a sales forecast is based?

II. Major Plans

The achievement of a business firm's objectives depends on the inter-locking effectiveness of so many plans that failure of any one of them would probably be a major setback. However, three plans stand out as being crucial: the sales plan, the production plan (for providing the service, or buying or manufacturing the goods that are to be sold), and the financial plan.

The sales forecast is an assumption about the probable demand for a firm's products or services. It can be prepared in such a way that it is both a forecast and a plan; but if it is, two steps have been taken, not just one. The basic plan for all business firms derives from the sales forecast; and, although it can be called a number of names, let us call it the sales plan.

From Sales Forecast to Sales Plan

The sales plan is the deliberate detailing of the actions that must be taken to make the sales forecast a reality. Probable sales do not be-come real sales until the firm does things to make them so. The type of sales effort that a firm exerts varies with the nature of its business. Efforts to produce sales for a restaurant, a retail store, a trucking firm, and a manufacturing company are different, but they all have the purpose of effecting an exchange of the firm's products or services for the customer's dollars. Therefore, every firm must either formally or informally define and schedule the actions that will be taken to produce sales.

Sales budget. Regardless of the kinds of sales actions that indi-vidual companies undertake, one thing that is common to all actions is that they cost money. Therefore, an essential feature of the sales plan is a time schedule of the costs of actions that will be taken to produce sales. This part of the sales plan is usually called a *budget*.

Sales schedule. In some kinds of businesses, sales are made at a constant rate, but in many other businesses, the rate of sales varies. In either case, a time schedule of expected sales should be developed.

Collection schedule. Some companies receive payment at the time a sale is made. Other companies, particularly manufacturing and industrial supply firms, must wait some time to be paid. For firms of this kind, an additional schedule showing income from sales by time period should be prepared.

Working from the sales forecast, a sales plan becomes a firm's basic planning document. This plan should detail sales actions, costs, resulting sales, and income—all scheduled by time.

Production Plan

A business firm sells either a product or a service, or both. In the case of a service, the source lies in the skills of the firm's employees. (For a discussion of manpower planning, see Section 35.)

If the firm sells a product, it obtains the product either by making it, as with manufacturing firms, or buying it, as with retail stores. Whether a product is made or bought, it is essential to develop a detailed plan for having the product available for sale at the times specified in the sales plan.

Purchase plan. Making a purchase plan involves determining from the sales plan the quantity and quality of the items expected to be sold, and when they are expected to be sold. Lead times, or the length of times between placing orders and receiving them, must be calculated; and inventory levels, or the amount of unsold goods that the firm is willing to have on hand at any one time, must be set. One way of determining lead times is to examine past records showing how long it took to receive goods after placing orders. With many items, such as the purchase of steel from the mills, the common practice is to get an approximation of lead times when orders are negotiated. Finally, suppliers must be selected, and the times scheduled for placing orders, receiving goods, and making payments.

Manufacturing plan. Developing a manufacturing plan is a highly involved process, especially if the product is made of many parts. The sales plan specifies when, what, and how many products are to be sold, thus defining when finished products must be available for delivery. Figuring backward from that target date, the time needed for assembling the finished product must be estimated, and assembly operations set early enough to have the finished product ready on schedule.

Preliminary steps that must be planned in this overall process are—in reverse sequence—making and assembling the parts so that they are available when assembly is scheduled to start, ordering and receiving raw material in time to start making the parts, and having required manpower available. Although the sales plan usually shows that sales will vary, it is undesirable to have abrupt fluctuations in the production rate. Therefore, the manufacturing plan must provide for some goods to be held in inventory when sales are slack.

Financial Plan

Although the sales plan is regarded as the basic planning document because all other plans derive from it, the most critical plan to a firm's survival is its financial plan. The costs must be scheduled for doing all of the things in the sales and production plans, for no matter how successful a company's sales record may be, if it does not have money to pay its bills, it will eventually become bankrupt.

There is a time lag between the incurring of costs in making or buying a product and the receipt of payments for sales. Also, there are investments that must be made in plant and equipment. Thus, all companies must carefully schedule by time periods the outgo of cash for all purposes. Balanced against this schedule is a schedule of income from sales. At any time, if accumulated cash outgo exceeds accumulated income, it will be known that additional cash must be obtained from sources outside the firm. If this is not possible, it will be known that the firm's scale of operations must be cut back.

*Jim Brewster sat uncomfortably in what he now knew to be the
overly plush outer office of Transcon, Inc. It occurred to him that it
was just like Eric Waino and Jefferson Hill, president and executive
vice-president, respectively, of Transcon, to keep him waiting, because from the beginning they had been unenthusiastic about engaging his services as a management consultant. It had only been his
proposition that he would do a five-day study for one third the normal
consulting fee that induced them to hire him at all, and then it had
been with the remark that the only reason they were doing it was to
satisfy their curiosity as to what function a consultant thought he
performed. Jim had been trying to build his own consulting practice
for three months, after having worked two years for a national consulting firm, and was beginning to wonder if he would ever get to
like the selling part of the profession. He certainly knew that he
didn't like having to cut his fee in order to get an assignment.*

*"Well, I guess that you have found out what a promising company
we have here," was Waino's opening comment when Jim was finally
admitted to the inner office. Waino and Hill had started Transcon
about nine months previously with $50,000 of their own savings,
$250,000 raised from a group of small business investors, and some
outstanding ideas for the design and manufacture of transistors, di-
odes, and semiconductors. Both men had brilliant backgrounds as
research and development engineers.*

*"In the time you allowed me, I decided to concentrate on your cash
position over the next twelve months," said Jim. "Because you said
that you were not interested in reading a long, wordy report, I have
condensed my findings on a single page. I have backup for all my
figures, however."*

*"You seem to avoid Mr. Waino's comment, which was really in the
form of a question," said Jefferson Hill.*

*Jim paused for a moment before replying. "I carefully checked the
basis for your sales forecast, and if anything, it is conservative. There
is an excellent potential market for your products. I used your own
sales projections to do my cash forecast."*

"You don't expect a fee for telling us something we already know, do you?" asked Waino.

"No, I have earned a fee for finding out that your company will probably go broke in May or June of next year," was Jim's calm response.

"Utterly absurd!" Waino exploded. "Don't you know that we have over $140,000 in cash right now, that our investment group is going to put in $200,000 more month after next, and that I am dickering for a $200,000 additional loan from the bank to be credited in January? And you have admitted that our sales will total over 3.5 million dollars over the next twelve months."

"I have taken all of those things into consideration," Jim said, "even including the highly improbable bank loan. If you will let me go over the figures with you, you will see what is going to happen. First of all, the average collection period on accounts receivable in this industry is forty-five days. In other words, you can expect to receive cash from one month's sales in the middle of the second following month. As you will notice, I have realistically lagged the cash receipts from sales in the forecast." (See Exhibit 11–1.)

"Maybe we can press our customers for faster payment," said Hill.

"Your customers are giant corporations, and can't be pressed," Jim replied. "What you had better start doing right now is try to talk them into some sort of an advance payment arrangement.

"Your main problem is that you will incur the expenses for generating sales before the sales are made," Jim continued, "and the buildup of payroll and purchase payments will be as impressive as the potential sales themselves. Wages and salaries must be paid when due, and payroll taxes must be paid at the end of each quarter. Trade creditors can only be stalled for so long before they will begin to take action. This firm is simply undercapitalized for the sales volume that you are trying to reach. As for the doubtful bank loan, you will observe that half of it will go out for new machinery in the month that you hope to get it, and that then you will have to start paying it back, which will be a further drain on cash. I see no feasible way for you to last until September, but if you could, and if you don't overexpand

Exhibit 11–1. Transcon, Inc., Cash Forecast, 12-Month Period, October 1971–September 1972 ($000).

	OCT.	NOV.	DEC.	JAN.	FEB.	MAR.	APRIL	MAY	JUNE	JULY	AUG.	SEPT.
CASH INFLOW:												
Cash Balance	143											
Sales	75	100	125	150	200	250	310	375	450	525	540	550
Receipts from Sales	25	40	75	100	125	150	200	250	310	375	450	525
Receipts from Loan				200								
Receipts from Stock			200									
TOTAL RECEIPTS	168	40	275	300	125	150	200	250	310	375	450	525
CASH OUTFLOW:												
Payroll	50	60	75	100	125	155	185	225	265	270	225	225
Purchases	35	40	50	60	80	100	125	150	180	210	220	225
Plant & Equipment	2	1	3	100	5	1	2	4	1	1	1	1
Loan Payment	8	8	8	8	25	25	25	25	25	25	25	25
Interest	1	1	1	1	2	2	2	2	2	2	2	2
TOTAL DISBURSEMENTS	96	110	137	269	237	283	339	406	473	508	473	478
Cash Surplus (INC.)	72	(70)	138	31	(112)	(133)	(139)	(156)	(163)	(133)	(23)	47
Cash Surplus (CUM.)	72	2	140	171	59	(74)	(213)	(369)	(532)	(665)	(688)	(641)

further, you would begin to reduce the negative cash balance at that time."

In view of the cavalier way that Waino and Hill had treated him, Jim couldn't help gloating a little as he watched their deflated faces. Finally Waino spoke up. "What do you recommend that we do about the situation?"

"As I have mentioned, you can try to get advance payments," Jim said. "This would certainly help, but you would still need to add substantially more permanent capital. You can try to get your in-,*vestors to put in more, but there is the risk that you and Mr. Hill will end up as only very minor stockholders in your own company. I suspect that several of your customers might be glad to acquire your firm, but there again, you would be back to working for someone else. At the present time, long-term debt is out of the question. My best suggestion is that you drastically cut back on your sales growth. Be the size of company that you can afford to be, and expand gradually as your resources permit."*

"Would you consider coming to work for us, and helping us get this company soundly established?" Hill asked.

"Right now I am interested in getting my own practice established," said Jim, secretly glad that he had a hedge on the venture. "But I will be glad to help you as a consultant. It will be at full fee, of course."

Discussion Questions

Reference Case A. The Case of the Unpredicted Variable (Section 10)

1. Explain how, in Reference Case A, the Moore brothers had developed a sales forecast but had apparently not implemented it with a sales plan.
2. In Reference Case A, what would be the effect of the expected reduction in sales volume on Central Texas Welding Supply Company's purchase plan? What would be the effect of the unexpected sales decrease?

3. In the Case of the Impending Disaster, how could the partners Waino and Hill have built a successful company, yet be so blind to the seriousness of their cash position?
4. Why would Jim Brewster tell Waino and Hill that it was improbable that Transcon would get a bank loan?
5. Speculate on some disadvantages of Transcon's getting advance payments from its large customers.

12. Supporting Plans

It is difficult to imagine any business firm that should not plan its operations—at least to the extent of having a sales plan, a production plan, and a financial plan. This is possibly enough planning for a small company. However, as the scale of a firm's operations increases, it is necessary to develop other plans—such as organization, manpower, management development, capital investment, and research and development plans—to support its major plans.

Organization Plan

As a firm grows beyond the size where all activities can be directed by the owner, it becomes necessary to divide the work into departments. Therefore, an organization plan is an important supporting plan for companies larger than the owner-operator type. There are alternative ways of departmenting, such as grouping activities by the kind of work done (finance, manufacturing, sales), the geographical area where the work is done (northwest region, central region, southwest region), and the requirements of different products or services (see Section 18). The choice of method is determined by the firm's objectives and by its sales plan.

Manpower Plan

Another important supporting plan for the larger company is a manpower plan. Even if the firm intends only to remain the same size, it will lose employees over time through resignation, firing, retirement, ill health, and death. But the managers of most companies realize that growth is essential for survival, so their sales plan will reflect the objective of some projected increase in size. Thus, a plan is necessary not only to replace employees who are lost to the firm for some reason, but to add to the complement of salesmen, production workers, clerical personnel, buyers, accountants, and others required to meet the increased demands imposed by a constantly growing scale of operations. (Details of a manpower plan, including recruiting, selection, training, and compensation are described in sections relating to the staffing function.)

Management Development Plan

The availability of competent managers is such an important factor in a firm's ability even to survive, let alone successfully grow, that a special plan is necessary to assure an adequate supply of managers. The number and qualifications of managers needed in the future at each organizational level can be determined from the company's organization plan. An inventory should be maintained of existing and potential managers now employed, with details covering their backgrounds and their potential for promotion. A comparison of managers currently employed with the number needed in the future, as identified in the organization plan, will indicate the number of potential managers that must be brought into the firm each year. In addition, the further education and experience needed by each managerial candidate must be determined, and the entire findings put together in a management development plan. (Management development is discussed in Section 40.)

Capital Investment Plan

What a firm does with its capital funds is crucial to its success. One test of a good manager is the ability to continuously produce good candidate investments for capital funds. (In this case, *candidate investments* primarily means improved production equipment and facilities.) A well-managed company will always have more candidate investments than it has capital funds. Therefore, a capital investment plan involves a careful analysis of the cost of each candidate investment relative to the savings produced by the investment over its economic life.

Some ways have been invented for establishing a numerical index of each investment's savings relative to its cost. One is called the *discounted rate of return,* which is the interest rate at which the cost of the investment and the present value of the estimated future flow of earnings from the investment equal zero. (Discounted rate of return is explained in Section 59.)

A firm's capital investment plan can be developed by rationing available capital funds among the candidate investments, starting with the investment with the highest rate of return, then proceeding to the next, and so on, until either the supply of capital funds is exhausted or the next candidate investment promises an unsatisfactory rate of return.

Research and Development Plan

This discussion, which in no way covers all of the supporting plans that business firms may make, will conclude with some comments on a kind of plan that is becoming increasingly important in these times of dynamic change—the research and development plan. This plan, by its nature, is relevant mainly to manufacturing organizations.

Change in products of all kinds is taking place at such a rapid rate that the average market acceptance of even a fantastically successful product is less than twelve years. Competition between products is so keen that something in the order of 80 percent of the new products brought on the market are failures. Therefore, for a firm to stay alive, it must constantly develop new product ideas to replace those on the market that will eventually become obsolete.

A firm uses the basic objectives and premises of its forecasts as foundations for its research and development plan. For example, a printing company whose primary product is checks for banks to provide for their customers might have as a premise that electronic systems are going to do away with the use of checks, and have an objective of getting into textbook printing. Its R & D plan would be shaped by these considerations. A restraint on the magnitude of the plan is the money that can be allocated to research and development. The details of such plans vary with individual firms, but the goal of all such plans is to come up with enough new ideas annually to keep the company alive and growing. (See Section 64 for a treatment of R & D from the perspective of the controlling function.)

Discussion Questions

Reference Case A. The Case of the Unpredicted Variable (Section 10)
Reference Case B. The Case of the Impending Disaster (Section 11)

1. Why might capital investment plans be the most important plans that managers make?
2. In Reference Case A, what kind of manpower planning should

Central Texas Welding Supply be doing, in light of anticipated and actual sales declines?

3. How might a small company like Central Texas Welding Supply maintain an R & D plan?

4. In Reference Case B, does Transcon need a management development plan? Why? If yes, what kind of a plan should it be?

5. Should Transcon develop and maintain an R & D plan? Why?

13. Long-Term and Short-Term Plans

Plans, both major and supporting, are further classified according to the period of time over which they are projected. The common time classifications for plans are *long-term* and *short-term,* although some companies also have what they call *intermediate* plans.

Priority

A firm's long-term plan is really a set of alternative courses of action, any one of which, depending on external conditions, could lead the firm to achieve its basic objectives over an extended time period. A short-term plan is for an immediate time period and is designed to meet objectives for that period. Therefore, short-term plans derive from long-term plans, and can be set only after long-term plans are made.

Current Practice

Business firms are apparently giving increasing attention to the development and maintenance of long-term plans. Except for the extremely large companies, this is a fairly new practice. The theory of long-term planning for business has been around for some time, and there has not been much improvement on what Henri Fayol had to say (see Section 3). However, it has been only during the past twenty years that most companies have practiced long-term planning of any significance. Probable reasons for the developing popularity of long-term plans include accelerating rates of change in products and markets, improved forecasting methods, computerization of data, and the increasing sophistication of business managers.

Length of Long-Term Plans

Surveys have found that the majority of companies doing long-range planning arbitrarily pick a period of five years as the time span for such plans. Some companies select shorter periods, others longer. The period really should not be selected arbitrarily, however, because there are objective criteria that a firm can use to determine the length of a long-term plan. One such criterion is how far into the future the firm's fixed commitments extend. Such commitments would include contracts and long-term indebtedness. If the firm is obligated to make debt payments covering principal and interest over ten years, for example, it would seem wise to plan for that long a period. Another criterion is the life cycle of its existing product line, as well as the life cycles of products in development.

Alternate Actions

As has been said, long-term plans spell out alternate actions. Assume that a firm's basic objectives have been set, and that they focus on a certain rate of growth and a certain return on investment. There are different ways these objectives can be achieved: (1) capture a larger share of the market; (2) broaden the product line and enter new markets; (3) acquire other companies. The long-term plan might include thoughtful analysis of all three alternatives. The final choice is made later on the basis of data obtained concerning factors in the environment in which the firm operates, such as changes in market demand, changes in competitors' strategies, or changes in government policy.

General Nature of Long-Term Plans

Long-term plans tend to be strategies, both for reaching the firm's objectives and for thwarting competitors' objectives. They are also designed to enable firms to accommodate to predicted trends in their industry. For example, firms in the aerospace industry, such as Boeing, North American Rockwell, and Aerojet-General, foresaw a steady lessening of defense orders several years ago and began to formulate strategies to diversify their product lines. Such plans are subject to change, and therefore should be flexible and not spelled out in detail. They are usually stated in gross, yearly terms. The type of thinking that goes into long-term plans has been called "nonprogrammed" decision making. That is, the strategies devised are novel, opportunistic, and uninfluenced by past actions.

The responsibility for developing long-term plans is almost always given to top managers of the firm, although they may enlist a planning staff, or lower level managers, in the plan's preparation.

Since a firm's major plans are those concerned with sales, production, and finance, its long-term plan will focus on these areas in broad perspective. Supporting plans in a long-term plan also stress objectives and policies more than they do details.

Short-Term Plans

With the long-term plan serving as a guide, short-term plans tend to be implementations of the long-term plan over the immediate period ahead. Because it is the function of the short-term plans to contribute to the realization of the long-term plan, they should be consistent with it. Opportunistic ventures, tempting though they may appear in the short run, must be avoided if they are in conflict with what has been planned for the long run.

Unlike long-term plans, short-term plans are prepared in detail, and are supposed to be carried out exactly as stated. Managers working under short-term plans are usually permitted only limited freedom to make changes. The plans are developed in at least monthly terms, and it is not uncommon, especially with the advantages now offered by the computer, to develop them in weekly terms. The best way to explain short-term plans is to say that they are budgets and offer a means of control, permitting actual results to be compared with projected performance.

Long-term plans are strategic, and short-term plans are tactical. The decisions involved in short-term planning might be called "programmed"; that is, they are routine, repetitive, and highly influenced by the action of preparing the long-term plan. Also, the decisions are made at the operational level by middle managers or supervisors.

The Case of the Markets
That Will Fade Away

"I don't mean to suggest that the two primary uses for petroleum products, namely, internal combustion engines and gas and oil furnaces, are going to disappear in the near future. In fact, the markets that they create for petroleum may not change much in our lifetimes. But, inevitably, gasoline will not be the fuel source for future modes of transportation, and nuclear or solar energy will heat our homes and factories. Plans must be made to enable Petro Corporation to cope with these changes." Thus, Paul Rosetti, chairman of the board of Petro Corporation, addressed the other four members of the newly formed planning subcommittee of the firm's board of directors.

"As I see this committee's role," Rosetti continued, "it is, for one thing, to establish the planning premises. The eventual disappearance of our markets is one planning premise, but we should time-phase the events leading up to this demise, which become premises themselves. We should also identify alternate strategies for use when each of the premised events occurs. This committee should then pass along the premises and the strategies to lower-level planning committees made up of operating managers."

"My thoughts are that there will not be dramatic impacts on either of the petroleum industry's two main markets for at least ten years," said Philip Coates, a director of Petro, and president of American Bank. "Over the very short run—say for the next year—I premise that gasoline marketing will be characterized by promotion of pollution-reducing additives. The board should authorize our president, Mr. Love, to adopt appropriate tactics to assure that Petro does not lose market position in the additives race."

"I subscribe to Mr. Coates' views," said Dr. Peter Benz, a director and vice-president for research and development. "A promotion plan for our special brand of lead-free gasoline is ready for implementation. The next thing that we must be ready for is reduction of other contaminants in gasoline. This will be forced on the petroleum industry, first by taxation, and later probably by legislation. The effect on Petro, and all other oil companies, will be obsolescence of our high-octane refineries, and a requirement for major capital expenditures for low-octane refineries."

"The need for a probable large amount of outside capital is a premise for your financial planning," said Rosetti to Justin Kast, another Petro director, and the firm's vice-president for finance.

"Our present financial plan extends to 1980," said Kast, *"but will have to be revised, and stretched out in gross terms to the year 2000, in light of what this committee is developing."*

"The reason that I agree with Mr. Coates' premise of a minimum ten-year period of little change," volunteered Dr. Neil Rogers, one of the outside directors, and president of the state university, *"is that the equipment to replace gasoline engines and oil furnaces has really not been designed yet. I suggest that plans be developed separately for what must be done about the elimination of the internal combustion engine, and what actions must be taken to compensate for the loss of the natural gas and heating oil markets. I put the serious effects of the latter contingency well into the next century, and suggest this as a premise. Moreover, I recommend two plans for the sustained sale of lead-free gasoline, one for a ten-year term, and another for a twenty-year term."*

"If there is agreement, let us adopt the premise that nuclear or solar energy will not be a threat to natural gas or heating oils on a major scale for forty years," said Rosetti. *"This gives us some time, but your people, Dr. Benz, should start planning on how Petro can fit into a new heat-source industry. Now, let's start talking about what Petro can do about the eventual decline in the market for gasoline."*

"As the company's greatest resource is its oil reserves, we must develop other uses for petroleum," answered Benz. *"We have expanded heavily in the petrochemical industry, but so have our competitors, both domestic and foreign."*

"One area in which Petro has gone too far is fertilizers," said Coates. *"Fertilizer plants all over the world are operating under capacity. I think that we might be better off getting out of this business."*

"At least one of our competitors has sold its fertilizer subsidiary," Kast supported, *"and our own operations have lost money."*

"Well, it looks like we have another product with an unfavorable market," said Rosetti. *"I will ask Mr. Love to have a detailed study*

made of fertilizer prospects. There is one obvious step that Petro can take, and that is gradually to change from strictly a petroleum company into a conglomerate. It will not be the complete solution, but one strategy that I suggest is that we begin acquiring firms in other industries. Perhaps the goal that in ten years Petro's sales should be 50 percent from products other than petroleum would be a desirable one to propose to the board."

"There is no question that Petro will have to go this route," said Neil Rogers, "but we must consider many additional strategies. Some of them may seem pretty wild at the present time. For example, this firm is in an extractive industry. The ocean floor is abundant with some minerals that are nearing exhaustion on the earth's surface. I suggest that serious thought be given to Petro becoming an ocean-mining company."

"Detailed planning for something like this would take years, and cost millions of dollars," said Rosetti thoughtfully. "But, I think it is something that should be done. I will ask Mr. Love to have a preliminary estimate and prospectus made for presentation to the full board of directors."

"One factor that should be kept in mind," Kast said, "is Petro's association with transportation. I think we should try to connect the firm with whatever modes of transportation will supplant the gasoline-powered automobile."

"I certainly agree that Petro shouldn't abandon transportation," remarked Benz. "What I suggest that this committee do is speculate on all possible replacements for gasoline-powered automobiles, and then determine how Petro can use its resources to associate with the new devices."

"It sounds like an excellent approach," said Rosetti. "Who would like to get the discussion started?"

Discussion Questions

1. Would a five-year plan be adequate for meeting the problems faced by Petro Corporation? If not, why not?

2. How might Petro's planning subcommittee of the board of directors utilize a planning staff?
3. What short-term plans will derive from the long-term planning that Petro Corporation has begun to formulate?
4. Why would some of the plans being developed by Petro's top-level planning committee be called "nonprogrammed" decisions?
5. In view of the directions taken by Petro's planning committee, what major long-term plan stands out as an imperative?

14. Standing Plans and Single-Purpose Plans

Besides classifying plans as major or supporting, and long-term or short-term, another way is to separate the ones that are used over and over again—called *standing plans*—from *single-purpose plans*. While the latter are applied to a single and probably nonrecurring series of future decisions, standing plans are composed of policies, procedures, and rules that are intended to apply to decisions made regularly, so that planning need not be repeated each time a decision situation recurs.

Policies

A firm's policies tend to reflect its attitude on various issues, some highly important and others relatively minor. Actually, a firm's most important policies are its objectives, which set the course for all managerial actions. Lower-level policies perform the same function; that is, they serve as guides to action, each in their own way.

Management decisions. Some of a firm's policies are the result of deliberate management decision, such as

- requiring at least a 20-percent estimated return on all capital investments.
- restricting inventories on hand to one fifth of expected annual sales.
- stipulating that all contracts, negotiations, and agreements with suppliers be made only by the purchasing department.

Policies of this kind are usually written, and deviations from them usually must be justified in advance.

Precedents. Other policies simply evolve from precedent. Without conscious managerial planning, various policies accumulate as a result of past behavior and actions, such as

- aggressive retaliation to a competitor's price cut.
- favoring graduates of a particular college when hiring new employees.
- continued use of machinery until it is completely worn out.

Evolved policies can have a great deal of influence in shaping a company's image, and they can be dangerous if they are in conflict with its stated objectives. Since evolved policies are usually not written, managers are often not fully aware of the extent to which they influence actions.

Imposed policies. A third kind of policy, largely beyond a firm's control, is imposed on it by outside forces, such as the government and labor unions. Such policies include

- regulated wage and hour requirements.
- restrictions on the hiring of nonunion employees.
- prohibition of misleading advertising.

A firm's actions are strongly influenced by such policies, which are almost always expressed in written form, as in published government regulations and in union contracts.

Procedures

Procedures are detailed, step-by-step methods for performing specific actions. Their supporting logic can be traced back to Weber's bureaucratic model and to Taylor's scientific management theory (see Sections 1 and 2). The one best way for performing any action is determined, and becomes the procedure to be used every time the action is performed thereafter.

The intention of setting up procedures is to reduce the need for planning. Once the decision to standardize a procedure is made, the action governed by that procedure becomes routine. No further time need be spent on planning that particular action until the procedure becomes obsolete. The key to efficient use of procedures is that they must continually be reviewed, and revised when necessary.

Generally speaking, the larger the company, the more extensive is its use of procedures. They are designed to govern every kind of repetitive action, including payroll checkwriting; requisitioning materials, supplies, and equipment; hiring new employees; processing a quality control report; requesting a budget increase; and so on.

Rules

Procedures specify how repetitive work activities are to be performed, while rules tend to stipulate what personal conduct is required of employees. Thus, firms have rules covering such matters as the care of company property, times for starting and quitting, safety precautions, and drinking and fighting on company premises. Most rules are accompanied by penalties for violation, which vary in degree according to the seriousness of the rule and the number of violations. Some rules and penalties are written and formally communicated; others are only informally understood.

Single-Purpose Plans

Single-purpose plans are often called *programs* or *projects*. They have identifiable beginnings and ends. In time, they often extend beyond a year. For example, a new factory, development of an advanced and unique system (like the Polaris system), or a drive for increased long-term capital would all require single-purpose planning.

Program planning involves
- the detailed determination of each step required to accomplish the end objective.
- the sequence with which each step must be performed.
- the time and resources required to accomplish each step.
- the measurements to determine that a step is accomplished.
- the dates for completion of each step.

Program plans tend to be as detailed as short-term plans, but extend over long-term periods. Individual managerial responsibility for a total program, and the parts of a program, are usually specified. Programs frequently cut across functional lines, that is, represent a complex of plans for engineering, production, procurement, and so on. (For a more detailed discussion, see Section 19.)

"One of the first things we have to do is establish regular calibration periods for all the shop gauges," said Stan Klopp, newly appointed quality control supervisor of Sum-ter Corporation, to his assistant, Allen Tanaka. "The way it is now, company-owned gauges are checked whenever the tool-crib attendant happens to have the time, and it's been left to the mechanics to ask to have their personal gauges calibrated."

Sum-ter Corporation manufactures golf carts and snowmobiles. It has grown rapidly over its five-year life, and employs about three hundred people. A serious accident caused by defective brakes on one of its golf carts made John Woodward, president, realize the need for formal quality control. This decision led to the employment of Klopp, who was given pretty much of a free rein to set up appropriate quality-control procedures.

Klopp's conversation with Tanaka continued: "In addition to the lack of control over the shop gauges, I can't find any evidence that the master gauges have ever been checked."

"At the last place I worked," said Tanaka, "the procedure was to calibrate all shop gauges except screw plugs every two weeks. Screw plugs were checked after every use. Arrangements were made with the manufacturers of the master gauges for calibration every six months."

"That was my experience also," said Klopp. "I'll send a memorandum to the production manager asking that all gauges be assembled this weekend. We'll calibrate them, and make up a record card for each one. Then I'll get the production manager to tell his foreman to make sure that the calibration schedule is followed."

Stan and Allen began patiently to build quality-control procedures in this fashion. An early event that required their attention was a bearing that had been left out of each machine in a shipment of snowmobiles to Sum-ter's most important dealer. Upon investigation, Stan found out that the assembly shop had no procedure for assuring that all parts were included in a piece of equipment when it was put together. His action was to design a form with a space for the date and the equipment's serial number, and a listing of every part that was supposed to go in the machine. As the parts were assembled, they were to be checked off on a form, and a completed form for every machine that was assembled was to be sent to his office.

While Stan was working on the checklist procedure, he assigned Allen to the task of planning which parts were to be inspected at the machines as they were being processed, and which parts were to be sent to a central inspection station after they had been processed. It would be desirable to have all processes that were producing defective parts discovered before unnecessary costs were incurred, but the limiting factor was that some operations required inspection by apparatus that could not be moved about through the shop. Allen's approach was to prescribe decentralized inspection for all operations that could be examined by portable gauges, such as micrometers. Instructions were written calling for central inspection of operations requiring such apparatus as Starrett height gauges or electronic devices.

The next matter requiring attention was inspection of incoming materials at the receiving dock. Until the arrival of Klopp and Tanaka at Sum-ter, there had actually been no inspection of items made by vendors to the company's specifications. Foremost among these components were engines, transmissions, and castings. Stan and Allen worked out performance tests for engines and transmissions, and persuaded John Woodward to invest in an X-ray machine for inspecting castings for blow holes and cold shuts. They then had to decide between 100-percent inspection of critical items and statistical acceptance sampling. Because of the high cost of inspecting every item, they opted for sampling, and then had to develop a sampling plan for the purchasing department to incorporate in its purchase contracts.

The work with the purchasing department on sampling plans made Stan aware that the company had no objective basis for evaluating suppliers other than by price. Together with Bill Leslie, the purchasing agent, he developed a point evaluation system to rank vendors on the basis of the quality reports on incoming shipments.

A system for communicating Sum-ter's quality performance to the company's top management was an obvious need, and Allen designed a system called Quality Rejection Reports. The reports were issued monthly, and recapped the number of quality rejections, the cause for the rejections, and the recommended corrective actions.

When parts were rejected because of failure to meet quality standards, two actions were possible. They could either be reworked or scrapped. To make the rework decision a routine one, Stan developed a list of criteria for incurring the costs of rework, and another list which sent defective parts to the scrap heap.

After about three months of quality-control effort, Stan remarked to Allen as he surveyed the pile of memoranda on quality that had been written: "You know, we could use these instructions to write up a Quality Control Standard Procedures Manual. We could assign a copy to everybody in the company who needed one, and keep adding to it as we developed new procedures. We would also want to give notice of the revision of procedures. The SPM would be the source of reference on any question regarding Sum-ter's quality assurance program."

Discussion Questions

Reference Case A. The Case of the Markets That Will Fade Away (Section 13)

1. Is it desirable that a firm commit all of its policies to writing?
2. How can an individual company (assume that it is a large one) exercise control over policies that are imposed by the government? By labor unions?
3. In Reference Case A, what is one of Petro's planning alternatives that should be formalized with the detail of a program?
4. In the Case of the Newborn SPM, how would you evaluate the development of the Quality Control Standard Procedures Manual for Sum-ter Corporation? Are there any advantages to the way it was done? Could it have been done in another way?
5. Should quality-control procedures be developed by top management, instead of by middle managers such as Stan Klopp, with the help of his assistant?

15. Human Factors in Planning

Planning would be a relatively simple process if the key element in the making of plans—people—always behaved predictably and controllably. However, they do not. Therefore, distortions and conflicts in the planning process often appear as a result of interpersonal conflicts and individual differences in perception, communication, needs, and interests.

Differences in Perception

There are differences in the way people perceive objectives, so that even if planning could be confined to the very top level of management, there would not be common agreement on the firm's basic goals. Because there is such disagreement, objectives must either be modified to get a unanimous opinion, or the vote of the majority must prevail. In the latter case, a dissenting minority could create ongoing conflict.

In addition to holding different views on objectives, the senior managers to whom we just referred will perceive different ways of achieving the stated objectives. These differences must somehow be reconciled, so that the objectives and main planning premises sent from top management to the lower levels appear to come from a united front.

At the lower levels, differences in perception about goals and the meaning of achieving them are magnified because of incomplete and often inaccurate information, plus conflicting personal interests. These factors are almost always present, and usually have some negative effect on plans.

Communication Channels

"Incomplete and often inaccurate" applies both to planning information that comes down from and that filters back up to the top levels of management. One reason is the transforming potential in the communication process. Fundamentally, communication is accomplished by written and oral messages. The channel through which messages pass may be direct: that is, from top to bottom and from bottom to top. The larger the organization, the more likely it is that the channel will not be direct, but indirect, which means that messages will be intercepted at the various management levels between top and bottom, and transformed. The reason for transforming the messages is to improve their clarity, but the result is often added confusion. (This subject is given further treatment in later sections, especially 53 and .65.)

Semantics

Changing the sense of the message in the communication channel is one cause of distortion in communication. Distortion also occurs as a result of imperfections in transmitting the message. Both written and oral messages depend on the receiver understanding what the sender wanted to say; ideal communication would result from perfectly expressed messages being perfectly understood. But words have different meanings to different people, and rarely does communication approach perfection. Some part of the intent of most messages is lost because of semantics problems.

Conflicting Goals

Every individual has a personal, specific set of needs, and a dominant interest in satisfying those needs. Individuals in organizations may perceive that their needs will be satisfied by complying with the objectives of the organization, but it is more likely that they will perceive other, perhaps conflicting, subgoals to be more satisfying. One such subgoal may be the individual's own work activity. Thus, production managers will seek to optimize the role of the production function in making plans; and engineering managers, the role of engineering, and so on. In like fashion, the manager involved in making plans for different product divisions, or major programs, will strive for allocation of resources in preferred quantities and qualities to their particular activities. With all managers competing to optimize their own job-oriented subgoals, the overall objectives of the firm may indeed be overlooked.

Another kind of goal that takes precedence over the firm's objectives, and thus interferes with rational planning, is the individual need for self-expression and job satisfaction. Expressed a different way, it is the need to feel worthwhile and to be influential to some degree, at least so far as one's own work is concerned. Organizations tend to inhibit people from satisfying this need. Thus, members of organizations are frustrated, and their frustration keeps them from giving wholehearted support to the company's objectives. The more the planning process is regimented and impersonal, with individuals directed to make a specified input to the plan without explanation or participation, the less fully successful the planning effort is likely to be.

The requirement for rigid conformity to plans once they are made, such as strict and unquestioning obedience to procedures, will produce the same bias against really working for the firm's objectives. In fact, people may achieve some need satisfaction by working against the company's goals.

Countering the Effect of Goal Conflict

One logical solution to the problem of conflicting individual and organizational goals lies in making people see that their personal interests are best served by working toward the achievement of the firm's objectives. This is an idealistic prescription, which in practice must rest on the motivational techniques that each manager employs in directing subordinates. One method that has been successfully used to offset the tendency of managers to optimize their own subgoals at the expense of overall goals is to engage them in the overall planning effort, so that they are faced with the task of helping coordinate their own subgoals with the subgoals of other departments or divisions. They also derive need satisfaction when they engage in planning if they are allowed to participate fully in making the decisions that govern their part of the planning effort. (This is known as management by objectives, and is discussed in more detail in Section 46; for other discussions of motivation, see Sections 47–51.)

By the summer of 1970, Sidney Green, president of Green Wholesale Grocers, Inc., knew that some drastic steps had to be taken to reduce operating costs or the firm was going to be in serious trouble. He first thought of imposing some economizing measures on his department managers, but then decided to let them develop a cost-reduction plan on their own. He called them together, and with complete frankness explained that the decline in business made a plan for running the company at considerably lower overhead costs absolutely essential.

"I appreciate the old man's confidence in us," said Jack Trask, warehouse manager. "Whatever we decide to do, we should try to communicate to the troops with the same candor that he has used. My personal contribution will be to stop putting in for the overtime that I work, which Mr. Green didn't have to pay, but always did. This might set an example for the guys in the warehouse to donate their overtime hours. Another thing that can be cut out is the cafeteria, which has always been much too small an operation to come close to breaking even."

"I am going to do the same thing with overtime," supported Al Mann, office manager. "If my people see me not charging my overtime, they should be able to sense the seriousness of our situation. Of course we should cut out all frills like the children's Christmas party and the Labor Day picnic. I think that if we just run the air conditioner in the late afternoon we could save some money. Also, I am going to ask my people to be especially careful with office supplies. What thoughts do you have for the sales department, Ike?" he asked Ike Comstock, sales manager.

"Well, we can't do the things that you fellows are planning," Ike responded, "and anyhow we must keep up appearances so that our customers won't suspect that Green is in trouble. I am going to tell the salesmen to try to work a little harder, however."

"I'll tell you what you can have your people do to reduce costs, and also eliminate what the other employees think is a gross inequity," Jack replied. "That is, do something about the salesmen using com-

*pany cars and company gas for personal business. I don't know how
I am going to get my people to work overtime without pay when
they see your salesmen lining up their cars at the company gas tank
every Friday afternoon. Who do they think they are kidding? They
sure aren't calling on customers on Saturdays and Sundays."*

*"That's right, Ike," said Al. "Unless you put the clamps on the sales-
men abusing their car privileges, this whole cost-reduction plan will
go down the drain. How about having the company cars parked in
the lot at night and over the weekends, and let the salesmen get to
work and get back home the same ways that the rest of us do?"*

*Comstock suddenly became very unhappy. He figured the use of the
company car was worth about $250 per month to him, especially
when his weekend trips to his mountain cabin at Big Bear Lake were
considered. "Absolutely absurd," he shouted. "The salesmen wouldn't
stand for that for a day. They count the personal use of company
cars as part of their compensation, and would look at your scheme
as a wage cut. Besides, quite a few of them live in their territories,
and they would have to get in here and then drive back each morning
before they could start to work."*

*"They would take it a lot better if you explained why the company
has to reduce costs, and what the rest of the employees are doing,"
Jack said. "I concede that some of the salesmen live in their territories, and perhaps their cars should only be parked in the company
lot over the weekends. Many of them come in here in the morning
before going out to their territories, and their cars could be parked
overnight. I think the key to getting this accepted would be for you to
set the example with your company car."*

*Ike Comstock was trapped, and he knew it. He realized that if he
presented any more arguments, Jack and Al would bring out what
was really on their minds, namely that as he spent most of his time in
the office, why did he need a company car at all?*

*"I'll see what the salesmen say," Ike snapped. "But I can tell you
right now that they won't go for it."*

*That afternoon at the sales meeting, Ike made his announcement,
"Green doesn't think he is making enough money," he said, "and he*

is trying to squeeze more out of the sales department. He begrudges us the use of company cars, and we are all going to have to park them here at night. I suppose the next thing that will happen is that you guys will have to walk to call on your accounts."

The response of the salesmen was predictable. They voted unanimously to refuse to call on their customers unless the overnight and weekend parking requirement for company cars was rescinded.

On the following day Ike reported back to Stan and Al. "I tried my best to convince the salesmen that it was for the good of the company," he said. "But they voted to strike if they are denied their personal use of the company cars."

"That's too bad," Stan said, and Al nodded in agreement. "Both my people and Al's agreed to cooperate 100 percent with our plan, provided that the salesmen would do their share. However, unless the salesmen will knock off using the cars and the gas as their personal property, the warehouse and the office workers will have no part of the plan. I guess we will have to tell Mr. Green that we can't do much for him."

"I really am disappointed," was Sidney Green's response when Stan, reluctantly acting as spokesman, outlined a greatly modified plan that promised only minor savings. "I was really counting on you men coming up with an emergency plan that would keep the company profitable. Now I am afraid that I am going to have to accept a purchase offer for the firm that has been made to me. My hope was that you three could show me that you could successfully manage the company, and I had a plan whereby you could eventually buy me out."

Discussion Questions

Reference Case A. The Case of the Many-Headed Monster (Section 9)

Reference Case B. The Case of the Newborn SPM (Section 14)

1. What is the likely effect of compromise on the quality of decisions? How eager are people to support the decisions of the majority, when their own plans have been defeated?

2. In Reference Case A, why were there so many interpretations of Harold Greely's statement of Tredco's objective?

3. In the Case of the Clogged Filter, did Sidney Green go as far as he should have in communicating to his key subordinates the need for a cost-reduction plan?

4. How could Ike Comstock have been prevented from deliberately distorting the sense of the plan when he communicated it to the salesmen?

5. In Reference Case B, is there potential for resistance by some individuals to the quality-control procedures that Klopp and Tanaka are developing?

16. Analytical Techniques
for Planning

Over the past ten to twenty years, there have been influences from two directions on the way management is practiced. The first influence has come from an improved, although still incomplete, understanding of human behavior. Some of the implications of behavioral science for management have been described, and are discussed in greater detail in the sections on organizing and directing. The second influence on management has come from the development of quantitative techniques for assisting in decision making.

Evaluating and Choosing Alternatives

Decision making, as noted earlier, is fundamentally the act of choosing from among alternatives. It would be rare for any goal not to have alternative means of achieving it. In real life there are usually so many alternatives that relatively few can be known or examined; consequently, decision making becomes a matter of evaluating those alternatives that stand out and choosing the one that appears to be best.

The following discussion briefly describes some important quantitative techniques for evaluating the tangible factors of such alternatives. The total decision process requires that, after the tangible factors have been evaluated, the intangible factors be brought into focus and then managerial judgment applied in making the final choice.

Decision Factors

Tangible factors are those that can be expressed numerically, such as hours of labor, units of production, and dollars of profit. Quantitative techniques arrange tangible factors into logical relationships and derive numerical solutions.

Intangible factors bear heavily on many decisions, but they cannot be expressed numerically. Reputation, community relations, and employee morale are examples of such factors.

Four quantitative techniques for decision making are critical-path scheduling, linear programming, simulation, and probability decision theory. Detailed examples of each of these techniques are presented as appendixes of this book. The following are general descriptions of them.

Critical-Path Scheduling

Critical-path scheduling, a program type of plan, employs the concept of network analysis to plan and control the performances of events in a time-phase relation to one another. The first step is to define the program's objectives, then each event to be accomplished must be identified, the time for accomplishing each event must be estimated, and finally, the events must be arrayed in a diagram (see Figure 16–1).

In the network diagram, circles are used to depict events, and those that must be accomplished first (preceding events) are placed on the left side, and those that cannot be started until preceding events are finished (succeeding events) are placed at their right. Succeeding events are connected to the preceding events by arrows.

Activity	Activity Code	Must Follow Activity
Get jack	a	—
Jack up car	b	a
Remove disk plate	c	—
Unscrew nuts	d	c
Remove flat tire	e	a, d
Get spare tire	f	—
Mount spare tire	g	e
Screw on nuts	h	g
Replace disk plate	i	h
Store spare tire	j	e, f

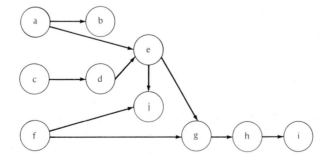

Figure 16–1. A Precedence Diagram for Changing a Tire.

For a program of any complexity, the resulting network will contain a number of paths from the start of the program to the finish.

The path through the network that takes the longest time from start to finish is called the *critical path*. The total time for the critical path is the time needed by the program.

Now you can see the benefit of critical-path scheduling for planning. Once a planner knows the time of the critical path, he can shorten it by shifting resources from events not in the critical path to events that are in the critical path, or by other devices, such as using overtime work to speed up critical-path events.

The benefits of critical-path scheduling are that

- a detailed plan must be drawn up of what has to be done to accomplish the goals of a program.
- total time to complete a program is estimated.
- the critical events in a program are identified.
- potential bottlenecks are detected before they occur.

The use of critical-path scheduling is becoming widespread for all kinds of firms, small as well as large, when they must plan for the performance of activities in sequence. Firms in the defense and construction industries, for example, have found this planning method especially useful. In fact, the technique was first developed as part of a major defense project, the Polaris program of the late 1950's. Some major parts of this system were the design, development, and construction of a nuclear-powered submarine, a rocket-propelled missile with a nuclear warhead, and advanced electronic guiding, tracking, and operating subsystems. Four or five prime contractors were involved in the Polaris project, plus thousands of subcontractors. Literally hundreds of thousands of sequential activities had to be performed in such a way that schedules for all of the parts would mesh together. It has been said that critical-path scheduling was one of the key factors in making the Polaris program successful.

Linear Programming

Linear programming is a mathematical system for allocating resources (constants) to alternative uses (variables) to get best (optimal) results. Resources can take such forms as labor capacity, materials supply, and available capital. Each of these resources can be allocated to a number of uses within a firm. Labor and materials, for example, can be assigned to any, or several, of the products within the firm's product mix, and capital can be rationed to different investment opportunities.

Resources may be called *constants* because they are available in fixed amounts, and the alternative uses may be called *variables* because the amount of a resource allocated to a potential use will vary. This amount may be called the *coefficient* of the use with respect to the resource. Finally, the certain amount of each resource that is gained or lost for every alternative use may be called the *gain* or *loss coefficient* of the use.

The objective in allocating resources is either to maximize something, such as a profit or a saving, or to minimize something, like a loss. If all of the variable uses are put into an equation, with each variable expressed in mathematical form and preceded by its gain or loss coefficient, we have what is called the *objective function*. Adding up the amounts assigned to each variable, and multiplying the total by the coefficients of that variable, gives the gain or loss resulting from the allocation of the resources.

The constant value (fixed amount available) of each resource imposes limits on *(constrains)* the amounts that can be assigned to the variables. Each constant, or resource being allocated, implies an equation in which the constant is equal to all of the alternative-use variables added up. In the equation, each alternative-use variable is expressed in notation form and preceded by its respective coefficient.

In linear programming, all of the equations bearing on a problem are solved simultaneously by a form of algebra to obtain the optimal values for each variable. In other words, each resource is allocated in such a way that maximum gain, or minimum loss, is achieved.

The linear programming example in Appendix B is as simple as can be expressed, yet it is fairly complex. In real-life uses of linear programming, it is necessary to do the calculating on a computer. Despite its complexity, linear programming is being used by an increasing number of companies for some parts of their planning effort. One example is a company like Sears, which has thousands of retail stores scattered over the country, and perhaps dozens of central warehouses from which goods can be shipped to retail outlets. From which warehouse is it most economical to ship to each of the stores? This question can be formulated into a linear programming problem, and the most efficient allocation of goods from warehouses to stores determined.

Simulation

Simulation is a term that covers many different techniques, but all have the common objective of imitating a set of real conditions in a way that predicts the outcome of the real conditions. Simulation techniques are much less expensive than actually trying out different alternatives, and the results are known much sooner.

One simulation technique is called "Monte Carlo." It is based on the assumption that events will occur with the same frequency in the future as they have in the past. To use Monte Carlo simulation, it is necessary to have records of some kind that show the frequency with which certain events have occurred in some time period; this is known as a *frequency distribution*. It is possible to project from such a distribution the average number of times each event will occur in the future. However, averages alone are not useful with many kinds of plans, where it is desirable to know how events will occur at random, which is the way they really do occur. This can be handled by relating numbers drawn at random (via a random number generator or a table of random numbers, in a manner like that described in Appendix C) to the cumulative frequency distribution. From this operation, projections can be made as to the probable occurrence of events in some future time period, and comparisons of alternative decisions can be made on the basis of these projections.

Monte Carlo simulation is not nearly so complicated as it sounds. One example is offered in Appendix C. Another practical business example of the use of Monte Carlo might have to do with preventive maintenance. Assume that the gear box of an important piece of equipment contains three main bearings. One of the bearings fails, and the gear box must be opened for the bearing to be replaced. Now the question occurs: Should one or both of the other two bearings be replaced along with the defective one? Through relating numbers drawn at random to the frequency distribution gained from past performance records, the likelihood of needed replacement of the other two can be simulated, cost comparisons of the alternative actions made, and an optimal decision reached.

Probability Decision Theory

The technique for decision making that generally is called *probability decision theory* starts with the assumption that the future will be characterized by conditions of certainty, risk, or uncertainty. If the future condition is certain, then only one state of nature is possible. Knowing exactly what will happen, a manager need only select the planning strategy that will produce the biggest payoff in terms of the use of the firm's resources. This kind of planning is relatively easy. Unfortunately, however, it is rare to have such certainty about future conditions. Very few absolutely certain conditions exist in the world, but there are many things that are relatively certain—for example, that actual time for doing work will conform to well-engineered work standards.

Under risk conditions, more than one state of nature can exist in the future, but the occurrence probability of each is known. To illustrate, consider a conventional deck of playing cards. Take the ace of spades as one state of nature. The probability that it will turn up if one card is drawn at random is 1 of 52. Thus, there is risk involved, but the amount of risk is known.

Under business conditions, possible future states of nature can be identified, and it is frequently possible to assign occurrence probabilities to each of them from data obtained from past records. The next step is to determine the firm's alternative strategies, and then to calculate the maximum payoffs that will occur for each combination of strategy and state of nature. The optimal strategy will be the one for which the greatest payoff is produced by the summation of each state of nature's probability times the payoff for that strategy/state-of-nature combination. Given the fact that risk conditions occur more frequently in business planning than do certain conditions, this technique can substantially improve the planning effort under risk conditions.

Most planning, however, is not done under certain or risk conditions, but under conditions of uncertainty. Under such conditions, thoughtful analysis will uncover the states of nature that possibly can occur, but records or other sources will be lacking to establish objectively the occurrence probabilities of each. One thing that can be done is to identify the firm's alternative strategies. Then, if each state of nature is for the moment considered to be certain, the payoff for each strategy/state-of-nature combination can be calculated. From this point on, there are numerous suggested methods for selecting the apparently superior strategy. The method that seems to be most popular is for managers to use their best judgment to assign subjective occurrence probabilities to the possible states of nature. When this is done, the final decision is made as though under risk conditions.

In fact, people constantly assign subjective probabilities in their daily lives without realizing they are doing it. For example, when most people undertake an important financial commitment, such as buying a new car or a house, they will have intuitively determined the probability of continued income from which to make payments.

Discussion Questions

1. Since the advent of quantitative methods, is the weighting of intangible factors the only way for managers to exercise judgment in decision making?
2. There are few more critical paths for a student than the path leading to a diploma. Put down in sequence each event that must be accomplished between now and your graduation. Perhaps the events will not be limited to taking courses; earning money to finance your continued education may be another kind of event to be diagrammed.
3. Explain why a system like linear programming, which helps in allocation-of-resource decisions, would appeal to the business planner.
4. What is the outstanding advantage of simulation techniques?
5. What are some decisions that you routinely make in your daily life, in which you intuitively assign subjective occurrence probabilities?

Summary

The first step that every organization must take when it attempts to plan for the future is to establish its objectives. Planning is not possible without some notion of what is to be accomplished. For the business organization, the process of setting objectives can consist of the senior managers' seriously answering questions about desired product type, market segments, and growth for the firm, and then developing quantitative measurements of these objectives.

Having set objectives, business planners must make some assumptions about the future environment in which the firm will operate. That is, they must forecast future demand for the firm's products or services. To get this forecast, they must establish premises regarding all the external factors bearing on the firm's operations.

A forecast of demand is only a potential; for it to be realized in the form of rules, deliberate actions must be planned. The result of such effort is a sales plan, upon which all other plans must be based. Two major plans derive from the sales plan. One is the production plan, for making or buying the products that are to be sold. The other is the financial plan, for having cash available to pay employees and creditors.

All sorts of more specific plans must be made to support the sales, production, and financial plans. Foremost among these supporting plans are ones for effectively grouping activities into departments, sustaining or increasing manpower, developing managers, keeping the firm's production equipment up to date, and finally, keeping the firm's product line viable.

A firm must plan ahead for a number of years in order to set alternative courses of action for all likely contingencies. These long-term plans are necessarily broad and subject to change. They are implemented by detailed short-term plans, which are relatively inflexible and which extend over the immediate period ahead.

Decisions that need to be made over and over again can be accommodated by standing plans. Such plans include (1) policies, which are broad guides to action; (2) procedures, which are detailed steps for accomplishing particular actions; and (3) rules, which prescribe employee conduct. In addition, program plans are often constructed for single, nonrecurring purposes.

The planning process is made more complicated by the human factor. That is, people are often biased in favor of personal interests that conflict with company goals. In addition, communication pro-

cesses are relatively inefficient and often result in distorted perceptions of objectives and the means to accomplish them.

The planning process has been refined and made more sophisticated by quantitative methods of analysis. Some of these methods
being employed are critical-path scheduling, linear programming,
simulation techniques, and probability decision theory.

Selected Bibliography

Carlson, Phillip G., *Quantitative Methods for Managers*. Harper, 1967.

Drucker, P. F., *The Practice of Management*. Harper, 1954.

Koontz, Harold, and Cyril O'Donnell, *Principles of Management*, 5th ed. McGraw-Hill, 1972.

LeBreton, P. P., and D. A. Henning, *Planning Theory*. Prentice-Hall, 1961.

Miller, D. W., and M. K. Starr, *Executive Decisions and Operations Research*. Prentice-Hall, 1960.

Newman, William H., Charles E. Summer, and E. Kirby Warren, *The Process of Management*. Prentice-Hall, 1967.

Steiner, G. A., "Making Long Range Company Planning Pay Off." *California Management Review,* Vol. 4, No. 2, Winter 1962.

Sweet, Franklin H., *Strategic Planning*. Bureau of Business Research, University of Texas, 1964.

ORGANIZING

As a managerial function, *organizing* is defined as grouping work activities into departments, assigning authority, and coordinating the activities of the different departments so that objectives are met and conflicts minimized. However, a discussion of only the deliberate actions that managers undertake when they perform the function of organizing would be an incomplete treatment of a highly complex phenomenon. Organizations evolve only partly as a result of what managers do; other characteristics derive from individual and group behavior, and are to some extent beyond the control of managers.

One approach to organizing involves the steps and decisions in the organizing function, and stresses mechanistic organization principles. Probably because static models are more easily explained than dynamic models, organizations are viewed as if they existed in a state of arrested motion. Variables that are awkward to explain, such as human behavior, are understandably omitted. The attempt is made in this book to explain the conditions that managers face when they organize in a dynamic environment.

An attempt is also made to deal with the paradox that the more efficiency that managers try to design into an organizational system, the greater are the problems related to the people in the organization. Systems designed for efficiency are impersonal; therefore, human frustrations multiply, and individuals feel a greater need to affiliate with informal groups, often ones that work against the formal organization. In addition, sharp boundaries between work groups foster frustration and conflict.

Finally, an attempt is made to put lateral relationships into clear perspective. Lateral relationships are far more varied and complicated than is implied by the traditional line-staff concept (Section 23), and one focus of contemporary management is to bring about a better understanding of these interactions.

17. Determining Activities

Organizing requires first of all the identification of the various work activities, or elements of work that are done by the members of an organization in carrying out their jobs. Determining exact work activities is one of the most important functions of the manager; it is also one of the most neglected, with the result that unnecessary activities can creep into the operations of an organization. Examples of such unnecessary activities are those that could be performed better and at less expense by outside companies during the infrequent times that they are needed.

Typically, the function of organizing is not performed without some kind of organization structure already existing. The exception is the brand-new company just getting started. However, organizing is not a one-time function that, once performed, is never to be done again. Organizing is a continual process that managers must do in order to keep their operations attuned to changing conditions. But in most cases, it is done within an existing framework.

Up or Down

One way to determine necessary work activities is to examine critically the work elements currently being performed. Two approaches are possible. One might be called "the top-down method"; that is, start with the highest manager in the organization and identify the activities of that position. Then go to the managers who report to the top manager, and determine the things they do. Continue on to the lowest level of employee in the organization. The opposite approach would obviously be "the bottom-up" method. Here the starting point would be the people who do the basic work in the organization, such as machine operators, salesmen, and clerks. Find out the activities each of these people perform. Work up to the first level of supervision, such as foremen, crew chiefs, and head clerks. Identify what they do. Continue on as high in the organization as desired. This process does not have to be done with an entire organization; any segment of an organization can be examined.

One Pitfall

The problem in asking people what they do is that they cannot be objective about their own jobs. Being human, they are motivated to protect their personal interests. Therefore, when they are asked what they do, their natural tendency is to exaggerate. The manager, or an organization analyst appointed by the manager, really has few standards for discriminating necessary activities from those which could be readily discarded. Since requirements for activities will vary greatly between one company and another of a different size, and between companies in different industries, there is nothing resembling uniform guides or policies to assist the analyst. Especially difficult is the problem of evaluating supporting activities, as compared with those that are central to the organization's main purpose.

Central and Supporting Activities

The structure of every business organization contains central and supporting activities. In a manufacturing firm, central activities include those concerned with engineering, producing, and selling a product; supporting activities include work elements associated with personnel procedures and records, accounting, and quality control. In an insurance company, central activities are those involved in generating premiums and investing funds; supporting activities would be those involved in office management and public relations. A similar breakdown could be developed for every kind of a business organization.

Determining the necessary central activities is a relatively straightforward process. Deciding which are the necessary supporting activities, and the extent to which they should be performed—by asking the people whose jobs and careers depend on performing these activities—is an entirely different matter. Generally speaking, to them everything they do is necessary and important. In fact, managers of support departments, given the chance, are usually prepared to aggressively offer new supporting activities.

Find Out What Support Is Wanted

One approach is to ask the people concerned with central activities what kind and how much of supporting activities they need. This has its limitations, however. The managers of central departments are also biased in favor of their own interests, and are often unfavorably disposed toward *any* supporting activities. This is a major source of conflict in organizations. These managers tend to look upon supporting activities both as a cost which their operations must bear, and as a source of potential rivalry. Actually, some supporting activities are essential to an organization's survival, and are becoming even more so in these days of advancing specialization.

A Better Way

The approach really should be to define the activities that must be performed to accomplish the organization's objectives under future conditions, rather than to find out what activities have been performed under past conditions. For example, firms in the aerospace industry which have found their past market for business to be drying up and are trying to develop new products for different industries, should project what future activities will be required, rather than perpetuating aerospace-type work. This approach challenges a manager's organizing ability, and must start with a sound long-term plan. It requires an intimate understanding of the firm's central activities and the impact on these activities of changing conditions and technological improvements. It then requires a thoughtful projection of the activities that must be performed to support the central activities. The whole process is one of determining the things that should be done, divorced as much as possible from the influence of the things that are being done.

The Case of the
Misguided Organization Study

"And I promise that if I am elected mayor, I will do everything in my power to reorganize the city government and reduce its costs of operation." This was the message that Frank Fawcett dinned into the ears of prospective voters in the city of Glenbank during the weeks preceding the 1972 election, and which ultimately was a major factor in his election victory.

Like some incorporated cities in central California, Glenbank had, up until 1968, enjoyed a period of prosperity dating back to the early 1940's. The reason, of course, was the presence in the immediate area of a large number of companies working on defense contracts. The employment opportunities generated by these firms had caused the population in Glenbank to more than triple. However, by 1968 the severe cutbacks in the defense industry had been felt in the form of significant reductions in the city's tax revenues, and the incumbent mayor did nothing to adjust Glenbank's governmental operations to a scale consistent with lower revenues and a shrinking population. This explains why economy in the city's management became a key issue in the mayoral election of June 1972. Some three months after the election, Mayor Fawcett began to be forcibly reminded by the City Council and Glenbank's newspaper and radio station of his campaign promise to reorganize the city government. This was a bothersome thing to the mayor because actually he was a retired dentist, and although he had enjoyed participating in civic affairs during the thirty years of his practice, he did not have the vaguest noton of how to go about reorganizing some quite substantial city departments. However, he knew he had to do something, so he decided to give the assignment to Bob Dale, a young attorney who had been his campaign manager, and who was now employed in Glenbank's Legal Department.

"I suppose one way to do it would be to just order a 10-percent reduction in personnel for all departments," mused the mayor as he acquainted Dale with the assignment, "but I did promise the voters that I would handle the reorganization on a systematic basis, and I think that is what the Council, and some others, are looking for. What ideas do you have?"

*"I read somewhere that when you attempt to reorganize an orga-
nization already in existence, you should first find out what activities
are absolutely essential, combine them, and then drop the ones that
can be dispensed with. The newspaper editor and some other business
people have been complaining for some time about what they claim
is a ridiculously large maintenance department. I just happened to
find out that salaries in that department amount to over $800,000 a
year. Suppose I start there by asking people what activities might be
done away with."*

*Bob Dale obtained a copy of the Maintenance Department's orga-
nization chart (Figure 17–1) before meeting with Jim Jonish, maintenance superintendent. He was somewhat surprised to find that there
were eighty-one employees in the department, and noticed that in all
cases the activities performed were offered as part of the services of
private business firms in Glenbank. As he had found Jonish to be
very cooperative in several previous contacts, he expected an open
mind when he suggested that Jonish identify activities in his department that could be dropped.*

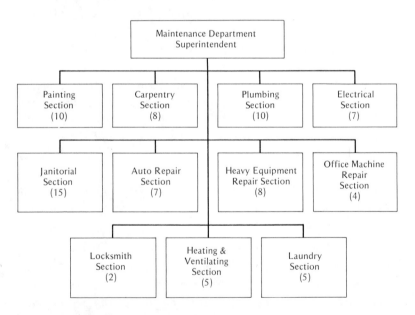

**Figure 17–1.   Organization Chart, Maintenance Department of Glenbank, California.
(Numbers = amount of filled positions.)**

"Eliminate some activities! You must be out of your mind," ex-claimed Jonish when Dale made his proposal. *"Why, what we should do is add some. I have been trying to get a machine shop in this department for years, and we still have to send our machining out. We are having the computer maintained by the leasing company, and we should be doing that work in-house. I could go on and on telling you of activities that should be brought into this department. If you don't believe me, go out and ask some of the section foremen. They will tell you how much money the city is losing by not having an adequate size maintenance department."*

With his enthusiasm considerably dampened, Dale began to make the rounds of the foremen. Dave Grier, electrical section foreman, almost exploded when Dale pointed out that four of the six electricians were obviously not doing any work at the time that they were talking. "Of course they're not," Grier said. *"We have to keep them on standby. Do think that if there is an electrical emergency in city hall that they don't want it taken care of right away? And, you talk of activities that can be cut out. I'll tell you some, like motor rewinding, that we should be doing and are not."*

Every foreman said fundamentally the same things about his own section, but the plumbing foreman did not see too much need for the city to maintain a laundry, and the heavy equipment repair fore-man thought that auto repairs could be better done by the service departments of the local auto dealers. He obviously had a grudge against the auto repair foreman, however.

Dale then went to the Public Works Department and the Parks and Recreation Department and talked to people there about activities needed to be performed by the Maintenance Department. He de-tected a wariness on the part of everyone he discussed the matter with—almost as though they were defensive about something.

"I thought that Fawcett was promising things that he couldn't do," said Luigi Ferraldi, head groundskeeper. *"Just try to name one ac-tivity done by Maintenance, or any other department, that the city could get along without."*

The city engineer, Melvin Rogers, was even more emphatic. "What Fawcett is going to do with your help is mess up the entire city organization. These departments have been carefully built up over the years, and nothing is being done in any of them that isn't essential."

As Dale began to write his report to the mayor on the findings of his organization study, his spirits began to rise. After all, as he rationalized, organization was not his field, but he had carried out the study on a logical basis. It was not his fault that the mayor had made a campaign promise that could not be kept, or that some people in town were biased against what appeared to be an efficient city government. He had carefully looked for activities in a sample department, Maintenance, that could be done away with, and could not find any. He felt he was justified in reporting to the mayor that any reorganization would be detrimental to Glenbank.

Discussion Questions

1. Explain how prosperity can lead to the buildup of unnecessary activities within organizations.
2. Was Mayor Fawcett's idea of a blanket 10-percent reduction in personnel for all departments any worse than the approach that Dale used?
3. Speculate how you would feel if you were Jonish or any of the foremen, and someone suggested to you that some of your organization's activities might be expendable.
4. Explain why people in Public Works and Parks and Recreation might seem defensive to Dale.
5. If you were given Dale's assignment, how would you go about it?

18. Conventional Departmentation

Departments are formed by grouping activities. In practice, the term *department* is used to identify a particular level in the organization at which activities are grouped, with other terms associated with higher and lower levels. Thus, a hierarchy of descending levels might be *plant, division, department,* and *section.* These various labels are useful in suggesting the relative importance of activity groupings within an organization, but since there is no set pattern in the way they are used by business firms, the general term *department* is used in this book to refer to any organizational unit, regardless of level.

Why Conventional?

Conventional is used here to differentiate the methods for grouping activities that have been used in the past from the new notions on organization, to be discussed in Section 19.

Historically, there have been three main groupings of activities at the primary level of management, that is, at the level of the managers who report directly to the top executive. The three groupings reflect (1) functional organization, (2) product organization, and (3) geographical organization.

Functional Organization

Functional organization groups activities by the kind of work done. Thus, all sales activities are grouped into a sales department, all production activities are grouped into a production department, and so on. Figure 18–1 illustrates a simple functional organization.

Functional organization is the method for grouping activities that small firms use most widely. It is the method that is intuitively chosen when a small company begins to grow beyond the size where the owner/manager can handle everything himself. When he has to create departments for the first time, he will do this by grouping the central activities into departments and appointing subordinate managers over them.

The advantage of functional organization is that it facilitates specialization in work tasks. When it is employed at the primary level, it ensures that the main functions to be performed get top man-

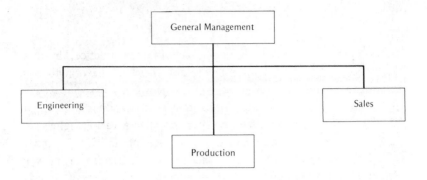

Figure 18–1.   Functional Organization at the Primary Level.

agement attention. Because of its emphasis on functions, it is the organization best calculated to optimize the performance of individual functions.

However, as firms become larger and more complex, the advantage of functional organization at the primary level becomes a disadvantage. The top manager of a small company with a single product can personally coordinate the activities of his functional managers so the goals of the firm are met. But at some stage of size and complexity, coordination of relatively independent functional departments becomes virtually impossible. There must at this stage be provision for directing top management's attention to broader dimensions, like the total requirements of products or geographical areas, rather than to specialized departments, like engineering, production, and sales. At this point an alternative method for grouping activities at the primary level must be chosen. However, regardless of the method used for grouping activities at the primary level, activities will be grouped functionally by the kind of work done at some level in the organization—and always at the operating level.

Product Organization

A second organizational form, product organization, groups activities at the primary level by specific products, or product lines. This form of organization permits companies to grow very large, as evidenced by such corporation giants as General Motors, General Electric, and Du Pont. In product organization, the central activities having to do with a specific product, and often the supporting activities, are grouped together under a product manager. Product departments tend to be semiautonomous, and often grow to the size of large companies themselves.

Specialization is the outstanding advantage of product organization, but it is a different kind of specialization than that found in functional organization. In product organization, human skills and production equipment can be specialized to meet the requirements of individual, and often highly complex, products. In addition, because of the location of the product departments at the primary level, as illustrated by Figure 18–2, each product receives top management attention.

Product organization is not without its problems, however. The main problem is how a company's top management can maintain effective control over independent product departments. (Techniques for such control are discussed in Section 60.) A second important problem is that product organization usually costs more, because it duplicates skills and equipment for each product department.

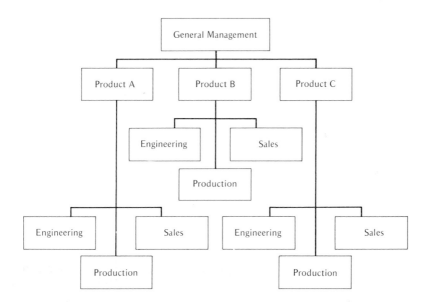

**Figure 18–2. Product Organization at the Primary Level;
Functional Organization at the Secondary Level.**

Geographical Organization

Widely scattered operations often justify a third form of organization, in which activities are grouped at the primary level by the territorial location at which they are performed. This form is known as geographical organization, and has logistic efficiency as its outstanding advantage. *Logistic efficiency* means that a company may locate operations close to the source of raw materials, or close to the markets being served, or both, and thereby significantly reduce transportation costs. A second advantage is the opportunity to provide specialized local services. Examples would be where the southern division of a national steel company would employ salesmen with southern backgrounds, and national supermarket chains would cater to the food-buying habits of people in the areas they serve. The main problem with geographical organization, as with product organization, is how to control the dispersed operations. Figure 18–3 illustrates a simple geographical organization.

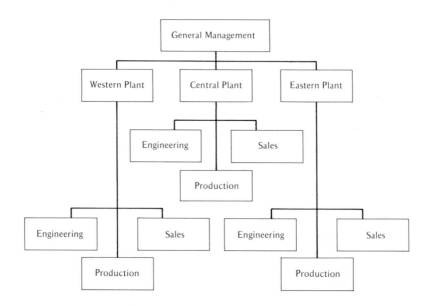

**Figure 18–3.   Geographical Organization at the Primary Level;
Functional Organization at the Secondary Level.**

Organization of Supporting Activities

Finance is one supporting activity that is always organized functionally at the primary level. This is because top-management attention to the control of funds is crucial to every firm's survival. Other strong candidates for primary-level location on a functional basis are personnel and purchasing activities in respective departments.

However, there is no set pattern for the assignment of supporting activities. If central activities are grouped functionally at the primary level, supporting activities may also be grouped functionally at the primary level, or under central activities at the secondary level. A product or geographical department manager may have supporting activities at the same level as central activities, or at a lower level under central activities. The implications of such locations of central and supporting activities are dealt with in Sections 21–25, which are concerned with vertical and lateral relationships.

The Case of the
Function That Wouldn't Fit

Bob McNulty was twenty-five years old, and just out of the Navy, when his father died and left the McNulty Steel Construction Company for Bob to retrieve from its creditors. The older McNulty had been a good engineer, and had built his company, which specialized in custom storage tanks, into an industry leader in the Phoenix area. Because of the virtual impossibility during World War II of getting steel for nondefense purposes, McNulty had successfully bid on a subcontract for making a bomber landing-gear component. He would have been all right on the contract if he had not tried to improve the design of the component at his own expense, and the pressure of trying to pay back the money that he had borrowed was probably the cause of his death.

Young McNulty began his industrial career by calling a meeting of the firm's creditors. The argument he gave them was that if they foreclosed on the company's assets they would be lucky to get back fifty cents on the dollar, but if they would give him time to reorganize the company to take advantage of the promising markets that were plainly visible, they would get back all of their money, and in addition have a good future customer.

The creditors seemed agreeable to the proposition; however, one of them raised the question: "It sounds fine, Bob, but are you going to try to do everything yourself like your father did?"

"No, I'm not," Bob replied. "I'm going to organize the company around the main functions of finance, engineering, manufacturing, and sales. I'm going to put good men in charge of these functions, and my job will be to keep everything coordinated."

With the blessings of his creditors, Bob started to build the company. Thanks to his father, there were both specialized equipment and a skilled work force for constructing steel tanks, and the firm branched out into pressure vessels of all kinds. A contemporary product using similar resources was steel buildings, such as gasoline stations and warehouses, and Bob moved aggressively into this field. The firm's engineers and salesmen, who were also engineering-oriented, fitted nicely into the expanded pattern that the company was following.

112

During the Korean War, Bob saw an opportunity to get into a new business that not only had a good profit potential of its own, but would also help the existing product line. The new venture was steel jobbing, which is buying steel in carload quantities from the mills, carrying it in inventory, cutting it to customer specifications, and selling it in small lots at prices substantially over the mill cost. The advantage to the tank and building business was the low cost of steel bought in large quantities.

A problem with the new business was that steel jobbing required a different kind of selling effort than tanks and buildings, and involved different customers—some of whom were actually competitors of McNulty Steel Construction. The apparent answer was to set up a steel supply division, in which the activities associated with steel jobbing would be independently grouped. Thus began the change from a functional to a product type of organization, although the question of where steel procurement and inventory control activities would be located did not have a really acceptable answer. As an expedient, these activities remained under manufacturing.

Bob McNulty had retained the engineer primarily involved in working on the landing-gear component design, and had subsidized a modest research and development effort until a payoff finally came in 1957. A design that was a marked innovation for both military and commercial aircraft was achieved, and excellent patent protection was granted. The firm had generated sufficient capital by this time to handle the complete manufacturing and marketing of the product, but its process characteristics did not integrate at all with the manufacturing capabilities for tanks and steel buildings, and the marketing effort for the aircraft component was entirely different from that of either of the firm's other product lines. Therefore, it was decided to create an aircraft products division, with its own engineering, manufacturing, and marketing functions.

The one thing that the new division had in common with the construction and supply operations was the requirement of large quantities of steel purchased at the lowest possible price. At the time of forming the aircraft division, it seemed appropriate to group the engineering, manufacturing, and marketing activities for the tank and building line under a product division designated as "construction." Strong pressure was then exerted by the manager of the steel supply division to have procurement and inventory management activities placed under his control. He persuasively reasoned with Bob McNulty that his operation would act as a steel supplier to the construction and aircraft divisions just as with any of the firm's large outside customers. The procurement manager countered with the argument that steel buying and storing, together with the purchasing and inventory of all of the other of the company's required supplies and equipment, was important enough to be set up as an independent functional division directly under McNulty. The view of the construction division manager and the new aircraft division manager was that they should each have their own procurement and inventory departments. For the time being, McNulty elected to go along with the supply division manager, so this organizational change was effected.

In the 1960's the company's name was changed to McNulty Steel Products, Inc., and its product-line expansion went in two directions. One was the fabrication of steel pipe for the transmission of petroleum and natural gas, and the other was a proprietary line of standard liquid petroleum gas (LPG) storage tanks for home use. Both the pipe and the LPG tank lines were complementary to the engineering and manufacturing capabilities of the construction division, and were dependent upon extremely efficient buying and storing of steel. However, they both required distinctly separate marketing organizations. McNulty set up two new product divisions, oilfield and LPG, with the respective managers reporting to him. Although this organizational arrangement solved some problems, it also created others, because the inevitable conflicts between the oilfield and LPG division managers, who had the responsibility for selling their respective products, and the construction division manager, who had the responsibility for making them, could only be resolved by McNulty himself. In addition, the construction division manager was increasingly critical of steel procurement and inventory being under the supply division manager. Finally, in 1968, McNulty centralized all procurement and inventory activities in a functional division called "materiel," and the company's organization chart at the primary level became as shown in Figure 18–4.

In the summer of 1972 Bob McNulty called in a management consulting firm for assistance with an organizational problem. "What I am thinking of," he said, "is setting up two decentralized materiel operations—one in the construction division and the other in the supply division. Making a centralized materiel division work in a

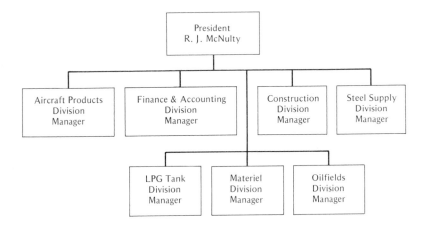

Figure 18–4.   Organization Chart at the Primary Level, McNulty Steel Products, Inc.

company like this seems to be impossible. Please make a study and give me your recommendations."

Discussion Questions

1. In the Case of the Function That Wouldn't Fit, was Bob McNulty right in organizing on a functional basis when he first began to run the company?
2. After the introduction of the steel supply division, no good answer was available for where to put procurement and inventory, so as an expedient these activities were just left where they were. Do you think it likely that many organizational decisions are made this way?
3. In the argument concerning the proper location for procurement and inventory management prior to 1960, take the side of each of the contending managers at McNulty Steel, including the procurement manager, and argue for their views.
4. If you represented the management consulting firm called in by Bob McNulty in 1972, what recommendations would you have made in response to his request?
5. In addition to the problem of where to locate steel procurement and inventory management activities, what other organizational problems might be caused by supporting activities? Name the supporting activities that you think may be sources of problems.

19. Project Organization

Sometime around 1955, industries working under government contracts became interested in project organization, which they thought was a new organization form. Today it is being used extensively by marketing and distribution companies; banks and insurance firms are experimenting with it; and some retail stores, laboratories, and hospitals have adopted it, at least in part. However, like most things which are claimed to be new, project organization has been around a while. The theatrical and construction industries, for example, have used the form, probably since the beginning of any kind of organized activity.

How It Works

Project organization is the team or task-force approach to getting a particular job done. It works this way: There is a specific mission with complex requirements (involving diverse skills) which must be accomplished in a limited time period. Such goals might be a product that must be developed and produced, a consumer product or service that requires a special marketing effort, or an unusual task with large and significant dimensions, such as a corporate merger or the creation of a new degree program in a university. The effort mounted to accomplish the requirements of the mission is called a *project*. The project is given a name—usually one associated with the mission—and a project manager is chosen.

Project Personnel

The project manager must bring various skills to bear on achieving the required goal, and does this in part by recruiting people as full-time staff members for the life of the project. These people tend to be highly specialized, and are usually drawn from permanent departments. They are under the direct authority of the project manager. The remainder of the work to be done, which is often the bulk of the project task, is executed by people temporarily assigned to the project who are permanent members of other organizational units. Although directed in their work on the project by the project manager or appointed deputies, they remain under the line authority of the manager of their parent department. The whole idea is to bring top efficiency to the convergence of specialized and varied skills— temporarily applied as needed—to a specific end item by cutting across organizational boundary lines and disregarding traditional organization theories.

Similarities With Other Organization Forms

Project organization has a marked resemblance to product organization, in that activities are grouped according to the requirements of a specific product or service, rather than by the kind of work or where it is done. As in both product and geographical forms of organization, at some level in the project organization activities are grouped on a functional basis. And within a project organization, there may be a level of activities grouped on a subordinate product basis; or a grouping may be made on a geographical basis, above a functional grouping of kinds of work done.

Differences From Other Organization Forms

A significant difference between the project organization concept and the other organization forms has to do with the life of the organization. Permanence is the normal intent in setting up a functional, product, or geographical organization. Project organizations are temporary on purpose. They are created to accomplish the requirements of a particular product or service, and when those requirements are met the project organization is disbanded.

A second difference of project organization is that it is not usually employed for the grouping of activities at the primary level. In the aerospace and electronics industries, for example, activities are usually grouped at the primary level according to product classification, and project organizations are created beneath the product level and in a matrix relationship to secondary functional levels. Figure 19–1 illustrates this matrix relationship, and points to the major distinguishing feature of project organization, which is plural command relationships.

Subordinates in a direct, formal relationship to one supervisor, and who are permanent members of one organization (in the figure, an engineering department) may be temporarily assigned to a project

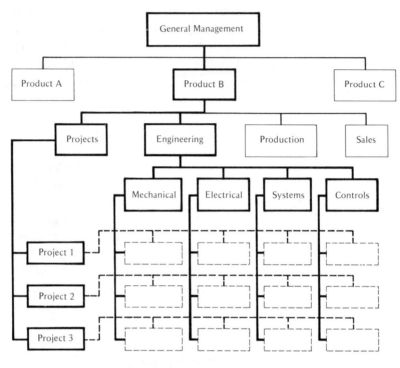

Figure 19–1. **Product Organization at the Primary Level;**
Functional Organization at the Secondary Level;
Project Organization in a Matrix Relationship to Functional Organizations.

department, and be in an authority relationship to at least one additional supervisor. In the figure, engineers would be reporting both to the manager of the functional engineering department and (temporarily) to the manager of the project department.

Advantages

Best solutions to difficult problems can be attained through project organization, which pools talent from various functional units. The people recruited for a project are freed from the constraints and prejudices of departments preoccupied with a single function, and become highly involved in contributing their share to a goal which depends on the successful performance of multiple functions. Project organization focuses group attention on a total process, rather than focusing individual attention on subprocesses.

Stages of project development can be completed faster and with greater integration because the shortened lines of communication facilitate information feedback. Cumbersome formal organization channels are bypassed, and the many reviews and approvals necessary when crossing traditional organization boundary lines are simply eliminated.

People assigned to a project identify strongly with the total process, and this tends to act as a motivator. The people can see themselves as part of an effort that has definable and measurable results, and a successful effort reflects credit on those who helped make it possible. They tend to get personally involved with a project, and perceive that their own needs are satisfied to some extent in meeting the objectives of the project.

In addition, permanent and costly organizational "empires" are avoided. The essence of the project system is to draw on skills as they are needed, and for only as long as they are needed, and then to release the skills for some other productive use. The system is set up deliberately to gain maximum efficiency from human resources. The success criteria of a project pressures the project manager to efficiently deploy the skills of the people assigned to it.

Unique Problems

It would be unrealistic to assume that project organization does not have some unique problems. One is that setting up a project is potentially disturbing to the total organization. Managers must accept giving up some of their key personnel to the project, often for an indefinite time. Functional managers find they are no longer in a key position but have been relegated to serving a project, or projects. When there are many projects, the project managers tend to compete vigorously with each other for the services of functional departments.

Authority for the Project

The authority delegated to the project manager is often ambiguous. Although in theory the manager is supposed to act with all of the authority of the president, or senior officer of the enterprise, in getting the project job done, in practice this authority is often more apparent than real, and the manager's accomplishments tend to be a result of personal persuasiveness and personality. However, the responsibilities are clear-cut: the project manager normally is blamed for anything that goes wrong on the project. To make project organization successful, a new state of mind must be achieved by all of the managers involved. The old system of command authority must be forgotten, and a new system substituted, based on coordinated lateral relationships. (These alternative relationships are dealt with in the next several sections.)

Effect on People

One of the major problems of project organization is that it can cause frustrations and anxieties for the people connected with it. Ideally, a forecast is made as to when a project organization must be broken up, and plans are developed for placing the people in some other organization at comparable status. But often in practice, after a project organization is disbanded, its people are either laid off or placed in lower-status jobs.

This is a serious problem of project organization. The known temporary life of a project organization can generate unusual worries about loss of employment or career setbacks. When individuals experience a successive series of bosses, they can become concerned that there is no one person looking out for their personal development. People who are continually being transferred from one department to another also may not develop a sense of loyalty to the larger organization.

Intuitively, it would appear that people would be frustrated by dual-command relationships. However, there has not been enough good research on the subject to reveal much about the effect on people of having to report to more than one direct supervisor.

Challenge to Managers

The problems of project organization are indeed formidable. However, proponents of the system urge that the problems are more than offset by the possible efficiencies. The challenge to managers considering project organization is to balance in each case potential gains against potential losses, and let the greatest weight determine the decision.

Criteria for Its Application

Just because project organization offers advantages does not mean that all other methods of grouping activities are obsolete, nor does it mean that the form has applicability to all business firms and social institutions. Project organization has had an impressive record of success, but only when it was thoughtfully and properly applied; managers must recognize where it is appropriate and where it is not. The following criteria, considered as a whole, may assist in deciding for or against project organization.

Scale of operation.   Project organization is generally appropriate for a unique endeavor, one that is
- definable in terms of a specific end.
- large enough to warrant special management attention.
- measurable in terms of having a definite beginning and end.

Unusual need.   Conventional organization forms are appropriate for meeting familiar needs. The choice of project organization is indicated when there is uncertainty, or even ignorance, about how to meet performance, cost, and schedule parameters. It is also warranted when unusual management controls are called for.

Integration.   Project organization is best for tying together dependent, diverse, and complex skills. It is especially appropriate when these skills must be applied all at the same time, rather than one after the other.

Significance.   The project should be important enough that a failure would represent a serious setback. In such a case, management might well decide that adopting project organization to cope with the problem is warranted.

"The mission of the project which you will head is to get our new Mexican subsidiary company ready for take-over by Mexican managers. My hope is that you will be able to do this in about two years," explained Robert Linderman, president of Linderman Industries, Inc., to Carl Conway, newly appointed project manager for "Operation Mexicano." Conway had been hired specifically for this assignment because of his experience in managing large defense projects in the aerospace industry.

"The first thing that I will have to do is put a project team together," said Conway. "I imagine that you have in mind my drawing people from the functional divisions."

"Yes, and I have already sent memoranda to the division managers informing them that you will be asking for some of their key people to work under you for about two years," said Linderman. "In addition, I have advised them to be prepared to process work orders from Operation Mexicano with the personnel and equipment of their organizations. Later on in the project's life, you will begin to get Mexican personnel, both managers and technicians, into your organization. These people will have Mexican supervisors, but until the mission is accomplished they also will report to you. I will have to admit that you are going to have some complex authority relationships, especially as you personally will be responsible to the president of the subsidiary, Felix Delgado, as well as to me."

Conway began to make his plans for the project team. The plant building was available and empty in Mexico City, and it was important to get equipment purchased and installed as soon as possible. A plant layout would have to be prepared, but before that could be done there would have to be a manufacturing plan. Therefore, he needed to recruit an industrial engineer, a production planner, and an equipment buyer. They, in turn, would have to build their own staffs.

He made an appointment with Sam Sargis, corporate manager of industrial engineering. "I have had a preliminary talk with Bob Cates about his joining Operation Mexicano, and he is quite interested," Carl said. "Will you release him to me?"

"Why, I'm grooming Cates to take over my job when I retire," replied Sargis. "He is my best man. Let me pick someone else for you, or better still, you just tell me what industrial engineering work you want done, and I will have it done for you."

"Sorry, I want Cates," said Carl firmly. "And besides, you are not due to retire for five years. This will be good experience for him."

For production planning, Carl had in mind Bert Mill, an older man with extensive experience in managing production operations, but Mill rejected his offer. "I talked it over with my wife," he said, "and we feel that at my age I shouldn't take a chance on not having a job to come back to when Operation Mexicano is finished."

Carl next talked to Emil Banowetz, who was assistant to Jim Burke, the vice-president for manufacturing, and Banowetz decided that he would like to join the project team. However, Burke told Conway that if Banowetz were forcibly taken away from him, he would give Mr. Linderman his resignation, so Carl decided to back down. He finally accepted a man that Burke recommended.

Filling the equipment buyer's slot was easy. The director of procurement phoned Carl and said that a senior buyer, Humberto Guzman, had requested permission to ask for the assignment, and that he strongly recommended him. Guzman had been purchasing agent for a large mining company in Mexico for about ten years.

Carl had about the same experiences in getting the people he wanted for the functions of engineering, quality control, cost, marketing, and advertising as he did for the first three positions; in other words, he won some confrontations with the division managers, and lost some. For personnel, he got Dr. Juan Perez, who was slated to be personnel director of the subsidiary company, to affiliate temporarily with the project team.

The first brush that Project Mexicano had in getting a functional division to do work for it came when Carl's engineering man, Frank Fong, reported to him that the engineering vice-president, who was formally Fong's boss, refused to authorize top priority to the changing of dimensions in the production drawings to the metric system.

Carl had to take this issue to Linderman, who ruled in his favor. The defeated vice-president, of course, did not take kindly to the decision.

The next incident revolved about Carl's desire to have a pilot run of products made with metric measurements for shipment to Mexico. The purpose was to test the market acceptance of the Linderman articles. Jim Burke stated flatly that there was no way that his production workers could be trained to work with metric drawings. Carl quickly saw that this was an issue that he was not going to win, so he had his buyer, Guzman, work with the newly appointed manufacturing manager for the subsidiary in getting a run of the products subcontracted in Mexico City.

Bob Cates made a special trip from Mexico City to present Carl with an interesting problem. The Mexican industrial engineer, whom Bob was supposed to be training, had his own ideas about plant layout. When they differed from Bob's, as they usually did, he would take his complaint directly to Felix Delgado, the president of the Mexican subsidiary. Because Delgado's competence was primarily in finance, he would not know how to decide the argument, and would simply table it. Carl took examples of some of the disagreements to Bob's formal boss, Sam Sargis, who quite unexpectedly ruled against Bob's proposed methods. Carl saw that there was bad feeling by Sargis against Bob for leaving his department, which boded ill for Bob's return. To solve the immediate problem, however, Carl asked Dr. Perez to try to reconcile the situation in Mexico City.

Despite these problems, and many more of a similar nature, Project Mexicano was successful, and the transition to Mexican management was made in just a little over two years. By a curious twist, through Dr. Perez' intercession Felix Delgado became very impressed by Bob Cates and convinced him to accept the job of director of industrial engineering for the Mexican company. Humberto Guzman also stayed on to head the procurement operation.

Other members of the project team were not so fortunate. Linderman Industries was laying off personnel when the project ended in 1970, and only the project production man was able to get a job in the company at as high a level as the one he had when he joined the team. The cost expert elected to leave Linderman because he said the glamor of Project Mexicano had spoiled him for any routine job.

Carl Conway had a difficult decision of his own to make. Robert Linderman said that he was extremely pleased with his performance and that something good would open up in the company for him soon. In the meantime, there was a staff assignment available for him. Carl had seen enough project managers in the aerospace industry who had figuratively rotted on staff assignments when their projects were completed to be somewhat wary.

Discussion Questions

1. Was Linderman Industries' adoption of project organization an appropriate one for getting the Mexican subsidiary started?
2. In consideration of Robert Linderman's letting the division managers know that the project manager would be asking for some of their key people, why would Conway have any difficulty in getting the ones he wanted?
3. Would you expect that many people would turn down a chance to join a project organization, as Bert Mill did?
4. Why would Conway take his problem with the engineering vice-president to Linderman and have it resolved in his favor, yet back down in two disputes with the manufacturing vice-president?
5. What could Linderman Industries have done to assure good jobs for the people coming off Project Mexicano, including Carl Conway, the project manager?

20. Spans of Control
Vs. Departmental Levels

Span of control refers to the number of subordinates that report directly to a manager. In the old days of management theory—almost up to 1950—a great deal of attention was directed to this issue. The thinking then was that an effective span of control involved some immutable number of subordinates, usually six. Often one of the first things done by an organization analyst or consultant was to count the number of subordinates reporting to each manager. In each instance where the number exceeded six, there would be a recommendation to narrow the span.

No Arbitrary Number

It is now clearly recognized that no general prescription can be made of an arbitrary number of subordinates. The fact remains, however, that each manager is somewhat limited on the number of direct subordinates that can be effectively controlled. When this number is reached a new management level must be created. Thus, the typical organizational structure is developed, with the top manager having authority over a certain number of subordinate managers, who thereby form a level. These managers, in turn, have a certain number of subordinate managers reporting to them, thus forming another level, and so on down to the lowest level of managers, who have only non-managers reporting to them. The number of management levels is determined by the spans of control. If spans of control are narrow, there will of necessity be many levels. As spans of control are widened, the number of levels will be reduced, and the organization structure will have a flatter look.

Factors Affecting a Manager's Capacity

Ideally, each manager's capacity for handling subordinates should be determined exactly, and a new organizational level should be created when this optimal number of subordinates is reached. There is no possibility, however, that this perfect arrangement can ever be achieved in the real world. There are simply too many variables that

126

bear on finding each manager's optimal span of control. Some of the more important of these variables merit brief discussion here.

The experience, personality, and attitude of the manager. A manager who is inexperienced and is learning the assignment cannot supervise as many subordinates as the manager who has been through all of the problems many times before. Some people have personalities that enable them to give direction to subordinates quickly and concisely, thereby enabling them to handle more subordinates than the deliberate and painstaking type. Some managers are inclined to delegate authority, which permits subordinates to make more decisions. Such delegation not only reduces the decisions the manager must make, but it also increases the number of subordinates that can be supervised effectively. Managers who are inclined not to delegate must spend more time making decisions, which restricts their span of control.

The experience and training of the subordinates. The extent to which subordinates are capable of performing their duties with a minimum of supervision and coordination is a determinant of how many subordinates a manager can control. The more of a manager's time that must be spent in directing individual subordinates, the fewer will be the number of subordinates who can be directed.

The incidence of change within the work environment. Frequent and dramatic changes in the nature and scope of the work assignments will restrict the number of subordinates, whereas if changes are few and job routines can be established, the span of control can be substantially increased.

External pressures on the manager's time and attention. Contact with direct subordinates is only one of a manager's continuous relationships. In the other direction, the manager will have contact with an immediate superior, and, additionally, highly demanding contacts through lateral relationships with other managers in the organization. If these contacts (which are external to the manager's relationships with subordinates) are severe, they will act to restrict the number of subordinates that can be handled effectively.

Arguments for a Wide Span of Control

Present-day thinking favors wide spans of control, as contrasted to the general belief, thirty to forty years ago, that narrow spans were the most efficient. The question of how wide the span should be is really best answered by considering the tangible and intangible costs of wide spans of control in comparison with the alternative, which is an increase in the levels of management.

It is difficult to think of tangible costs resulting from stretching the span of control, unless it would be from mistakes that subordinates would make by not getting adequate supervision. Intangible costs might result from subordinates' feelings of insecurity and frustration at not receiving as much of their boss's time as they would like. But, the advantage of a manager having a large number of direct subordinates is that the subordinates have to be left relatively on their own. They get a chance to learn and develop by making decisions, and well may get more satisfaction out of their jobs as a result.

There are some definite tangible costs associated with excessive management levels. The number of managers is increased, and this is accompanied by an increase in managerial salaries. In addition, managers require secretaries and extra office space, both of which add to overhead costs. A significant intangible cost comes from the way communication is distorted when it passes through multiple filters, which is what each management level tends to resemble. At each succeeding level downward, members are apt to feel less important in the organization and more like anonymous contributors. This feeling is damaging to their motivation to produce effectively. Their job satisfaction may be further diluted because their managers, having few subordinates, will tend to exercise close supervision. As a result, all decisions affecting the subordinates are made for them, and their opportunity to grow by learning is blocked.

On balance, there appears to be substantial justification supporting wide spans of control.

The Case of Piggyback Management

The organization structure of the contracts administration division of Philips-Aerodyne Corporation evolved as the firm acquired more and more space weapons contracts. In the company's early days, Jim Mario personally handled all of the activities associated with contract negotiation and administration. As the company grew, it became necessary for him to hire contract administrators to do the actual work, and his role became that of a manager. Despite continued expansion of the firm's defense contracts, Mario resisted for a long time adding a second level of management to his organization. He personally supervised his administrators until he finally had nine reporting directly to him. Most of them were new to contract administration work, so there was much training that he had to perform. In addition, changes were taking place on all of the contracts constantly, which necessitated Mario's close involvement with each of his administrators. Finally, when one administrator neglected to request a progress payment from the Navy far enough in advance and the company had to borrow money for working capital for ninety days, it became apparent that a reorganization was essential.

Jim Mario separated the current contracts into three groups according to the nature of the work required, namely, development, production, and field support. He appointed a supervisor over each group to report to him, which meant that he had reduced his span of control to three subordinates, and each of them supervised three contract administrators. At the time, this was a needed innovation, and there was a considerable improvement in the performance of contracts administration, which had now gained the organizational status of a department.

The contracts on which Philips-Aerodyne was the successful bidder continued to increase, and each of Mario's supervisors had to hire additional contract administrators. When the number of subordinates reporting to the development contracts group supervisor reached eight, he came to Mario with the request that he be allowed to reorganize. He wanted to add a level of three supervisors to report to him, with each of them being responsible for approximately one third of the development contracts. They would supervise two or three contract administrators.

There was some logic to this appeal, but Mario perceived that if he granted the request of this particular supervisor, he would have a problem with his production and field-support group supervisors, who would feel that a former peer had moved a level above them. A solution was to add an additional management level to each group. Mario was secretly motivated in this direction anyway, because the company's controller had recently been made a division manager, primarily on the basis of adding personnel to his organization. So, Mario effected this new reorganization.

After about a year, some subtle differences began to occur in the work characteristics of Philips-Aerodyne's contract administration. One difference was that the contract administrators had become highly skilled in their duties. Another was that the contracts themselves began to stabilize, and significant changes were the exception rather than the rule. A third difference was that the total number of contracts began decreasing, so that each administrator had fewer contracts for which he was responsible. Jim Mario either didn't know, or didn't want to know, about these things that were happening.

One day Mario was told by his boss, the plant general manager, that a doctoral candidate named John Moore had requested permission to collect research data from various divisions within Philips-Aerodyne. Mario was asked to cooperate in this endeavor.

"The purpose of my research is to investigate human problems within organizations," Moore told Mario, "that is, problems that cause people to become frustrated and upset."

"Young man," said Mario condescendingly, "we have no human problems in the contracts administration division. However, if you wish, you have my permission to talk with the administrators."

Moore had developed a research instrument comprised of ten problem statements. He would read a statement to a research subject, and then ask two questions: First, is this a problem in your organization, and second, if it is a problem, what is the perceived severity of it on a scale of from 1 to 5? He invited the research subjects to make any comments that would explain their responses.

There was nothing particularly significant about the responses of the twenty-one participants to any of the statements except the last one.

This one read: "The number of management levels in the organization causes a stifling of individual initiative." Only two of the administrators said that this was not a problem, and they were both new to the organization. The mean perceived severity was 4.

As Moore analyzed the comments to the management-level statement, he found marked evidence of considerable frustration. Quite a number were in this vein: "The supervisors don't have enough real managing to do, so they stick their necks into our work." Another common one was: "Everything that comes down to us is filtered through those guys, and then they screen and distort everything that goes back up." One comment was: "Can you believe formal morning section meetings when there are only two people in the section?" Three responses were in almost identical words: "My supervisor religiously comes to my cubicle twice every morning and twice every afternoon to check on my work." A comment with important implications went: "The company is now screaming about reducing costs, yet it tolerates this piggyback management. If it wants to cut costs, why doesn't it eliminate one whole level of supervisors?"

Discussion Questions

1. If it could be determined what is the optimal number of subordinates that a given department manager can effectively handle, would it mean that the manager should continue with that same span of control in the event of a promotion? Or should the new job carry with it the same number of subordinates who reported to the previous manager?
2. In the Case of Piggyback Management, did Jim Mario have an alternative to establishing a second management level when his personal span of control stretched to nine subordinates?
3. Can you explain why the top management of Philips-Aerodyne could have accepted the adding of management levels when the principal reason for the reorganization appeared to be the improvement of the status of individuals?
4. How could Jim Mario not know that the real work in his division was shrinking? Why might he not want to know?
5. How could the attitudes learned by researcher John Moore be related to Philips-Aerodyne's declining business?

21. Vertical Relationships

Vertical relationships in an organization are those between individual managers and the subordinates reporting directly to them. The act of departmentation creates these vertical relationships; when activities are grouped into departments, managers are appointed to head them, and are granted authority over the subordinates reporting to them. Earlier notions on management theory perceived vertical relationships as practically the whole of organization, and authority as the cement holding an organization together. The predominant organizational interest in those days was with the hierarchy of supervisor-subordinate relationships. Modern thinking is that there is a great deal more to organization than this, but vertical relationships and authority are still recognized as highly important factors.

What Is Authority?

There are a number of ways of defining *authority*. One is that authority is the right to command. Another is that authority is the power to limit choice. One that seems particularly meaningful is that authority is a right granted to a manager to make decisions, within certain limitations, to assign duties to subordinates, and to require subordinates' conformance to expected behavior.

Source of Authority

There is an upward-downward dispute over the source of authority, in which the conventional view is at odds with the acceptance theory.

The conventional view. Conventionally, authority in business organizations has been viewed as having its origins in the rights of private property. Consider that the ownership of a corporation is vested in its common stockholders, whose individual authority is proportionate to the number of common shares they own. The stockholders centralize their authority by electing a board of directors. Thus having possession of all the authority granted to them by the stockholders, the directors delegate a large part of it to the corporation's chief executive. This officer, in turn, delegates portions of that authority to subordinate managers on the primary level, and they delegate pieces of their authority to their subordinates. And so on down through the organization.

The acceptance theory. Sharply conflicting with the above "downward" view of the source of authority is the one which holds that authority is a right granted to a manager by subordinates. The extent of the authority thus granted is determined by the subordinates' judgments concerning whether they stand to lose more by conforming to the manager's commands than by not conforming. This acceptance theory was discussed in Section 5, which related to the contributions of Chester Barnard to management theory.

The downward-upward dispute over the source of authority actually tends to oversimplify a highly complex relationship. A strong argument could be made for the case that authority derives from both poles, with effective authority being that which is generally supported by a manager's supervisors and subordinates both. And it is highly probable that the recognition that at least some authority may rise from the bottom has had a modifying influence on the behavior of managers who otherwise might have acted despotically toward their subordinates.

Responsibility for Using Authority

If we accept the premise that authority is a right granted to an individual, then responsibility is the obligation owed by the individual to execute the right properly. In the traditional theory of management, authority and responsibility were thought of as static qualities. It was assumed that authority and responsibility could be spelled out exactly in job descriptions, and it was emphasized that the two must be equal. It is now recognized that rarely does a manager have any unilateral authority, either in decision making or in relations with subordinates. The modern manager may expect to be held responsible for departmental actions, even though the actions may have to be effected through a pooling of authority with that of other managers. The project manager, discussed in Section 19, is a case in point.

Two main management functions, directing and controlling, derive from the setting up of vertical relationships within the organization. (These functions are discussed in detail in later sections of this book.) But, in addition to the obvious vertical relationships in which the manager gives direction to subordinates' activities and monitors their performance, a web of less apparent relationships is created.

Managers' Roles in the Vertical Structure

Relationships in the vertical structure cast managers in various roles, each with different requirements.

Roles toward subordinates.   Subordinates seek assurances as to their security and career development. They need reinforcement of their perceptions of their role status; they want help in resolving personal conflicts; they often need technical assistance in performing their jobs; and they want to be represented effectively on such issues as raises and promotions. These requirements put varying pressures on the manager. Sometimes the manager is cast in the role of a parent, other times as a psychologist, and occasionally as a judge, a teacher, or a promoter. Each of these roles calls for a different supervisor-subordinate relationship; and it appears clear that authority for directing and controlling work performance has no primary significance in any of these other roles. Yet, the way the manager performs in them will influence the way the subordinates respond in their formal duties. Merely having a supervisor tends to generate conflicting feelings on the part of subordinates—with respect, admiration, and affection being at odds with fear, frustration, and contempt.

The role of communication transmitter.   The manager performs still another role in the formal vertical relationship structure, which is to transmit messages upward and downward in the organization. Serving both as an amplifier and a filter for this communication, the manager connects the two organization levels.

The Location of Decision Making

As mentioned earlier in this section, the conventional theory of authority is that pieces of authority are precisely defined and delegated downward to lower individual managers in the organization. To the extent that this is done, decentralization is said to have taken place. It is more accurate, however, to say that decentralization takes place when the location at which managers may pool their authority to make decisions is fixed lower in the organization. Section 22 is concerned with decentralization, and with its opposite, the location of decision making higher in the organization.

Discussion Questions

Reference Case A. The Case of Piggyback Management (Section 20)

1. Speculate on reasons why early management theory stressed supervisor-subordinate relationships.
2. Why should managers behave differently toward their subordinates now that there is some question concerning the real source of authority?
3. Is it fair and reasonable to hold the managers responsible for actions over which they have incomplete authority?
4. How will the performance of informal roles toward subordinates, such as security guarantor, psychologist, and representative, affect the authority a manager exercises over them?
5. In Reference Case A, trace and explain the probable changes in effective authority granted to Jim Mario by the contract administrators.

22. Decentralization
Vs. Centralization

A *decentralized* organization is one in which conditions have been created to permit more decisions by lower-level managers, whereas in a *centralized* organization, the bulk of the decisions are made by top-level managers. The terms are relative; an organization cannot be completely decentralized, because all decisions would be made at the lowest level of the organization, and they would therefore be uncontrolled and without an integrated direction. Nor can an organization, other than a very small and simple one, be completely centralized, because all decisions would be reserved for the top manager, and would significantly restrict the scale of the organization's operations. The terms refer to tendencies to disperse or concentrate the location, within the vertical relationship structure, of decision making. They have no connection with the geographical location of decision making.

Factors Involved in Decentralization

The primary requisite for a decentralized operation is maturity on the part of the organization, and the people in it. An undeveloped organization, still trying to find its place in the larger social system, has a strong need for the central determination of goals, along with plans for achieving them. Decisions in such a case should be restricted to only the most experienced managers, who presumably would be at the top level. Only when an organization can survive the mistakes likely to be made by less experienced managers, should it take the risk of decentralizing in order to capitalize on increased growth and success opportunities.

Not only does decentralization require maturity on the part of the subordinates to whom the decision-making responsibility is entrusted; it also requires maturity on the part of the higher managers, who, though still responsible for the outcome of their subordinates' decisions, must refrain from interfering with their decision processes. The higher managers need, above all else, a faith in the axiom that management is accomplishing things through others, not doing the things themselves. Managers must never decentralize, however, until they have means for objectively evaluating and controlling the performance of their subordinates. The subordinates must possess demonstrated judgment, confidence in themselves, and a drive to be on their own.

As decision making is essentially a matter of choosing from alternatives, what is really involved in decentralization is the dispersal of certain amounts of the planning function. This can be accomplished in various ways and degrees. One way is to have the firm's long-term plans developed from the integrated contributions of the lower-level managers. Another is to disseminate the long-term plan developed centrally to the subordinate managers, and hold them responsible for implementing it with short-term plans. Still another way is to specify the areas in which subordinates can make decisions, such as whether to produce or buy parts and larger components, which channels to use in marketing distribution, and even what style and characteristics should identify the product line. Firms are revealing a growing tendency to decentralize by forcing profit-making responsibility down into the organization. In this approach, human and physical resources are made available to lower-level managers, who are challenged to utilize these resources in such a way as to yield some expected profit.

How Far to Decentralize?

Textbooks on management are replete with guides on how far a company should go in decentralizing. Generally, they approve the delegation of decision making to a level at which

- the facts needed for making a decision can be readily and accurately obtained.
- individuals have a proven capacity to make sound decisions of the order required.
- costs would occur if the decision in question were delayed.
- the probability of costly mistakes is low.

Advantages of Decentralization

One outstanding effect of decentralization is democracy in industry. People become involved in decisions which affect them, and therefore, in a sense, guides of their own destinies rather than pawns to be manipulated. Another advantage, both to individuals and the firm, is that decentralization provides excellent opportunities for the development of managers who may rise higher in the organization. And to the firm itself, decentralization permits almost unlimited size and scope of operations, and it might lead to improved profitability.

The Present Trend

Some companies are tending to re-centralize decision making. One reason is the difficulty of controlling highly decentralized operations; over the past ten to fifteen years, a number of large corporations in the United States have encountered serious problems because decentralized divisions got out of control. Another reason for re-centralizing decision making is the difficulty of coping with the pressures of big government and big labor unions. These two forces are making it essential that business firms operate under uniform policies, strictly administered by top-level managers. A third reason for centralization is associated with the increasing use of the computer. For one thing, the computer is said to be eliminating some middle-management positions and causing others to be reduced in importance, and it is at this management level that decisions are made under decentralization. Primarily, however, the computer influences a firm to centralize because it can furnish information regarding all phases of the company's operations to top managers with incredible speed. No longer is it necessary to have the "man on the spot" make the decisions; through the computer the firm's most experienced managers can keep abreast of every decision-making situation.

The following three sections are concerned with nonvertical relationships within organizations.

As Charles Leghorn often remarked, "With my last name, and the nickname of 'Chick,' there was really no way that I could stay out of the chicken business."

Chick Leghorn got started in business for himself with a catering service in a large midwestern city. He would undertake to provide every detail connected with banquets, weddings, conferences, etc., including the room itself, food, beverage, waiters, bartenders, decoration, and transportation to and from the location, if required. He developed an outstanding reputation for the quality of his service, and he became particularly recognized for the fact that the final bill that he presented never exceeded his original estimate. As was to be a characteristic of his later business life, he developed a system for handling every size and kind of a catering assignment, and he would meticulously check the performance of his employees, whom he informally called his "arrangers," and who supervised the actual work at the catering occasions. By 1963, he had seven arrangers working for him in the city in which he started, and three in each of two smaller cities within a radius of seventy-five miles.

The success of the catering business convinced Chick that many people in the United States were affluent enough to be willing to pay for the convenience of having things done for them. Take-out food service shops, which were then just beginning their phenomenal growth, especially attracted his attention. Through his contacts with local restaurants, he met a chef who was unusually proud of his ability to prepare fried chicken. Chick commissioned the chef, Tony, to experiment with his recipe until he developed an original process for the mass frying of chickens that really had superior qualities. Chick paid Tony $5,000 for exclusive rights to the process.

After an intensive study to determine the most promising location sites for take-out food shops, interior and exterior architectural styles, pricing, advertising, kitchen equipment, and even attendants' uniforms, Chick opened his first shop under the copyrighted name of Chick's Heavenly Chicken. He had a long-term lease on the site, but owned the building and all of the equipment. As he said: "I'm going to spend a year with this one operation until I feel that I really under-

stand the business." He hired and trained employees to prepare the food and wait on customers, and methodically tried different approaches to increasing sales and reducing costs. In the meantime, he remained extremely active in his catering business.

In the middle of 1964, Chick felt that he was ready to expand the Heavenly Chicken operation, and he decided to do it on a franchise basis. He ran display advertisements in the financial sections of local newspapers, and in the newspapers of neighboring cities. The minimum requirements were $35,000 in cash, an impeccable character background, and some business experience. Chick interviewed each applicant intensively, and found that he was accepting only about 20 percent of those who met the minimum standards. Those who were accepted were obligated to a contract wherein Chick would select and negotiate for the site, specify the architecture, prescribe all operating methods, and retain the option to terminate the franchise if, on the basis of periodic reports and his regular visits, he found that the franchisee was departing from established procedures. In spite of the rigid requirements, franchises were in great demand because Chick's Heavenly Chicken shops were making the franchisees prosperous.

The growth of the take-out food industry made desirable sites increasingly difficult to find, and Chick was required to widen his geographical sphere of operations. By 1967 there were 89 franchised Chick's Heavenly Chicken shops in 11 states, with 13 as far away as California, and 7 in Florida. The strain on Chick's personal time was tremendous, and he tried to meet it partially through agents whom he would engage as needed in the various geographical areas. For example, there was an attorney whom he would call on to help with new franchise deals in Los Angeles, a retired ex-banker often did similar things for him in Miami, and around his headquarters city he had trained one of his catering arrangers to relieve him of some of the load.

The huge annual payments by franchise holders to poultry wholesalers made Chick realize that he was missing a bet by not raising, processing, and distributing his own chickens. With his typical thoroughness, he first studied poultry raising, and then started an experimental farm near his headquarters city. Initial results were highly satisfactory, and he expanded the original farm to mass-production scale, and started two others, one in southern Oregon and another one in Florida.

A small wholesale restaurant-supply firm in Los Angeles got into financial trouble in 1968, and Chick's attorney friend mentioned to him that it could be picked up at a bargain. Chick had been thinking for some time that the thousands of take-out food shops all over the country offered a virtually untapped market for an aggressive supply operation, and he figured he could learn how to capture this sales potential with an already going business in a closely related field. Therefore, he made an offer which was accepted, and after spending about three months personally running the company, he found the prospects were really better than he had estimated. He decided that when sales doubled, which he calculated would be by 1974, he would start a branch in the midwest.

One day as Chick and his architect were flying to Seattle to get construction started on three new Chick's Heavenly Chicken shops, the architect remarked: "I admit that I don't know much about management, but it seems to me that what you need more than anything else is an organizaion. You are personally stretched to the breaking point."

Chick's reply was: "My physician tells me the same thing, but I can't get things done the way I want them with an organization chart and fancy titles."

In the early afternoon of Tuesday, April 27, 1970, Chick walked into his office and said to his secretary, "Miss Forrest, please remind me to get to the banquet hall for the political party meeting by five o'clock. I want to be sure to check out the catering details."

Ten minutes later a call came in from San Francisco, where it seemed that a lease on a new shopping center site had bogged down. He buzzed Miss Forrest, "Get me on the late afternoon flight to San Francisco."

Just before 2:30 P.M. he received a call from the poultry farm in Florida. A trucking strike had stopped the delivery of chickens, and nobody there knew what to do about it. "Miss Forrest," he said, "get me to Florida as soon as possible, and arrange for a car to meet me."

A few minutes later Miss Forrest came in and said: "Mr. Leghorn, I simply have to ask you a question."

"Yes, what is it?" replied Chick as he impatiently looked up from his study of the fast-growing "fish and chips" shops.

"Just which part of you is going to the banquet, which part to San Francisco, and which part to Florida?" answered Miss Forrest in a resigned voice.

Discussion Questions

1. *Decentralization* and *centralization* refer to the location of decision-making authority within the organization structure—irrespective of geographical location. What effect on the locus of decision making, however, would geographical dispersal of a firm's operations have?
2. Why should a young and struggling company avoid much decentralization?
3. Argue from the position that the computer may foster decentralization, rather than centralization.
4. In the Case of the Chicken With Its Head Cut Off, what criteria justify decentralizing Chick Leghorn's enterprise?
5. Should Chick undertake the organization of his enterprises himself?

23. Advisory Relationships

Advisory relationships represent one of the types of interaction between members of an organization that are distinguished from the supervisor-subordinate relationships described in preceding sections. Typically, an advisory relationship is established when a member or members of one department (usually a supporting department) counsels a member or members of another department (often a central department) on some specific subject area. The counseling function may carry with it some authority, but the authority is confined to the subject area.

The Line-Staff Concept

Line-staff is a traditional management concept that implies a sharp distinction between two key areas. On the one hand, *line* has historically been used in reference to two things: (1) vertical authority relationships and (2) departments in which central activities have been grouped. *Staff,* on the other hand, has been used in reference to (1) the locus of a type of authority ambiguously called "the authority of advice," and (2) departments in which supporting activities are grouped. Literally dozens of management writers have struggled with the contradiction that their so-called staff departments are involved in many more relationships than just advisory ones.

In this book the position is taken that in any organization there are two kinds of departments, central and supporting. Vertical relationships always exist within both kinds of departments. In addition, there are relationships that take place between departments, one type consisting of advisory relationships, wherein advice is tendered by a supporting department to another department—central or supporting. For example, the personnel department may advise the production department, which is a central department, and also the purchasing department, which is another supporting department.

Reasons for Advisory Relationships

The two principal reasons for instituting advisory relationships are to make specialized knowledge available to every department and to assure uniform interpretation of policies. The necessity for advice based on specialized knowledge derives from the ever growing complexity of the activities performed within a business organization. It is no longer possible for a single individual to be really well informed about more than relatively few of its activities. Thus, there has come about the development of specialists in such areas as public relations, office procedures, and employee compensation, to name just a few, whose special competence is made available to other people within the organization. The complexity of organizations also makes it necessary that policies intended to guide decision making be consistently followed. Policies governing such affairs as labor relations, contacts with vendors, and overhead cost allocation need to be explained to people, and questions regarding the policies satisfactorily answered.

Change in Role—Advisory to Prescriptive

Since a purpose for setting up specialized supporting departments is to make expert advice available to other departments, the conduct of newly established supporting departments will be confined to providing information and counseling others on how to use it. However, this level of effort tends to be unsatisfying after a while, because highly trained specialists would naturally get greater satisfaction out of telling people what to do than merely advising them. Thus, they often begin to move toward having prescriptive control over the way their specific activities are practiced. Frequently they gain this authority through the issuance of a formal edict by a manager high in the organization to the effect that other departments shall abide by their prescriptions for doing things in their areas of specialization. The superior manager in such a case is motivated to grant this limited authority to the specialists either because of a conviction that things will thereby be done better, or because of the influence of their personalities and persuasive arguments. Specialists will often be highly aggressive in changing their roles from merely advisory ones to ones of limited formal authority.

Another way that specialists can gain the right to prescribe specific conduct in departments other than their own is by the other managers' voluntarily granting it. This can often come about by the managers' being so impressed by the specialists' technical competence that they envision improvements in their operations if the specialists are permitted to implement their advice. Managers may also grant specialists authority over some activity within their departments because they simply do not want to be bothered with it themselves. Another reason for granting such authority lies in some managers' sensitivity to the power of a supporting department manager, and their doubts concerning who would win in case of a direct confrontation.

Adverse Impact on Authority

Obviously, the authority of the central department manager will be reduced when specialists have prescriptive control over the performance of certain activities in the department. However, as indicated in Section 22, the manager's responsibility will probably remain the same. In addition, there will be a disturbance of the department's vertical relationships. Subordinates, for example, will receive direction not only from their own supervisor, but also from each of the specialists in their respective areas of authority. Thus, a subordinate in the production department may receive instructions not only from the manager of that department but also from a personnel department specialist, an accounting department specialist, and an industrial engineering department specialist. The reality of this situation violates the traditional concept that no subordinate should have more than one boss.

Reactions to Advisory Relationships

The pure advisory relationship can be highly successful if managers have the right to request the advice, and if specialists make sure that managers get credit for any benefits achieved from following their advice. Similarly, when managers themselves grant specialists certain authority within their departments, the relationship can be quite productive. There is no question that many managers resent having advice forced on them, and having specialists make a big show of how valuable their advice is. The practice by top management of authorizing specialists to prescribe certain policies and procedures in other managers' departments has become so common that it is tolerated, but it carries the potential for explosive conflict. (Conflict, as a general subject, will be discussed in Section 28.)

*Curtis Tool Company, a leading manufacturer of oil field equipment,
employed about 1500 workers. A new president, Loren Whipple,
had been appointed in early 1969. Whipple was a former senior
partner in a large management consulting firm, and had extensive
ideas about introducing up-to-date methods in all of the company's
operating divisions. In June of 1969, he issued a memorandum to
all division managers announcing the establishment of a new department, Management Controls, to be headed by a former junior associate of his, Bill D'Agostino. In the memo Whipple told the division
managers that the new department's function would be to help them
in the areas of systems, organization, and planning. He urged them
to cooperate with D'Agostino and his staff.*

*"Actually, I don't think it's going to be too bad," said Bob Mill,
manufacturing division manager, to his assistant, Ken Beeson. "Remember how apprehensive we were under the old regime when a
labor relations department was appointed. Now we wouldn't think of
doing anything that would have an effect on our various union contracts without getting the advice of the labor relations people. Let's
hope that we have the same good relationship with this new advisory
department."*

*Bill D'Agostino arranged a meeting with Bob Mill for the purpose of
explaining what his department's role would be. He brought along
three of his assistants; Gail Drinkwater, a systems specialist, Ralph
Thompson, whose forte was organization, and a planning specialist,
Ed Litvak. "What you should do," D'Agostino told Mill, "is think of
us as being your own private consultants. We are here to take some
of the load off your back. Our only purpose is to give you help when
you need it. A way of getting started would be for you to let my
people roam about your organization in order to learn what is going
on."*

*After about a month, each of D'Agostino's specialists requested sepa-
rate conferences with Mill in order to present their findings. Mill
asked Ken Beeson to sit in. The first meeting was with Gail Drinkwater.*

146

"I have spent most of my time studying your inventory and production control systems," Drinkwater said, "and I have some ideas that should help you. For one thing, your inventory policy is a two month's coverage for all items. I suggest that the carrying costs for many of the high-value items could be reduced by shortening the coverage period, and the ordering costs for the low-value items could be reduced by increasing the quantities carried in stock. Another thought is that instead of having expediters reporting the progress of work in process in the shop, you could require the foremen to phone notice of completion of operations to the production control office."

Ralph Thompson was next to describe what he had done. "I have prepared charts of authority relationships for your organizational units, starting with the sections, then leading into the departments, and finally culminating with the division itself. Each chart shows the number of people in various experience and educational brackets, and the subordinate/supervisor ratios."

Mill next heard from Litvak. "My work has been to get your supervisors to start thinking about planning in two dimensions," said Litvak. "First, I have been helping them plan the extent and timing of their section's effort in terms of labor hours for each of the current and potential work orders. Second, I have been advising them on how to project their section's total operating expenses by month in terms of the aggregate of the work orders for which they have some responsibility."

"See how well it's working out," Bob Mill said to Ken Beeson when the two of them had finished studying the three written reports that had been submitted. "These reports contain some really good ideas."

"It's working out well for D'Agostino too," said Beeson reservedly. "You will notice that a copy of each of these reports went to Whipple, and they might make him wonder why we haven't thought of these ideas."

Over the next year, changes began to take place gradually in the relationships between Management Controls and all of the operating divisions of Curtis Tool Company. The following are some examples of things that happened in the manufacturing division:

Drinkwater first began selling Bob Mill on the notion of a computer-ized inventory and production-control system. Before long his pre-sentations got beyond Mill's technical competence, but they sounded plausible. Without fully realizing the consequences of the action, Mill authorized Drinkwater to implement a computerized system. Ken Beeson finally brought to Mill's attention the fact that the inventory and production control personnel were taking their operating orders directly from Drinkwater.

Ralph Thompson partially convinced Mill that the educational level of the supervisors in the manufacturing division was too low. With some reluctance, Mill approved a policy statement prepared by Thompson to the effect that two years of college was the minimum educational requirement for a supervisory job.

D'Agostino and Litvak together presented Mill with a new planning system. It was keyed around a five-page input form which was to be filled out by each supervisor, approved by the department heads and finally by Mill, and submitted to Management Controls quarterly. Mill's objections that the system involved too much red tape were quelled by D'Agostino's remark that it had been developed by Loren Whipple, the president, when he was in the management consulting business.

In July 1972, a memorandum was sent to all division managers by D'Agostino. It was countersigned by Loren Whipple. The thesis of the memorandum was expressed by the following statements:

1. *Sole authority to design and implement an integrated in-formation-flow system, cutting across all divisional lines, is vested in Management Controls.*
2. *Organizational changes in all divisions, including expansions, promotions, transfers, subordinate/supervisory ratios, etc., must first be approved by Management Controls.*
3. *All variations between a division's plans and subsequent events must be explained by the responsible division man-ager in quarterly reviews conducted by Management Con-trols.*

"Well, Ken, it looks as if the division managers' jobs have been pretty much taken over," Bob Mill commented as he handed Ken Beeson the memorandum.

"That's a polite way to say it," was Beeson's tight-lipped reply.

Discussion Questions

1. Is the term *staff department* necessarily obsolete?
2. Why would members of a supporting department strive to expand their role from advising to prescribing?
3. In the Case of the Subtle Takeover, could Loren Whipple have had a personal motive in establishing and expanding the authority of the new department, Management Controls?
4. Was there anything apparently wrong with the way Drinkwater, Thompson, and Litvak executed their advisory relationships in the beginning?
5. Would the authority vested in Management Controls (as expressed in D'Agostino's memorandum of July 1972) be detrimental to the future operation of Curtis Tool Company?

24. Service Relationships

Like advisory relationships, the service relationships set up within an organization induce a type of interaction where the supervisor-subordinate question of authority is not a factor. Service relationships accrue from the service activities that must be performed in the organization.

Any supporting department will probably engage in both advisory and service relationships with other departments. In the former, as noted in Section 23, the other departments perform an activity under the guidance of a supporting department, whereas in service relationships a supporting department is responsible for the performance of a grouping of specialized activities. Although the activities will be in the same functional area whether the relationship is an advisory or service one, the nature of the relationships will be distinctly different. For example, the personnel department, in an advisory relationship, may inform the production department concerning the prevailing wage rates in the industry for schedulers, or may go further and specify that schedulers are restricted to some maximum wage rate. In a service relationship, the personnel department may recruit and screen applicant schedulers in response to a request by the production department.

Reasons for Service Departments

In a small organization, the necessary service activities, such as personnel, purchasing, and maintenance, will probably be performed on a part-time basis by members of the central departments. An exception will almost always be the accounting activities, because even in a simple organization accounting is usually set up as a supporting department at the start.

For the service activities that are performed in the central departments, problems will begin to appear as the organization becomes more complex. First of all, when an activity is performed only as a sideline by individuals, it will not be done as well as it would be by people who are specifically trained in its routines, and who give it full-time attention. Second, when an activity (such as one pertaining to personnel or purchasing) is performed in two separate departments (such as production and sales), many aspects of the activity will be similar, but a different policy may be applied with respect to its accomplishment. And third, costly equipment and facilities will be duplicated when various central departments independently perform services that are commonly required throughout the organization.

In order to reduce these problems, at some point in the development of any organization specific service activities will be broken out of the central departments and grouped into semiautonomous supporting departments. It is important to note that the creation of different supporting departments will not usually happen simultaneously; the establishment of each should be at the time when the advantages of having the department appear to justify the outlay of effort and expense.

Characteristics of Service Relationships

Although in many respects service relationships resemble conventional buyer-seller relationships—with the object of the service being to meet the standards of those to whom it is rendered—they differ from the buyer-seller relationship in an important way: The services are arbitrarily imposed. Usually there is no option in the matter of utilizing this service or some other one; the specialized services of a supporting department are utilized to the exclusion of all alternatives. Thus, the supporting departments, in effect, have captive customers. Central departments within the organization having need for industrial engineering, or market research, or traffic activities to be performed, for example, may not choose whether to do the work internally, hire an outside company for the service, or use the service of the respective supporting department. Not only must the supporting departments be patronized; but also the costs of operating the supporting departments are usually arbitrarily allocated to the production and sales department budgets.

As implied above, managers of central departments would often prefer to have direct control over their own service activities. The production and sales managers, for example, will reason that their authority has been diluted when important activities in such areas as personnel and purchasing are not permitted to be performed in their own departments. Therefore, these managers are quick to point out flaws in the quality, quantity, and timing of the various services that they are forced to have done for them.

Most service activities are distinguished now by the necessity for them to be performed by specially trained people. Many of these people believe that their skill is really at the professional level, and perhaps several degrees above the status level of the people in the departments they serve. This preoccupation with status often breeds an attitude of superiority, and puts an additional strain on the service relationships.

The combined pressure from outside the supporting departments for faster and better service, and from the specialists themselves for wider scope and increased professional recognition, often causes the size of supporting departments and the number of services offered to expand far beyond original expectations. This seems to be particularly true with business firms in the United States, where the entire subject of service relationships appears to have a far greater significance than it does with firms in foreign countries.

Resolution of Problems

When expansion of a service activity is being considered, the problem arises of how large a department to provide some service should be. The problem can be handled by a critical evaluation of the costs of any expansion proposal vs. the real expected benefits. In addition, a comparison can be made of the costs of alternative ways of providing any proposed expanded service, such as by purchasing the service from outside firms.

The supporting department managers have the important function of preventing "prima donnas" in their ranks from destroying necessary service relationships. One way is by impressing upon the people responsible for performing these specialized activities the fact that their organizational purpose is indeed to serve, and that their success is measured in the way their services are received by other departments. The frequent resentment by other departments over being captive customers can be partially handled by the supporting department managers' conscientiously "selling" the best service possible. If the problem becomes aggravated, and especially if the organization grows large enough to adopt the product form of departmentation (see Section 18), the next move may be to relocate the service activities under the central managers.

Discussion Questions

Reference Case A. The Case of the Function That Wouldn't Fit (Section 18)

1. Explain how performing all maintenance services in a centralized maintenance shop could be less costly than having the engineering development and production shops perform their own maintenance services.
2. Why should a company insist on exclusive use of its service departments by the other departments?
3. Why should managers feel kindly toward having some services performed for them, and resent other services that they have to accept?
4. What implications does the trend for many people in service departments to perceive themselves as professionals have for the acceptance of their services by other departments?
5. In Reference Case A, the central problem revolves about where to locate a service department in the organizational structure. Was the problem really based on conflicting ideas of how to best serve the company's interests, or were there other factors?

25. Other Lateral Relationships

From the foregoing descriptions of relationships within an organization, the position might well be taken that the typical organization is composed of relationships so complex and numerous that any attempt to describe them graphically with a very fine pen on a very large chart would produce a solid background of undifferentiated lines. Indeed, this is the case for all organizations—nonbusiness as well as business. Up until very recently, writers on management were preoccupied with the supervisor-subordinate relationships in organizations, and gave varying attention to the so-called line-staff concept. In this book, part of the old line-staff relationships are identified separately as advisory and service relationships. These are *lateral relationships,* in that no resemblance to supervisor-subordinate relationships is present. They are, however, far from being the whole of the possible lateral relationships. Just a few of the other important ones include functional-sequence, evaluative, plural, and nonvertical, unequal-status relationships.

The Significance of Lateral Relationships

Perhaps an analogy using the human body will illustrate the significance of lateral relationships. The heart, and its blood-pumping function through the veins and arteries, might be likened to an organizational subsystem of vertical relationships. There is no question that this process is important, but consider the countless additional subsystems of organs, nerves, and muscles that relate together to make the total system of the human body. Lateral relationships are the counterparts within organizations of these human subsystem relationships. All of them that exist in an organization cannot possibly be described, but the members of the organization are either consciously or subconsciously affected by them. The work that gets done within an organization, and its successes or failures, is as much—or possibly far more—the result of lateral relationships as of vertical relationships.

Functional-Sequence Relationships

Highly important nonvertical interactions between members of organizations occur as a result of functional-sequence relationships.

These relationships exist because the tasks necessary to produce an end product or service must usually be performed in series. Again resorting to a manufacturing firm for purposes of illustration, assume that the engineering design of a product is the initial task in a series. An immediately following task is the development of a prototype model. Thus, there will be interactions between individuals involved in the two tasks with regard to schedules, drawings, and so on. The development people depend on the design people doing their job on time, and doing it in such a way that the prototype can be made, but they have no real authority over them to assure desired performance. In turn, the task of producing an approved product will follow the development of the prototype. If the development work in either the design or prototype stage is delayed, the manufacturing schedule will be affected, so the production people will engage in interactions with individuals in both development areas. And finally, the people involved in selling the product will depend on the whole series of preceding tasks to provide a salable item in the quantities and at the times desired, and so they, too, will engage in a complex network of relationships. People late in a series will influence their peers who are early in the series by every possible tactic, including friendly inquiry, referral to a higher manager, bullying, pleading, and reciprocation.

Evaluative Relationships

Members of organizations, particularly those at some managerial level, are continually involved in evaluative relationships with peers in other departments. These are not formal evaluations having to do with raises and promotions (which will be discussed in Section 41). Nevertheless, these informal evaluations have an important bearing on people's career progression, and on their ability to get support for their own department's objectives. Evaluative relationships are two-directional, in that while person A is evaluating person B, the evaluation of person A by person B is also taking place. The evaluations are sometimes based on objective, measurable parameters, but often they are founded only on superficial judgments. Typically they are not kept private but are communicated throughout the organization by the "grapevine" (see Section 26).

An example of evaluative relationships can be drawn from the context of the project type of organization. The project manager will evaluate the manager of the functional engineering department according to the way engineers assigned to the project from that department have performed. Simultaneously, the engineering manager will be evaluating the project manager according to the project's engineering accomplishments.

Professional ability is one criterion for performance evaluation. Another is the opinion of peers; do they mark an individual as someone who is going to move ahead in the organization, or as someone whose proper level has been reached or passed? This latter judgment is based largely on the nebulous factor of how a person behaves in the various organizational relationships.

Plural Relationships

Group meetings tend to be a way of life in the modern organization. Here the individual is exposed to plural relationships, which require interaction with two or more members of the same, or other departments. In the departmental meeting, people may propose or defend issues that have a bearing on their personal roles. In the interdepartmental meeting, an individual represents the department and must try to serve its needs. While ostensibly the purpose of the meeting will be to effect coordination of various activities for the good of the organization, personal and departmental pressures will motivate the individual to gain something for the department, or at least prevent it from suffering some loss.

Group relationships are often characterized by frictions resulting from the divergent motivations of the participants, and by alliances which pit participants holding sympathetic views against those with strongly opposing views. Unless controlled, such frictions can impair the coordination which is supposed to result from the group meetings. Fundamentally, four things can happen as an outcome of frictions. The first is that one faction will win and the other faction, or factions, will lose. Second, there can be an impasse, and all factions will withdraw. A third possibility, and a very common one, is compromise. Finally and ideally, the factions may discard their parochial interests and try to work together toward mutually agreed-upon goals.

Nonvertical Unequal-Status Relationships

We have already considered vertical, unequal-status relationships which exist between direct supervisors and their subordinates. There are also, within an organization, many occasions for nonvertical, un-equal-status relationships to occur. These take place when individuals in one department must interact with individuals in another depart-ment who are at a level as high, or higher, than the first individual's supervisor. Both levels of individuals are aware that authoritative directions need not be followed, but both are also conscious of a status differentiation. The lower-level individual will characteristically be somewhat subdued, although there will be instances when hostility is expressed. It might be expected that some condescension will be evident in the attitude of the higher-level individual. An example of this kind of relationship would be where the production manager proposes a drawing change to a nonmanagerial design engineer. The two individuals can resolve the problem together, but stress can result if there are sharp differences of opinion. If stress does occur, the issue will probably be referred to the manager in design engineer-ing at the production manager's level, and fresh negotiations will begin.

Discussion Questions

Reference Case A. The Case of the Mexican Crazy Quilt (Section 19)
Reference Case B. The Case of the Clogged Filter (Section 15)
Reference Case C. The Case of the Newborn SPM (Section 14)

1. Explain functional-sequence relationships by using the analogy of a runner on first base planning to steal to second base on the pitch, and the interactions between the pitcher, catcher, and second baseman.
2. Consider the case of a waiter and a chef in a restaurant, who are in a functional-sequence relationship with each other; that is, the chef's tasks precede those of the waiter. The waiter's tips from customers depend to a large extent on quality of food and service, and the chef can largely determine these factors. Explain how the waiter might alternatively use friendly relations, referral to a higher manager, bullying, pleading, and reciprocation to influ-ence the chef.
3. In Reference Case A, discuss an obvious instance of an informal evaluative relationship.
4. In Reference Case B, discuss the implication for Ike Comstock of the meeting he had with his peers, Trask and Mann.

5. In Reference Case C, it is entirely possible that Klopp, the quality-control supervisor, would be at a lower organizational level than the production manager. However, the production manager would have no authority over Klopp, and it is apparent from the case that Klopp's assistant, Tanaka, could have many interactions with the production manager. What would you do if you were Tanaka, and the production manager let you know that he felt considerably superior to you?

26. The Informal Organization

Up to this point, the discussion of organizing as a managerial function has focused on the processes, concepts, and relationships of the formal organization. Formal organization, as has been indicated, is the deliberate and conscious grouping of activities and melding of relationships for the purpose of achieving some predetermined objective. Now attention is directed to informal organizations, which inevitably are a part of every formal organization.

Distinguishing Features

Informal organizations originate spontaneously rather than deliberately. Members of informal organizations may be conscious of the fact that they are members, but often they are not. Relationships among members are never spelled out, but somehow status and position distinctions do exist and are perceived as highly important. If informal organizations have goals, they are undefined, and reflect the personal goals of members. In short, informal organizations differ in every way possible from formal organizations. However, in every formal organization, whether it be a business firm, a military unit, a church, or whatever, the members will instinctively join together in informal groups disassociated from the formal structure. The force that causes such groups to form is a need that cannot be satisfied through the formal organization.

Need Deprivation in the Formal Organization

Maslow's theory of needs, and the implications of needs for motivation, will be discussed in some detail in Section 48. However, it is appropriate to the present discussion to mention that informal groupings represent an unconscious attempt by individuals to satisfy a special kind of need. This is the need that virtually all people feel for close relationships with other people. It is the need for sociability, for emotional support from other people, for a sense of a personal identification, for protection against feeling alone. The larger the formal organization, the more impersonal it becomes; members feel some isolation even in belonging. Therefore, they form informal groups, but instinctually, without analyzing what makes them do it.

Roots of Informal Groups

The work environment within the formal organization naturally fosters informal groupings. For example, workers on an assembly line, clerks in a specific area of an office, engineers in a "bull pen," and managers on the same corridor of the executive suite will tend to be found associating off the job. Cultural ties also bind people together. Thus, groups will form made up of people with similar ethnic, racial, or religious backgrounds. Outside interests represent another basis for informal groups; golfers, stamp collectors, and garden enthusiasts, to name a few, will naturally gravitate to their respective interest groups. Dissenters, or persons with unresolved grievances, will be inclined to merge their dissatisfactions and find some solace in collective unhappiness.

There are countless other bases for informal organizations in addition to those named. Some are formed just for sociability, some for exchanging information, and some for gaining allies for future action; and some combine these functions. It should be plain, also, that a given individual may belong to many such groups.

Inner Workings of Informal Groups

An interesting characteristic of each informal group is the way in which status hierarchies develop. An individual's position within a group is, of course, in no way formally designated. But through some subtle process of perception and understanding, members have a rank and status accorded to them by the group.

Each group will have an informal leader, or possibly leaders. These leaders are neither appointed nor elected. They are leaders simply because the other members of the group—somehow perceiving that the leader can either help them advance toward their personal goals or hold the group together, or perform both functions simultaneously—simply become followers.

Another characteristic of informal groups is their tendency to separate themselves from other groups and withhold coveted membership. The word which describes this element in grouping is *clique*. Cliques will be in rivalry with each other, and an individual's status in some large informal organization will be largely determined on the basis of membership in a particular clique. Cliques will be perceived by outsiders as snobbish, but internally, members might not even recognize that they are in a clique. A clique system and a caste system have marked similarities.

The cohesiveness that a group develops has significant implications for group conduct. That is, the group will set norms of conduct and behavior to which all members will be expected to adhere. These norms are extremely important to the formal organization because they are applied to quantity and quality of work produced, response to authoritative commands by the formal supervisor, dress, punctuality, absenteeism, competition with other groups, and so on. An informal group thus has power to facilitate or thwart the attainment of the formal organization's objectives.

Grapevine

The grapevine is the unofficial, unauthorized channel of communication in the informal organization. It flourishes on information which is not openly available and which appears to have indications of privilege and confidentiality. Contributions to the grapevine come when two or more people gather informally and exchange rumors, gossip, or vaguely supported items of opinion. Information channeled via the grapevine proceeds with amazing speed and incredible penetration. Like the informal organization in which it has its origin, the grapevine is inevitably and unavoidably present in every formal organization.

Discussion Questions

Reference Case A. The Case of the Many-Headed Monster (Section 9)

Reference Case B. The Case of the Markets That Will Fade Away (Section 13)

Reference Case C. The Case of Piggyback Management (Section 20)

1. In Reference Case A, what might cause the division managers (Johnson, Hayes, and Richardson) to group together despite their divergent views on how to increase profits?
2. In Reference Case B, what possible informal groups could form within the formal planning subcommittee of Petro's board of directors?

3. In Reference Case C, what bases exist for the formation of informal groups?
4. How can informal groups be used to benefit the formal organization?
5. Is the grapevine something that management should attempt to eradicate?

27. Power Politics in Organizations

All organizations, of either a formal or informal nature, are arenas for power struggles, and politics is the means for gaining mastery in these struggles. Any perceptive person experienced in the affairs of organizations will testify to the dominant influence of power politics.

Machiavelli's Prescription

Despite the intuitive knowledge that most people have of the existence and the workings of power politics, there is little textbook information on the subject. Except for what we can find in the writings of current political scientists, our best source is Machiavelli, who developed a classical prescription for the use of power politics in *The Prince,* written over five hundred years ago. Although Machiavelli's purpose in writing *The Prince* was to advise his benefactor, the dictator of an Italian city-state, on the use of political strategies, his precepts may be seen operating in any modern-day striving for power.

Will for Power

The striving for power may be instinctive in human beings. On the other hand, it may be a cultivated drive, resulting from a cultural emphasis. Many people, for example, are impressed from childhood with the idea that competition is the mode for goal achievement. Whatever its source, the will for power appears to be active, or at least latent, in most people. And for managers, the will for power must be accompanied by the ability to obtain and manipulate power, if success is to be attained.

Definitions

Power may be defined as the capacity of an individual to restrict the alternatives available to other people to those of his choosing. It follows then that *politics* is the complex of intuitive and deliberate strategies and tactics through which power is acquired and manipulated. Another way of looking at politics is that it is the means whereby an individual gains promotions and power-wielding status other than by, or in addition to, demonstrated job competence or nepotism.

Both *power* and *politics* have somewhat unpleasant connotations, but the fact is that people who govern the affairs of organizations seek power and know how to use it. This does not necessarily imply that they are immoral or unethical; it is simply that from a practical standpoint, they can gain the power to rule most readily through politics.

Steps in Organizational Politics

The following outline of steps by which an individual becomes a successful organizational politician is based chiefly on an analysis (unpublished) by Norman Martin of New York University.

Preparation stage.   The power-seeking individual must first go through the preliminary stages of preparation. This may be done intuitively, but the really professional politician makes a deliberate and thoughtful process of it. Essential at the beginning is the manager's creation of a unique personal image. Components of this image, which is the way that the manager wants to be perceived by others, will include physical characteristics, interactional behavior, past accomplishments, and a projection of potential accomplishments. The manager will want to convey a sense of ease and quiet confidence and to be consistent in behavior, so that every attitude and action reinforces the desired image.

The next preparatory stage involves the development of external power resources. These resources will include individuals and cliques who can be relied on for support. The individual's existing power will be added to and strengthened by pooling the power of these supporters, who will be characterized by loyalty and positive response to requests.

Following the enlistment of a personal team, the power seeker will need to develop an efficient intelligence system. Privileged significant information, although not readily available, is the key to power; thus, the aspirer for power will want feedback regarding the effect of self-initiated moves and of retaliatory moves by opponents. To a large extent, the team will represent an information-gathering system.

The most important information that the aspirer to power will need concerns individual competitors—their strengths and weaknesses, their approaches to situations, and their defense mechanisms. Also, their social connections, their enemies, and their sponsors and proteges will be matters of utmost importance, for above all the power seeker will want to know where blocks will occur and what their strength is. With the development of this intelligence system, all the steps in the organizational power seeker's preparation stage have been completed.

Planning stage. Next, political strategies must be developed. The starting point will be a clear statement of the individual's ultimate objective in the organization. Then, by working backward to the present, the sequence and timing of the subgoals that must be accomplished in order to reach that final goal must be established. Involved in this process is a projection of the general lines of conduct to be pursued, including a forecast of possible obstacles and a description of means to overcome them. The political plan thus will not be confined to a single course of action, but will include contingency paths to be followed in the event of power shifts within the organization.

Tactical stage. Finally, the power seeker will reach the tactical stage. It is at this point, when the political plan goes into motion, that the individual will proceed patiently and carefully to negotiate the required actions in their predetermined sequence—typically following certain practices that date back to Machiavelli. Some of these Machiavellian maneuvers include:

- Maintain mobility. Be able to switch to alternative plans readily, without apparent compromise or loss of face.
- Maintain tempo. Always be one move ahead of opponents in the power arena.
- Avoid entanglements. Seek counsel only when you want it, not when others wish to give it.
- Beware of being overwhelmed by success. Never relax; always move forward; do not drop guard.
- Beware of friends. Use people; do not be used by them.

Realistic Appraisal

Whether people really behave in the manner described, the reader may be able to decide by thinking back to membership in some organization and asking whether there was not a strong resemblance to the Machiavellian prescriptions listed here in the behavioral patterns of individuals who rose (or may still be rising).

Discussion Questions

1. How is success determined in most endeavors, at least in the United States? The endeavors to which you apply the question may be scholastic, athletic, vocational, etc.
2. Give reasons supporting the notion that the striving for power is an instinctive drive in human beings.
3. Are the student activists on college campuses seeking to do away with power?
4. Why is it important for a power seeker to project a consistent self-image?
5. If very little has been written on the subject of power politics, explain how successful power seekers seem to follow similar behavior patterns.

28. Organizational Conflict

So much has been written on the subject of organizational conflict that management literature abounds with treatments of

- conflict between the organization and external systems, such as unions.
- conflict between individuals in an organization over cultural, ideological, and racial values.
- conflict between subsystems (or departments) within an organization.

To keep the present discussion within reasonable bounds and permit adequate development, the focus will be on the conflict between subsystems. In this context, *conflict* is defined as a behavior of rivalry and hostility between formal subgroups whose goals are incompatible and who are working against each other.

The Development of Conflict

Conflict may be viewed as a natural human state, because people are constantly in many conflict situations, of which conflict between work groups is just one. However, this view does little to explain how conflicts occur and what are the contributing factors. One major contributor to conflict in organizations is the hierarchical structure. Departments are established like independent little islands, with highly effective boundaries separating the duties and prerogatives of each group of activities. In complex organizations, the grouping of activities at the top management level may be by product line or geographical location, but eventually, at some place in all organizations, departmentation occurs according to the function performed. Thus, as we have noted earlier, there are central functional departments, such as engineering, production, and sales, and supporting functional departments, such as accounting, personnel, and purchasing.

Each functional department is staffed with people who are specialists in that function. These specialists naturally are inclined to confer priority status on their own function. In addition, each department has goals—both assigned and internally developed—associated with the performance of the specific departmental function and with the receipt of preferential status recognition for that function in the hierarchy of functions. The members of each department will also have personal goals, which are likely to be different from the departmental goals; however, they will perceive that some of their personal goals can be achieved through achievement of departmental goals. As a result, they tend to become highly prejudiced in favor of their departmental function.

When the members of different functional departments survey the availability of departmental rewards and status symbols, they will perceive that the supply is limited. For example, there can only be so many departments at the primary (top) level of an organization. Competition between departments naturally arises; and when there is competition there is the chance of losing. Each department therefore will perceive other departments as threatening sources of loss, and conflict will result.

Likely Locations for Conflict

Management literature seems to stress the incidence of conflict between line and staff departments, which, in the terms of this book, are central and supporting departments (see Sections 17 and 23). Some writers contend that staff departments try too aggressively to prove their worth, that they are condescending to personnel in the line departments, and that they resent being measured by values set by the line departments. And for their part, the line departments are described as fearful lest the staff departments usurp some of their authority, and jealous of the rising importance of the staff departments.

Observations by many experienced managers, however, suggest that the degree of conflict between departments tends to reflect personality differences between department managers rather than a difference in the functions performed. Departments whose managers are driving, domineering, and highly motivated toward goal achievement, will reflect these characteristics and be continuously involved in a high degree of interdepartmental conflict. Conflict will be at a much less stressful level between these departments and departments whose managers are placid and easygoing; and it will be practically nonexistent between departments whose respective managers are of the latter type.

Disruptive Effects of Conflict

A certain amount of competition, and hence conflict, is essential within organizations. Up to some level, competition is a motivating force and ensures efficient achievement of objectives. It is when competition becomes an end in itself that the conflict becomes destructive. In destructive conflict, energies are drained away from the direction of productive effort and directed almost exclusively toward strategies of defense and attack. Such conflict results from continuous and violent win-lose struggles, in which neither party will capitulate, so each issue must be referred to a third party for resolution.

Retaliation. Often, after a decision to resolve a win-lose struggle, the losing party will begin plotting retaliation. A real-life example of such conflict, related to this writer by a company vice-president, took place between an engineering department and a production department. The managers of both departments assigned first order of importance to their respective functions and continuously fought for supremacy over such issues as final authority over part configuration, make-buy decisions, quality deviations, and work-order responsibility. Each conflict precipitated an impasse, which had to be resolved by a higher-level manager. The loser in each case then would begin developing strategies to assure success on the next occasion.

Isolation. If the losers of destructive conflict do not react by plotting retaliation, they may take a position of isolation. Often this attitude develops in a department which is a constant loser in win-lose struggles. Its manager takes the position, which is adopted by the other members, that the department will simply perform duties precisely spelled out in the operations manual and sever all nonspecified contacts with other departments. One example of such withdrawal told to this writer concerned a reliability department that was withdrawn by the manager from all but formal interdepartmental contacts because it was not accorded primary-level status.

Compromise. A less disruptive consequence of conflict, but one which still can thwart organizational objectives, is compromise. Like win-lose struggles, a compromise usually involves a third party. To avoid the bitterness inevitable in win-lose situations, the third party will try to find some level in the dispute at which both parties can agree. Often this conclusion is not really satisfactory to either party, and is only partially satisfactory in terms of the goals of the organization.

Reduction of Destructive Conflict

As noted earlier, the compartmentalized structure of organizations makes conflict inevitable. It cannot be expected that conflict-free, productive cooperation will ensue from an organizational network in which each department's boundaries are rigidly defined, in which the members of each department identify more with their functional goals than with the goals of the organization, and where efficient lateral relationships between departments are left to chance. These are common conditions in organizations at the point where departmentation is on a functional basis.

What is needed is an entirely new approach to organization. The first step might be to relax the functional boundary lines and create loosely knit subsystems within an organization that are oriented toward an end item or product rather than toward functional specialization. Such subsystems would be multifunctional, rather than single-functional. A second step might be to study the necessary lateral relationships between the subsystems and define how they should be conducted. And finally, a third step seems blindingly obvious—that is, to build into the organization's formal appraisal structure a system of rewards for managers who accomplish their objectives without destructive conflict, and sanctions for managers who do not.

Discussion Questions

1. Is conflict between departments a natural and inevitable condition?
2. Explain why people identify so strongly with their particular department.
3. In what ways are interdepartmental conflicts connected with power politics?
4. Are there constructive aspects to interdepartmental conflict?
5. In the text, an example is given of continuous win-lose struggles between an engineering department manager and a production department manager. If you had authority over these managers, how would you resolve the conflict?

29. The Individual in the Formal Organization

The discussion in this section summarizes the nature of human alienation in the environment of formal organizations. Possible resolutions of the problem, together with a discussion of what is known about human needs, are presented in sections of this book dealing with the managerial function of directing.

Formal organizations only partly come about by the deliberate actions of managers. As has been pointed out, the development of such elements in formal organizations as informal groups, the maze of lateral relationships, politics, and conflict are largely beyond the control of the manager engaged in the function of organizing. But, to the extent that organizing is controllable, it is geared toward the rational objective of maximum efficiency. Basic departmentation, job design, vertical authority relationships, policies, procedures, and rules are all calculated with this objective in mind, and the entire process is at odds with the needs of individuals for security, self-esteem, and opportunities to grow to the limit of their capabilities.

Indifference to Efficiency

It is probably not so much that people are opposed to efficiency as they are indifferent to its goals. Below the higher levels of managers, the people in organizations simply feel no sense of personal involvement with the organization. They are frustrated by the means employed to achieve efficiency. And, the curious thing is that although most people in organizations know that they are frustrated, few of them can point to the reasons. All organizations of which they have ever been a part, starting with kindergarten, have fundamentally been structured the same way. Most people have little trouble adapting to new organizations because the regimen is the same; it is merely the paper work that is different. So people infer that the organizational way of life is normal, and through a business organization they earn a living. The understanding that the mechanics of organizational efficiency are unnatural to man, and induce frustrations, has come to us from the studies of psychologists and sociologists.

Frustrations

An observation of conditions in a formal organization suggests a number of reasons for human frustration.

Monotony. Division of work is one principle of efficiency, the theory being that if work is fractionalized into parts and people are trained in performing the various parts, the end result will be better than if people must learn all the variables in the total job. This is very likely true, and application of the principle causes few or no problems to people of low IQ and limited education. However, to individuals possessing more than basic intellectual qualifications, such jobs become repetitive and boring. Moreover, after a few years of such work they become known as specialists in it, and will have great difficulty breaking out of the rut.

No room for individual differences. Another aspect of work assignments is that they are designed for some conceptualized "average person." People whose aptitudes and education seem to fit them for particular jobs are trained in performing the carefully engineered requirements. Recognition is rarely given to the probability that a job would be a great deal more satisfying if an individual's qualifications were considered first, and a job designed to fit them. As a result, most individuals rarely have a chance to use more than a few of their abilities. There is no place in organizational efficiency for individual differences.

Lowering of self-esteem. The conventional vertical authority relationships appear to be taken for granted as the logical way to organize, with little thought ever given to the fact that such a relationship cannot fail to have a psychological effect on the subordinates. Naturally experiencing dependence and submissiveness toward their supervisors, and looking upward at tiers of supervisors, subordinates at a lower level in an organization will not likely have their opinions of themselves improved very much by their quite obvious low caste. And self-esteem is a major human need.

Regimentation. Although it is undoubtedly highly efficient to routinize repetitive decisions through the media of policies, procedures, and rules, such regimentation is stultifying to individual growth. It is hard to imagine any personal satisfaction to be derived from looking in a manual to find the prescribed action for a particular situation. The need that individuals feel to have some control over their work environment, and to be able to create something on their own, is denied them when everything must be "run by the book."

Pressures for conformity.   A tenet of organizational efficiency stresses the need for conformity, because conformists are predictable and therefore controllable. Individuals soon learn that rewards are given for conformity and that nonconformists are passed over for raises and promotions. Therefore, they conform, but at a possible cost to their dignity.

Status discrepancies.   Defects in a firm's system of promoting employees will be readily perceived by individuals in the ranks, and their resentments will fester when they see people rise higher for reasons other than merit. The cognition of status discrepancies will be particularly galling when individuals, to keep their jobs, must appear contented to take orders from a supervisor whom they do not respect.

Effect of the Goal Divergence

If conditions in an organization are as described, and they frequently are, then paradoxically the result will be low efficiency in an efficiently designed system. If the implication of organizational efficiency is that individuals have no goals other than those associated with their organizational roles, then their response typically will be to learn whatever the organization expects of them, do it at the specified level of performance, and do nothing more. Their own needs will be unsatisfied; or if satisfied, in some system other than the formal organization. Sometimes the external system providing satisfaction is in conflict with the formal organization, such as a labor union. A better coordination of organizational and individual goals depends on how the managerial function of directing is performed, and on breaking away from strictly mechanistic organizational models.

*Sally Inouye felt her familiar impatience growing as she read the
newly received insert page for the Standard Practices Manual entitled
"Rules of Personal Conduct for Female Buyers." In fact, she had to
muster her sense of humor in order not to be insulted at some of the
instructions, for example, "2.2. Female buyers are requested not to
accept evening entertainment from suppliers' representatives." She
thought to herself that her husband had some prescriptions of his own
on that issue. Another nagging thought crossed her mind, which was
that five years ago when she started as assistant chinaware buyer
for Rinehart Department Store, she would have been far less resigned
to receiving instructions from her employer as to her personal behavior. Yes, she was becoming brainwashed, or maybe just more
realistic about the present state of affairs.*

*Ms. Inouye was a thirty-year-old, highly intelligent college graduate
who had started her business career with visions of becoming one of
the first woman presidents of a large merchandising organization.
Beginning as assistant to Mary Tilford, chinaware buyer, Sally
thought that she would soon be promoted past the older woman, and
move solely on the basis of ability through successively higher levels
on the way to her goal. The finding out that although Rinehart had
a lot of women at the buyer level, there was an unwritten law in the
company that said that no woman can ever rise higher, was a bitter
pill for her to swallow. Being single at the time, she had been willing
to leave Rinehart's and start over in a different store in another city,
but her investigations disclosed that she would probably encounter
the same discrimination wherever she went.*

*Now, still working under Mary Tilford, Sally found herself tormented
by a complex of frustrations. She wanted to work; a housewife's life
was boring to her; besides, she and her husband had been unable to
have children. She had a grudging respect for Mary Tilford's efficiency in running her department, but rebelled at having to take
orders as though she were an insignificant underling. In the earlier
years at Rinehart's she had had several opportunities to transfer to
other departments, but she then thought that she soon would succeed
to Ms. Tilford's position. In any case, two incidents in which she was*

involved diminished the enthusiasm of other buyers to have her in their departments.

One incident occurred when Sally was acting in her role as salesperson. Her taste in all beautiful things, including fabrics, fine furniture, and paintings, attracted some of the store's most valued customers, and in serving them she became intolerant of departmental boundary lines, and would take them from department to department, landing large sales. The personnel in the other departments became extremely resentful of the way she would ignore them as she escorted customers through.

Sally's reputation as a nonconformist reached the attention of the store's top managers when she submitted a written proposal to the effect that certain customers be assigned to her for all of their shopping. The flat rejection of this idea met with her barely concealed contempt, because it had been inspired by the customers themselves.

Another unfortunate incident occurred at a semiannual buyers' market in New York. Mary Tilford was ill and could not attend, and Sally handled her selections and negotiations with marked ability. The trouble came when she observed Ted Egan, buyer for flatware, trying to negotiate a large purchase in an obviously drunken condition. She overheard a term being entered in the contract that she knew would be prejudicial to Rinehart's, and moving Egan aside, she negotiated with the supplier's representative until the term was finally resolved in Rinehart's favor. She might have picked up some credit with the senior buyers had it not been for her remark: "I don't know why Rinehart's always sends a bunch of lushes on these buying trips."

In Ms. Inouye's fourth year at Rinehart, the company opened a branch store in a suburban shopping center, and there were many managerial positions to be filled. She requested an appointment with the company president, Wilbur Rinehart III, and asked for his personal intercession in getting one of these posts. He was polite but reserved in his conversation with her, and when the staff for the new store was announced, her name was omitted.

One day soon afterwards, Mary Tilford asked Sally to meet her after the store closed. "I suppose you feel mistreated because you didn't get a promotion," Mary began. "Well, let me tell you something. I had in mind recommending you up the line. But, instead, you had to go over the heads of about five people to try to get Mr. Rinehart's help. This irritated the personnel vice-president, the merchandise manager, the assistant merchandise manager, the group buyer, and me. One thing you have never learned, young lady, and that is how to play the organizational game. You have refused to conform ever since you have been here, and that's the cause of all of your problems. You have one chance left, and that is for my job when I retire in five years. However, the only way you are going to get it is to drastically change the way you act."

The following year saw Sally outwardly begin to adjust to the system. In fact, she began to receive a few mildly favorable comments from persons more highly placed in the organization. Inwardly she felt contempt for herself. By her values, she had put a price on her self-esteem in resigning herself to wait five years to get a job that would be a complete dead end.

One day she snapped at a sales clerk: "Haven't you read the Standard Practice Manual on how to handle a charge sale when a customer doesn't have her charge plate? It might do you some good to find out how things are supposed to be handled around here."

Mary Tilford, overhearing the remark, smiled triumphantly. Sally Inouye wished that she could crawl into a hole.

Discussion Questions

1. Describe some system, organized for maximum efficiency, that has been extremely frustrating to you as a student.
2. What inefficiency will probably occur when an organization strives for conformity by its members?
3. In the Case of the Encroaching Rut, Sally Inouye suffered one frustration in finding that women could advance only so far in the company. How can business firms justify such a policy?
4. What is the effect on people when, as with Ms. Inouye, their jobs permit them to use only part of their abilities?
5. What effect will the Women's Liberation movement have on women's opportunities for promotion to management jobs?

30. Coordination

It should now be clear that organizations are made up of subsystems, or groupings of activities, conveniently called *departments*. Within each department there are smaller subsystems, with the smallest being the job roles of individual members. Each subsystem has a defined contribution to make in a certain form and at a certain time to the total system that is the organization.

What Coordination Is

One way of looking at coordination is that it is the function of assuring that the contributions from the subsystems are made as required, and that they are linked together into a harmonious whole.

Another, complementary, way of looking at coordination is that it is fundamentally the management of change. Through the managerial functions of planning and organizing, objectives are established and the means are created for implementing them. Among these means are defined divisions of work, vertical authority relationships, managerial spans of control, decentralization of decision making, and the definitions of some lateral relationships. Plans are disseminated downward through the organization, and channels are provided for feedback of the results of plans upward. Policies to guide nonroutine decision making, and procedures specifying how to make routine decisions, are established. At one static moment in time the system is theoretically synchronized; every gear is apparently in mesh, and there is a high probability that all events will conform to plan. But an organization operates in a dynamic environment, not a static one. Changes of all kinds that cause the system to get out of synchronization take place continuously. Coordination is thus the effort of managing the changes to the end that the system is brought back into a state of synchronization.

Actually, coordination is the essence of management. The purpose of performing the functions of planning, organizing, staffing, directing, and controlling is to achieve coordination. Coordination therefore is the composite of the functions performed by all managers at all levels. The importance of coordination seems to stand out more in the organizing function, however, than in some of the others.

Achieving Coordination

Fundamentally, there are three approaches to achieving coordination. These include

- planned coordination.
- corrective adjustments resulting from the analysis of feedback.
- motivated coordination.

These approaches are not mutually exclusive; all three must be employed continuously within an organization in the never ending battle to eliminate the obstacles to coordination.

Planning.   Planned coordination is the deliberate action taken by managers to hold the organization together as a single working unit. It is recognized as necessary because coordination will not automatically result from even the most perfectly defined structure of departments, policies, and relationships. Misinterpretation of organizational goals, and divergent subgoals, can be predicted to cause the various subsystems to move in tangential directions unless they are tied together. Therefore, formal groups composed of representatives from different subsystems are either permanently established, or provisions are made to call them into being as required. These groups are commonly called *committees.*

Committees permit the airing of various views on goals and on the means for accomplishing them—views which are often in violent conflict. Simply the act of meeting together reveals to the members that there are objectives bigger than their own narrow ones; and the exchange of information and viewpoints often discloses more similarity than dissimilarity in personal interests. Because committee decisions are normally reached by consensus, even dissenting members will be deterred from actively working against the expressed views of the majority.

Adjusting to feedback.   A manager's day-to-day work activities consist primarily of looking for existing or potential friction points in the subsystem or of being notified of them by subordinates or higher management, or by fellow managers in a lateral relationship. Friction points are signs that the system is getting out of synchronization and corrective action is needed. The manager, alone, may decide on the appropriate action, or may confer on remedial means with vertical and lateral contacts. Coordination takes place when the prescribed action is communicated to all persons who must respond to the action and when positive response is obtained. The communication may be channeled via face-to-face instruction, speeches to assembled groups, written memoranda or directives, or written changes in policies or procedures.

Motivating. Motivated coordination primarily involves the task of getting individuals to identify with the goals of the total organization rather than some subsystem of it. Obviously, for this to happen, organizational objectives and plans for implementing them must be communicated to the individuals and be understood and accepted by them. Then, benefits to be derived from working with members of other subsystems toward common goals must be made to appear of greater personal value than those to be gained from specialized goals. One way of achieving this end is to break down the boundaries between subsystems so as to facilitate problem solving by teams made up of various kinds of specialists. This is the project management concept, as discussed in Section 19. Another approach is to rotate individuals among subsystems on a periodic basis. In this way, they will come to see the necessary interactions of all parts of the organization, and avoid becoming biased toward any one segment.

Accomplishing Through People

There is certainly no problem involving the coordination of the parts of a physical system, such as the parts of a machine, that is comparable in complexity to that of coordinating human organizations. Some progress has been made as a result of findings by the behavioral scientists. The more important of their contributions toward an undersanding of people and how they can be motivated are summarized in the parts of this book devoted to the staffing and directing functions. The subject is of such depth, however, that only the surface has been scratched; much more investigation needs to be done.

Discussion Questions

1. What are some examples of change that can cause an organizational system to get out of synchronization?

2. Why might more coordinating effort be required in an electronics firm than in a firm in the railroad industry?

3. Coordination is an extremely important reason for forming committees. What are some other reasons justifying committee formation?

4. It is often said that "what a manager does mainly is put out fires." Explain the statement.

5. When effort is directed toward getting individuals to identify with the goals of the total organization instead of the goals of some subsystem, such as the marketing department, is there the possibility that achievement of the marketing goals will not be optimal?

Summary

If the steps in the managerial function of organizing can be discussed in chronological sequence, the first one is identification of the activities to be performed in accomplishing the organization's purpose. This can be effected by either reviewing the activities currently being done or by deducing, from the purpose of the organization, what activities should be done. Regardless of the approach, activities will fall into those which are central to the main purpose of the organization, and those which support the central activities.

After necessary activities have been identified, they must be grouped into departments. Conventional methods for grouping activities are by the kind of function performed (functional organization), the requirements of a specific product or service (product organization), and the geographical location at which the activities are performed (geographical organization). At some level in all organizations, activities related to the same function are grouped together. Thus, functional organization tends to be the predominant form of departmentation.

Over recent years there has been an increasing interest in a form of departmentation called *project organization*. Under this form, dissimilar activities are temporarily grouped so as to result in a specified product or service. The project requirements are not continuous; that is, they have a definite beginning and end. The project team members are drawn from functional organizations, and are temporarily assigned to the project for as long as their skills are needed.

There would be no need for departmentation were it not for the limit to the number of subordinates that a manager can effectively control. When this number is reached, a secondary management level must be established. The number of subordinates under any manager, known as the *span of control,* will vary with the manager's characteristics, the subordinates, and the internal and external work environment. Costs of wide spans of control must be weighed against costs of multiple management, and some optimal balance arrived at.

When departments are established, supervisor-subordinate relationships are created. Called *vertical relationships,* they are characterized by the supervisors' having authority to specify what duties subordinates will perform, and to require that the duties be done as directed. Having authority implies that the holder is responsible for the effective performance of the activities over which the authority extends. Vertical relationships also cast supervisors in roles other than command-obedience ones; that is, they are likely to be called upon to perform as protectors, defenders, and communicators.

Decentralization and *centralization* refer, respectively, to tendencies to permit decision making at lower management levels, and to restrict decision making to top management echelons. Decentralization requires maturity both on the part of the organization and of the subordinate managers. When practiced properly, decentralization encourages democracy in industry, develops managerial skills, and permits organizations to grow almost indefinitely. Problems incurred in controlling decentralized operations appear, however, to be sparking a trend toward more centralization.

Lateral relationships exist between people or departments on the same hierarchical level. One type of lateral interaction within an organization occurs when a supporting department offers advice to central departments, as well as to other supporting departments, in its specific area of competence. The advantages of making the services of such specialists available to other departments—one of which is the uniform implementation of policies—often leads to an extension of the specialists' role. From a purely advisory function, they assume a prescriptive one over some limited affairs of other departments.

A second distinctive lateral relationship occurs when a supporting department offers a service to other departments. Such service departments usually have the exclusive right within the organization to perform their respective services, so that managers are, in effect, captive customers. Economy and improved performance are supposed to result from the grouping of work tasks, but a plaguing problem is how to determine the optimal size and scope of service departments so that these objectives may be achieved.

Advisory and service relationships form only a part of the complex network of interactions between departments in an organization. A high level of interaction exists between departments that are responsible for operations performed in sequence. Moreover, on an individual basis, managers engage in a constant process of evaluation of other managers; representatives of departments meet continually, thus setting up a chain of group relationships; and individuals having unequal status in their respective departments must often interact, thus creating another unique relationship.

Members of formal organizations instinctively come together in various informal groups for the purpose of satisfying personal needs that are left unsatisfied in the formal organization. Informal groups unconsciously develop status hierarchies, choose leaders, and set norms of behavior and performance. The grapevine is their channel of communication.

A highly significant force within organizations, but one which is almost "unmentionable," is that of power politics. The will for power—a potent drive in many people—is essential for those who aspire to success as managers. Political tactics are used in gaining and using power. Patterns of behavior, either intuitive or deliberate, by managers seeking power can be predicted; and the steps by which power seekers mount their campaigns are usually well delineated into preparation, planning, and tactical stages.

Conflict within organizations, one of the most popular topics in contemporary management literature, is generally ascribed to the typical compartmentalized structure of organizations. The dividing of work into specialized functional departments creates sharp boundary lines between them, with the effect that each feels that it is a separate entity. The members of each department seek a preferred position for their specialized function within the organizational status system, with the result that conflict situations beween the departments become a continuous occurrence.

The divergence between the goals of the formal organization and the needs of the individual within the organization accounts for the alienation of employees. Where individuals are frustrated by efficient organizational concepts and become apathetic toward them, the general result is paradoxical: inefficient performance within a system designed to produce the opposite effect.

The fundamental purpose of management is to create conditions that make it possible to coordinate the subsystems of the organization. Human nature presents the main obstacle in the way of coordination of organizational and individual goals. Managers strive to synchronize the parts of their system in three ways: by establishing coordinating committees, by analyzing system feedback and communicating corrective action, and by attempting to motivate people to work toward system goals rather than subsystem goals.

Selected Bibliography

Argyris, Chris, *Personality and Organization*. Harper, 1957.

Barnard, C. I., *The Functions of the Executive*. Harvard University, 1938.

Baumgartner, John Stanley, *Project Management*. Irwin, 1963.

Cordiner, R. J., *New Frontiers for Professional Managers*. McGraw-Hill, 1956.

Dale, Ernest, *Management: Theory and Practice*. McGraw-Hill, 1969.

Dalton, Melville, "Conflicts Between Staff and Line Managerial Officers." *American Sociological Review,* Vol. 15, June 1950.

Etzioni, Amitai, *Modern Organizations*. Prentice-Hall, 1964.

Jacques, E., "Too Many Management Levels." *California Management Review,* Vol. 8, No. 1, Fall 1965.

Janger, Allen R., "Anatomy of the Project Organization." *Conference Board Business Management Record,* Vol. 20, November 1963.

Katz, Fred E., "Explaining Informal Work Groups in Complex Organizations: The Case for Autonomy in Structure." *Administrative Science Quarterly,* Vol. 10, No. 2, September 1965.

Koontz, Harold, and Cyril O'Donnell, *Principles of Management,* 5th ed. McGraw-Hill, 1972.

Lawrence, Paul R., and Jay W. Lorsch, "New Management Job: The Integrator." *Harvard Business Review,* Vol. 45, No. 6, November–December 1967.

Litterer, Joseph A., "Conflict in Organization: A Re-examination." *Academy of Management Journal,* Vol. 9, No. 3, September 1966.

March, James G., and Herbert A. Simon. *Organizations*. Wiley, 1959.

Mechanic, David, "Power of Subordinates in Complex Organizations." *Administrative Science Quarterly,* Vol. 7, December 1962.

McGregor, Douglas, *The Human Side of Enterprise*. McGraw-Hill, 1960.

Sayles, Leonard, *Managerial Behavior*. McGraw-Hill, 1964.

Sloan, A. P., Jr., *My Years With General Motors*. Doubleday, 1964.

Suojanen, W. W., "The Span of Control—Fact or Fable." *Advanced Management,* Vol. 20, No. 11, November 1955.

STAFFING

An organization's success depends on how well its managers develop and maintain its various resources. To a business organization, important resources include capital, raw materials, plant and equipment, and markets for products or services. However, to a business organization, as to all organizations, the most important resource is people. The managerial function of staffing is concerned with the development and maintenance of the organization's human resource.

The things that managers do in performing the staffing function include

- determining what work has to be done and segregating this work into jobs.
- analyzing the relative worth of jobs so that equitable compensation levels can be established.
- forecasting future job openings that must be filled.
- recruiting and selecting people for these openings.
- providing opportunities for new employees to become of greater value to the organization while improving their own self-image.
- appraising the performance of people on their jobs.

Many managers become impatient with having to perform these activities, and feel that they can be shunted off to the personnel department. It is true that modern personnel departments render a valuable service to the managers of other departments in helping them perform the staffing function, but in the final analysis managers cannot neglect staffing without compromising their full managerial role.

The various functions that managers perform cannot be looked at in isolation, for each is an integral part of the total management activity. Planning would lead nowhere unless the plans could be implemented via the organizing function. And organizations must have people, via the staffing function, to give them life. Still, an organization adequately staffed with people would only randomly achieve its objectives without the directing of various contributions into efficient channels. And finally, controlling is necessary to assure that the functional parts of management are integrated and meshing smoothly.

The following sections deal with the building of human resource, and the sections relating to the directing function are concerned with the use of this resource.

31. Job Design

As noted previously, the job is the smallest subsystem or grouping of activities within an organization. It is made up of a combination of work tasks performed by individuals, and each job is distinctive from other jobs in terms of its component work tasks. The main reason for creating jobs is to make sure that necessary work tasks get done. The job requirements provide the basis for selecting, training, evaluating, and compensating the individual members of an organization.

Job and Position

There is a distinction between a *job* and a *position*. Basically, the terms are convenient for differentiating between a classification of work, which is a job, and the number of slots authorized for that particular classification, with each of these being a position. Thus it might be said that in a firm there are ten positions authorized for the job of machinist; of these ten positions, seven are presently filled and three are open. Each person performing a job occupies a position.

However, many companies use the terms to differentiate between high- and low-status work. For example, a manager would be said to have a position, while a machinist would be said to have a job.

The Composition of a Job

The traditional and allegedly efficient approach to building jobs has been to combine a limited number of similar work activities. Such jobs require minimum skills; simple techniques can be used to train people to perform them; and repetition presumably leads to improved quantity and quality of work produced. Any notion that this approach has been used only in grouping routine manual tasks should be dispelled, because it is currently being used in all types of organizations for designing jobs in such categories as engineering, personnel, accounting, and other white-collar classifications.

Growing recognition of the fact that many people become frustrated by highly specialized jobs, and thereby alienated toward the organization, has led to a new concept called "job enlargement."

The idea behind job enlargement is that worker satisfaction can be increased by broadening the scope of jobs and making them richer in terms of variety, interest, and significance. Many companies are experimenting with job enlargement, and preliminary findings suggest impressive improvements in worker performance, as well as in their attitudes toward their jobs.

Related to the job enlargement approach to job design is another new approach called "human engineering." Its principles are to design jobs, and the equipment and work environment associated with them, to fit human physiological, psychological, and sociocultural characteristics, rather than to require people to adjust to jobs that have been impersonally constructed.

The Job Designer

In simple organizations, job design has historically been performed by the worker's immediate supervisor. In more complex organizations, professional job designers, such as industrial engineers or management consultants, have performed the role. Another fairly recent change in job design involves enlisting the participation of the people who are going to do the work in deciding the content of jobs. Reports from firms that have tried this approach, such as IBM Corporation and the Colonial Insurance Company, suggest that it has exciting possibilities for improving worker satisfaction and performance. The two companies cited have encouraged workers to help in the design of their own jobs since the 1950's, and in their experience it has increased productivity and improved job satisfaction.

Job Descriptions and Specifications

Two complementary techniques are those which are used to record what jobs consist of (job descriptions) and to set forth qualifications for the jobs as so described (job specifications).

Job descriptions. Although there are various forms for devising job descriptions, generally they provide

- the job title and classification grade, the latter being an identification of the relative worth or significance of the job.

- a concise summary of the nature of the job, often specifying the person to whom incumbents on the job report.
- a description, in intentionally broad terms, of the duties of the job—the objective being to describe the average duties of many individuals occupying job positions.

Job descriptions are used to inform and remind individuals what is expected of them; they serve as a basis for training people to perform jobs; and they provide criteria for measuring performance. In addition, they provide a basis for preparing job specifications; and they are used in still another way to assist in manpower planning.

Effectiveness of job descriptions. Simple jobs can be described quite adequately because the duties are routine and interactions with other jobs are minimal. Problems occur in describing complex jobs, where there are hosts of unpredictable and indescribable lateral relationships, and where each position of the job is performed differently by the incumbent. Thus, descriptions of complex jobs are rarely precise, and as a result, are not as useful as they should be for their intended purposes.

Job specifications. Job specifications derive from job descriptions. For a given job, the specification enumerates first the personal qualifications required to perform it. These qualifications are described briefly under such headings as education, experience, ability to work with other people, capacity for responsibility, initiative, and so on. Next, the physical demands of the job are identified. These might include such items as descriptions of physical exertion required, noise and contaminant levels, and heat ventilation. If appropriate for the particular job, the specification will attempt to describe the mental effort required.

Job specifications are used in the recruitment and selection processes to differentiate between people who have the potential for performing particular jobs and those who do not. In addition, they are used in job evaluation, which is the process of determining the relative worth of jobs.

Effectiveness of job specifications. Most job specifications have the common fault of being unnecessarily restrictive regarding applicants' qualifications. The required qualifications are either inferred from the job descriptions or are determined through induction, by checking the qualifications of people who are performing or have performed the jobs. Both approaches tend to inflate the qualifications unnecessarily. For example, college educations are becoming so prevalent that an impressive title on a job description usually leads to an assumption that only a degree holder can do the job. And when people performing a job are asked about qualifications for it, their natural tendency will be to exaggerate so that their own importance might be better appreciated.

*In the summer of 1970, Skil Mor, Inc., a manufacturer of power
lawn mowers, hedge trimmers, and chain saws, employed about 200
people in all job classifications. The highly satisfactory market acceptance of the firm's products had warranted an approved plan to
expand the work force to 500 employees by 1972. Before any substantial recruiting or hiring was to be started, however, the company's
managers agreed that objective descriptions and specifications should
be prepared for all new jobs. The personnel manager, Dick Awenius,
offered to lend his help in designing new jobs, and many of the
managers volunteered to help each other. Among the new jobs that
would have to be designed was that of buyer in the purchasing department. Up until then, all of the purchasing work had been handled
by Ralph Smith, the purchasing agent, and his secretary, but the
firm's expansion necessitated filling three positions in the job classification of buyer.*

*"I have asked Mrs. Scheuler to join us while we talk about the
buyer job, Dick," said Ralph Smith. "She knows the purchasing part
of this company as well as I do. In fact, she would be a prime
candidate for buyer if it weren't for the fact that she has decided
to move to the West Coast."*

*"Fine. To get started, Ralph, what do you generally see a buyer
doing?"*

*"Well, first of all, I have in mind three different kinds of buyers—
one for raw materials, one for supplies of all types, and another for
subcontract parts. Should there be separate descriptions and specifications for each one?"*

*"A case could probably be made for separating the job of buying
subcontract parts from the others, but let's try to write a blanket
description and specification covering all three," said Awenius. "I
suggest that the description start out: 'Under the general supervision
of the purchasing agent, the buyer . . . ,' and then go on to specify
the duties."*

"I am afraid of the word 'general.' As I am ultimately responsible

for all purchasing, I feel that I should exercise close supervision," said Smith.

"Mr. Smith," said Mrs. Scheuler, "the main reason for having buyers is to relieve you for more important matters, such as policy. If you exercise close supervision you will get so bogged down that you can't get past the routine details. And another thing, if you put the buyers pretty much on their own, within a policy framework, they will be motivated to better effort."

"I must agree," replied Awenius, "and besides, if you specify 'close' supervision the job will be evaluated lower than if you say 'general' supervision."

"All right. At least on paper I will go along with it. Well, a buyer will maintain a list of qualified vendors. He will receive and evaluate purchase requisitions. He will . . ."

"Excuse me for interrupting, Ralph," said Awenius, "but about the word 'evaluate.' Does this mean that a buyer can question a requisition, or that he can change what someone in a requisitioning department has asked for?"

"The issue revolves primarily around requisitions that specify brand or vendor. We must allow the buyer to make the decision as to what make is best for a particular purpose, and from whom to buy it," replied Smith.

"Perhaps we can take the threat of a change out of the wording by saying 'receive and process,'" said Mrs. Scheuler. "Then we can leave any possible interpretation conflicts to the individual buyers."

"We are going to have to find people for the buyer positions who are particularly good at handling potentially explosive situations if we are going to even imply that the production manager, for example, can't have his steel bought from a certain source, if that is the way that he wants it," said Awenius. "Somehow, we will have to get this qualification written into the job specification. However, let's be straightforward and say 'evaluate,' if that is what a buyer really does."

"To go on," said Smith, "a buyer will send requests for quotation to approved vendors, and analyze the returned quotations. He will select the vendor, with the approval of the purchasing agent, and issue a purchase order."

"Now we are back to the matter of the closeness of your supervision," said Awenius. "Are you saying that you are going to make the final selection of every vendor?"

"No, of course not. In many cases the buyer will simply award the purchase to the vendor with the lowest price. However, with some of the things that we buy I want to spread the business among several vendors, provided that the prices are the same. There will also be occasions when we will select the vendor with the lowest price to start negotiations for a better deal. These are the kinds of situations where I want to be consulted before a purchase order is sent out."

"Those are contingencies that are rather hard to spell out in a job description," said Awenius. "I guess we will have to say it your way, and then you will have to work out understandings with each of your buyers."

"I think that will be best," replied Smith. "Finally, a buyer will follow up on all purchase transactions to assure that the terms are met, and authorize the payment of the vendor's invoice."

"I guess those duties are clear enough in general terms," said Awenius. "Now about the job specification. I suggest that for minimum education we specify four years of college. This is so that we can fit the job into the proper salary grade."

"I don't have four years of college myself," conceded Ralph Smith, "and I don't think that it is necessary for a buyer. A bright, aggressive individual with some good work experience, like inventory or production control, is what I would like for the job, regardless of his formal education."

"How about saying 'four years of college or equivalent,'" said Awenius.

"What exactly is the equivalent of four years of college?" asked Mrs. Scheuler. *"It seems to me that this will always be a matter of personal judgment."*

"You are probably right, but we have to specify some educational level. Now about experience. We should specify some number of years, such as five, in similar or related work," said Awenius.

"Suppose we get an applicant with three years of intensive experience. Do we screen him out because he lacks two years?" asked Smith.

"That will be another matter of judgment," admitted Awenius.

"How are we going to say that the buyer must have high ethical standards, and make it meaningful for hiring? You can only tell whether an individual is susceptible to commercial bribery after you have worked with him awhile," was Smith's next comment.

"And, getting back to the kind of personality that a buyer should have," said Mrs. Scheuler, *"just saying 'must have the ability to get along with people' is pretty vague. I don't suppose Skil Mor would hire a person for any job who did not have the apparent ability to work with others. How do we say in the specification that a buyer must be reasonable, but be firm when he thinks he is right, and must be able to make people—perhaps higher in the organization—defer to his opinions? Moreover, how do we screen people for this quality?"*

Discussion Questions

Reference Case A. The Case of the Encroaching Rut (Section 29)
Reference Case B. The Case of the Mexican Crazy Quilt (Section 19)

1. In Reference Case A, Sally Inouye proposed a new job designed to suit her interests and capabilities. What practical problems would have arisen if Rinehart Department Store had permitted her to have her way?
2. In Reference Case B, what difficulties would be encountered in writing a description of the job of project manager at Linderman

Industries at the completion of Operation Mexicano, assuming that project management was destined to continue?

3. In the Case of Picking the Right Words, will Dick Awenius' insistence on the words *general supervision* in the job description change Ralph Smith's views on how he will supervise the job? What are the implications of Smith's comments?

4. How useful will the buyer's job description be if understandings must be worked out privately with each buyer concerning vendor selection?

5. What potential problems are being created by setting the specification for education as "four years of college or equivalent"?

32. Job Evaluation

In every organization all members have the implicit understanding that the various jobs are not equal in worth or significance. This statement does not refer to the performance by individuals on different jobs, but to the jobs themselves. With some jobs, of course, value differentiations are obvious; no one would deny that the job of general manager is more important to a firm than that of stock clerk. With many others, however, distinctions are not nearly so clear. Since the relative worth of a job is reflected in the compensation paid for doing it, job evaluation is extremely important; and since in all organizations there are compensation differentials between jobs, somehow job evaluation always occurs. The way it is done will vary, however, from the making of highly subjective judgments to the formal application of objective standards.

Evaluation of Top-Level Jobs

Although there appears to be a trend toward introducing objective evaluation methods for high-level managerial jobs, many companies still use completely subjective methods for setting executive salaries (with *salary* used here as an index of a job's worth). A common basis for fixing the salary of a chief executive of a business organization is to equate it to what other chief executives in the same industry are being paid. Another basis for setting the chief executive's salary is the effect it will have on the company's desired image. In other words, it might be set low to indicate that the firm is sober and prudent, or it might be high to suggest that the firm is prosperous enough to afford only first-class managerial talent. The chief executive's salary might also reflect an ability to negotiate to personal advantage.

When there is no formal job evaluation program, the salaries of the managers at the first level will have some percentage of the chief executive's salary as a ceiling. Below this ceiling, their salaries will actually be determined by the compensation level of similar titles in the industry, effect on company image, and ability to negotiate in their own interest. Determination of managerial salaries at lower levels will be in the same pattern. Where managerial jobs are evaluated formally, the criteria and terms are different, but the systems themselves are quite similar to systems used to evaluate nonmanagerial jobs. Therefore, in the following discussion of evaluation systems, no job level distinctions will be made.

Purpose and Kinds of Job Evaluation Systems

When a firm adopts a formal system of evaluating jobs, it is with the intention of providing an equitable basis for compensating people according to the worth to the organization of the job they perform.

Ranking. The simplest job evaluation system, and one that is only a slight step beyond not having any system at all, is to rank jobs in the order of perceived importance. A simple way would be to use cards on which job titles have been entered, or to use the job descriptions, and try to decide which job is most important, which is next, and so on. This approach does not involve any detailed analysis of the components of job, and a request for an explanation of a ranking can often be difficult to fill.

Grade. The next system above simple ranking is what is called a *grade,* or classification, method. Concise descriptions of a number of different grades are developed, and assigned to each grade will be requisite degrees of such factors as skill, experience, and responsibility. Using job descriptions as a guide, the method involves fitting jobs into the grades which appear to be most appropriate. This system can have enough substance built into it to be quite workable for an uncomplicated organization, such as a university, where there are only four academic grades—instructor, assistant professor, associate professor, and full professor.

The point method. At the opposite pole of systems, so far as complexity is concerned, there are two which have basic similarities. One is called the *point method,* and the other is called *factor-comparison.* Each method has its proponents, and although some reports suggest that the point method is the more popular, the evidence is not conclusive. However, the general nature of sophisticated job evaluation systems can be explained by describing the point method.

The point method involves the use of a manual, or guide, which probably should be custom-made for a specific company. There are, however, many standard manuals available which a company might use with varying degrees of success. The main features of the manual are the thoughtful development of the elements that are common to some extent in all of the jobs that will be evaluated, and clear descriptions of a number of gradations of each element.

Examples of elements might include education, experience, physical effort, mental effort, responsibility for equipment, and responsibility for the safety of others. Examples of gradations, using experience as a typical element, might include: (1) Job can be learned in less than three months. (2) A minimum of one year's experience is required in order to perform the job satisfactorily. (3) Progressive experience totaling two years leading up to the job, plus three years' experience on the job, is necessary for expected job performance. (4) A complex of related job experiences totaling five years, plus five years' experience on the job, is the minimum required to assure acceptable competence.

The next step is to assign some number of points to each gradation of each element. It should be noted that each element does not require the same number of gradations, and that the total points assigned to the various elements will probably be different. This is because the elements will not usually be of the same importance.

The objective is to establish an evaluation for each job that is measurable in points. The procedure, then, is to take the job specification, and decide which gradation for each element is applicable for the job. The points for each element are then summarized, and the total is the evaluation for the job.

The final step is to group the various jobs into grades, or classifications, according to total points. Thus, Grade I might include jobs with less than 100 points, Grade II, jobs with point totals of from 100 to 125, and so on. After that, wage or salary ranges must be developed for each grade (a discussion of which is included in Section 33).

Problems in Job Evaluation

The point method and the factor-comparison method both suffer from the same defect, which is that although they have the appearance of being objective, they are still based on what may be described as "systematized subjectivity." Every step in the point method, for instance, actually requires a value judgment. Answers to such questions as what elements should be included, how many points should be given for each gradation, and which gradation best fits a particular job, must all be influenced by human biases. The detail of the analysis, and the use of group judgments, compensate for this subjectivity to some extent.

Another significant obstacle that must be overcome is resistance by the people in the organization to formal job evaluation. Whoever is sponsoring the program must gain the confidence of the people who will be affected by the evaluations so they will perceive that the program is fair, will not be prejudicial to them, and that, despite its weaknesses, is better than no system at all.

Still a further problem arises when there are sharply different groupings of jobs within the organization, such as factory, clerical, and technical. Should different evaluation systems be used for each job type, or should the same system cover all types? Problems will arise no matter what action is taken.

*Workers in a number of job classifications at the Littleton Steel
Company had been disgruntled for some time over what they held
were wage inequities between their jobs and other jobs in the company. By far the most vocal were the 23 holders of the job classification "furnace repairman," who argued that the conditions under which
they had to work warranted top wages in the mill. What the job
amounted to was for the worker to don asbestos clothing, crawl into
a furnace in which the temperature had been allowed to cool to
around 180° F., dig out bricks that had deteriorated under up to
3000°-F. operating temperatures, and cement in new bricks. The
workers were in a furnace for fifteen minutes, then were out for thirty
minutes to recuperate from the heat exposure. There was no disagreement by anybody that it was a miserable job.*

*Ray Miller, personnel director of Littleton Steel, and Harry Frank,
job analyst, had recognized for some time that the grade system of
job evaluation that the company used was inadequate for the number
and varieties of jobs in a steel mill. The many complaints by workers
that their jobs were unfairly rated induced Miller to request sufficient
funds to design and install a more comprehensive system. Upon approval of his request, he held a meeting with the union stewards to
let them know that the company was going to try to do something
about the alleged inequities. He went a further step and invited the
stewards to select three of their number to make up an ad hoc job
evaluation committee with him, Frank, and another management representative. The purpose of the committee was to select a new system,
and then to reevaluate every job in the mill. Concurrent with the
study of various possible systems was a review and updating of all
job descriptions.*

*The committee finally selected a point system tailored after the one
approved by the National Metal Trades Association, but with the
wording of the gradations, or degrees, for each element written in the
context of steel mill work. The committee then spent almost one year
in careful reevaluation of each job. Particular attention was given to
such jobs as furnace repairman, where gross misjudging of worth under the old system was claimed.*

When the final scores for each job were tabulated, it was found that the new system established the relative worth of furnace repairman one classification lower than it had been under the old system. The immediate response of the furnace repairmen was to file a formal grievance, after which a meeting was arranged between the union grievance committee and the ad hoc job evaluation committee, not including the union members.

Joe Graber represented the furnace repairmen and was supported by the two shop stewards and the local union business agent. The meeting had not even been called to order when Graber burst out, "Miller, you and the rest of these fancy pants guys had better learn to crawl in a furnace because I and the rest of the gang are going to walk out."

The business agent, Bob Chewning, said calmly, "Now let's not talk about walking out. We're here to learn if your job was not properly evaluated."

Ray Miller first went over the table of point values for each of the factors considered important in steel mill jobs (Exhibit 32–1). He was

Point Values for Job Factors

Factors	1st Degree	2nd Degree	3rd Degree	4th Degree	5th Degree
SKILL					
1. EDUCATION	14	28	42	56	70
2. EXPERIENCE	22	44	66	88	110
3. INITIATIVE	14	28	42	56	70
EFFORT					
4. PHYSICAL DEMAND	10	20	30	40	50
5. MENTAL DEMAND	5	10	15	20	25
RESPONSIBILITY					
6. EQUIPMENT	5	10	15	20	25
7. MATERIAL	5	10	15	20	25
8. SAFETY OF OTHERS	5	10	15	20	25
9. WORK OF OTHERS	5	10	15	20	25
JOB CONDITIONS					
10. WORKING CONDITIONS	10	20	30	40	50
11. HAZARDS	5	10	15	20	25

Exhibit 32–1.   Littleton Steel Company Job Evaluation System.

about to go over the way the committee had evaluated the job of furnace repairman, starting with the factors where the job had received a high number of points, but Graber beat him to it.

"How about working conditions and hazards?" he demanded. "How did you rate the jobs on those?"

"Furnace repairman was rated at the 5th Degree for working conditions, which is 50 points, or maximum," said Miller. "It also received the maximum points for hazards, but the 5th Degree for this element is only 25 points. This is because our safety program has eliminated really serious hazards, as is testified to by Littleton's extremely low accident rate. Another element for which the job of furnace repairman received the maximum number of points was physical demand, which is also 50 points at the 5th Degree. So you can see that everything that you claim makes your job worth more has been agreed to by the evaluation committee."

"Now for the factors where furnace repairman did not receive a high evaluation," Miller continued. "It was rated at the 1st Degree for education."

"As I only have an 8th-grade education myself, I guess I can't complain about that," conceded Graber.

Miller went on, "There are four new men on the job who are doing satisfactory work with experience that compares to the 2nd Degree, so we think that is a fair rating. About the only initiative that is required for the job is deciding whether a brick has started to crumble, so it is also rated at the 2nd Degree for that element. For the three skill factors, furnace repairman has 86 points out of a possible 250 points."

"Do you see anything unfair about this, Joe?" asked Chewning.

"No, but I know the job isn't being paid enough," said Graber.

"To continue," said Miller, "the job was rated at the 1st Degree for mental demand. It was rated fairly high, at the 3rd Degree, for both responsibility for equipment and for material, but at the 1st Degree for responsibility for safety of others and work of others. To sum-

marize, the job received a total of 256 points out of a maximum of 500 points. 256 points places it in the fifth highest classification in the mill, which means that it is considered to be an important job to the company."

"Not important enough to be paid what it is worth," said Graber heatedly. "I might admit that the job rates are low on some of those things, but not enough points are given for others like working conditions."

"That is a matter of opinion," said Miller.

"Yeah, and my opinion is as good as yours. The boys and I are walking out," shouted Graber.

"Oh no, you're not," was Chewning's response to this outburst.

Discussion Questions

1. Suppose you were in your early sixties and the chief executive and a large stockholder of a company whose stock was on the stock exchange. What would be your inclination for setting the amount of your own salary? How would the amount affect your subordinate managers?
2. What reason would there be for a company's having a different evaluation system for factory, clerical, and technical jobs?
3. In the Case of the Heated Furnace Repairmen, what were some evidences of good judgment shown by Ray Miller in implementing an improved job evaluation system?
4. What foreseeable problem came up in explaining the evaluation of the furnace repairman job to Joe Graber?
5. What have you noticed to be an obvious result of Ray Miller's careful planning for the implementation of the job evaluation system?

33. Financial Compensation

After job design and job evaluation, the next process is to determine wage or salary ranges for each grade of jobs. It seems to be general practice to use the term *wages* when compensation is on an hourly basis, and *salary* when compensation is based on a longer period, such as a week, month, or year.

A *range* is the spread between the minimum and maximum compensation for a job grade. The purpose of a range is to permit merit compensation increases. The maximum is usually some fixed percentage increase over the minimum for the grade; thus, each higher grade will have a larger range value in dollars. Ranges usually are established only for nonunion jobs, because unions typically are against merit increases and want raises to be on an across-the-board basis.

Basis for Compensation

As has been mentioned, the purpose of identifying the relative worth of each job is to develop an equitable basis for compensation. However, other factors, external to the organization, also will usually enter in as determinants of compensation. That is, the relative worth of jobs within the organization will be the starting point, but after that adjustments will commonly have to be made because of demands by unions, the going market value of jobs, and government wage legislation.

Using a Scatter Diagram

The first step in equating compensation with job worth is to construct what is called a *scatter diagram,* with job evaluation points on the horizontal axis and existing compensation on the vertical axis. Figure 33–1 illustrates this type of diagram. A plot point will be made at the intersection of the number of points evaluated for a job and the compensation currently paid for the job. The plot points will tend to cluster around a diagonal line that rises as the number of points increase. In other words, there will be a strong tendency for points to be proportional to compensation, even at the start of systematizing the compensation structure. However, there will be some plot points that are significantly below the diagonal line, which indi-

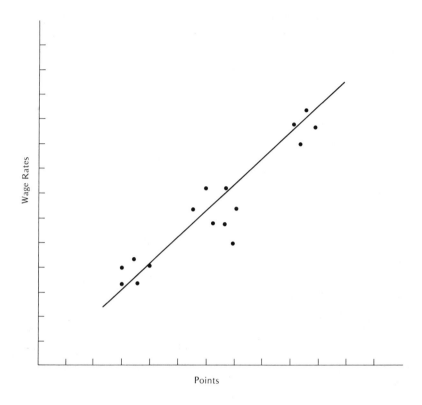

Figure 33–1.   Wage/Points Scatter Diagram.

cates that the associated job is being underpaid. Other plot points may be considerably above the line, and this condition suggests that the associated jobs are being overpaid.

Adjusting plots above or below the line.   When jobs are found to be paid less or more than they are worth, the first step should be to carefully check the evaluations for possible errors. Next, the practice with most companies is to increase the compensation of jobs that are underpaid to bring them up to the average. Jobs that are overpaid present more of a problem. If compensation is reduced to where it should be, the workers will be dissatisfied and productivity will probably suffer. If compensation is left where it is, workers whose jobs are worth more than the overpaid workers, but whose pay is the same, will feel inequitably treated. Most firms elect not to change the compensation until all existing workers on the overpaid jobs have left the company or have been transferred to other jobs.

Achieving internal balance.   Reviewing and adjusting the compensation paid for jobs, relative to the worth of the jobs as indicated by the evaluation points, will bring the jobs into proper internal balance. From this point on, raises can be applied proportionally for individual jobs without disturbing the balance.

Factors That Necessitate Adjustments

As indicated above, external factors such as union demands, labor supply, and government legislation will create imbalances in a firm's compensation system.

Union pressure.   Management's strategy in wage negotiations with the unions will be to try to keep the wages paid for jobs in proper balance with their worth. Often union pressure will force wages for union jobs higher than their relative worth, in which case management can either let the nonunion jobs be paid a relatively inequitable compensation, or can restore the balance by raising compensation for nonunion jobs. Choosing the first alternative will cause the nonunion people to be dissatisfied with their pay, and election of the second alternative will significantly boost the company's total cost for compensation. Management will be faced with the dilemma of choosing between two unattractive alternatives.

Labor supply.   If a review of a job's evaluation shows that its compensation is internally equitable but the firm still cannot attract new people—or hold existing employees—then the demand for qualified applicants must be greater than the supply. The company's alternatives include hiring people with less than required qualifications, but at the compensation established for the job, or increasing the compensation in order to get qualified people. The first alternative will probably cause performance to suffer, and the second will cause an imbalance in the compensation structure.

Government legislation.   Other than the requirement of overtime pay under specified conditions for stipulated kinds of jobs, the main impact of government legislation comes from the minimum wage requirement, which was established under the Fair Labor Standards Act of 1938, as amended. Since jobs which formerly were not evaluated as worth this amount of compensation must legally be paid it, the effect of the minimum wage requirement has been to force the compensation of higher-grade jobs up proportionally, thus increasing the total compensation cost.

Other Forms of Financial Compensation

Financial incentives to produce more or better work were briefly discussed in Section 2 as part of the management concepts promoted by Frederick W. Taylor. These incentives can be built into either a piece-work system, in which individuals or groups receive increased compensation for production beyond a certain standard, or into the commission system, in which salespeople, for example, are paid in direct proportion to what they produce.

Various profit-sharing systems seem to be increasing in popularity among firms in the United States. The objective is to increase the total net profits of the company by motivating the employees to greater productivity. The share of the profits going to the employees is usually distributed on an individual basis by a formula in which the direct compensation paid to the job is the key variable. Other variables are the employee's length of service and, of course, the profits available for distribution.

Discussion Questions

1. What is the purpose of plotting job evaluation points against existing compensation?
2. What justification is there for not reducing the compensation of jobs found to be overpaid? Argue for and against the practice.
3. Why are unions typically antagonistic toward merit increases?
4. What difficulty might you have comparing your company's compensation for a job classification with compensation paid by other companies for the same classification?
5. Can the legislated minimum wage be more hindrance than help to some job seekers? In what way?

34. Indirect Compensation

Indirect compensation refers to the fringe benefits that individuals receive from employers as supplements to wages or salaries. The amounts of many forms of indirect compensation tend to reflect an individual's relative worth to an organization; pension contributions, for example, are based on direct compensation. The amounts of some other forms do not vary with job grade, however, being equally available to all. An example of this form would be a company's recreation program.

Importance of Fringe Benefits

Two aspects make indirect compensation a highly significant factor to managers.

- As a percentage of total compensation costs, fringe benefits rose from an average 14.6 percent in 1941 to 29.9 percent in 1967 in a representative sample of companies in the United States. This fact alone suggests that management control over indirect compensation is seriously needed.
- Generous fringe benefit programs have come to be expected by workers, and firms whose programs are relatively austere will experience much difficulty in competing for skilled personnel in the labor market.

Classifications of Fringe Benefits

There is one category of indirect compensation which a firm must provide. It comprises the legally required payments to federal and state social welfare programs, which include Old Age, Survivors, and Disability Insurance, Unemployment Compensation, and Workmen's Compensation. The estimated proportion of this category of indirect compensation to total compensation cost is about 5 percent.

The next two categories of indirect compensation are not legally imposed, but may either be volunteered by the company or negotiated between the company and the employees' bargaining representatives. The first of these comprises the service costs of deferred or contingent monetary payments by the company to its employees, including pension plan costs, life, accident, health, and hospitalization insurance costs, and termination pay allowances. The average cost of these benefits is about 11 percent of a company's total cost for all compensation.

Another category of benefits that may either be volunteered by the company or result from negotiation comprises the cost of payment for time not worked by employees, including rest periods, get-ready time, wash-up time, vacations, holidays, and sick leave. Benefits of this nature are coming to be expected by employees more and more, and, on the average, represent about 10 percent of all compensation costs.

A final category of fringe benefits comprises such elements as recreational and educational programs, suggestion awards, and parties and picnics. Generally, these benefits are not negotiated, but tend to be granted at the company's option. In the total compensation picture, they average a little over 3 percent.

Returns to the Company

Other than problems, business firms appear to get little in return from the costs of indirect compensation, except by way of attracting and retaining qualified employees. At the same time, benefits tend to bind marginal workers to the company. There is virtually no evidence linking higher productivity to fringe benefits, but it is possible that lower productivity may result if the fringe benefit program is reduced.

Indirect compensation has evolved to its present magnitude without any deliberate intention by managers. The real start was during the World War II wage freeze, when employers competing for workers offered them so-called fringes. Those fringes have now grown into what many managers perceive as a Frankenstein, and the paradox is that fringes are also resented by many workers. These workers' main complaint is that the employer is exercising discretionary choice over part of their merited compensation. Thus, the argument runs that the company should add a pro-rata share of the costs of indirect compensation to each paycheck and let the individuals decide whether to spend the additional amount for insurance, a retirement income plan, or anything else that they might have in mind.

Control of Fringe Benefits

The reason that fringe benefits are uncontrolled in many companies is that the objectives of such benefits have never been established, nor plans made for administering them. Certainly, the first thing a company should do is carefully determine the cost of each item in a fringe benefit program. Probably the next step should be an attempt to assign a priority to benefits. That is, the cost of each item might be related to the value that the company might receive from it, and the items arrayed in the order of their estimated return. Another vitally important step is to project how much money the company will have available for all items in a fringe benefit program over some future period of time.

After the above steps are completed, the program fundamentally becomes one of rationing available future funds to the items in the order of their priority. The first rationing would be to the legally required items, the next to items already agreed to by contract or other commitment. If there is not enough money to cover these latter items, then the company should renegotiate. When all of the money that the company feels is reasonable for indirect forms of compensation, and that it can afford for such purposes, has been rationed, then the items to which funds have been assigned will comprise the fringe benefit program.

Discussion Questions

1. In what respect does a retired employee's pension reflect his or her past relative worth to the organization?
2. Do you see a connection between the Great Depression of the 1930's and legally required fringe benefits? In what way do you suppose the Depression influenced relevant legislation?
3. If fringe benefits do not noticeably improve worker productivity, how can business firms finance them?
4. On what grounds can a lowering of productivity be seen to result from a reduction of fringe benefits?
5. Employees of what age groups would be most prone to resent fringe benefits—preferring instead to get comparable compensation directly in the form of wages?

35. Manpower Planning

People are the most important resource of any organization, yet business organizations too frequently rely on chance to assure the future availability of this resource in proper quantity and quality. And although the trend is toward better planning, most managers feel that the effort must be improved still further.

Prerequisite: Detailed Appraisal

Manpower planning is an involved process and should start with full information concerning the different jobs that must be performed within the organization, the qualifications for each job, and the annual total compensation cost of each job. How to develop this information has been discussed in Sections 31–34. The next step requires an assessment of the current manpower inventory, that is, the age, promotion potential, need for additional training, and health of every individual holding a position of each job. Thus, as a prerequisite to manpower planning, an organization needs a detailed appraisal of its current human resources.

Looking Into the Future

A beginning step in manpower planning might be to hold the existing scale of operations constant, and project over a number of years what will happen to the manpower of the organization if no new personnel are added. Quite obviously, voids will begin to appear immediately and become increasingly manifest the farther into the future the projection is extended. The reasons are several. First of all, there is the firm's normal attrition rate, which can be calculated from past records; a certain number of employees will quit each year and another predictable number will be fired. Absenteeism is another factor; each year a proportion of the labor force will be absent from their jobs for lengthy periods because of accidents or sickness. Promotions will account for some vacancies; employees will be promoted to higher jobs, for which they will need some training, and they will leave voids in their old jobs. And eventually, employees who stay long enough will either retire or die. The word for what will happen is *entropy*, which means that every system has the built-in tendency to run down unless it is rejuvenated. In the case of an organization, the rejuvenation must come about through taking in new employees at a rate comparable to the occurrence of voids and through upgrading existing employees through training to assume jobs of greater responsibility.

At What Level to Hire?

Ideally, employee development should prepare candidates for higher-level jobs, with everyone starting at their level of capability and advancing up the structure through promotion. But practically, some jobs at higher levels will have to be filled from the outside because the required qualifications will not be generated internally. Plans for the exact kinds of people who will have to be brought into the organization each year must be developed by applying the manpower inventory, both present and forecast, to the job voids that are predicted to occur.

Plan for Change

An organization cannot grow if its manpower plan is based simply on a constant scale of operations. However, the assumption that a constant scale will be maintained provides a good starting point for planning. When the preliminary assessment of personnel replacements and their training needs has been done, the manpower plan will need to be adjusted in accord with the firm's long-term objectives. This means that in most cases the plan will be expanded, because the majority of business firms see no alternative to growth. There are exceptions to planning for manpower increases, however, as evidenced by firms in the aerospace industry in the United States. These firms have been doing their manpower planning in contemplation of a future environment of reduced operations.

Planning for growth usually involves more than just planning to do more of the same things. New or different products or services, different markets and channels of distribution, and changes in technology will force a company to plan for jobs not currently being performed. The crucial impact of technological change upon almost all companies can be illustrated by reference to a firm engaged in metal manufacturing. Currently, some of its key jobs would be those of machinist and tool and die maker. These jobs will soon be relatively obsolete, however, because of the sweeping advances of automation. The firm thus faces two manpower problems: how to get the programmers for the inevitable computer-operated equipment; and what to do with persons possessing obsolete skills who are too young for retirement and not trainable for the new skills.

Integrate With Other Plans

After a determination has been made of the number and kinds of new employees that must be assimilated into the firm each year, and systems provided for continual upgrading of the company's human resources through training and development, the next step is to assess implied costs of the manpower plan. Projections must be made of the future increases in both direct and indirect compensation for each job, and then extended by multiplying compensation by the number of future positions for each job so as to arrive at the firm's total wage and salary bill. This final amount then becomes an essential element in the cash forecast. It may be found in the process that the company's objectives are too ambitious because it cannot afford the manpower to carry them out; its long-term plans may then have to be cut back. Or, other plans, such as those for equipment and research and development, may have to be modified downward in light of an unexpectedly high rate of expenditure for personnel. Another crucial plan that may be affected is the firm's projection of permanent capital needs. The discovery may be made that it simply cannot do the things it wants to do without increasing its capital base.

The culmination of decisions revolving about the company's whole complex of plans will be a manpower plan that has been approved by top management. This then will be the authorization to proceed with the subsequent processes of the staffing function.

The Case of the
Defensive Defense Contractor
and the Pitiful Pawn

*It was in the early 1960's that Dr. Charles Lane, planning director
for Spacetech, made his plea for a relaxation in the manpower ceilings before the top managers of the company and their staffs. The
main thrust of his address was as follows:*

*"In summary, my warning is that unless Spacetech drastically in-
creases its ability to apply direct labor hours, particularly engineering, according to our proposal schedules, we are going to lose out
in the race for the weapons contracts coming up. On some of our
present contracts we have charged only 50 percent of the engineering
manhours that we said we would have committed by this date. We
have promised the customer for so long that the big surge in our
engineering effort is just ahead of us, that the government negotiators
are beginning to joke about it. I can see the space weapons business
booming for at least the next ten years, but we are not going to get
our share unless we double the number of engineers that we now
have on board."*

*Ralph Stevens, engineering vice-president, led the applause that fol-
lowed Lane's somewhat emotional presentation. "What I urge,"
Stevens said, "is that we start building an inventory of engineers, so
that when we submit a proposal we can actually identify the technical
people who would work on the project by name and badge number.
There is no question that the Department of Defense is committed to
a long-term program of building and improving the nation's space
weapons arsenal, and we simply must get ready for it."*

*The vice-president and general manager of Spacetech, Dr. Lloyd Al-
lison, looked quizzically around the room before quietly commenting:
"It appears that my manpower ceilings are not as popular as they
might be. However, I am not nearly as confident as the rest of you
seem to be that the government will, or can, continue the present
rate of defense spending much longer. Does anyone else have anything to say?"*

*Bob Blake, personnel director, got to his feet: "Forecasting defense
spending is not a strength of mine, as it is Dr. Lane's, so I won't at-*

214

tempt to differ with him. I do know this, however, that if we expand our personnel base and the defense contract well does dry up, we are going to cause some human suffering. In our relatively isolated location, we will have to import any additional engineers that we hire from other parts of the country. Suppose that they go to all of the stress and expense of moving, then after a year or two we have to lay them off. They can't get any other job in this area, and will have to move again, with probably a house to sell. Let me ask Don Hyde, our professional recruitment manager, what he thinks."

Hyde had prepared some statistics in case he was asked to talk. "Like Mr. Blake," he began, "I don't know how long these weapons contracts are going to go on. I am familiar with the supply of engineers in this country right now, and it is unbelievably tight. Dr. Lane suggests that we double our present number of engineers, which is approximately 400. There is no way that I can conceive of getting 400 qualified people in the foreseeable future. I will stick my neck way out and say that we can have a net increase of 100 engineers in eighteen months, if we are willing to incur any expense in order to obtain them."

Dr. Allison studied the flip charts arrayed along the walls of the room showing manpower assignments to existing contracts and to proposal efforts, as well as Dr. Lane's projections of future requirements. Somewhat reluctantly he finally said, "I am willing to authorize requisitions for 100 additional engineers, as well as requisitions for 100 positions in other job classifications. Before any of you start complaining that this isn't enough, let me advise you that I would feel a lot more comfortable if I could predict job security for the bulk of the people already employed by Spacetech."

. . . . .

The following is taken from the exit interview with Jim Wilson, one of the 87 engineers hired by Spacetch recruiters between the time of Dr. Allison's opening of the additional engineering requisitions and the time, fifteen months later, when he cancelled the remaining unfilled positions.

"Getting my layoff notice didn't come as a surprise, but what makes me sick is the five years of my life that I literally wasted at Space-

tech," was Wilson's opening remark as he took a seat in Tom Trump's small interviewing cubicle.

Tom answered sympathetically, "We have talked together several times since you have been here, Jim, and I think I know how you feel. Dr. Allison knows generally what the conditions have been like at Spacetech over the last five years, but he would like to give each person who has to be laid off an opportunity to express his personal feelings. Please believe that anything that you tell me will be reported anonymously."

"Well, at least it will give me a chance to get some things off my chest," Jim began. "Would you believe that when I got here in 1963 there were already rumors about impending layoffs. This really startled me, particularly when I found out that I hadn't been hired for any specific job. I was assigned to a section in the engineering controls department, but the section supervisor told me that he was so busy personally doing engineering work on a contract that was having slipped schedule and overrun costs that he couldn't take the time to train me. He suggested that I read the contract work statement and the proposal and acquaint myself with what was going on. I read these documents so many times that I almost memorized them, and finally in desperation began to spend my days in the company library, reading anything that happened to interest me. This went on for about six months before I got any kind of a job assignment. By this time I knew I had made a mistake signing on."

Tom said, "If there were layoff rumors, and you didn't like not having definite work to do, why didn't you either complain or look for another job?"

Jim flushed slightly, "I guess I have to admit that it was the money —about $250 a month more than I had been making. But, to go on, my first work assignment was on a new proposal. I was given the job of estimating part of the engineering costs."

Tom commented, "I've often wondered how you, as an engineer, ever got into cost work."

"Of course this is one of the things that gripes me," Jim replied. "As long as I have been here I have never done any real engineering. The

*proposal got me typed as a cost man. When we negotiated the con-
tract I went on the project to work on the budget. Then the company layoffs really started, but I had a secure job as long as the project
lasted, and finally became cost supervisor. Now the contract is finished
and I am laid off. I have a house to sell, and I have been out of engineering for so long I'm obsolete. And in nondefense companies,
they want accountants for cost work, not engineers."*

*"Forgive me for saying this, Jim," Tom said, "but I can't help won-
dering how many of your present problems you couldn't have avoided
by looking to the obvious future, and doing some good, sound reasoning of your own."*

Discussion Questions

Reference Case A. The Case of the Markets That Will Fade Away
(Section 13)

1. In Reference Case A, what is a formidable manpower planning
    problem?
2. In the Case of the Defensive Defense Contractor and the Pitiful
    Pawn, what example do the remarks of Lane and Stevens provide
    of an engineering approach to manpower planning?
3. Unemployment resulting from curtailed defense spending is a
    problem in the United States. Could not Spacetech, and actual
    aerospace companies, have foreseen the decrease in defense con-
    tracts?
4. Other than the miscalculation of the defense contract market,
    what was a major mistake in Spacetech's manpower planning?
5. Spacetech's manpower planning was obviously deficient. But
    what about the personal planning of the engineers who were
    hired, if Jim Wilson is a typical example?

36. Recruitment of New Personnel

Within the limits on the number of positions of each job that may be filled during a specified time period, as set by a firm's manpower plan, department managers are authorized to requisition new employees for unfilled positions. Some personnel to fill them will come from within the company, but the present section is concerned only with recruiting applicants from outside the company.

A Centralized Service

Recruiting, in most companies, tends to be a centralized service performed by the personnel department, with actual hiring being subject to the requisitioning manager's approval. Many managers would prefer to recruit applicants personally; for example, sales managers might feel that they know best how to look for potential salespeople. By and large, however, they must cooperate in the recruiting function. Aside from suggesting likely sources or names of likely applicants, they ordinarily must leave the mechanics of recruiting to the specialists. An exception to this practice may be observed in the recruiting of new managers, which is often removed from the personnel department and assigned to a top-level manager or a committee of top-level managers.

Sources of Applicants

Sources of applicants will vary according to the types of jobs to be filled. For simplicity of explanation, jobs can be divided into the three classifications of (1) wage and commission jobs, such as those for clerks, machine operators, and salespeople; (2) jobs for management trainees and professionals; and (3) jobs for experienced managers.

Class 1. Wage and commission jobs. Applicant sources for jobs in this class include:
- Public employment agencies. Although there is no known way of arraying sources in the order of their effectiveness, the fact that all persons applying for unemployment insurance

benefits must register with their state employment agency as being available for work makes listings of job openings with agencies in different locations a productive source.

- Newspaper classified advertising. As this source involves an expense for the recruiting company, its use tends to increase as the supply of qualified applicants decreases. When unemployment is low, prospective employers try to outdo each other in the size and number of their advertisements, and descriptions of benefits to be derived from working for them. In times of short labor supply, this is also a very popular source of professional applicants (who are grouped in Class 2).

- Commercial employment agencies. Although the applicants from this source usually must pay a fee if hired (unless the recruiting firm assumes all or part of the obligation), the charge made for the placement service often makes applicants more serious about performing well on a job. Commercial agencies also do some screening of applicants for qualifications before referring them to a prospective employer.

- Union hiring halls. In many industries, such as all construction trades, transportation, steel, and automotive, the union hiring hall constitutes virtually the only source of applicants for certain jobs. The problem to the employer is that these applicants are usually referred on a basis of "first on the list, first referred," and the top of the list is usually occupied by the least desirable workers because unions tend to resist differentiating between workers on the basis of ability.

- Educational institutions. Trade schools, high schools, and junior colleges are usually cooperative in referring qualified applicants to recruiting employers. An advantage of this source is that the applicants' grades provide one indication of their ability.

- Referrals by present employees. When present employees refer their friends or acquaintances for employment, there is some indication that they are satisfied with working conditions. A potential problem that must be considered, however, is the building up of powerful cliques.

- Unsolicited applications. The number of people who just "drop in" looking for jobs varies with the supply of labor, and in times of high national or regional unemployment provides a good source of qualified applicants. The task of maintaining an active file of such applicants can be costly and relatively unrewarding, however, because in so many cases the applicants become unavailable soon after making their application.

Class 2. Jobs for management trainees and professional employees. Sources of applicants in this class include:

- Universities. By far the leading technique for generating a supply of young applicants for managerial jobs, and those educated in some engineering or scientific discipline, is the conducting of formal recruiting campaigns on college and university campuses. Depending on the extensiveness of the demand, these campaigns can be highly competitive, as trained recruiters strive to interest senior and graduate students who have the most impressive qualifications in joining their respective companies.
- Professional societies. Technically trained individuals frequently register with societies representing their particular discipline, indicating that they are seeking employment; recruiters therefore often find these organizations to be productive sources of specialized kinds of applicants. In addition, many of these societies publish journals in which advertisements of job opportunities may be presented.
- Newspaper classified and display advertising. The competition for management trainees and professional employees with high potential is acute enough at times to prompt recruiters to go beyond classified advertising into the more expensive display advertisements to attract applicants with outstanding qualifications.
- Professional placement agencies. There are some agencies in most large cities that specialize in finding engineers and scientists for client companies. During the shortage of this type of worker during the 1960's, the fees were paid by the employing firms. Because of the oversupply of technical workers in the early 1970's, however, many of these agencies began charging the fees to the applicants whom they placed in jobs.

Class 3. Jobs for experienced managers. Sources of applicants in this class include:

- Industry contacts. Often the names of qualified individuals throughout the country for certain management jobs can be learned, either through published information on their accomplishments, or through underwriting houses, banks, law firms, management consulting firms, or comparable sources. Inquiries may be made of these individuals as to interest, and more direct approaches employed if they offer some encouragement.

- Executive recruiting firms. Since the early 1960's, many hundreds of firms specializing in executive placement have developed in the United States. These firms can pinpoint presently employed managers with the required qualifications who might be interested in relocating. The cost to the companies using such firms is high—running as much as a full first year's salary of an applicant who is placed as a consequence of the service.
- Display advertising. Publications specializing in financial news —The Wall Street Journal in particular—are serving as clearing houses for executive talent via display advertisements inserted either by the firms seeking managers or by managers looking for a change in jobs.
- "40 plus" associations. Because of the layoffs of executives in the late 1960's and early 1970's, many unemployed managers have banded together in some cities to help each other find jobs. They constitute an excellent source of seasoned executives.

Discussion Questions

1. What advantages might be gained from centralizing the recruitment function in a firm's personnel department? (See Section 24.)
2. What implications are there for the personnel department in recruiting heavily from people referred by public employment agencies, so far as investigatory work and screening of applicants are concerned?
3. What investigatory work of commercial employment agencies should a recruiter do before soliciting applicant referrals from the agencies?
4. How long should a firm maintain an active file of applicants who were not hired?
5. The term *pirating* is sometimes used to refer to the activities of executive recruiting firms. Explain this allusion.

37. Selection of New Personnel

The recruitment process is intended to produce enough applicants for job openings to permit differentiation between those who appear to have the necessary qualifications and those who do not. The word *appear* is used, because despite the diligence with which the selection process is conducted, the applicants chosen for employment represent largely unknown quantities.

Validity of the Selection Process

Only after the applicants' actual trial on the job (and in many cases the trial requires years) will the validity of the selection process finally be known. Selection techniques will be considered valid if employees were hired on the basis of predictions that they would do well on the job, and they did. The techniques will also be considered valid if they indicated that applicants would not do well on the job, and they did not, although the signs were ignored and they were hired anyway.

Preliminary Screening

Usually the preliminary screening of applicants is done by the personnel department, but the final choice among applicants is usually made by the immediate supervisor over the job.

The screening procedure will vary according to the level of jobs for which applicants are being considered, but a usual first step is to let the applicants know something about the job for which they are applying. At this point some applicants will automatically remove themselves from further consideration because they are not interested in the job or are obviously not qualified.

Most companies will next request the applicants to fill out application forms. These forms vary in the extensiveness of the information requested, but usually the information asked for includes name, address, phone number, age, sex, physical characteristics, marital status, work experience, and education. Generally, different application forms will be used for higher-level jobs than for those at the lower grades. A practice being used by many firms is to have a short form filled out at the preliminary stage, followed by a more comprehensive form later if mutual interest toward employment develops between the company and the applicant.

Courtesy toward job applicants is now an accepted standard by most companies, so the completion of the application form is almost always followed by an interview. These interviews are customarily conducted by the personnel department in the preliminary screening, and some applicants will be weeded out because of readily apparent deficiencies in qualifications. Again, courtesy requires that applicants be told, tactfully, the reason for their rejection. Implicit in continuing the selection process, or stopping it at the initial interview, is the understanding that the information contained on the application form and supplemented in the interview is in some degree predictive of success on the job. Applicants who are not rejected at this stage are almost invariably referred to the departments with the job opening for which they are applying.

Subsequent Screening

For lower-level jobs, a second interview conducted by the person under whom the applicants would work if employed often terminates the selection process; that is, an employment agreement is either reached or it is not. However, even for lower-grade jobs, psychological testing, physical testing, and reference checking are quite frequently used to supplement what is decided in the interview. In addition to these testing and checking techniques, which will be discussed later (in this section and in Section 38), the number and comprehensiveness of interviews tends to increase as the job grade for which the applicant is being considered rises in importance. Thus, an applicant might be (1) given a series of interviews by superiors on successively higher levels; (2) interviewed by a group of potential superiors together; or (3) asked to talk with potential peers, either singly or in groups.

Interviewing Methods

Probably the most important requirement for effective interviewing is a plan. In other words, random conversation will not produce much in the way of benefits for either the interviewer or interviewee. The plan must start with objectives, which are usually twofold:

- find out more about the applicant's qualifications than has been revealed thus far.
- convince a promising applicant that the employment opportunity under discussion is better than others that may be available.

Accomplishing both objectives in the same interview requires considerable skill in whatever technique is used.

The patterned interview.   Among the interviewing techniques that have been devised, the "patterned" interview has become quite widely accepted. Patterned interviews are conducted by asking the applicant questions contained on forms and summarizing the applicant's answers after the questions. Forms vary for different jobs, but all applicants for the same job are asked identical questions. Consistency is the outstanding advantage of this method because all applicants are evaluated on the basis of the same criteria. Although patterned interviews are not guaranteed predictors of job performance, they are considerably more valid than the nondirective and the stress types.

The nondirective interview.   This technique involves asking broad, general questions and then permitting the applicant to talk freely. The purpose is to learn some of the inner feelings of the applicant, who in responding is led to ever increasing depths. The interviewer must not lose control of the interview, however, and should give just enough direction to assure that the same feelings of every applicant are probed. This is the most common kind of interviewing method, despite the fact that it is generally a random predictor of the interviewee's performance on the job if hired.

The stress interview.   The purpose of the stress interview is to find out the applicant's tolerance for unpleasantness, nonroutine situations, and threats to personal defenses. Some jobs involve a high order of these variables, and the stress interview is intended to predict how well the applicant is able to cope with them. For example, applicants for selling jobs may be deliberately insulted and otherwise treated rudely in an attempt to learn their tolerance for this kind of behavior. Stress interviews have a low validity in predicting job performance, and have pretty much fallen into disuse in industry.

A common misconception is that interviewing skill just comes naturally to people, but the fact is that it requires intensive training. Personnel department specialists usually have it, and as a result can predict an applicant's success or failure on a job with a fair degree of accuracy. The problem is that managers who are not trained in interviewing must usually make the final decision concerning selection or rejection of applicants.

Interviewing Mistakes and Pitfalls

"Don'ts" of interviewing are implied in the following practices.

Unplanned interviews.   Often in an interview the interviewer will do most of the talking, and when realizing at its conclusion that very little information has been learned about the applicant, will make a snap judgment from some superficial bit of evidence.

Basing judgments on stereotypes.   The common tendency in people to base judgments on stereotypes leads to many selection errors. In other words, fixations can develop within people to the effect that individuals of certain appearance or background are hardworking, honest, and intelligent, and others are indolent, untrustworthy, and stupid; and they make selection decisions accordingly.

Placing undue emphasis on one characteristic.   Untrained interviewers tend to be influenced by the "halo effect," which means that if one of the applicant's characteristics is liked or disliked, all other characteristics will be judged on the basis of that feature. For example, many managers find it difficult to evaluate unfavorably applicants who happened to graduate from their own alma mater.

Other Techniques; Checking References

A physical examination is often required of applicants, both to assure that they are physically capable of doing the work, and to preclude persons with chronic ailments from being potential financial burdens to the company. An additional highly important selection technique that will be discussed here is reference checking. Psychological testing as a selection device will be discussed in Section 38.

Certainly past employers constitute a prime source of information about applicants who have a previous work history. An easy way of exploring this source is to mail a standard form, requesting that gradations of such criteria as industriousness, loyalty, initiative, and so on, be checked off. These forms are of relatively doubtful value, however, because past employers usually will not give a bad written referral to any but the most derelict of employees. Somewhat more useful is a request from past employers for letters describing the applicant's attributes and weaknesses. This technique develops more specific information than a checked-off form, but it still requires that anything against the applicant be put in writing. A third alternative, which can be more productive, is to call past employers by phone to learn their opinions of an applicant. Finally, face-to-face discussions with past employers tend to yield the most candid appraisals of the applicant's performance, and may be among the best predictors of the way an applicant will perform on the job if hired.

In addition to past employers, former teachers and work peers or subordinates can provide illuminating information about job applicants. Here, also, face-to-face communication produces the best results but is not often feasible.

Personal references listed by the applicant are of questionable value except to affirm the applicant's good points, because who is going to name as a reference someone who would stress, or even point out, negative characteristics?

The Case of the
Un-Merry Widow

The widow of Patrick Moynihan was a diminutive Korean who had married Pat when his Army unit was stationed near Seoul. Soon after their son was born, Pat was transferred to Fort Lewis, and the Moynihans settled in an apartment in Tacoma. Then, tragically, Pat was killed in an automobile accident, and Ms. Moynihan was left with the decision of whether to try to make a life in the United States or to return to Korea. For the sake of her son, she decided to stay in the States.

Ms. Moynihan's father was a professor of English at the university in Seoul, and she had been a legal secretary for three years in a Seoul law office. Therefore, in seeking the employment that was absolutely necessary, she had two things going for her, a proficiency in English and a high competence in typing, shorthand, and office procedures. However, she knew nothing about the customs that have become ingrained in the process of getting a job in the United States.

Upon the advice of her landlord, Ms. Moynihan took a bus into Seattle and went directly to the Acme Employment Agency. She arrived there at 11 o'clock on a Monday morning, and the office was jammed with people. It was early afternoon before an interviewer finally got to her, and after a short discussion about her employment background, she was asked to return the following day to take a typing test.

To a former legal secretary, the typing test was ridiculously easy, and the interviewer was quite impressed with Ms. Moynihan's performance. "I think I will send you to Washington Equitable Insurance Company," the interviewer told her. "They are looking for someone like you, and the offices are on the top four floors of this building. The starting salary is $450 per month, and you should be there at 9:00 A.M. Friday."

In her naivety, Ms. Moynihan thought she was being told that she had a job. She spent the balance of that day finding a day nursery for her son, and paid a deposit. She located an apartment near downtown Seattle and the nursery on the following day, and moved in on Thursday. On Friday morning she reported to the Washington Equitable Insurance Company to go to work.

227

"If you will make out this short application form, an interviewer will see you in about thirty minutes," was her greeting by the receptionist in the personnel department of the insurance company.

"But I came here to start to work," said Ms. Moynihan.

"I'm sorry, but there must be some mistake," said the secretary. "You have been merely referred to us by the employment agency."

The interviewer talked with Ms. Moynihan only briefly, but seemed to be interested. In any event, he was quite polite, and finally said: "This shouldn't be necessary, but this company has a requirement that all applicants for a secretarial job must take a typing test. Could you arrange to do this on Monday?"

"Please tell me when I start to work," answered Ms. Moynihan, and then told the interviewer about the apartment and the nursery.

"I can't tell you how sorry I am that we have unintentionally inconvenienced you, but due to the layoffs in Seattle there are a lot of people available, and we are intending to screen a number of applicants for this job opening," was his reply.

After resignedly telling the interviewer that she would take the test on Monday, Ms. Moynihan stopped in at the Acme Employment Agency. There she was told about three other job openings, but they were all in the suburbs, and she had paid the first month's rent on the downtown apartment. She knew that she couldn't afford to forfeit this money, and was further shocked when the agency interviewer said to her: "I'm sorry you didn't understand that you were just referred to the insurance company. Perhaps you also don't know that if you get a job through the agency you will owe us 35 percent of your first month's gross salary."

On Monday, Ms. Moynihan took the typing test and passed brilliantly. She was then asked to fill out a four-page application form, and bring it in the next day for an interview with the personnel manager.

"Tell me in your own words, Ms. Moynihan, why you want to work for us," this gentlemen purred in a friendly way.

Ms. Moynihan was momentarily speechless. Other than to tell him that she desperately needed a job, and that because of the apartment she had committed herself to working in the downtown Seattle area, she couldn't think of anything else to say.

The personnel manager frowned slightly as she somewhat embarrassedly stated these reasons. "The kind of people that we really like to employ here at Washington," he said gently, "are those who feel dedicated to the objectives of the company, rather than just wanting a job. However, you appear to have exceptional ability, and I would like to have you meet the man whose department has the job opening. Can you arrange to be here on Friday afternoon?"

Feeling increasingly discouraged, Ms. Moynihan spent the next two days calling on other employment agencies. She had one referral, but at that company she was asked to return the following day to take a typing test, which she elected not to do. On Friday she kept her appointment with Mr. King, who was her prospective employer.

"Do you think that you may not be too well qualified?" asked Mr. King, after he reviewed Ms. Moynihan's background and described the duties of the job that was open. "The girls in this office have a pretty tight little group," he went on, "and are apt to resent someone who might show them up, especially if the new person happened to be a foreigner."

"What mistakes have I made now," thought Ms. Moynihan. She then proceeded to try to play down the qualifications that she had so carefully built up a few minutes earlier.

"I like your determination," said Mr. King finally, "and would like to see you get the job. However, there are a few more things that the personnel department has to do. Suppose you go back to their office."

Ms. Moynihan dutifully waited to see the personnel manager. "Well, it looks like you are getting close to being a member of our happy family," he said to her. "You will have to have a physical examination, which you can do next week."

"Will that be all? If I pass will I get the job?" asked Ms. Moynihan.

"Not quite yet," answered the personnel manager. "We will have to wait for a reply to the letter that we sent the law firm that you worked for in Seoul."

"I will be in Seoul on Monday, and will probably be back on my old job. the next day," said Ms. Moynihan quietly. "Korea is really not such a bad place to raise a boy."

Discussion Questions

1. Why is it so important to select new employees carefully?
2. What can firms do to improve the interviewing skills of managers who make the final selection decisions?
3. What are some jobs for which the use of a "stress" interview might be appropriate?
4. What are some advantages of face-to-face discussions with former employers of applicants?
5. In the Case of the Un-Merry Widow, what was fundamentally wrong with the methods used by both the employer and the employment agency?

38. Psychological Testing

Probably most people in the United States have had some exposure to psychological tests. School systems at all levels use intelligence tests as predictors of scholastic ability, the Army and Navy started using various tests as far back as World War I as a means of directing servicemen to the most appropriate duty, and adoption of psychological tests by business firms appears to have risen steadily over the past fifty years. The main purpose of psychological tests in industry is to assist in the selection process, although secondary uses include appraising employees for types of training requirements, promotion potential, and counseling needs.

Supplemental Value

Interviews, reference checks, and the information on the application form are all inefficient, to some extent, in predicting an applicant's future success or failure on the job. It is so important to avoid mistakes in selection decisions that any technique offering additional clues toward potential performance will be welcome. As with the other screening methods, psychological tests are not infallible, but they help narrow the possibility of selection errors when they are used in conjunction with the other selection techniques. This is particularly true if the conclusions of all of the techniques point in the same direction.

Characteristics Measured

The various tests used for selection can be grouped into one of three categories—those measuring native skills and abilities, interests, and personality traits. All three categories of tests are used primarily for fitting new applicants to jobs, rather than appraising existing employees for promotion.

Native skills and abilities. Of all the attributes which an individual is born with and which presumably do not change, probably the most important is intelligence. Intelligence tests, such as the Wonderlic Personnel Test, have as their objective the measurement of an individual's relative capacity to comprehend facts and their relationships to other facts, and to reason about them. Other important native attributes whose relative capacity tests have been devised to measure include mechanical aptitude, mathematical aptitude, and dexterity. Of all tests, these are the most accurate in measuring what they are supposed to measure.

Interests.   Tests in this category have the purpose of discovering an individual's inclination, or resistance, toward particular kinds of work. Some people are fortunate enough to know instinctively what they want to do; probably most people do not, and many find their way randomly into an occupation. Tests such as the Strong Vocational Interest Blank are intended to reduce the incidence of assigning people to types of work for which they are not well suited.

Personality.   These tests are used to assess such characteristics in the psychological makeup of job applicants as sociability, hostility, and emotional stability. The Gordon Personal Profile and Inventory is one example. Tests to determine personality traits reportedly have the lowest degree of dependability of the three test categories under discussion, one reason being that these traits vary within individuals and the tests do not show the extent of the variance. For example, in tests to measure an individual's ability to get along with other people, it is not entirely clear whether the results show that the individual can get along with all people, just some people, or no people. For another thing, test responses can be faked more easily than on the other two types of tests. The right answers are often quite obvious, and in giving them an applicant can conceal his real attitudes.

Problems in the Use of Tests

The most serious problems in the use of tests are related to the validity and reliability of test results.

Validity of test results.   An assumption underlying the use of tests is that they truly measure what they are supposed to, or in other words, that the tests are valid. The big problem, however, is how to derive some criteria of validity. For example, if success or failure in job performance could be related to test results, it could be determined whether the tests were truly valid. A commonly used criterion is the performance appraisal (Section 41). But performance appraisals constitute problems themselves, rather than solutions, because more often than not, they are based on subjective judgments. Only where job performance can be measured in terms of numerical output, such as units of product made or sold, can job success or failure be identified and related back to test predictions. Otherwise, test validity is difficult to establish.

Reliability. Test reliability, which means the consistency of test results, poses another problem. A reliable test generates the same result for an individual on some characteristic regardless of how many times he takes the test. Quite apparently, tests that do not produce consistent results are valueless as predictors. As mentioned above, a factor contributing to unreliable tests is that people are becoming educated in how to fake responses to test questions; and if faking cannot be prevented, the accuracy of the test score is highly suspect.

Attitudes Toward Tests

Until recently, managers tended either to be strongly for tests or strongly opposed to them. There is possibly a growing trend toward taking a more neutral position with respect to the proper role of tests, namely, that they are not totally reliable by themselves, but are useful in supplementing other selection techniques.

Some management writers denounce tests on the grounds that they are universally worthless, that they have become popular because of the appeal of a scientific base, which is false, and that they constitute an unwarranted invasion of human privacy. Other writers argue that tests are based on careful research, that they are steadily improving as professional instruments, and that they are better than having no alternative to interviewing and background investigations as selection methods.

A growing resistance to psychological testing as a screening device is coming from minority ethnic groups. Charges are being made that tests, either intentionally or not, discriminate against people whose cultures, education, and even vocabularies differ from those of the majority of the population. The essential issue is that while tests may be valid for the majority of applicants, they may be invalid in predicting failure in job performance for applicants from minority ethnic groups. It is held that if given a chance on the job, these people would be able to perform successfully.

Requirements of the Testing Program

A company that is setting up a psychological testing program should observe first of all that it is not a job for amateurs. The personnel assigned to administering the program should be specially trained and experienced in performing this activity, and the interpretation of test results should be done only by a qualified psychologist. If a company cannot afford to retain individuals with these skills on a full-time basis, it is possible, and often very practical, to engage consulting firms to handle the entire program.

The purpose of tests and how they will be used must be carefully explained to all concerned personnel within the organization, as well as to the applicants to whom the tests are administered. Every effort should be exerted to remove any implication of threat or fear from the testing program.

Finally, it should be recognized that for a testing program to be worthwhile, time and money must be continually expended for improving it, primarily in the direction of refining the validity and reliability of the tests used.

Discussion Questions

1. For what level of applicant would tests for native skills and abilities appear to be most appropriate?
2. "Mortality" rates for beginners in certain selling jobs, such as insurance or securities, are extremely high. What kind of tests might reduce the incidence of failure?
3. Explain the position, held by some critics, that psychological tests invade human privacy.
4. Some people feel that there is a factor of impartiality in psychological tests. What would cause them to hold this view?
5. What is the practical determinant of a firm's decision to undertake the cost of psychological testing?

39. Employee Training

The skill level of new employees hired into a business organization will vary from virtually none at all up to a high degree of occupational competence. Individuals in the first category obviously must be taught some rudimentary skills, because otherwise they would have no productive value to the firm. Individuals at the opposite extreme of initial capability, and at all gradations of skills between, should have opportunities to upgrade their capacities in order to satisfy their personal needs for growth, to keep abreast of new information and changing technology, and to provide a pool of steadily improving workers upon which the company can rely in moving toward its objectives. For these reasons, the role of formal training programs within industry is growing in importance.

Getting Started

If a firm has constructed a comprehensive manpower plan, this document would be the starting place for designing a training program. In it would be detailed the kinds and quantities of skills needed at stated times in the future, plus an inventory of skills possessed by workers currently employed. An analysis of these categories of information would identify the required scope of the training program. However, most companies do not have manpower plans that have been developed in such depth.

An alternative method for determining training needs, and the programs to satisfy them, is through initiation by top management. Through an analysis of performance records, perception of skill deficiencies in the labor force, and observation of training programs adopted by other companies, senior managers may recognize the need for formal training opportunities, and put the mechanism into action via policies, appointments, and budgets. Perception of the need for training may also occur at the foreman or supervisor level. These managers may be frustrated by their inability to meet performance standards with the level of skill that their workers possess, and will communicate recommendations for formal training upward until they reach a management level at which positive action is taken. Others who may recognize the need for upgrading workers' skills may be specialists in the personnel department. Their inability to recruit applicants with required qualifications will be a strong motivating factor for them to urge for a comprehensive program of skill training.

Prerequisite: Accomplishment Goals

.An essential first step, and one that is, surprisingly enough, not always taken, is to identify exactly what the accomplishment goals of a training course are and how the achievement of these goals will be measured. What this amounts to is establishing means for validating the training. For example, assume that a course in welding is being considered. Before the course is started, it might be established that the criterion for measuring the effectiveness of the course is that all persons completing it be capable of performing three-position welding in accordance with Army/Navy specifications.

Training Methods

Probably all business firms, large or small, rely most heavily on training people on the job. Sometimes an experienced worker is assigned the duty of teaching a newcomer; at other times, the foreman or supervisor takes responsibility for on-the-job training. Such training may advance the new worker to the stage of adequate performance, but because the training is usually unplanned, it may result in significant voids in the trainee's preparation.

An opposite approach is to use formal classroom teaching methods. With this approach, considerably more of the theory underlying the optimal performance of various jobs can be imparted to the trainee. To be effective, however, this method must provide for the theory to be supplemented by practical experience under simulated work conditions.

A fairly new technique for classroom instruction is programmed instruction, often used with a teaching machine. The technique involves organizing course subject matter into a sequence of dependent steps. Material in each step, which may be in the form of narrative, graph, formula, and so on, is printed on a frame, and all the frames together make up the program. To describe the principle simply, the trainee digests the material frame by frame, and to progress from one to another must answer correctly a question concerning the preceding frame. In case of a wrong answer, advice may be given to go back and review material in earlier frames.

A balanced approach would be to combine on-the-job training with formal classroom instruction. Many of the apprenticeship programs leading to journeyman status in a craft or trade now incorporate the two methods, and the practice seems to be followed in less formal training programs as well, such as short-term training in a specific skill.

An Essential Factor

The desire to learn is essential if any training is to be effective. And if trainees are to want to learn, they must see that they will get something out of the training. In some cases, tangible benefits, such as promotions or raises immediately following completion of some specific training, provide the incentive. In other cases, the only immediate tangible reward might be a certificate of completion, but if the trainees perceive that the certificates will lead to more money or higher status in the long run, they can be effective incentives. Success is another powerful motivator. If the trainees' confidence in their ability to complete a training course is periodically reinforced, they will be much more inclined to stick with it until completion than if they perceive themselves as failing. The training must therefore be organized so that the trainees can perceive incremental progress.

Retraining

Management's responsibilities to workers whose skills are made obsolete by automation are included in an overall treatment of the social responsibility concept in Section 68. Helping people displaced by machines is one responsibility accepted by the management of many companies. These managers believe that it is wrong for a firm to cast workers aside simply because their skills have been made obsolete. Therefore, numerous companies in the United States are currently undertaking the retraining of employees in skills that have future usefulness so that they might continue a productive working life.

Discussion Questions

1. At how low a skill level should a company's training program commence in order to make productive workers out of new employees?
2. Regardless of the management level at which the need for a training program is recognized, what positive actions are required by top management to get the program started and sustained?
3. What problems may be caused by having an experienced worker train a newcomer?
4. What would be some effects of enrolling more people in a training course than are needed in the job they are being trained for?
5. What obstacles—psychological or otherwise—might a company encounter in an attempt to retrain workers whose skills have been made obsolete by automation?

40. Management Development

Up until the years immediately following World War II, the absence of any planned efforts by most business organizations in the United States to develop managers suggested either that managerial ability was regarded as something certain individuals were just naturally endowed with, or that a development program was considered as too awesome to be attempted. Since the early 1950's, the situation has definitely changed, and today few companies beyond those of simple scale do not have some kind of program for management development. Much of the emphasis seems to be misguided, however.

Mistaken Belief

Despite the current emphasis on management development, there are too few well-planned, systematic programs. Indeed, the current popularity of the notion of "management development" has led many companies to randomly adopt unintegrated courses, so-called packaged training programs, and out-and-out gimmicks, such as one-day sensitivity sessions, all in the mistaken belief that these things will "train" managers. The first thing that is needed is a better understanding of the complexities of developing managers.

Development Vs. Training

Whereas skill training implies the teaching, in accord with known principles, of how to do some technical tasks that require determinate physical and/or mental effort, it can be engaged in with predictive success. Management ability, on the other hand, being largely an art, cannot be taught with predictive success. Potential managers can be exposed to the existing body of knowledge about management, as summarized in this book, but this will not make them managers. However, with this knowledge, plus motivation and judgment, they may grow to be managers if provided with successive management experiences. This is the way management development should be viewed; any notion that people can be trained to be managers is misleading.

Development Opportunities

It must be recognized that there are gradations of management jobs within an organization, which for the sake of simplicity can be categorized by levels—supervisory, middle management, and top management. Every organization, in order to survive, must assure that there is continuous accession of qualified individuals to each level. However, the required qualifications at the successive levels will differ; therefore, the developmental experiences must be different also.

Supervisory positions.   Individuals being groomed for positions at the supervisory level may be presumed to have had no previous management experience. They will tend to come from two sources— either technical jobs within the organization, or college campuses. The former will know something about the company, but together with the recent graduates, they will need to learn in detail company policies and procedures regarding personnel, budgeting, scheduling, and other matters. These things can be taught via classroom instruction, reading assignments, and instruction provided by the candidates' own supervisor. The next step should be to expose the candidates gradually to management problems, and permit them to participate in solutions. Ideally, this experience should probably come as a result of the candidates' being in the role of "assistants to" their immediate supervisors. Predictively, some candidates will find at this stage that management is not to their liking and disqualify themselves. Others will be disqualified because of lack of potential not apparent to them. The remainder will succeed to their supervisor's job, or some other job at a comparable level, when an opening occurs and their performance indicates that they are ready for such responsibility. The experience that first-level supervisors gain is primarily in directing technical workers, making routine decisions within the framework of procedures, and facing the sobering results of mistakes in judgment.

Middle-management positions.   Opportunities for experience in middle-management jobs are usually reserved for individuals who have demonstrated managerial competence at the supervisory level. By this time they will be familiar with the routines of the company's operation, but will need closer acquaintance with its objectives and policies. In addition, they will need to acquire a broad view of management theory. The first requirement is usually taken care of through instruction by the managers immediately above them—to whom, in their first exposure to middle-management responsibilities, they will likely be assistants. The broadening of these employees' theoretical knowledge of management is facilitated by university programs geared to the development of managers, by conference programs offering more condensed instruction, and by courses sponsored by the company itself. The experience that individuals gain in middle-management positions includes directing subordinate managers, pooling judgment and authority with peers in arriving at group decisions, and participating in the setting of goals, along with guides for implementing them. It is becoming increasingly popular to rotate middle managers from job to job in order to broaden their experience.

Top-management positions.   The criterion for consideration of individuals for top-management posts is almost always singularly impressive performance in middle management. Some outstanding middle managers may have a general management background as a result of job rotation or of experience in product management. More often, however, their experience will tend to be specialized, and what they will need most at the top level is a general management background. Here again, the "assistant to" role can be used to provide this rounding and maturing exposure. In addition, top-level committee appointments and special study assignments can have a broadening effect. Assignments whereby the individual is put in contact with systems external to the firm, such as government, labor unions, the public at large, or potential foreign markets, are also of substantial benefit. And finally, many university programs, some lasting as long as a year, are especially adapted to providing managers headed for the top echelons with a broad theoretical base in both management and cultural subjects, and are well suited to supplementing the planned management experience.

Need for Criteria

There is one glaring weakness of management development programs that plagues most companies, and that is the lack of objective criteria by which to measure management performance. Without such criteria, there is no way to validate any program, that is, to determine if it is truly developing qualified managers. Section 41, which follows, deals with the various performance-appraisal systems now being used, but the admission is made that few business organizations are more than moderately satisfied with the results of any of these techniques.

The Case of
Four Roads to the Top

It was the evening of the bimonthly dinner meeting of the presidents of the member stores of International Department Stores, Inc. As was their custom on these occasions, four of the executives who had become fast friends over the years met for cocktails in one of their hotel suites before joining the other officers at dinner.

"I have a problem at my store which is not a new one, and I am sure that it is shared by the rest of you," said John Hopkins, president of Hunt-Marshal. "That is, how to develop qualified managers. We have two stores now, and a third one under construction, and we badly need managers at all organizational levels. I have tried pirating good ones from our competitors, but they simply reciprocate by pirating from us. We have experimented with various kinds of management development programs, but with indifferent success. What does it take to develop good managers?"

"You're right, it is one of our most difficult problems," answered George Moranian, president of Huntley Brothers, Inc. "But I have an idea of something that we can talk about while we are enjoying our drinks. Suppose each of us tells the others the steps that he took on the road to the top job in his company. John, since you brought up the question, perhaps you would like to start."

"Well, I got out of college in 1940. Hunt-Marshal had what they called a management training program, and I was hired for it along with five other new college graduates. The philosophy of the company at that time was that management trainees should have the experience of working at the lowest jobs in the store before very gradually moving up. I suppose the vague objective was to expose the trainees intimately to every activity in the company. Anyhow, my first assignment was unpacking dishes. I suppose there is some value in knowing how to unpack dishes, but the knowledge can be learned in a day. I was kept on this task for over three months. After numerous complaints, I was transferred to men's suits. There my training consisted of assuring that suits in different sizes were carefully segregated. After two months of this, I was about to quit the company, as three of the other trainees had already done, but I got

drafted into the Army. When the war was over, I told the people at Hunt-Marshal that there was only one job that I would take, and that was selling appliances. I not only sold on the floor during the days, but I followed up prospects by calling at their homes at night. My record was good, and in a year I was made department manager. Within four years I was assistant merchandise manager, and from there became merchandise manager, and so on up. Other than the first abortive training experience, the only company-sponsored development that I had was at some American Management Association Conferences."

"I joined the Navy right out of high school," said George Moranian, "and when my hitch was over I started to work under my father, who was head carpet buyer at Huntley's. I also began to study accounting at night school. My father retired about the time I got my degree, and I moved into his job. I heard about the summer management training program at Stanford, and I asked the then president of the company to send me. About two years after that experience I was asked if I wouldn't like a change from carpets, and was made assistant controller. Next came the controller's job, which carried a vice-presidency, and then finally I became president six years ago."

"I think there was a lot of planning to the trainee program that I got started on," said Richard Johnson, president of Scott-Anderson Company, and the youngest of the four men. "In the first two years after I joined the company out of college, I worked as an assistant to five different buyers. During this time I was really given some responsible assignments. Then I was made buyer for the notions department, which was one of the buyers' jobs reserved exclusively for trainees. The company usually kept a trainee on the buyer's job for about a year, while watching his performance very closely. My next assignment was at the corporate office, where I became involved in appraising European department stores that seemed ripe for acquisition. That was really an interesting job and I hated to leave it after three years, but the people at central headquarters felt that I should have more experience in store operations. I came back to Scott-Anderson as buyer of men's shoes, and in two years was made assistant to the president. Three years on this job led to merchandising manager, and four years later I was made president."

"I think you all know most of the story of my life," said Irving Levine,

president of Goldblach-Levine, Inc. "I dropped out of high school and began selling pots and pans door to door. When the Korean War ended, I opened a war surplus store. This operation did extremely well, and I got three others started. When I saw my sources of supply drying up I took a long trip to Japan and made hundreds of contacts for good, cheap merchandise. I gradually converted my surplus stores to discount houses just when the boom in this kind of merchandising was taking off. Goldblach's had been the principal department store in the area, and was expanding to the suburbs. However, every time they built a department store, I built a discount house close enough to capture the market for low-cost merchandise. Finally Goldblach's decided that I should be on their team, so we merged. I was executive vice-president for a couple of years, and then moved to the top job. I haven't had a day of formal management development in my life, but I feel that a good part of my personal development has been through my interest in the arts."

"Those are certainly four entirely different stories," said John Hopkins. "Dick obviously had the best company guidance, and he has given me the kind of ideas that I was hoping to get. Let me ask you this question, Dick. Would the kind of program that you were on make good managers out of anyone with the normal prerequisites?"

"I saw too many apparently good men who didn't make it to reply yes," Dick answered. "No matter what kind of program that a company sets up for developing managers, the only individuals who will ultimately be able to handle senior managerial responsibilities are those who are more motivated by the drive for success than by anything else."

Discussion Questions

1. How can you explain the emphasis given by most medium-size and large companies to management development programs?
2. What kind of experiences do you suppose are most valuable in the development of managerial ability?
3. In the Case of Four Roads to the Top, John Hopkins got into management as a result of an outstanding record as a salesman. What would you think of a company policy requiring that all managerial aspirants prove themselves through outstanding per-

formance in some technical function, such as selling, accounting, or engineering?

4. Apparently, business firms cannot rely on getting good managers by looking for individuals with the "knack" for managing of an Irving Levine. Explain why not.

5. What do you think of Richard Johnson's statement that "drive for success" is the most important quality that managers must have?

41. Performance Appraisal

Very likely, the performance by individuals of their assigned duties has in some way been appraised by supervisors since the beginning of any form of organized activity. If the performance were measurable in numerical terms, such as length of ditch dug in a day, it has always been easy to evaluate. Assessment of nonquantitative performance, on the other hand, has always posed a problem.

Until comparatively recently, evaluation of nonquantitative performance was made on the basis of overall impressions, scaled into relative degrees of good or bad. Yet efforts have been under way—dating back to about World War I—to reduce the subjectivity of such performance appraisals through the development of techniques whereby numerical measurement could be applied to components of the performance. The resulting techniques—still largely unsatisfactory—for differentiating the performance of individuals via development of a total score are discussed in this section.

Appraisal Techniques

Determination of scores has varied with the appraisal technique used. Some of the most widely used appraisal techniques include the graphic rating scale, rank order, critical incident, and forced choice methods.

Graphic rating scale. One of the oldest appraisal methods, and the most frequently used, employs the graphic rating scale. The essentials of this technique are, first, a list of traits or characteristics that are deemed important to job performance. Categories commonly found on appraisal forms include quality of work, quantity of work, dependability, initiative, and cooperation. Second, descriptions of gradations of each characteristic are provided on the form, ranging from various connotations for *outstanding* to terse synonyms for *poor*. A certain number of points is established for each gradation of each trait. In using the form, the appraiser considers the performance of the subordinate relative to each trait, and decides on the proper gradation. The points given for the various traits add up to the total score of the individual being appraised.

Rank order. Like the graphic rating scale, the rank order method also involves rating employees according to characteristics of performance, but here all employees in a given job classification are rated against each other. The number of employees being rated is the same as the score to be given the one showing the best performance in any category, and the others are successively lower on the scale according to their relative performance. From this analysis in each category, the appraiser is able to develop a total score for each person. For example, in the rating of five customer service employees on the basis of such characteristics as quality of work, quantity of work, dependability, and customer contacts, the appraiser would rank each person from 1 to 5 for each characteristic, and then add the individuals' scores in all categories to determine their standings.

Critical incident.   The critical incident method departs from characteristics of performance, in that the manager keeps a record of extreme impressions formed of each subordinate over some past period. These impressions are both of the unusually good and the unusually bad varieties. This method is not adaptable to totalling a score, but presumably a preponderance of either favorable or unfavorable incidents leads to some overall impression.

Forced choice.   Although the forced choice method is not widely used, proponents urge that it has significant advantages. The appraisal form consists of four sets of statements. The appraiser does not know the value assigned to any of the statements, but is asked to check the statement in each set that best describes the individual being evaluated, plus the description that is least appropriate. Some of the statements have good connotations; others, bad; and a scored evaluation can be developed after the appraisal checks have been entered on the form.

Use of Performance Appraisals

Most companies that employ formal appraisal methods require periodic performance interviews. Ideally, in these interviews the supervisor carefully reviews each appraisal statement with the individual concerned. Again ideally, the scene involves the wise and patient supervisor not only counseling the attentive and earnest subordinate on correcting deficiencies, but also stressing competencies and offering encouragement concerning advancement. From most reports, however, the situation rarely is so constructive. For one thing, neither supervisor nor subordinate has confidence in any of the appraisal methods that have been described. The outstanding fault of all of them is that they lack objective standards against which performance can be compared. The typical performance interview is characterized by the supervisor being embarrassed and defensive because the appraisal cannot be backed up if challenged, and the subordinate feeling resentful of the vagueness and subjectiveness of it, not to mention a sense of indignity at being appraised by a person perceived to be quite fallible. Often the performance interview will culminate with the supervisor identifying the amount of the merit increase that the subordinate will receive for the next period. In many cases, this is all that makes the experience palatable to the subordinate, and the typical interview ends with both parties being glad that it is over.

Unsatisfactory Results

The director of industrial relations for a large aerospace company told the writer that over a twenty-year period his company had gone full circle in the types of appraisal systems used. The firm had started with the graphic rating scale, then abandoned it in favor of rank order, next tried critical incident, went next to forced choice, and finally readopted the rating scale. According to this senior manager, none of the methods tried were satisfactory, but the rating scale method was being put back into practice because it was felt that the company had to have some kind of appraisal system, and the graphic rating scale technique was the easiest to administer.

Methods Under Development

There are some new methods of performance appraisal that are still in the development stage.

Peer rating.   One method that has been used extensively in military organizations, and which is now being experimented with by some business firms, is peer rating, or sometimes called "buddy" rating. As the name implies, in this system all members of a group with equal status evaluate each other. So far, the value of peer rating seems to be restricted to identifying potential leaders, but this is a benefit not to be lightly regarded. Leadership is an important characteristic of managers, and if individuals who have this attribute can be discovered early in their careers and provided with management experience, the supply of qualified managers in the future will likely be increased.

Appraisal by specialists.   Apart from some inherent weaknesses in the conventional appraisal methods, an additional problem in making them effective is that most managers are not well trained in using them. A relatively new approach being taken by some companies is to have appraisal specialists from the personnel department gather information on the performance of individuals in all departments. These specialists compile the information through patterned interviews with each employee's superior, peers, and sometimes, subordinates. They then prepare an appraisal, usually of the graphic rating scale type, and have it approved by the superior of the respective subordinates. On the surface, at least, this system appears to have considerable merit.

Appraisal within management by objectives.   A concept that is partially an appraisal system, but primarily a new view on how to perform the managerial function of directing, is management by objectives, or results-centered management. It is important enough to warrant a section in the part of this book concerned with the directing function (Section 46). Apropos to the present discussion, however, are its provisions for letting subordinates decide upon goals for their jobs over some future time period, subject to their superior's agreement that the goals are appropriate, and then for having the subordinate and superior together, at the end of the period, assess the degree to which the goals have been reached. Called "the hottest thing in management" when it was introduced, the concept offers some valuable insights into how to manage. It is, however, not without weaknesses, which will be reviewed.

Discussion Questions

1. What advantages would result from a good system of appraising performance in numerical terms?
2. When a manager appraises a subordinate on the basis of some characteristic, such as initiative, what standard could be used for differentiating between "outstanding" and "good"?

3.   What implications, unsatisfactory to both parties, have been associated with the announcement of merit increases at the end of performance appraisal interviews?

4.   It is common in colleges to have students evaluate their instructors. Could this practice be carried over to performance appraisals in business?

5.   A main purpose of performance appraisals is to make decisions concerning who gets promoted when higher job openings occur. An alternative way for deciding promotions is on the basis of seniority. In view of the weaknesses of performance appraisal methods, would you rather have your own promotions based on your years of service?

42. Managing Change of Status

The decision to change the status of an employee is usually based either on merit—or the lack of it—or on seniority. It would be logical to think that if a company has a formal performance appraisal system, the relative merit of individuals could be determined by an analysis of past appraisal records. This writer's hypothesis, however, is that in business organizations such records are not often consulted, and that when changes of employees' status are said to be based on merit they are typically motivated by general impressions created by the subjective judgments of managers. At the same time it is probably true that important change decisions, such as the promotion of a top-level manager, are based on the pooled collective judgments of a group of managers.

Unlike merit, seniority is exceedingly easy to determine, being simply the length of time that an employee has been with the company, in the department, or in a particular job classification.

Promotions

The kinds of status changes that are probably the most crucial to the company are promotions, because of the importance of continually moving up qualified people, as opportunities occur, to jobs of greater importance. Promotions are highly significant to qualified people also, because they symbolize recognition and progress, as well as representing tangible rewards, such as more pay. From the company's viewpoint, the filling of a job opening should always be with the most competent person available. In other words, ideally, all promotions should be based on merit. The problem is that the weaknesses of existing appraisal systems often make the relative merit of alternative candidates for promotion difficult to determine, and managers must strive to make merit decisions with the means that they have available.

Promotions based on seniority convey the implication of stagnation. Length of service, of course, favors older employees and works against younger ones, who often have the drive that a firm needs to move ahead. However, seniority has one thing going for it, which is its objectivity. Whereas merit is a matter of opinion, seniority is incontestable. In an array of candidates for promotion, one will clearly be senior. Additionally, individuals passed over for promotion because someone is senior to them might not be happy about it, but at least they understand the basis. On the other hand, most people are intolerant of the suggestion that someone else *merits* a promotion more than they do.

In view of the fact that managers often have difficulty in supporting merit promotions, very likely more promotions are based on length of service than managers would like to admit.

Demotions

Questions of merit and seniority enter into demotions as well as promotions. When individuals have been assigned to jobs for which they are obviously not qualified, relocation at a lower level in the organization where they can perform satisfactorily is based strictly on lack of merit. Such an action is rarely satisfactory to either the company or the demoted employee. The employee will usually be disgruntled and resentful, and those attitudes will "rub off" on co-workers. Often the best decision is to discharge, rather than demote, an employee who cannot perform a job.

Another possibility for demotions occurs when declining business forces a company to cut back its scale of operations. It would be to the firm's advantage to demote its least qualified people, and to the extent that these merit decisions can be made with confidence, managers make them. However, if merit distinctions are not clear-cut, those individuals with the least seniority will be the ones who are demoted.

Terminations

Termination refers to the action taken by a business firm to rid itself of an employee. The finality of the action may be one of degree, as indicated by the terms *discharge* and *layoff*. An employee who is discharged has either been considered to have violated company rules, or to be incompetent in the performance of a job. The decision to discharge an employee should be faced carefully by the managers involved because of its potentially damaging effects on the individual. In addition, a discharged employee who is a union member may get the union to contest the discharge as unfair; and a discharged non-union employee may take the case to court. Either action may result in a reversal of a discharge decision if the firm cannot objectively support it. The problem is aggravated if the discharged employee has had extended service with the firm; here the management might be at fault for not detecting cause for discharge earlier.

Layoffs are necessitated by the contraction of a firm's business. Often they are considered temporary, with the laid-off employees expecting to be recalled. Union contracts are usually quite explicit regarding how layoffs are to be handled—the majority specifying that seniority shall be the single basis for determining who goes last and returns first. Given its option, management would prefer to base layoff and recall of workers on merit, but even having that option, it will often resort to seniority as a criteria because of the difficulty of making objective merit distinctions.

Lateral Changes

Job transfers are changes in which a person moves laterally in an organization. The transfer may be from one kind of job to another, with equal pay and status, or may be from one location to another in the same job.

A strong reason for transferring individuals from one job to another, particularly managers, is to broaden their experience. Such transfers benefit both the company and the employees, even though the employees may not appreciate the advantages at the time. People have a natural resistance to change, and an unsolicited transfer may be perceived as a threat, particularly if there are no tangible rewards connected with it.

Transfers of employees from one geographical location to another in the same job classification are frequently made for the convenience of the company. When a firm's operations are dispersed, the demand for particular job skills will vary over time from place to place in the total organization, and individuals will be transferred to the points where the current demand exists. Employees, and their spouses, are often extremely resistant to such moves, because they mean uprooting and the severing of ties with friends, schools, and neighborhoods. Companies with operations that require frequent location transfers often stress this as something to be expected and tolerated when interviewing applicants for employment.

Transfers may also be made with the employees' needs as a primary factor. For one thing, persons may have been assigned to jobs for which they are not suited for various reasons, such as too high or too low qualifications, lack of interest, or emotional problems. If these people are judged to have potential value to the firm, efforts will often be made to transfer them to jobs that seem more appropriate. Another reason for transferring people is to eliminate personality clashes—sometimes with other workers, and in other instances with a superior. A third reason is that the employee might request a transfer in order to get a change, either in job duties or in location.

The Case of the
Out-Moded Vice-President

The other officers of Weber Corporation found various ways of distracting their attention from Bob Reith's disjointed harangue at the weekly meeting of the executive committee. Some doodled, one or two looked out the window, several engaged in whispered conversations, and a few simply stared down at the conference table before them. "Before any of you start interrupting me," Reith rambled on, "let me remind you that I was here when the old man was running the show, and I know what he would have said about acquiring a company that is losing money. All this talk about its tax loss carryover and its leverage position doesn't make any sense to me."

As he had done many times in the past, Verne Weber, son of the founder of Weber Construction Company, and president of Weber Corporation, the successor company, patiently let Reith have his say before directing the committee's discussion into productive channels.

Bob Reith had started to work for the senior Mr. Weber when he was eighteen years old. His drive soon became apparent to Weber, and by the time he was in his early twenties he was successfully managing construction projects. The military building boom caused by World War II resulted in a tremendous growth of Weber Construction Company, and Reith's ability to force a project to completion gained him a vice-presidency and the designation of Weber's "right hand man" when he was just thirty. When the war ended and young Verne Weber joined his father's company, he was assigned to work for two years under Reith's tutelage.

Upon his father's death in 1954, Verne Weber succeeded to the presidency of the company. After several years of making certain that the company was firmly established in a growth position in the construction industry, Weber began to consummate his plans for diversifying the company's operations. He had hoped that Reith, who was the only remaining top manager from the old company, would be able to run the construction division part of the new company that he envisioned, but came to the reluctant realization that Reith's ability level was to boss an individual construction project, and that the managing of an international construction organization was completely over his head. Weber's expansion plans were delayed for two years until he finally attracted Tom Hoslett, a highly experienced manager in the largest construction company in the country, to accept the challenge of building Weber's construction division.

In 1960 the company's name was changed to Weber Corporation, and the firm branched out into equipment distributorships, auto leasing, resort hotels, and insurance. Weber was very careful not to enter a new field until he was able to entice the most competent managers that he could find to align their interests with the corporation in heading the diversified operations. As a result, Weber Corporation grew on a foundation of highly qualified top managers. The only exception was Bob Reith, who still held the title of vice-president, and whose role was formally defined as advisor to Mr. Weber. In a practical sense, the scope of the company's operations had gone beyond his ability to contribute anything of value, but he lacked the perception to recognize his inadequacies. His persistent meddling in all of the firm's affairs was a source of increasing resentment to the other senior managers.

Many times during the prosperous 1960's, Verne Weber's thoughts dwelt on the problem of what to do with Reith. He regularly suggested early retirement, but Reith's predictive reply was always, "I'm too healthy to think of retirement yet. And besides, I promised your father that I would always be around to give you a hand when you needed it." Once in 1967 he talked Reith into taking over the managing of the construction of a huge shopping center, thinking that would get him back into the area where he had shown ability as a young man. However, construction technology had passed Reith by, and when Hoslett finally demanded that he be replaced as head of the project, Reith's bungling had caused such delays that the shopping center resulted in the largest loss that the corporation had ever suffered.

Weber's success in putting together an industrial empire earned him the respect of all of the managers he had reporting to him. The only time there was serious disagreement was when they periodically, either individually or collectively, asked him to get rid of Reith. On an objective basis, Weber knew they were right. He realized that he should have discharged Reith years before. Had he done so, the man might have been able to build a new career at a job level compatible with his abilities. Thus, as Weber reasoned, his own weakness had caused the situation to get beyond the point where a discharge was an equitable solution.

One day in 1972, shortly after Reith's emotional stand against the acquisition that all of the other company officers strongly favored, Weber asked the advice of Lane Smith, a management consultant who was doing some work for the company. "Actually, Mr. Weber," said Smith, "many companies have drones in their management ranks. You might even be surprised to learn that some of them are much worse than Mr. Reith. For example, he apparently is neither an alcoholic, a compulsive gambler, or a woman chaser—and that is more than can be said for the problem of personnel of other firms. What trouble is he really causing?"

"Actually, it is just his talking at the meetings," Weber answered. "I can keep him away from the other managers except for those occasions. He has no decisions to make that could cause problems for the company. The dollar cost of his salary and office expense to this company is meaningless. I can put up with his well-meant counsel to me without any personal difficulty. It is just that the other managers can't stand him, and my conscience won't let me fire him."

"How about removing him from the executive committee, and all other committees that he might be on," Smith suggested. "You could think of plausible reasons to explain the action to him, and it would at least be a lot less damaging to him personally than a discharge."

Discussion Questions

1. Discuss a factor other than merit or seniority that may result in some individuals receiving promotions. (See Section 27.)
2. In the Case of the Out-Moded Vice-President, what would be wrong with demoting Bob Reith to the level where he could perform competently?
3. What do you think of the consultant's advice to simply remove Reith from any contact with the other senior managers?
4. If you think the best decision would have been to discharge Reith, when was the most appropriate time to have done it?
5. What effect do you think Verne Weber's reluctance to discharge Reith would have on the attitudes of the senior managers toward Weber himself?

43. Assurance of Justice

The Constitution and the Bill of Rights guarantee justice to all citizens of the United States, yet the members of subsystems, such as business organizations, have not always enjoyed full protection of their rights. One reason for people joining trade unions has been to gain assurance of fair treatment through collective means when it was not obtainable individually. Nonunion employees of business firms, including managers, have also joined forces to exert leverage for the same level of justice in their job environment as promised by the national social system.

Meanings of Justice

Justice is a term that goes back to the Greek philosopher Aristotle, and refers to the fair distribution to individuals of the good and bad things of life according to the way they are deserved. To be precise, this is "distributive" justice, which often needs to be supplemented by "corrective" justice. By means of the latter form, individuals may try for the reversal of errors made in the allocating of benefits or in the levying of punishments.

Distributive Justice

In a business organization, distributive justice is associated with assuring that
- pay raises, promotions, and other tangible benefits are granted without discrimination, except by supportable merit variations or seniority.
- differentiated privileges are decided by equitable standards.
- disciplinary actions are administered impersonally and without bias.

Many of the staffing processes that have been discussed in the preceding sections are either directly or indirectly intended for the purpose of assuring distributive justice. For instance,
- job evaluations are attempts to determine the relative worth of different jobs to the organization and to establish compensation scales proportional to their worth.

- modern selection policies provide that relative ability to perform on a job be the only discriminatory factor in choosing among applicants, and that race, religion, age, or sex are not recognized as legitimate employment factors.
- training programs are generally open to all employees who are interested in improving their skills in areas related to their jobs, or to jobs that they might hope to be promoted to.
- performance appraisals are attempts to objectively place a value on the worth of individuals to the organization, and to differentiate compensation and change of status on the basis of worth, except where seniority is the overriding factor.

Other means for assuring justice are formal rules that specify acceptable conduct and penalties for violations; these are often distributed in booklet form so that all employees may be informed of them. If some of a company's employees are union members, the labor contract will spell out criteria applying to wages, hours, working conditions, and promotion, demotion, layoff, and disciplinary action in an attempt to guarantee fair allocations of rewards and penalties to all union members.

Problems in the Administration of Justice

Trouble arises in a system of distributive justice primarily because of conflicting opinions on what is fair between the people who make decisions and the people who are affected by them. The processes designed to assure distributive justice have the appearance of being objective, whereas they are based on human judgment, which is fallible and inconsistent. Human judgment is such that if only one individual in an organization were administering justice, decisions on a single issue would be inconsistent to some degree, from case to case. This inconsistency will be compounded to the extent that additional individuals make independent decisions on the same issue. Further compounding of inconsistencies results from the multitudes of issues on which decisions are made. Thus, justice is a variable, rather than a constant, in the way it is administered.

At the other end, the recipients of justice have varying perceptions of what is fair and what is discriminatory. Individuals will be inconsistent in their evaluations of fairness on an issue from case to case; and the more people and issues involved, the greater will be the variations in the perceptions of justice that is administered. Therefore, the differences in opinions on what is fair, from both the administering and receiving ends, cannot fail to generate friction.

Consider the single issue of merit increases. Assume that Manager A is a "low grader," and regards as only average what would be superior performance to another manager. Moreover, this manager is strongly influenced in evaluating subordinates by their "loyalty," which means their willingness to work overtime, for which they are compensated. Now assume that Manager B tends to be a "high grader," but places top priority on the qualities of punctuality and regular attendance. In this manager's view, if people are never late or absent from work, overtime will not be necessary, and if it is, it is the fault of the workers and they should not be paid for it.

Some subordinates of Manager A will feel unjustly treated because their merit wage increases are low in comparison with their counterparts in the other department. Others of these subordinates will not perceive inequity, because to them the overtime pay more than makes up for the merit increase discrepancy. Subordinates of Manager B will show similar variations in their opinions of how they are treated. To some, high performance ratings satisfy both their desire for a little more money and their need for recognition. To others, punctuality and attendance will appear as shallow criteria for appraisal, and the refusal to pay for overtime work will be perceived as unjust. (Note that it must be assumed that these employees are outside the coverage of the Fair Labor Standards Act, which provides that in some jobs hours worked in excess of forty per week must be compensated for on the basis of time and a half.)

Corrective Justice

A discussion of corrective justice will have to consider union and nonunion employees separately.

Union employees. Virtually all union contracts specify a formal procedure whereby union employees may file a grievance for alleviation of what they perceive to be unfair treatment. The typical procedure comprises a series of steps that the aggrieved employee and the union representatives may take in the effort to get satisfaction. The steps move the dispute up through the levels of managment, if decisions unsatisfactory to the employee are rendered at the lower levels, until it reaches top management. However, a decision unacceptable to the employee and the union even at this level does not necessarily end the matter, because the ultimate step is submittal of the grievance to arbitration. At this step, an impartial person, or a tripartite board comprised of a union representative, a management representative, and an impartial person acceptable to both union and management, listens to the arguments of both sides, and finally renders a binding decision.

Nonunion employees.   Surveys indicate that about 50 percent of the medium-sized and large companies in the United States have some kind of formal grievance procedure for unorganized employees. These procedures tend to follow the general lines of those specified in union contracts, although it appears that they offer less protection to the aggrieved employee. For one thing, the nonunion worker is not buttressed by a powerful representative. Second, the nonunion grievance procedures restrict the issues that may be presented. Finally, no procedures that have been discovered by this writer provide for arbitration as the ultimate step.

In lieu of formal grievance procedures, most business organizations, at least in theory, provide some means for redress of unfairness. There is the so-called open-door policy, whereby dissatisfied employees may bypass their immediate superior and go to a higher manager to present their case. Many companies provide that serious disciplinary actions must be reviewed by a panel of managers higher in the organization than the one who meted out the punishment. In addition, there appears to be a trend for firms to offer their personnel departments as places to which an employee who perceives injustice may submit a grievance for impartial review and decision.

Discussion Questions

Reference Case A. The Case of the Encroaching Rut (Section 29)
1. Differentiate between justice as the distribution of good things according to the way they are deserved, and justice as the distribution of good things according to the way they are needed.
2. How is distributive justice concerned with the assignment of penalties to individuals?
3. What human characteristic makes us frequently perceive inequities in all systems for distributing rewards and penalties?
4. In Reference Case A, did Sally Inouye receive unjust treatment? What provisions for corrective justice were available to her?
5. Using Reference Case A as a basis, what do you think of the "open-door policy" as a medium for corrective justice?

Summary

In grouping activities that must be performed in an organization, the design of the individual jobs provides the starting point. Today, this staffing function is revealing a growing trend toward enriching jobs with broader and more stimulating activities, whereas in the past it has been assumed that jobs are most efficiently performed if they are comprised of similar, limited tasks. Another trend is toward encouraging people who are to perform the jobs to share in their design, rather than have it come from above in the organization. Job description forms are used to define and record the composition of jobs, while job specification forms identify the requirements that people must have in order to perform them.

The worth of various jobs to the organization varies, and as compensation should be proportional to the worth of jobs, systems for evaluating jobs have been devised. One system consists simply of ranking jobs according to their relative worth; a step beyond that is a system in which certain criteria are applied in the ranking of jobs, such as the skill and experience required for their performance. The point method and the factor comparison method are more comprehensive systems of job evaluation, in which gradations of required elements are calculated for each job.

In establishing financial compensation level for jobs, the attempt is made to relate compensation for a job directly to its evaluated worth. But exceptions will have to be made when compensation for some jobs has, by precedent, been set too high, when union pressures force wages for certain jobs above their apparent worth, and when labor scarcity requires the raising of compensation for some jobs in order to attract skilled workers. Government legislation has acted to force wages up by setting a minimum wage that a company has to pay regardless of the jobs' calculated value to the company.

Indirect compensation (fringe benefits) represents an important cost element to business organizations. Social legislation in the United States has made some indirect compensation mandatory, but other fringe benefits have grown without plan until they are almost out of control. This accumulation of benefits does not seem to yield much in return by way of increased productivity.

Although planning is essential to assure the future availability of human resources, managers often overlook the development of systematic manpower plans. Elements of a manpower plan include an analysis of the jobs performed in the company's operations, the development of a current manpower inventory, and a projection of job openings that must be filled over successive time periods. The manpower plan must then be integrated with the firm's other major plans in order to assess the feasibility of its objectives.

An organization cannot rely on qualified applicants gravitating to it when job openings occur; it must deliberately seek them out. Sources of applicants, which vary with the type of jobs to be filled, include employment agencies, educational institutions, advertising media, unions, professional societies, and industry contacts.

Applicants who have been recruited by various means must undergo increasingly discriminating screening processes until a confident selection decision can be made. In each case, qualifications will be judged by the information the applicant provides on an application form, by comprehensive interviews, and by reference checks. Much reliance is placed on interviewing as a screening device, without the realization that efficient interviewing is an acquired skill, and that untrained interviewers can make significant selection mistakes.

Psychological tests provide a supplementary way of screening applicants. The assumption underlying their use is that future job performance can be predicted by test scores; and the validity of tests is measured by the accuracy of their predictions. Another important criterion of the tests is their reliability, or the consistency with which identical characteristics in various people will be scored the same. There are sharply conflicting views on the significance of tests, with the neutral opinion being that they are useful in reinforcing selection decisions formed by other screening techniques.

Since new employees cannot be assumed to possess all the skills needed for successful performance on the job, and present employees should have their skills upgraded to improve their value to the company and their own self-image, business organizations must institute and maintain skill training programs. Crucial elements of these programs are, first, to know what results are to be expected from training, and second, to assure that trainees are motivated to learn.

Management development cannot be accomplished in training programs because managerial ability cannot be taught. Individuals can become managers only through managerial experiences of increasing breadth and responsibility, and this development can be supplemented successfully by formal studies in managment theory. Opportunities for experience must be planned, and should include rotation to different managerial assignments, involvement in increasingly complex decision making, participation in policy making, and exposure to interactions outside the firm.

It has always been necessary to appraise the performance of subordinates, and over the last fifty years or so, systems have developed whereby this process can presumably be done objectively. These include the graphic rating scale method, in which characteristics of an individual's performance are evaluated separately and a total score reached; the rank order method, in which employees in the same job classification are assigned a rank according to their relative demonstration of various characteristics under consideration; the critical incident method, in which assessment is based on the appraiser's extreme impressions of an individual's performances, both good and bad, over some past period; and the forced choice method, in which scored evaluations are based on the appraiser's checking of descriptive statements most appropriate and most inappropriate for a given employee. With any of these appraisal methods, the culmination is usually an interview in which the subordinate is informed of both good points and shortcomings, and often of a merit salary increase. Some new developments in appraisal techniques include peer ratings, appraisal by specialists, and appraisal associated with management by objectives.

The status of individuals rarely remains the same. Some people warrant promotion and others, demotion. Discharge and layoff decisions often must be made. Management would like to have such changes governed by merit, but lack of objective merit standards very frequently requires that seniority be the basis for decision. In addition, lateral movements, or transfers of employees, must be accomplished. The basis for these changes is usually either company convenience or the good of the employee.

In these times, employees are intolerant of perceived unjust treatment. They want the rewards to which they feel entitled, and they resist being punished undeservedly. All business firms have some systems for distributing benefits and assuring penalties. However, fairness is perceived differently by different people, so systems must be set up for correcting mistakes made in administering justice. Union employees have the advantage of a formal grievance procedure for this purpose, while it must be admitted that nonunion workers appear generally to be more on their own in seeking redress of perceived inequities.

Selected Bibliography

Belcher, David W., *Wage and Salary Administration*. Prentice-Hall, 1962.

Bower, M., *The Will to Manage*. McGraw-Hill, 1966.

Buffa, Elwood S., *Modern Production Management*. Wiley, 1969.

Chapple, Eliot D., and Leonard R. Sayles, *The Measure of Management*. Macmillan, 1961.

French, Wendell, *The Personnel Management Process*. Houghton Mifflin, 1964.

Gellerman, Saul W., "Personnel Testing: What the Critics Overlook." *Personnel,* Vol. 40, May–June 1963.

Gross, Martin L., "Personality Tests—Science or Cult." *Personnel,* Vol. 40, March–April 1963.

Haire, Mason, "Managing Management Manpower." *Business Horizons,* Vol. 10, No. 4, Winter 1967.

Herzberg, Frederick, Bernard Mausner, and Barbara Snyderman, *The Motivation to Work*. Wiley, 1959.

McCormick, Ernest J., *Human Factors Engineering*. McGraw-Hill, 1964.

Patton, John A., C. L. Littlefield, and Stanley Allen Self, *Job Evaluation*. Irwin, 1964.

Spriegel, William R., and Virgil A. James, "Trends in Recruitment and Selection Practices." *Personnel,* Vol. 35, November–December 1958.

Tiffin, Joseph, and Ernest J. McCormick, *Industrial Psychology*. Prentice-Hall, 1965.

Whisler, Thomas L., and Shirley F. Harper, *Performance Appraisal Research and Practice*. Holt, 1962.

DIRECTING

Through the functions of planning, organizing, and staffing, discussed in preceding parts of this book, a management system will be brought into a state of readiness. The various processes can be compared with the stages of getting an engine to the idling stage, ready to be put into gear. Designing the engine, and determining its objectives (in terms of horsepower, torque, and displacement) and the means of achieving them, compares with the managerial function of planning. Developing the relationships between the engine components, such as gears, levers, and pistons, compares with organizing. Creating the hardware and putting each engine component in its proper place compares with the staffing function. And, finally, putting the idling engine into gear and keeping it going can be compared with the directing function. With a management system, the activation comes from managers directing the efforts of subordinates in the performance of their work tasks.

As mentioned earlier in this book, management theorists have long sought to systematize their ideas into a body of principles that could be learned and followed with predictable results. To a large extent, the planning function has proven adaptable to such regulation. Many aspects of controlling, also, can be systematized, as shown in later sections of this book. The staffing function, too, is relatively straightforward, there being a discrete sequence of activities to be performed in building manpower resources. But the variability of human behavior, which causes so much inexactness and unpredictability in the organizing function, is present to an even greater degree in the directing function. There are within each manager and subordinate unknown personal characteristics that have a powerful influence on the effectiveness of direction.

A study of the directing function, then, is really a study of human behavior and the factors that motivate it—the behavior of leaders and the behavior of followers. Thus, it is undestandable that what now exists as a foundation for understanding the directing function should have come from the research of the behavioral scientists. The following discussions present the directing function's essential features.

44. Leadership

There have been numerous attempts to isolate leadership as a variable so that it can be understood and predictions can be made about it. One early attempt was that of Max Weber, whose contributions were discussed in Section 1. In essence, Weber's theory was that a very· small number of people are born with a phenomenal leadership trait called "charisma."

Charismatic Leadership

Historically, charisma has been associated with persons, such as profoundly influential religious leaders, legendary military commanders, and certain outstanding statesmen, who have inspired their followers to embrace lofty ideals or accomplish heroic feats. Followers of charismatic leaders often appear blindly devoted to them, as though they were superhuman. Frequently the charismatic leader tends to be a revolutionist who opposes some established order.

Natural Leaders

In the strictest sense of the term, a charismatic business manager is very unlikely. However, who has not heard some fairly ordinary individual described as a "natural leader"? The description implies that leadership is a trait with which some people are born. If that is true, it does not necessarily follow that the trait is manifested in every situation. Some individuals who are identified as leaders in one environment, such as a lodge or church, may be identified as followers in another environment, such as their work situation.

Trait Theory of Leadership

Until recently, the view was widely held that leadership could be predicted according to an individual's possession of certain traits, and on this premise lists of so-called leadership traits were compiled. Two approaches were used in developing the lists. One was to try to determine by deduction what traits leaders *should* possess. The other was to study leaders to learn by induction what traits leaders *do* possess. But both approaches were inconclusive; variations in kinds and degrees of traits possessed by leaders proved so great as to make the theory of traits meaningless, and it has since been largely abandoned. The only single factor that all leaders have in common is a group of followers.

Influence on Subordinates

From a functional point of view, leadership is effective if subordinates can be influenced to
* choose the leader's interpretations of organizational objectives over opposing views.
* follow the leader's prescriptions for achieving those objectives.
* perceive that their personal goals can best be gained by consenting to the leader's authority.

Acceptance of objectives.   Subordinates must be convinced of the legitimacy of the manager's perception of objectives. Several elements are necessary.
* Subordinates must not feel that they are being manipulated to support the manager's personal interests.
* The manager must be open-minded toward subordinates' views and willing to modify concepts for the sake of improvement.
* The manager must be consistent and rational in approaching objectives.
* The manager's interpretation of objectives must be socially acceptable and desirable.

Acceptance of prescribed methods.   Subordinates' acceptance of prescribed methods for gaining objectives can range from marginal to unquestioning—depending on their degree of confidence in the manager's technical ability or judgment, and their view of the manager as a person inspiring confidence and respect. The greater the subordinates' confidence in the manager's technical competence and integrity, the more effective the leadership.

Perception of the manager as influential.   The manager perceived by subordinates as influential in helping them achieve their personal goals is an effective leader. This can be accomplished in a negative way. All managers have some power to fire employees, or withhold privileges and rewards. But the amount of leadership influence that can be obtained this way is probably minimal. A real generator of fervent followers, on the other hand, is a manager's positive power to reward. A main difference between ineffective and superior leaders is their degree of influence on the organization's reward system.

Leadership As an Acquired Ability

It would appear that having a properly balanced ability to influence subordinates in each of the three ways described above would mark a manager as an effective leader. It is easy to see that a lack in any one area would mean weakene 1 leadership; however, it does not seem that a person must be born with this ability to influence others in order to be a leader. Perhaps charismatic or natural leaders have an indefinable force in attracting followers, but there is no reason to suppose that a manager cannot develop leadership effectiveness in the areas mentioned.

Section 45 focuses on the subject of leadership styles, which has to do with the ways that different types of managerial behavior affect subordinates' performance and satisfaction.

Assumptions About Human Nature

The leadership practices of managers are powerfully influenced by the assumptions they have about human nature—and every manager has such assumptions, whether aware of them or not. Douglas McGregor proposed two sets of such assumptions (recall Section 6). The conventional management view, which he called Theory X, is that workers must be motivated and controlled through direct pressure from management, because they are lazy, lack ambition, dislike responsibility, prefer to be told what to do, and are passively resistant to achieving organizational goals. Money is the only way to motivate them. In the next section, you will see the probable connection between this view of subordinates and the authoritarian or production-centered leadership style.

The other set of management assumptions about workers' motivation, McGregor called Theory Y. If given the opportunity, people will be self-motivated to achieve organizational goals through striving for personal growth and development. Their natural traits are the opposite of those assumed by Theory X. The theory further holds that if people *appear* to be behaving according to Theory X, it is because the organization has forced them to do so. By this view, the task of the manager is to arrange matters so that people can satisfy their higher-order needs for self-actualization and achievement (see Sections 48 and 49) in the process of accomplishing organizational goals. You will see the probable connection between the assumptions of Theory Y and the democratic or employee-centered leadership style in the next section.

The Case of the
Loyalty-Loving Ex-Colonel

The sixty-year-old Taggart Construction Company had reached the point in 1970 where it was doing about $25 million in construction business annually. The firm was headed by Alex Taggart, grandson of the founder. Except for approximately 5 percent of the common stock that was dispersed among employees, the company was owned by members of the Taggart family.

Alex Taggart decided in 1970 that he was trying personally to watch over too many of the company's activities. The construction jobs on which the firm regularly submitted bids often were as high as $7 million, and because of the magnitude of the stakes Taggart wanted to spend most of his time reviewing and approving estimates and checking the progress of the major projects. He felt that if he could group the purchasing, personnel, safety, and equipment maintenance functions in a department to be called Administration, he could direct his own attention more to the activities that he considered central to the firm's operations. Purchasing was headed by Ted Reeves, fifteen years with the company, who supervised two buyers, a chief storeskeeper, and a secretary. A ten-year man, Sid Cohen, handled the personnel activities with the help of a secretary. The safety engineer, Frank Tanada, had been with Taggart eight years, and had an assistant and a secretary. John Petersen, also with eight years' seniority, supervised five foremen, and had a total equipment maintenance organization of about forty people.

Among the applicants for the newly created job of manager of administration was Lt. Col. Bob Laird, who was retiring from the Air Force. Laird served his last tour of duty at the local air base, and as Taggart knew many of the senior officers, he was able to get some first-hand information about this promising candidate. The officers under whom Laird had served spoke extremely well of his administrative experience and ability, and each singled out loyalty as one of his outstanding traits.

In due course Laird retired, and he immediately started to work for Taggart Construction Company. On the first day Laird said to Taggart: "The people who will be working under me seem to be loyal, and with that quality, plus their good experience, we're going to have a great team."

It was in early 1972 that Taggart called Bob Laird into his office to have a serious talk: "I have been putting off saying this to you for a long time," he began, "but it is obvious that something is wrong between you and the men directly reporting to you. One place I sense it is when we have meetings. Before you came, Ted, Sid, Frank, and John always had worthwhile contributions to make to agenda items in their particular areas. Now they don't say anything, but merely look down at the table. This happens even when I specifically ask for their opinions of some of your proposals. When I try to talk to them in the hall, or in the coffee room, or out on the construction sites, it's the same thing. They either find an excuse to move away, or change the subject to some trivial topic. The climax came this morning when Frank Tanada asked to be allowed to go back to his old job of running a survey gang, which he was promoted out of five years ago. Can you tell me what the trouble is?"

"Mr. Taggart, I have made one mistake since I have been here," Laird heatedly replied, "and that was in assuming that these men would be loyal. They don't know the meaning of loyalty, and that is one thing that I cannot stand."

"Well, I owe it to them to hear their side of the story. With your consent, I am going to have a talk with them as a group," said Taggart.

"Ted, and Sid, and Frank and John, we've known each other for a long time. I used to think that we knew each other pretty well. Lately you have put up a barrier between us, and you seem very unhappy. I suspect that has something to do with Mr. Laird, and although I have never before asked people to talk about their superior, this time I am breaking my own rule. What is the matter?" was the way Taggart opened the talk that afternoon.

There was nothing but silence. Taggart finally broke it by saying: "Ted, you have been with this company for almost as long as I have. Can't you help me figure this thing out?"

Ted looked away, and then said: "Mr. Laird is one of the hardest working men I have ever known. In addition, he always tries to help the people working under him—like getting me authorized to have a company car."

"That's right," John spoke up, "he has been helping my son with algebra for the past six months."

Taggart thought for a moment before he commented: "One thing that I have observed about Mr. Laird is that he makes up his mind on things pretty quickly."

The others looked sharply at each other. Sid then made the opening remark: "I guess that's it in a nutshell, Mr. Taggart. He makes his decisions off the top of his head. Then, once he has made them, he is absolutely convinced they are right."

"I go along with that," Frank put in. "I'm scared every time an issue comes up that has to be decided. He doesn't even start to think something through before he has an answer. Then he gets mad at me if I suggest that we should consider some alternative."

"An example that comes to my mind," John supported, "is when I suggested that we start thinking about a winter repair program. He immediately decided that we should schedule a major overhaul for every piece of equipment with over 2000 hours on it. When I mentioned that this would include equipment we plan to sell in the spring, he said that this would help us get more money for it. He then refused to look at figures showing that we only recoup about half of an overhaul cost even when we trade in equipment on a new purchase."

"I have no confidence in his decisions," Ted reluctantly said. "He is smart enough, and he has plenty of experience. But when he decides something as capriciously as he did the other day, I lose respect for him. We were trying to objectively decide between three makes of tractors. He was sitting in the meeting, and became more and more impatient as we compared specifications, past equipment records, dealer spare parts inventories, and so forth. He finally broke up the analysis by saying he thought we should have an equal number of each make of tractor in our fleet, and therefore we should buy tractors of the make that we have fewest of."

The following morning Taggart entered Laird's office and sat down. "Bob," he said, "this is a question that I should have asked you two years ago. What is your definition of a loyal subordinate?"

"One who doesn't debate and question every single thing that his superior decides," Bob Laird replied.

Discussion Questions

1. What is a drawback of the "natural leader" concept?
2. Why study leadership from the standpoint of the evaluations of subordinates?
3. In the Case of the Loyalty-Loving Ex-Colonel, was anything unacceptable to Laird's subordinates in the way he interpreted organizational objectives?
4. What qualities did Laird have that could almost have made him a leader? What factors were present in the situation that could have helped make him a leader?
5. What quality essential for leadership did Laird lack?

45. Leadership Styles

Descriptive terms which imply extremes in leader behavior provide a useful conceptual base for explaining leadership. For a number of years, management writers have employed *authoritarian* or its synonyms to describe one kind of leadership, and *democratic* for the opposite kind. Similar opposites were implied by the terms *production-centered management* and *employee-centered management*.

Meaning of the Descriptive Terms

All of the above terms aid in putting in perspective alternative styles which managers may elect in dealing with subordinates.

Authoritarian. The authoritarian manager relies heavily on the formal authority vested in the managerial position. Toward subordinates, the manager's role is that of an order giver and performance monitor. A lack of confidence in their judgment is implied by the manager's habit of making all important decisions.

Most individuals who rise to managerial positions probably have a natural tendency to authoritarianism, because they have dominant, self-assertive personalities. The impressions such people usually receive from parental influence, school experience, and early employment often condition them to view authority as unilateral. Moreover, the reward system in most organizations influences managers to be authoritarian. Raises, bonuses, and promotions are given to managers who meet or exceed quantitative standards.

Realistically, however, it is unlikely that pure authoritarianism can exist in a modern organization. First of all, managers simply do not have enough absolute authority to behave as dictators. (Possible exceptions are owner-managers of small businesses.) Second, unless the firm is very small, the limitations of the managers' span of control forces them to delegate some decision making, whether they want to or not. And third, the educational level and other job opportunities available to most people make them intolerant of purely authoritarian leadership.

Democratic. The democratic manager relies on the consensus of subordinates rather than on unilateral authority. Here, the manager's role tends to be that of a moderator in group discussions, where subordinates and manager alike deliberate over issues requiring decisions; or the managerial role is sometimes that of a coach counseling subordinates as individuals. Delegating decison making as far down in the system as possible, this manager exercises loose supervision over the performance of subordinates, giving them the opportunity to learn by making mistakes.

Production-centered.   The production-centered manager focuses attention on quantitative standards. This individual's zest in life is in meeting schedules, working within budgets, and exceeding quotas. Subordinates are merely cogs in the system, to be used in accomplishing a purpose; their individual needs or concerns are irrelevant.

Employee-centered.   The employee-centered manager is deeply concerned about subordinates' welfare and is willing to listen to their troubles and try to learn their individual needs. This manager affords each subordinate the opportunity to grow to maximum capacity, and demonstrates through positive actions that their best interests are being consistently represented.

Usefulness of the Models

The foregoing descriptions are useful as models for analyzing styles of leader behavior. However, one danger in applying them is to infer that the types are mutually exclusive—that a person is supposed to be all one type or all another, and never a combination. In addition, there has been a tendency for some management writers to prescribe democratic leadership and employee-centered management as ideals to which managers should aspire in all situations.

Achieving a Balance

As a generalization, managers may achieve better results in the long run by inclining in the direction of democratic rather than autocratic leadership. The outstanding advantage of democracy in industry is that it affords people an opportunity to grow to their full potential, which in an organization should be viewed as important to the extent that it benefits the organization. Thoughtful managers recognize that the chances of meeting standards are improved if all members of the organization are working toward the same goals, and that cooperation can best be achieved if subordinates can be made to see that they stand to gain personally if the goals are met.

On the other hand, since managers are rewarded for achieving or exceeding production standards, they are likely to be production-centered. And some individuals can accomplish significant managerial feats when they practice authoritarian leadership, but are relatively ineffective when they try the democratic style, because their personalities are better suited to the former. Furthermore, some subordinates prefer to work for a strong boss, and become upset if they are asked to become intensively involved in decision making. Subordinates' preferences usually depend on the nature of their job. An R & D scientist probably works best under democratic leadership, but it is likely that an assembler doing repetitive work on a production line wants clear-cut direction.

Time, circumstances, and the manager's expertise relative to that of subordinates are also factors. If a decision must be made quickly, perhaps in response to competitive pressures, and only the manager has the necessary knowledge to make the decision, then democratic leadership is obviously not appropriate. But if the market demands made on the firm are changing and unpredictable, and the technology involved (say, electronics) is complex, then managers who do not tap the knowledge and skill of subordinates are doing themselves and their firm a disservice.

The successful manager will seek to understand what it takes to motivate each subordinate individually toward maximum productivity, and will adopt a style that is a balance of democratic/autocratic and production-centered/employee-centered. The real criterion of leadership is which style gets the desired results.

The Case of the
Leopard That Couldn't Change Its Spots

Al Kirschman became interested in rocketry and rocket design while he was in high school, and when he began his engineering education it was with the intention of entering the then budding aerospace industry. After receiving his engineering degree, he spent two important years with a small developmental laboratory, and then five years in the aerospace division of a large aircraft company. By the time he joined Consolidated Technology he had established a reputation as a successful manager of rocket engineers, rather than as an engineer himself, and despite his youth had an impressive record of projects that he had managed.

Al drove himself relentlessly to get a goal accomplished, and expected the same kind of discipline from the people working under him. When a project was in trouble, an 80-hour work week was normal with him. In fact, he often made the comment: "If I weren't married, I would put a cot in my office and spend my entire time on the job." Just as he demanded perfection from himself, so also did he demand it from his subordinates, and as he suspected that most persons' performance standards did not measure up to his, he ran his organization with an iron hand.

He held many meetings, but they were of an interrogation type, rather than group discussion. He was indifferent to people's feelings, and, in a room filled with people, would sarcastically probe into a subordinate's defense until it was plain to everyone that a blunder or oversight had been committed. It couldn't be said that Al was very well liked personally, but he was respected because he was almost always right in the final outcome. His superiors and the Air Force representatives thought he was great, because his project was one of the few aerospace missions that was successful by any criterion.

Al had been with Consolidated Technology for about two years, and the project he headed was about half completed, when the company employed Dr. Hugh Stetson to set up and administer a management development program. Dr. Stetson's approach to management development was through sensitivity training. He would form groups of peers within an organization, take the group to an isolated retreat away from the day-to-day operations, ply the novitiates with con-

temporary literature on human relations, and then through informal group processes enable each member to become aware of his own behavior as other people perceived it. He would then individually counsel the managers who had gone through the experience on correcting their managerial shortcomings, as measured by human relations norms.

Al Kirschman was a member of the first group to experience Dr. Stetson's therapy, and he had a rude awakening. Most of the other members had at one time or another been temporarily assigned to Al's project, and in that sense had been subordinate to him. In the group discussions Al's way of managing was identified as the worst possible managerial behavior. He became the butt of jokes, many of which were not meant to be too funny, with the result that the exposure to what other people thought of him made quite an impact. He was most receptive to Dr. Stetson's offer of counsel.

"Al, your problem is that you are 'thing' oriented, rather than 'people' oriented," Dr. Stetson began. "To you, people are just tools that you use to get things done. Your attitude is that people won't produce unless they are driven, which is not true. You would be surprised to find out how much can be accomplished by getting your subordinates to work with you, rather than for you. Let them bring out their ideas, not just obediently follow yours. You plainly saw in the group discussions how those people resented the way you have made fools out of them. That's not the way to manage. Why don't you try complimenting them instead of tearing them down? You will find that your projects' performance will be greatly improved."

Al was a confused young man. For the past seven years he had received raises, promotions, and bonuses because of the accomplishments of the projects he had managed. Now it had been forcefully brought to his attention that everything he did as a manager was wrong. He was intelligent enough to know that he was not perfect, and to accept the possibility that a way of managing different from his might be better. He decided to find out.

"Fellows," Al began at the next meeting that he held, "I hate to say this, because I know how hard you have all been working, but the Air Force wants much better performance out of the pump. You are all the best in your respective fields, and I invite you to state what you think is wrong, and what you would do to correct it."

For a while the group sat in shocked silence. They were so used to being told what to do that they didn't know how to respond. Finally some thoughts began to be expressed, and as Al didn't rip them apart, the discussion picked up momentum. Al inwardly fumed, as he thought they were only scratching the surface of the problem, but he let the discussion run its course. When all of the ideas seemed to be exhausted he said: "I have confidence that you can work this out by yourselves, so see what you can do. And another thing, I am going to stop calling Saturday and Sunday meetings. I know that a lot of you would like to spend the weekends with your families, and if you think you can spend the time away from your jobs, that's up to you."

Al continued like this for about three months. His cigarette consumption went from two packs a day to four as the project's progress reports got progressively worse. There were no signs of a correction of the pump problem, and Al observed that each weekend there were fewer pump engineers working. Inevitably, Al was called to the office of his own boss, Ray Wilt.

"What is going on out there?" Wilt demanded. "All of a sudden I have another sick project on my hands, and it is last one I would have expected."

Al explained how he was trying to change his managerial style to conform to what Dr. Stetson said was right. He said that he was so frustrated that he was thinking of leaving management and going back to research work.

"Al, what Stetson says might suit some people, but it won't work for you, and it wouldn't work for me," said Wilt. "I want job results, not well-balanced people. Now you get out there and run that project like you used to."

Al called a meeting that afternoon. "Heath," he said, "How do you solve an engineering problem?"

"Why, I do an analytical overhaul."

"Are you sure that you know what an analytical overhaul is?" asked Al.

"Of course I do," heatedly replied Jack Heath. "It is tearing a system

down, part by part, examining for actual or potential malperformance, making the necessary corrections, then rebuilding the system."

"Have you done that with the pump?" said Al.

"Absolutely," said Heath.

"Is the hydraulic seal part of the pump?" Al probed.

"You know it is," Heath said, as he became more angry.

"What did you find with the seal?" Al continued.

"It was worn, and we replaced it," Heath spit out.

"Why was it worn?" Al asked.

"I don't know," Heath almost yelled. "Maybe because it isn't the right material."

"Maybe," Al sneered. "Don't you think that an expert like you should find out?"

The meeting went on like this until two o'clock the next morning, with each member receiving his share of Al's seething interrogation. When it finally broke up, one member remarked to Jack Heath: "Well, it looks like the vacation is over, doesn't it?"

"I know damn well it is for me," said Heath grimly.

Discussion Questions

1. In what way does the limitation of a manager's span of control necessitate some delegation, or departure from pure authoritarian management? (See Section 20.)
2. What is missing in most reward systems that might motivate managers to try harder to cast off authoritarian tendencies?
3. Would you have liked to work under Al Kirschman?
4. What was wrong with Al's attempt at democratic leadership? Could he have made it work? What other style might he try?
5. If you were in the position of Ray Wilt, and saw the efficiency of Al's project drop off suddenly, would you have done as Wilt did? If not, what would you have done?

46. Management by Objectives

A management technique which combines a variation of the democratic style of leadership and a different approach to performance appraisal is called *management by objectives* (MBO). Its significant feature is the setting of short-term performance goals for subordinates by subordinates themselves, subject to the supervisor's approval. In other words, each subordinate defines what assignments he is willing to be held responsible for over some future time period, along with standards for measuring them. The goals are derived from the subordinate's understanding of what his responsibilities are and what his organization must accomplish in the immediate future.

When the subordinate has defined his goals and standards for measurement, he and his supervisor review them together. Ideally, in this review the supervisor does no more than offer such counsel as seems to be needed. When the time period for accomplishing the goals has expired, the subordinate and the supervisor together review the plans and their degree of achievement. The supervisor at this review may advise the subordinate as to how mistakes, if any, could have been avoided. The next step is for the subordinate to formulate goals and measurement standards for the subsequent period.

The manager in this situation is taken out of the role of order giver, and cast as a counselor or coach. And for judging performances, there are objective standards which have been agreed to as equitable by both parties. In this way the personality characteristics of the subordinates will not weigh so heavily in the performance assessment.

In organizations using MBO, the managers will have a double role. Not only must they consider what objectives of their own to nominate to their superiors, but in addition they must bring into meaningful focus what they expect subordinates to accomplish. Management by objectives does not mean management without order. The objectives put forward by subordinates must be integrated by the manager of each department so that they are consistent with organizational goals.

Advantages of MBO

A desirable by-product of management by objectives is that it forces conscious attention to the overall goals of the organization. When identified, these goals must be communicated to the participating subordinates.

Another advantage of management by objectives is that the subordinate, in effect, is self-directed. Because of being "put on his own," the subordinate will often set more difficult targets and more stringent standards of measurement than might be tolerated if they were established by management. It is reasonable to think that many individuals might choose tough goals in areas where they are relatively weak, in order to further their personal development. The kind of people who would do this are the ones who really want to get ahead, and who are perceptive enough to recognize weaknesses that they have that might hold them back.

Preparation for MBO

The installation of an MBO program must be carefully planned if it is going to succeed. One requirement is that it should be introduced gradually, and then only in departments where the managers are open-minded about it. A feasible way of getting it started is to initiate it at the top level of the organization, with senior managers who report to the chief executive. If they get accustomed to more freedom in guiding their destinies, and like it, they are apt to be enthusiastic about introducing it at lower managerial levels. Another way of beginning an MBO program is to ask for a manager of some department to volunteer to try it on an experimental basis. In this way, experiences in using it can be recorded, and the performance results of the experimental department can be compared with those of similar departments abiding by conventional direction methods.

If experiments indicate that the company may be ready for management by objectives, widespread adoption of the program should be announced well in advance of the time it is to be formally started. Every person involved should understand it and have opportunities to discuss it with others. In addition, they should be encouraged to think seriously about what they consider to be the contributions of their job.

Results of MBO

Some organizations in the United States have been using MBO since about 1958. Reports in management literature about it are conflicting. Some writers have considered it the "hottest thing in management," and there have been statements to the effect that "no modern company should be without it." Not only have business firms adopted it, but the approach is also employed by government and military organizations.

On the other hand, some companies that have tried MBO have registered disquieting complaints. One complaint is that subordinates accomplish the objectives that they commit themselves to, but that they often fail to include other desirable, and often essential, objectives. Another problem is that subordinates are inclined to pursue objectives after changes have occurred to make them irrelevant. Still another problem is that the whole concept is often looked at as a game, with managers using it as a speedup tactic, and with subordinates perceiving how it can be played in order to win.

The problem of setting objectives of comparable weight seems to plague managers; for instance, one subordinate may set objectives that can be accomplished without difficulty, while another establishes almost impossible goals. A final problem is that the concept may not be appropriate for supporting departments, where subordinates often simply cannot establish discrete, measurable objectives that can be accomplished in a specified time period. The concept appears to be more appropriate for central departments, such as engineering, production, and sales, where quantitative standards can be set.

Tool for Appraisal

Obviously, if MBO is used as intended and kept under control, and if the objectives nominated by subordinates are inclusive, consistent, and subject to measurement, it will offer a powerful tool for appraising performance. And, apparently, many companies are finding it so. It certainly has the potential of being more valuable for performance appraisal than some of the routine and more common devices, such as graphic rating scales (Section 41). However, it is weak as a general-purpose performance appraisal method because of the difficulty of comparing objectives, and the degrees of their accomplishment, between subordinates. With objectives which vary in nature and difficulty, how can this approach point with accuracy to the subordinates who should receive raises or promotions in preference to other subordinates?

In conclusion, MBO has considerable potential power as a motivator, but it must be applied with thoughtful skill and honesty if it is to be effective as a direction device.

*Joe Parsons was manager of the mechanical design section in the
engineering department of Medco, Inc., a prominent manufacturer
of hospital equipment. One evening toward the end of 1972 he was
trying to compile a ranking of the engineers who reported to him in
connection with the company's policy of awarding annual bonuses to
the top 50 percent of the salaried employees in all departments, and
found to his surprise that the newly instituted management by objectives program had not made the task any easier. He was completely convinced that the performance of at least eight of the twelve
engineers in his section had improved since he had volunteered to
try "managing by objectives," but now he was bogged down in trying
to rank their contributions according to their value to the company.
As a separate problem, he was going to have to decide what to do
with the four engineers who had felt threatened by being put relatively on their own, and whose performance had actually declined.*

*Until 1971, Parsons' method of directing subordinates had been
along the traditional lines of a boss giving specific and limited assignments to the people working under him. He set the goals that he
expected to have accomplished, and the standards by which he would
measure accomplishment. He kept a record for each of his engineers,
on which he would note examples of good performance, and instances
where the subordinate's performance exhibited shortcomings. At the
end of each year he would meet privately with each of his people,
and appraise them of how well they had done in his eyes. Then he
would announce any raise or bonus that was forthcoming.*

*Parsons had been reading independently about management by ob-
jectives, and so was familiar with the concept when the president of
Medco called a meeting of all management personnel in May 1970
for the purpose of hearing a talk on the subject by a professor from
State University. At the end of the meeting, the president announced
that he would like to try the new management approach on an experimental basis, and asked for some volunteer managers, who would
first attend a six weeks' conference conducted by the professor. Joe
Parsons was one of the volunteers.*

Parsons introduced management by objectives to the people in his section in a way similar to that used previously by the president of the company. He had the professor give his talk, then explained that he had volunteered to try the program. He said that no one was forced to participate in the program, but for those who wanted to, the main objectives of the section that should be kept in mind were improvement in product quality and reduction in cost. A list of the assignments made to the section by the engineering department manager would be posted on the bulletin board. The participants were to choose the ones that they would like to work on, then prepare a plan as to how they would proceed, and develop a time-phase milepost schedule whereby their progress could be measured. They were invited to suggest any relaxation of restrictions in their job description that might be inhibiting. After these preparations each would be asked to discuss their plans with him, and with his approval could set about accomplishing the objectives that they had established for themselves. Review of their progress with him would be on the dates specified in their own plans.

Response to management by objectives was generally enthusiastic. Dave Young, whom Parsons rated as one of his top men, was the first to present his plan. "I think that we have all fallen into the habit of specifying unnecessary frills in our designs," Dave said. "For example, every knob on every one of our products is machine knurled. Knurling is an expensive process, and really adds nothing to the quality of our product. Another waste is our customary specification of seamless tubing. In think that with tests I can prove that welded tubing will do just as good a job, and it costs a lot less. We have machined parts that could just as well be die castings, with a substantial savings. I propose that my objective will be to effect an annual savings of $50,000 per year through design changes that will not deteriorate the quality of the product in any way. I will accomplish this in three months. I would like permission to contact vendors, because I would like to get price estimates on some of the ideas that I have."

Your plan sounds fine, Dave," said Parsons. "Go ahead with it. However, I am afraid that we would start a war with purchasing if you began going to the vendors direct. You had better continue requisitioning estimates from them. What you might do, though, is get one of the buyers interested in working with you."

Tom Wells was waiting to see Parsons as Young left the office.

"What I would like to do is take a crack at perfecting the German patents that we bought on the cine-radiography unit," Tom said. "The unit is not quite right now, but I have been talking with a radiologist who has given me some ideas that I know can be developed. It will take a while to get the design ready for production, but I think that I can show you enough progress in three months to convince you that Medco will have the most accepted cine-radiography unit on the market."

"I was hoping that you would want to tackle this," said Parsons enthusiastically. "Let me suggest that you turn over everything that you develop to our patent attorney, Bob Allen, as soon as you finish it. That way he can get patent applications started immediately."

Over the next two weeks, all of Parsons' engineers discussed their objectives with him. Some plans sounded as promising as Young's and Wells', others had good possibilities, but a few were unimaginative. Parsons tried to stimulate the proposers of the latter plans, but it was apparent that what they really wanted was for him to tell them what to do. He decided to force these people to be on their own awhile; then if that didn't work he would try something else.

Dave Young asked Parsons for a review of his accomplishments ten days before his three months had expired. He was almost bursting with pride as he announced: "$50,000 savings in a year was just a drop in the bucket. I got Dick Hardesty in purchasing and Sam Buck in production to work with me as a team. We also got a salesman to evaluate what effect any changes that might be made would have on the product acceptability. Here is a report showing the details of every change that we propose. The conservative estimate of the annual savings is $117,000."

Before Tom Wells reported on his progress, Joe Parsons received a call from Medco's sales manager, Allen Pruitt. Pruitt said: "I have taken the ideas that your engineer, Wells, has on the cine-radiography unit to the administrator of the Hillsboro Hospital, and he wants to buy the first one that we make." Parsons told Tom about this the next day when Tom came in to see him.

"That's great," Tom said. "And the patent attorney has filed four separate patent applications on my new designs which he says, with the German patents, will give us complete protection."

Parsons reviewed these incidents in his mind on the evening that he had allocated to ranking his subordinates. Under the company's reward system, which Parsons frankly didn't particularly like, first place ranking was quite important. Who should receive this position, he pondered, Young or Wells?

Discussion Questions

1. What would be the worst way for a company to try to get a management by objectives program started?
2. What are the dual—and not necessarily complementary—aspects of management by objectives?
3. In the Case of Deciding Which One Was Best, what performance appraisal method was Joe Parsons using prior to introducing management by objectives? What alternative conventional methods could he have considered? (See Section 41.)
4. In what way was Joe Parsons not completely candid with subordinates when he introduced management by objectives?
5. What problems do you see for Joe Parsons as a result of the performance reports of Dave Young and Tom Wells?

47. Motivation Through Incentives

As stated in Section 44, the leadership a manager provides is the crucial variable in the effective performance of the directing function. In the rational organization, a manager's leadership ability is measured by the degree to which subordinates are motivated to improve their productivity. It may be that as a result of the manager's motivating acts, the subordinates are happier, more secure, and less prone to frustration, but these are actually by-products. The efficient leader, in the practical sense, is the one whose subordinates are motivated to work to the limit of their capacity for the good of the organization. It should be noted that these subordinates may or may not reach their optimal performance, but at least they are motivated to try for it.

Definitions

Motivation is a force that induces people to act. Within each human there is a complex of such forces. An individual is aware of some of the forces, but may be unaware of others. One category—called *drives*—includes many forces, of which aggression, conscience, and childhood impressions are just a few. Another category is that of *needs*. Maslow's theory of the basic needs that all people have is treated in Section 48, and McClelland's theory of the need for achievement, in Section 49. In a complementary relationship to needs and drives, which are internal to the individual, there are external forces which stimulate action by satisfying some of the internal forces. There are the *incentives,* or payoffs. Positive incentives (rewards) are motivators for taking action; negative incentives (punishments) are motivators for avoiding some action. Motivating a subordinate thus has two aspects. One is to create positive incentives; the other is to establish negative incentives.

Negative incentives range downward in severity in a business organization from discharge to such minor punishments as oral or written reprimands. In periods of prosperity they serve to motivate subordinates to some minimum level of acceptable performance, whereas in times of depression the threat of unemployment sometimes spurs people on to the maximum performance of which they are capable. Ordinarily, however, positive incentives tend to be the primary means that managers must rely on to stimulate subordinates to move beyond merely acceptable performance.

Only recently, through the contributions of behavioral scientists, have we come to realize that all people are not motivated by the same incentives; moreover, individuals are not consistent from one time to another in being motivated by the same incentives; different incentives work at different times.

Recognition

It is difficult to imagine anyone who would not be motivated by recognition. Money and promotion (discussed below) are recognition symbols to some people. And if handled properly, praise is an almost unfailing incentive. In addition, most people can be motivated by more tangible recognition symbols, such as preferment in working conditions or special privileges. The danger always exists, however, of negatively motivating people who are not favored by such advantages, and who perceive the bases for bestowing them as inequitable.

Money

Financial rewards have, until recently, been looked on as the most effective of all incentives, and Taylor's scientific management theory (recall Section 2) has been interpreted to mean that people will work harder for an increase in wages than for any other thing. There seems to be general agreement that it is the incentive of "more" money, rather than the sustenance of some level of money income, that has motivating power. In other words, simply the assurance of a constant flow of money will not induce people to significantly extend themselves, regardless of how great this flow might be; it is the possibility that the flow might be increased that will cause people to put forth extra effort.

Over the last forty or more years, there has been a tendency in management literature to disparage the effectiveness of money as an incentive. Many research studies have been made in which people at all organizational levels have been asked to enumerate in order of importance the things that they most want out of their jobs. In every such study that is known, money has been ranked after such factors as opportunity for advancement, security, working conditions, and so on. However, these findings may be misleading. For one thing, money is either a symbol for, or can buy, most of the factors that are usually listed ahead of it. Second, people do not always express their true feelings when responding to these surveys. It may seem crude to many people to list money as their primary want, yet it is possible that if the same people were asked what they think *others* want most from their jobs, money might be a strong candidate for first place.

Promotion

Some way of phrasing "opportunity to get ahead" commonly leads lists of what people say that they want out of their jobs, so it would appear that managers can effectively use promotions as incentives. The issue is not as clear-cut as this, however. For one thing, it is not known how many people are motivated by promotions because they indicate career progress, and how many value promotions because they usually mean more money. Another factor is that in most promotion decisions one individual is promoted while others are passed over. Thus, the act of promoting may dampen the motivation to produce for more people than are stimulated by it. This factor becomes important if the incidence of promotion opportunities is low. Still another element that bears on the effectiveness of promotions as incentives is the criteria used by managers to decide who will be promoted. If the criteria are perceived by the subordinates to be unfair, again promotions may depress motivation to improve productivity. A further complicating factor is that there are at each organizational level some people who have reached the limit of their aspirations. These people would actually feel threatened by promotion, and must be motivated to higher productivity by some other incentive than promotion.

Competition

Some people seem motivated to extra effort when placed in a competitive situation. There has been a tendency in industry, especially in firms doing business with the federal government, to artificially create conditions in which departments are matched against each other in striving to reach or exceed certain common goals. Compensation systems, such as quotas used to motivate salesmen, also have competition as an incentive base. There are at least two questions connected with competition that managers ought to explore when they use it, however. One is, how many people who appear to thrive on competition are actually motivated by a fear of failure? And second, how many potentially productive people feel so threatened by competitive situations that their real usefulness is inhibited?

Security

Security is considered to be a basic human need, and as such will be discussed in the next section. The way that security is conventionally used by managers as an incentive is through conditional guarantees of continued employment, assurance of retirement income, and commitments of financial relief in event of accident or sickness. Most organizations provide such security benefits, yet the question exists as to whether they really motivate people to produce to their optimal effectiveness. It has been suggested earlier (Section 34) that they are not; these benefits are comparable to punishments, in that they motivate people to perform only at some acceptable minimum level. People will set their productivity high enough so that they will not lose their jobs and the security benefits that go with them, but they will not be motivated to produce more because of having security.

Participation

For a decade or more, considerable interest has been shown in the notion that people can be motivated by being given an opportunity to participate in the decisions that affect them and their jobs. Management by objectives, which was discussed in Section 46, has this type of motivation as its central thesis. As was mentioned, the concept has both its proponents and detractors. In addition to what was stated, a problem in using participation as an incentive is that no one really knows how many people want to participate in their job decisions and how many would prefer to be excluded from such responsibility. An assumption is that the proportion of people for whom participation is an effective incentive will grow along with the steadily increasing education level of the working population in the United States.

Motivation by Example

An incentive that is not mentioned as prominently as perhaps it should be is the example that is set by the senior managers of the organization. By their personal conduct and job-related conduct and working habits, these managers have the potential of stimulating lower-level organization members to higher productivity through the desire to be like the boss.

Discussion Questions

Reference Case A. The Case of the Leopard That Couldn't Change Its Spots (Section 45)

1. In Reference Case A, the character of Al Kirschman was based on an actual person. At the time described, the kinds of specialists that Al directed were in short supply, and any of them could easily have obtained other jobs. Yet virtually none made any effort to avoid working under him. What kind of incentives did Kirschman use?
2. How will money rate with you as an incentive to extend your efforts on your jobs?
3. When promotion opportunities are used as incentives, how can the people who are necessarily passed over continue to be motivated?
4. What differences do you suppose there might be between the incentives that motivate young people and the ones that have the most motivational appeal to older members of the work force?
5. What is the essential requirement in any incentive system based on competition?

48. Human Needs

One prominent theory of motivation is that incentives are perceived by people to be need satisfiers; that is, more money, promotion, recognition, and the rest, are presumed to assist in the fulfillment of some fundamental human need. A widely accepted classification of human needs is attributed to the psychologist Abraham Maslow, and the following discussion is based primarily on his analysis and interpretations others have made of it.

Hierarchical Arrangement of Needs

The basic thesis of need theory is that

- human needs can be grouped into five categories: physiological, safety, love, esteem, and self-actualization.
- these categories can be arranged in a sequence of ascending order.
- humans are motivated to move from partial satisfaction of a lower need to a striving for satisfaction of a higher need.

Humans are viewed as insatiable in their drive upward toward need fulfillment; they are in a perpetual condition of wanting more.

Physiological need. On the lowest order is the physiological need for elements essential to life itself, such as air, water, food, and the rest. It is plain that this need is fundamental; until it is satisfied, consideration of any higher need would be irrelevant. Companies quite rightly concern themselves with meeting this need of employees in their work environment—for example, by assuring proper ventilation and other conditions essential for their physical welfare. But where the physiological needs of workers have been met, they cannot be motivated to further productivity through an appeal to their physiological needs, because an important tenet of need theory is that a satisfied need is not a motivator. Of course, workers will be dissatisfied if these needs are not met, and productivity can be expected to suffer (see Section 51).

Safety need. At this stage, the next need, for safety, emerges. The safety need is construed to mean the need for clothing, shelter, and avoidance of physical danger. It is often expanded to include the need for economic security. At present, the need of most people for protection against the elements and predators and abject poverty is largely satisfied, but the need for psychological security appears to be less than fully met in many instances. Within organizations the greatest threat to psychological security is change. Some proportion of the working population is so upset by change that the potential or actual introduction of it in any form may reduce productivity; and even the most urbane of senior managers will feel insecure and probably be less productive at the prospect of some dramatic change, such as the takeover of the firm by another company. Managers must be conscious of the fact that change does cause insecurity, which in turn induces worry and drains energy away from productive effort. To the degree that they can control the introduction of change, they should do so in ways that will have minimal negative effects. (There is a further discussion of change in Section 54.)

Need for love or belongingness. In Maslow's hierarchy, the next need is that for love or belongingness. The logic of having the love need come after the physiological and safety needs is that the need for affection from other people is felt only after partial satisfaction of the preceding needs. As part of this need, people need to belong to groups and feel natural support through their membership. Most people are moved to satisfy this need, a factor of significance to the manager, who in motivating subordinates must understand the influence of the group on individual behavior. (This need is discussed further in Section 50.)

Need for esteem. From some degree of fulfillment of the need for love or belongingness, the individual is motivated to satisfy the need for esteem. This is the need that a person has for self-respect, and for the respect of other people. Here, many of the incentives that managers may use come into play, because esteem is largely represented by symbols. The material things that money can buy are symbols; a higher title is a symbol, and a fancy office or public recognition are also symbolic of esteem. Probably for most employed people in the United States, the esteem need is highly important.

Need for self-actualization. The final need is for self-actualization, which may be unattainable by many people. It is the need felt by an individual to "be what he was meant to be," or in other words, to achieve his full potential. It will never be known how many people ever find outlets for their abilities that are exactly appropriate, but the number is undoubtedly small. Some people will be so motivated by the need for self-actualization that they will at least partially satisfy it, while other people will give up in frustration at its unattainability. It is important that managers understand that jobs can offer people opportunities for self-actualization, and that they can attempt to increase the potential for self-actualization by making jobs more interesting and satisfying.

Application of Need Theory

The central problem in applying need theory in managing is the difficulty of knowing the present dominant needs of subordinates; they cannot be known with any precision unless the manager is exceptionally well trained in psychology. This limitation becomes more impressive with the observation that probably very few individuals even recognize their own needs accurately, or what is required to fulfill them. Need theory offers an explanation of human motivation; it does not show us explicitly how to motivate.

The Case of Why
Some Engineers May Join Unions

"The reason I have asked you to come here," said Preston McNair, senior vice-president of engineering, Amalgamated Aircraft Corporation, to Dennis Cloud, industrial psychologist in the personnel department, "is to see if you can help me understand why any individual with an engineering degree would join a union. When I was a young man moving up the ladder, engineers looked at themselves as professionals, just like physicians or attorneys, and considered that unions were for the blue-collar workers. We got everything that we needed, such as security, status, and challenge, from our jobs. Yet, the bulk of the engineers in this company have voted for a union. Why?"

Cloud glanced about McNair's luxurious office. With its drapes, thick carpet, oil paintings, and expensive furniture, it looked like a room in a private club. "Tell me, Mr. McNair," he asked, "how long has it been since you have had any contact with the working engineers in this company?"

"Well, to tell you the truth, it has been a long time. My responsibilities are concerned with engineering policy at the corporate level. There are engineering division managers for the product groups whom I see frequently, and sometimes I have contact with a few of the managers of engineering departments. However, I haven't talked with a first line engineer in years."

"I suggest that we take a walk through one of the engineering buildings," said Cloud. "You may get the answer to your question through your own observations."

As McNair and Cloud opened the door leading to the interior area of the Commercial Aircraft Division engineering buildings, their view was obstructed by a large bulletin board. Despite the warning, "Use of this board for nonbusiness messages is expressly forbidden," a page from that morning's newspaper had been thumb-tacked to the board. The headlines of an article, which had been circled in red, were: "TEXAS AIRCRAFT TO LAY OFF 2000 ENGINEERS."

"I suppose the implication is that if a layoff can happen at our competitor's plant, it can also happen here," remarked McNair. "Let me

take a minute to read this company communication." The communication was headed: "RULES OF CONDUCT FOR ALL ENGINEERING JOB CLASSIFICATIONS," *and listed fifteen statements, of which the following are examples:*

1. *Hours of work are from 7:30* A.M. *to 4:00* P.M., *with a lunch break from 11:30* A.M. *to 12:00 noon. A ten-minute coffee break is permitted in the morning and in the afternoon.*

2. *Except for the designated breaks, all employees are expected to be at their work stations during the work day, unless authorized to leave by their supervisors, or for the relief of personal discomfort.*

5. *Nonbusiness conversations between employees at their work stations or in the corridors is not permitted.*

8. *Incoming personal telephone calls will not be transmitted by the control switchboard. With the approval of their supervisor, employees may place outgoing personal calls of not more than three minutes' duration at the pay telephone booth.*

"Those are rather restrictive conditions for people that I called 'professional,' " McNair commented. "Let's see what the inside of this place looks like."

The scene that met his eyes would be staggering to a person not accustomed to it. The windowless interior covered acres of space. Half of the area was occupied by rows of drafting tables placed end to end. A draftsman was busily hunched over each table, with the exception of some groups of two or three people who appeared to be discussing the drawings on the tables. The other portion of the huge room was partitioned into cubicles. The portable walls of the cubicles were six feet high, and there were two sizes of cubicles in the main area, one size to accommodate four desks and the other size to hold eight desks. A labyrinth of corridors permitted access to the various cubicles. Each of the four walls of the building were lined with cubicles large enough to hold one desk, a table, and four chairs. These were the offices of the supervisors.

"I know what you are thinking, Cloud," said McNair, "but let me

remind you that when I started out as an engineer I worked in an airplane hangar. Of course, I'll have to admit that I would rather work in a hangar than in this place. By the way, who is that guy walking around with the clipboard?"

"His job is to take notes at random of what the people in this room are doing at all hours of the day. He notes what proportion appears to be working, what proportion seems to be occupied with nonbusiness activities, what proportion is away from the assigned work stations, and so on. The results are tabulated into comparative scores for the various supervisors' sections. Each week the five highest and the five lowest sections are listed on the bulletin board. Supervisors of sections with low scores are reprimanded, and they in turn chew out their subordinates. It's supposed to be a motivating device."

"It sounds about as motivating as a rawhide whip," said McNair caustically. "What is the education level of the people working in these cubicles?"

"78 percent have at least a bachelor's degree, 35 percent have a master's degree, and 17 percent have their doctorate," replied Cloud. "Perhaps you would like to talk to some of them," he said as he directed McNair into a cubicle occupied by four men.

After the introductions and some opening conversation, McNair asked the question: "What about the work itself? Are the assignments that you are given challenging to you?"

"Sir, I am willing to speak for all four of us," said Tom Jefferson, who had a master's degree. "The practice here is to force engineers into specialization on fragments of work. As a result, we simply do the same things over and over again. We become good at some micro portion of our engineering field, but we don't have the opportunity to expand our abilities. Actually, I haven't been stimulated by my work in over two years."

Just then the 11:30 bell rang, and the men reached for their metal lunch containers. McNair and Cloud walked out of the building. "Before going back to your office," said Cloud, "let's take a walk through the machine shop."

At the entrance to the machine shop, there was a bulletin board with a rules of conduct list prominently displayed. The shop was a vast windowless area filled with rows of machine tools. Several analysts could be observed entering work-sampling notes on clipboards. Because the machine shop was on a different schedule, the bell rang at noon, and the workers reached for their metal lunch containers.

Back in his office, McNair sat thoughtfully for a few minutes. Finally he said: "You are right. I did get the answer to my question, Mr. Cloud. Except for higher pay and cleaner clothes, there is no difference in this company's treatment of engineers and machinists. The engineers are worried about being laid off, the working conditions couldn't possibly make them proud of their status, and their work is boring to them. Why shouldn't they think that a union might not satisfy some of their needs?"

Discussion Questions

1. Explain, in the context of need theory, why an individual leaves a secure job where he has many friends and risks his life's savings to start his own business.
2. What are the implications, to a manager trying to motivate subordinates, of the tenet that a satisfied need is not a motivator?
3. In the Case of Why Some Engineers May Join Unions, what evidence is there that Amalgamated Aircraft's engineers may feel a threat to their security need?
4. Has Amalgamated Aircraft accorded professional esteem to its technically trained employees?
5. What needs of Amalgamated Aircraft's engineers could a union satisfy?

49. Motivation Through Need for Achievement

A somewhat different view of needs as motivational drives has been developed by the psychologist David C. McClelland. McClelland's theory is that some people have a compelling need to achieve—that is, to achieve simply for the sake of achievement—and that this drive sharply differentiates them from most other people, who might wish or even strive for the symbols of success but not for achievement itself. Implicit in this theory is that the need for achievement—or "n Ach" in McClelland's notation—is the key element in achieving. In other words, people who do achieve *need* to achieve.

Characteristics of n Ach People

The driving need for achievement makes n Ach people preoccupied to an unusual degree with doing things better, as contrasted with others, whom McClelland designates as "n Aff," or need for affiliation, types. These n Aff types are more preoccupied with having fun, being with friends or loved ones, or other topics not related to achievement. Another characteristic of n Ach people is that they favor situations where they can influence outcomes through their personal efforts. For example, they might be inclined to bet on their own performances in a golf match, but not be interested in gambling at racetracks or casinos. Winning by chance is not a big thing to them.

People with n Ach can also be identified by the way they set goals for themselves. Goals that are easily accomplished do not interest them, nor do goals that are impossible to attain. Their inclination is to set goals that are challenging, but which with effort they can achieve, and thereby get the satisfaction they need. By the same token they tend to calculate the risk of failure, and strive for goals where the predictability of success is greater.

A requirement for feedback concerning their performance is typical of n Ach people. They want to know how well they have done, obviously, to get the satisfaction of having done it. Work like running a business, where lower costs or higher profits are positive indicators of success, appeals more to n Ach individuals than a job such as teaching, where the effectiveness of efforts is more difficult to verify.

How to Identify n Ach People

One approach to identifying people with a strong need for achievement is to ask them questions concerning their values, interests, and attitudes. But the problem with this approach is that people often do not know precisely what motivates them. McClelland favors a more indirect technique, which is to show people a picture and ask them to describe in a story what is taking place. The stories reveal their relative tendencies to be either n Ach or n Aff oriented.

For example, one picture is of a man at a work table, with a small family photograph clearly in evidence. One story goes like this:

"The engineer is at work on Saturday when it is quiet, and he has taken time to do a little daydreaming. He is the father of the two children in the picture—the husband of the woman shown. He has a happy home life and is dreaming about some pleasant outing they have had. He is also looking forward to a repeat of the incident which is now giving him pleasure to think about. He plans on the following day, Sunday, to use the afternoon to take his family for a short trip."

The man who wrote the above story is obviously more interested in family life than in achievement. He would probably be classified as n Aff.

Here is another man's story of the same picture:

"The man is an engineer at a drafting board. The picture is of his family. He has a problem and is concentrating on it. It is merely an everyday occurrence—a problem which requires thought. How can he get that bridge to take the stress of possible high winds? He wants to arrive at a good solution of the problem by himself. He will discuss the problem with a few other engineers and make a decision which will be a correct one—he has the earmarks of competence." (McClelland, 1962)

Observe the preoccupation with achievement in the second man's story. He gives passing notice to the photograph, but the rest of the story focuses on getting things done. Stories like this one mark people as n Ach types.

A third category suggested by McClelland is "n Pwr," or the need to exercise power over other people. Stories revealing a desire to influence, control, or manipulate people—or in a more positive sense to arouse them by direct influence to greater accomplishment—would indicate n Pwr. If n Pwr is a valid category, we can see how it might identify people who want to become or might enjoy being managers.

What Makes an n Ach Person?

McClelland found that family influences are important factors in developing a person's need for achievement. Such people often come from families where the parents have high standards of achievement, where there is warmth and encouragement, and where the father is not dominating and authoritarian.

Another source of n Ach values is the Protestant Ethic, translated into the work ethic. Many writers, Max Weber for instance, have held that there is a transfer from striving for a perfectly pious life to striving for business achievement. McClelland suggests that beliefs in other value systems, such as nationalism and communism, can also transfer to a personal need for achievement. Finally, McClelland has apparently come to think that the n Ach characteristic can be an acquired one.

How to Train People to Be n Ach Types

McClelland runs seven- to ten-day courses to train business people to increase their n Ach. The goals of the course are as follows:
- to train people to think and act like n Ach types.
- to motivate them to set attainable goals for themselves over some period of time, such as two years.
- to teach them to really understand themselves—to perceive how they behave and why.
- to create a feeling among all the trainees in the course that they have the support of each other in striving to achieve their goals.

Is n Ach Training Valid?

During the mid-1960's McClelland carried out an experimental program in India to see if the quality of small business management in that country could be improved. (See McClelland and Winter in the bibliography.) The programs were ten days in length, and were run four times in one city and twice in another, with follow-up two years after the training. Seventy-four trainees were compared with seventy-three people with comparable backgrounds, except for the training. After two years it was found that the trainees were working longer hours, had made more definite attempts to start new businesses, had actually started more new ventures, had made more investments in productive assets, employed more workers, and had relatively larger increases in the gross incomes of their firms.

The results of McClelland's program in India suggests that n Ach is a useful characteristic for business success, and that it can be stimulated or acquired through training.

Discussion Questions

1. Explain how people might want symbols of success, but not have a high need for achievement.
2. Evaluate McClelland's theory that n Ach people can be identified by the way they tell stories from pictures. Why could not n Ach be faked if you were aware of the theory?
3. How do you suppose McClelland would explain n Ach people who grew up in an orphanage, or in a broken home?
4. How much effect do you think the Protestant Ethic has on developing n Ach people today?
5. Do you agree that people who are not n Ach types to start with can be trained to develop n Ach characteristics?

50. The Work Group As a Motivating Force

The existence of informal organizations within all formal organizations was discussed in Section 26. This section will go further in explaining the influence that work groups have on the motivation of the individual members.

Norms of Group Behavior

In discussions of how the work group acts as a motivating force, *norms* is a term frequently used. The term refers to standards of behavior, both work-related and unrelated, which are common to the group members. It is probably better said that norms are the accepted modes of behavior of the *majority* of the group's members, because there are usually some members of any group who deviate from the norms.

For managers, group norms which influence subordinates' actions apply to such areas as group-established productivity standards, attendance, tardiness, and respect for rules. It can be recognized that norms established by groups can be either favorable or unfavorable to the goals that the managers feel are in the best interests of the organization.

Group Cohesiveness

Group cohesiveness is another term frequently used in discussions of group behavior; it refers to the attraction that the group has for its members, and this will increase as individuals perceive that membership satisfies their needs. Strong group cohesiveness will motivate members to accept the group norms as compelling and to pursue the group goals, whether or not they are also the goals of the managers.

Some of the characteristics of a group that make it attractive to members were touched upon in Section 26. Additional aspects may now be noted in relation to the need theory developed in Section 48. For example, security has been identified as a basic human need. A business organization has the potential of threatening the security of an individual in many ways, such as a discharge or layoff, a cut in wages, or a requirement to work under undesirable or dangerous conditions. Except where protected by government regulations, the individual, acting alone, is relatively powerless in coping with threats of these kinds. However, when a number of individuals act as a group in warding off potential security threats, their collective power becomes significant.

A work group also satisfies the fundamental need for belongingness, or affiliation. Just the social satisfaction that is obtained from fellow workers may prompt an individual to tolerate low wages, stultifying work, or bullying supervision. The importance of the social life within a work group has often been underestimated, and there have been many reports of attempts by management to increase productivity by reducing social interaction on the job—with diametrically opposite effects. Most people need the social contact that they get from their work groups.

Informal groups also satisfy the need for esteem that all humans have. As mentioned in Section 26, informal organizations develop status systems, with individuals occupying recognized positions within the hierarchy. All persons, of course, will not be leaders in their groups, but those persons who earn the respect and approbation of their peers will be at least partially satisfying a need that is highly important to them. In addition, the need for esteem may be met from just being an accepted member of some powerful informal group.

Behavior in a Cohesive Group

From the voluminous research on group behavior, only a small portion of the results can be noted. One important finding is that the norms of a cohesive group will generate tendencies in the members to uniformity of behavior. The members will, in fact, feel obligated to conform, and if some do not, the group will put pressure on them to change. The most effective tool that the group has to pressure nonconforming members is rejection.

It can be reasoned that the more attractive a group is to a member, the greater will be the power of the group over him. The personal ethics of the members, for example, will be strongly influenced by the group. Moreover, it has been shown under experimental conditions that individuals will often defer to group judgment, even when their own is obviously better. And the more cohesive the group, the more it will present a unified front to external threats—such as the introduction of change by management. The group will act as a protector of its members, extending support that ranges from help with their jobs to material aid in family crises.

Levels of Cohesiveness

There is no known research upon which to base an objective evaluation, but it seems probable that the most cohesive work groups are comprised of individuals on a nonmanagerial level, and that the higher the organizational levels, the less cohesive are the informal work groups formed by members. The inference is that managers tend to get their need satisfaction from the reward system of the formal organization, and to identify their personal goals with the organizational goals.

The Scanlon Plan

Some group incentive systems, of which the Scanlon Plan is probably the best known, attempt to motivate workers toward positive goals via group pressures. The Scanlon Plan was created by Joseph Scanlon, who started out as a laborer in a steel mill and eventually became a key figure in the United Steelworkers of America. The basis of the Scanlon Plan within a business organization is a hierarchy of committees, with the committee on each level made up of management and union representatives. Lower-level committees develop recommendations for improving departmental productivity and devise equitable means for distributing the gains realized from the increased productivity to the company and the employees. Higher-level committees integrate the recommendations of the departmental committees into a company-wide system.

   Typically, the application of the Scanlon Plan first involves the determination, through agreement by the representatives of management and labor, of a "normal" labor cost for a department. Employees are then encouraged to submit to their departmental committee suggestions for improving productivity. The committee considers the suggestions and recommends adoption of the likely ones. The workers' share of any gains realized from these suggestions go to the work group of which the initiator of the suggestion is a member, and distribution is made according to wage classification.

The singular feature of the Scanlon Plan is that it focuses on motivating the individual through the group, rather than isolating the ambitious individual from the group, as other incentive systems do. When an individual does something worthwhile, the entire group benefits. The esteem felt by the group toward the individual naturally increases, which satisfies one of the individual's higher needs. A norm will develop within the group to the end that members are expected to initiate productivity suggestions, which puts pressures on members to be innovative. In short, the Scanlon Plan ingeniously tries to take advantage of what is known about group behavior. The few studies that have been made of the Scanlon Plan in operation suggest that the results are impressive, with companies using it achieving productivity gains in excess of 20 percent, on the average.

The following section also deals with motivation, but work itself will be seen as the motivating agent.

*The invoice processing section of the New York Wholesale Hardware
Company's accounting department had a normal complement of
seventy-five women clerks who were divided into five groups. Each
group was headed by a woman group leader, and they in turn reported to Walter Miller, section supervisor. The section occupied
one wing of the top floor of the company's Brooklyn headquarters
building. The invoice clerks' desks were arranged in rows facing the
desks of the group leaders. Miller occupied a glassed-in cubicle in a
corner of the wing. The work performed by the invoice clerks consisted of deriving the details of sales from the customers' purchase
orders and the shipping reports, and typing invoices to be mailed to
the customers.*

*One day in the summer of 1972, Miller was visited in his cubicle
by Harvey Smith, payroll section supervisor. "Walt, I have a problem
with one of my clerks," said Smith. "She has the potential of being
a good worker. However, she seems to rebel at conforming to any
standards or rules of conduct. The groups in my section are not
very closely knit, perhaps because I have purposely kept moving individuals from group to group to prevent them from developing
loyalties other than to the total section. As a result, some of the
others are beginning to copy this girl's behavior. Her name is Linda
Jones, and although I don't want to, I will have to discharge her
unless you will be willing to give her a trial. The reason I am asking
you is because of the excellent morale that you have developed in
your section."*

*"The morale in my section is more the result of what I call 'the in-
visible hand,' which is an inaccurate paraphrase from Adam Smith's
'The Wealth of Nations,' than from anything that I have done,"
replied Miller. "By 'invisible,' I mean that the employees are motivated by some force that exists within their groups. I'll be glad to
give this girl a chance. What does Linda look like?"*

"She is in her early twenties, and is small and pretty."

*"She sounds like a perfect fit for the 'Mighty Mites,'" said Walter
Miller.*

"What do you mean, 'Mighty Mites?' That sounds like a name for a girls' softball team."

"Well, I used to designate my groups by the letters of the alphabet corresponding to the names of the customers that they handled," Miller replied. *"For example, there was A-E Group, F-L Group, and so on. One day, quite by accident, in complimenting the F-L Group I called them 'the mighty mites,' because they are all rather short, petite types. The name stuck, and the girls seemed to take more pride in belonging to the group. And surprisingly, the group's productivity began to improve. Pretty soon the other groups began to invent names for themselves, so now instead of having cold alphabetical designations, we have the Valkyries, the Suffragettes, the Florence Nightingales, and the Gray Ladies, in addition to the Mighty Mites."*

"Do these names pose any personnel problems for you?" asked Smith.

"They definitely do," answered Miller. *"I have to be extremely careful when I assign a new employee to a group to put her where she fits. Each group has taken on distinctive characteristics. For example, the Gray Ladies are all older women, the Suffragettes are in their thirties and early forties, the Valkyries all have last names like Olsen, Kruger, or Hackenschmidt. The Florence Nightingales have the highest educational level and the largest proportion of women of the black race. It's remarkable, but the women in all groups are obviously pleased when I make a perfect fit in placing a new employee. On the other hand, performance of the entire section drops immediately if I don't fit a new person to the proper group. For instance, productivity would fall 50 percent if I put Linda Jones in the Gray Ladies."*

"Do you think the Mighty Mites can change her behavior?" asked Smith.

"She will either conform to the group's norms, or she will be made so miserable that she will quit," said Miller. *"All of the groups have set productivity standards in terms of average number of invoices processed each month, average number of errors, etc. The groups compete with each other to have the best monthly records. In addition, the Mighty Mites have adopted a certain style of dress. They use low-key makeup. They don't smoke at their desks. If Linda*

flaunts these norms, the other girls won't talk to her. She will eat lunch by herself. She won't be invited to parties and the other things the girls do together. I think she will change, not only to keep the job, but in order to belong to the group."

On the next day when Miller interviewed Linda Jones, he made the following mental observations: Her appearance was seemingly in defiance of conventional business standards. She used heavy makeup, she wore a tight, low-cut black dress, and had on black net stockings. She smoked cigarettes in an ornate holder. She was defensive, with slight undercurrent indications of fear. On the positive side, she had better than average grades from high school, her typing proficiency was high, and her responses to questions were quick and articulate.

About a month later, Miller came to the office early, and to his surprise found Linda at her desk working. "What are you doing here at this time of the morning?" he asked, noting a complete change for the better in her dress and general appearance.

"I didn't make my quota yesterday, and I came in early to be sure to get it out," she answered.

"How do you like your job?" asked Miller.

"I hated it the first week," she replied. "Now I love it. Can you believe that the group got together a donation to send flowers to my mother who is in the hospital? And one of the girls got me a blind date with her brother, and now we are going steady." She looked up shyly: "I like being a Mighty Mite."

Discussion Questions

1. What can a manager do on finding that the productivity norms set by the group are lower than the standards established for the group?
2. Is it to a manager's interest that subordinates be cohesively grouped?
3. Would all people respond positively to the provisions of the Scanlon Plan?

4. In the Case of the Invisible Hand, what factor is leading to high morale and productivity, in addition to the "invisible hand" that Walter Miller modestly identifies?

5. What practical problems would there be in attempting to fit a new employee to the group for which he or she appeared to be most suited?

51. Motivation Through Job Satisfaction

Managers' concern with improving subordinates' productivity, and behavioral scientists' attempts to better understand human behavior, have led both groups in a search for the key to worker motivation. And a notion that has long appealed to both is that satisfaction gained from work itself has motivating power. The answer to why managers and theorists alike should conclude intuitively that work is a motivator is straightforward: Like people in many other professions, they are strongly motivated by their own work; therefore, why should not satisfaction with work move all people toward higher productivity, in whatever terms productivity is measured in connection with their own jobs?

Thus, personnel programs have been structured with a view toward increasing job satisfaction and improving productivity. And, for some twenty years, research studies have been conducted by behavioral scientists expecting to prove that higher productivity is a consequence of job satisfaction. So far, however, the belief that job satisfaction is a motivator for most people has not been substantiated. The apparent problem is in the oversimplified ways in which *job satisfaction* has been defined and measured.

Definitions and Criteria for Management

Semantic confusion exists in management literature over the terms *job satisfaction* and *morale*. While some writers perceive the terms as synonyms, others ascribe *job satisfaction* to a feeling by an individual, and *morale* to a group condition. A paraphrasing of various definitions leads to the definition of *job satisfaction* as "a state of mind that varies in a favorable degree with the worker's positive impressions of the total job environment."

In accord with this generalized definition, personnel policies of business firms have focused on job factors that are thought to be important to workers, such as equitable compensation, pleasant working conditions, fair differentiation in job status, communication of company policies and progress, and various fringe benefits. Although there has been little standardization in the research instruments used to measure job satisfaction, studies have tended toward trying to learn workers' attitudes relative to these same factors, plus the pride they feel in their group's performance, their perception of the work itself, and the regard they have for their supervisor.

Findings

A summary of the reported investigations indicates that actually only about one third of the workers sampled are dissatisfied with their jobs, as measured by the above criteria. However, there appears to be no statistical difference in the productivity of the dissatisfied workers and the workers who are construed to be satisfied with their jobs. In other words, the research findings would indicate that job satisfaction and productivity are not related.

Dual Emphases of Recent Research

The research of Frederick Herzberg and his associates offers some newer insights. The significant feature of this research is that it differentiates between two sets of factors related to job satisfaction: those that must be perceived to be present in a job for the worker *not to feel dissatisfied,* and those whose presence can enable the worker to achieve true job satisfaction.

Prevention of dissatisfaction.   The first set of factors include
- acceptable company policies and rules.
- approved, or at least tolerable, management methods on the part of the immediate supervisor.
- equitable compensation.
- desirable interpersonal relations with co-workers.
- agreeable working conditions.

Although the perception of these factors is sufficient to prevent dissatisfaction with a job, the worker will not be motivated thereby to produce any more than necessary to maintain the acceptable conditions. The theory on which this reasoning is based is that a satisfied need is not a motivator. The factors listed have the potential of satisfying the individual's need only up through the need for esteem. The next and highest-level need, for self-actualization, is very likely beyond satisfaction for most people through such prosaic rewards.

Fostering of personal satisfaction. The second set of factors is related to what an individual can obtain from a job in personally satisfying terms. These factors, which do have the potential of meeting the need for self-actualization, include

- a sense of achievement, or the knowledge of having done something worthwhile.
- recognition, by persons whose opinion is valued, that one's work has merit.
- the gratification that may come from the work itself.
- a high degree of responsibility, which some individuals need in order to perceive themselves as complete persons.
- open-endedness, with opportunity for advancement.

Herzberg and his associates suggest that the presence of this second set of factors has the strong potential to motivate individuals to higher productivity. What is obtained from these factors is *intrinsic* job satisfaction, whereas the satisfaction obtained from the first set of factors is *extrinsic*. Those factors, which may be observed to be similar to the criteria used by other researchers to constitute the whole of job satisfaction, merely relate to conditions associated with the job.

Discussion Questions

Reference Case A. The Case of Why Some Engineers May Join Unions (Section 48)

1. What effect have the "divisions of work" principle and the scientific management movement had on motivation through job satisfaction? (See Section 2.)
2. How have personnel policies focused on the wrong factors, if their intent has been to motivate workers through job satisfaction?
3. How do some of the hobbies of many individuals refute the proposition that there is no satisfaction to be obtained from hand labor?
4. Why be concerned with such factors as fair compensation, good working conditions, and equitable treatment if they are not motivators? (See Section 34.)
5. How can Herzberg's second set of factors, that he claims motivate individuals to higher productivity, be applied to the engineers in Reference Case A?

52. Nonrational Influences on Motivation

The attempts to explain motivation that have been summarized thus far have all been based on the assumption that human behavior is rational, or based on reason. However, rational influences only partially explain human behavior; what must be added are the inherited or acquired characteristics of humans that induce them to action. No attempt will be made to examine all of the theories of nonrational motivation, nor to defend any. The only objective is to establish that motivation is a complex of forces, rather than a single, easily understood model.

Animal Ancestry

The theory of evolution was propounded by Charles Darwin in the late 1800's, and has recently been expanded by Robert Ardrey in *The African Genesis*. According to this theory, man is descended from lower predatory animals, and is motivated by latent instincts to survive through aggression. If we consider this theory as a possibility, some human behaviors become more readily explainable. For example, what is the basis for conflict between diversely specialized organizational departments, if not the instinct for territorial protection? How are the power arenas in organizations different, except for a civilized façade, from jungle fighting grounds? At the same time, many human behaviors elude explanation by this model; other forces obviously come into play.

Ethical Teachings

The teachings of most religions prescribe norms of moral conduct that cannot fail to have some influence on the behavior of people who were required to learn them. Although the ten commandments and the golden rule are not closely followed by everyone who learned about them as children, they have contributed to the development of conscience as a guide to behavior.

One of the major influences on people's attitudes has been the Protestant ethic of John Calvin, which included the notions of hard work, thrift, and avoiding debt as being virtues in themselves. Max Weber was the first to write about the work influence of the Protestant ethic, the idea that "Work is a virtue, sloth is a sin." Benjamin Franklin's *Poor Richard's Almanack* carried the same sort of message intended to inspire hard work. Although today the strong motivational influence of the Protestant work ethic is apparently weakening, it is still a model that shapes the behavior of many people.

Freudian Psychology

The Austrian psychologist, Sigmund Freud, in the early 1900's proposed a theory of motivation that has had a significant impact on the understanding of human behavior. Freud's central thesis was that the acts of humans are dictated considerably more by their unconscious minds than by conscious determination, and that the unconscious mind is a complex of impressions made on the individual in early childhood. In addition, Freud postulated two basic human drives: the life instincts, which consist of all activities that are positive and constructive, and the death instincts, or hate instincts, which are destructive. He urged that man's behavior is typically ambivalent, based on an unpremeditated mixture of these instincts. Nothing could be more damaging to the notion of rational motivation than the suggestion that people are moved to actions without even knowing what is directing them.

Amos Hull's family had farmed the same rocky forty acres in an isolated area of Vermont for nearly three hundred years. The original Amos Hull had left England with other members of a small religious sect in order that they might worship God and interpret the Bible in the manner of their choosing. The valley they selected for settlement had enough resources to provide a frugal living, and the sect was able to stay in existence and remain relatively independent of outside material influences through nine generations.

The congregation survived the minor disasters of nature that a farming community could expect over the time that it occupied the valley, but in 1968 two catastrophes occurred in series that destroyed its means of livelihood. First, a fire swept across the fields ready for harvesting, the orchards, and the grazing lands. Several lives were lost, much of the livestock was killed, and the homes and barns were leveled. Then came an early blizzard that killed most of the remaining livestock; and without shelter, the families were forced to flee to the nearest town. The congregation's way of living over the centuries had not been calculated to generate much cash, and the communal wealth, of which Amos Hull was custodian, was slightly over $1100.

Through the efforts of some of the leading townspeople, the valley was declared a disaster area, and the inhabitants were entitled to a rehabilitation loan at low interest. When this information was communicated to the valley residents, Amos Hull, acting as spokesman, explained their refusal: "In our religion we consider debt to be a sin. The heads of the families are going to find work. We will pool our savings, and when we have enough we will rebuild our farms."

Although Amos Hull had no specific job skill, he could work with hand tools, and he moved his wife and three daughters to Waterbury, Connecticut, where he got a job as an assembler at the National Valve Company. Although Amos was not by inclination a friendly man, his co-workers sympathized with his plight, and helped him acquire the skills necessary to perform his duties. In fact, they might have taught him too well, because within a few months he was progressively exceeding the daily output of every other worker in the assembly crew.

One day Sam Bolton, who seemed to be the informal leader of the work group, came over to Amos' work bench. "Huh! Sixty valves assembled so far today, and there are still two hours to go," Sam said as he looked at Amos' tally sheet. "Didn't I let you know last week that the gang has set about fifty valves a day as the bogey? What are you trying to do—mess things up for everybody?"

"I'm sorry you feel that way," said Amos, "but I can't do less than a full day's work for a full day's pay. I feel an obligation to turn out as many valves as I can."

"Buddy, we don't go for guys like you," Sam replied. "You either cut back to fifty valves per day, or it's going to be pretty rough for you around here."

Amos' daily production continued to increase, and things began to happen. The freeze was put on—not one member of the assembly crew said a word to him. His tools would mysteriously disappear. Sometimes when he opened his lunch pail he would find it filled with greasy rags. One evening as he walked home he was grabbed from behind, and punched in the stomach. His productivity finally leveled off, but at a rate almost double the standard set by the work group.

Bill Eztey, assembly lead man, met Amos one morning as he entered the shop. "Well if it isn't the tin hero," said Bill. "The guy who shows up everybody, including me, his boss. Now the foreman wants to know why I let the rest of the gang get away with doing only about half the work that you do. You had better get in line, or I'm going to find some reason to get rid of you." Amos proceeded to his work bench, and knelt to pray as he did each morning. He then turned to his work, and assembled the most valves that day that he had ever done.

About two weeks later, the company's personnel manager passed down word that he would like to talk to Amos. "You know, you are the only employee who has not made a donation to the Community Chest," he said to Amos. "The company prides itself on getting 100 percent participation each year. Why don't you make a small donation, like $5.00, just so that everybody will be in."

"I don't believe in accepting charity, or in giving to charity except to

my own congregation," Amos answered. "This is a deep conviction with me."

At about this time, after several attempts to get a union shop, the International Association of Machinists received a majority vote by the employees of National Valve Company. Amos cast his vote against the union, and made up his mind that he would never join, regardless of the outcome of the election. Because of the completely ostracized conditions under which he worked, he knew little of the implications of National Valve Company being certified as a union shop by the NLRB. He disregarded the form that he received in his pay envelope, which he was supposed to sign authorizing the deduction of union dues from his paycheck.

Once again Amos was called to the office of the personnel manager. "Secretly I applauded the way you stood up for your rights on the Community Chest matter," the personnel manager said to Amos, "but this issue is different. Unless you authorize the check-off of union dues, the company will have to let you go."

"Badly as I need the job, that's what you will have to do," Amos said. My principles are against an individual having to belong to anything."

Discussion Questions

1. How could the process of motivating be simplified if people's behavior were consistently rational?
2. Argue against Freud's thesis that the behavior of humans is largely determined in childhood by impressions on the unconscious mind.
3. In the Case of the Contrary Conscience, Amos Hull's precept against going into debt seems completely out of date. However, what constrains you, and most of the people you know, from using credit to the limit in getting material things?
4. Do you believe Amos Hull was acting rationally, or irrationally, when he refused to conform to the pressures of his work group and his boss to reduce his production of valves?
5. Do you agree or disagree with Amos that an individual should have the right to accept or reject membership in any organization? What makes you think as you do?

53. The Communication Process

Just as coordination is the end for which the managerial functions of planning, organizing, staffing, directing, and controlling are performed, communication is the means whereby the performance of these functions is made possible. Communication could just as readily be treated in the parts of this book dealing with the other managerial functions as well as here (some key communication concepts are, in fact, reserved for consideration under controlling; see especially Section 65), but the importance of communication to directing warrants its inclusion here.

The Communication Model

In the business organization, communication is generally construed to mean the exchange of information, but some additional variables will have to be added to provide a basis for analysis. Communication involves at least two persons, or two machines, or one person and one machine. One person, or machine, is a sender. Another person, or machine, is a receiver. There must also be a message. Communication is achieved when the receiver understands and responds to the message in the way intended by the sender, based on the sender's choice of information. However, when persons, rather than machines, are the communicating agents, variables are present which may impede this achievement. One set of variables consists of the possibly divergent values of the sender and receiver, and another consists of potential distorting forces external to the sender and receiver. Figure 53-1 represents the communication process in schematic form.

The model will have to be viewed from different perspectives. First, consider the exchange of information via the formal organiza-

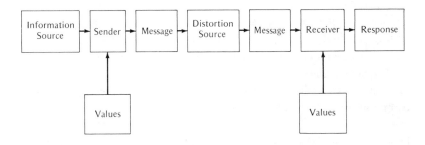

Figure 53–1. The Communication Process.

tion hierarchy, that is, through the channel of vertical authority relationships (discussed in Section 21). We can start with one of two alternatives. Either the manager or a subordinate can be the sender. Assume at the beginning that the manager is the sender.

The Manager As Sender

Of the number of different kinds of messages that a manager will want to communicate downward, there are

- directions concerning performance of work tasks.
- information about the company, such as prospects, product news, and operational developments.
- personnel policies and procedures.
- important changes, such as promotions or the firm's entrance into a new market.

Sources for such messages will be the organization's formal plans, management decisions, economic surveys, and industry or nationwide trends. Influencing the manager's transmittal of information downward will be the organization's goals, along with the manager's personal goals, judgments concerning what subordinates should know, perceptions of what they want to be told, and choice of vocabulary.

Vocabulary level.   The vocabulary a manager uses when communicating with subordinates may not always be as intellectual or technical as when conferring with board members. An individual's judgment should determine what expressions are appropriate, in terms of the message itself and the persons to whom it will be directed.

Downward message media.   A sender must choose between oral and written messages, or might use one to supplement the other. A manager, as a sender, in choosing oral communication may use mass addresses, conferences with a selected group, or face-to-face meetings with individual subordinates. Written messages may range from widely disseminated ones, such as newsletters, bulletin-board announcements, and standard-practice instructions, to personal letters or memos. The nature of a manager's messages will usually be information providing, information seeking, or order giving.

Downward distortion.   Distortion of downward communication may be caused by prematurity or delay in the transmission of the message. For example, a message can be transmitted so early as to be ineffective, as when a schedule of summer vacations is issued in January, thus overlooking many factors that employees would perceive as important later in the year when they really begin to think about vacations. An example of a message delivered too late to be effective might be one requiring compliance immediately with a request that would entail a week's preparation. Such a message will usually be resented, as well as not being filled properly.

Another distortion source not specifically related to the original sender or ultimate intended receiver is the organization hierarchy. If organization policy requires that communications be transmitted via the formal chain of vertical authority relationships, messages may be misinterpreted, amplified, and filtered, as well as delayed, when they pass through the various organization levels.

Other than distortions caused by the time required to pass a message through a series of levels, the primary distortions result from the impact that the values of the intercepting receiver-senders will have on the message. That is, an interceptor in the chain will interpret the message according to personal understandings of the word meanings, and may also amplify it, or add more to the message than was originally intended. As an example of such distortion, assume that an original message states that an impending strike in the steel industry warrants increasing steel inventories. This message is amplified by the first receiver to include a direction to cover a six month's inventory. The next receiver might add another three months, and when the message finally reaches the people responsible for controlling specific items in the steel inventory, the instruction might be for well over a year's supply. Additionally, an interceptor may filter a message by removing details considered unessential for the next receiver. Thus, through the values of the interceptors, messages may be distorted by interpretation, amplification, and filtering before they reach the ultimate receiver.

The ultimate receiver will assess the message according to personal values and interpret it according to personal understandings of the word meanings. The receiver's interpretation of company goals and their congruence with personal goals will dictate his or her response to the original aim of the communication.

Subordinates' Messages

The kinds of messages that subordinates may wish to communicate upward include

- performance reports to an immediate superior.
- work-related matters requiring coordination with people in other departments.
- suggestions for improving operations or working conditions.
- personal or group grievances.
- political maneuvers calculated to gain favor with the manager.

Sources of information will include the performance criteria of the jobs, the work environment, the work group (including the union), and what can be learned outside the immediate department. The subordinates' values which will influence them in transmitting messages include their personal goals, the extent to which they are influenced by their group's norms, what they think managers want to know rather than what they should know, and their vocabulary.

Upward message media. The subordinates' choice between oral and written messages is quite often made for them. For example, managers may specify that certain performance reports be made periodically in written form, with additional oral reports on a continuous basis. Requests by subordinates for assistance in dealing with members of other departments, or their reports to the manager of such dealings involving lateral relationships, may again be oral or written, depending on department policy. Many organizations require that employee suggestions be made in writing. Grievances usually start as oral but may evolve into a specified written form, especially if they must pass upward through several organization levels. When subordinates maneuver for favor, they use whatever mode of expression best suits their purpose.

Upward distortion. Probably more communication from subordinates stops at the department manager's desk than proceeds upward through organization levels, but the messages that do pass upward have the same potential of being distorted by time, and by the interpretations, amplifications, and filtering of interceptors, as those moving downward. However, the frequency of dead-end communications at this point suggests that the distortion potential is especially significant.

Obstacles to communication include not only the difference in values between subordinates and supervisors, but also the more formidable obstacle of status differentiation. Few subordinates are indifferent to the fact that the manager controls their rewards from their jobs. This realization induces defensive behavior on their part, and a tendency to flavor messages in a way to put themselves in a good light. The techniques of this flavoring will be deliberate amplification and filtering. Put these conditions together with the strong possibility that the subordinate and the manager figuratively do not speak the same language, and the potential for garbled messages becomes impressive.

Avoiding the Authority Chain

When people bypass formal lines of authority, they may communicate with someone in a vertical or a lateral relationship.

Bypassing managers with downward messages. A senior manager wishing to communicate with subordinates several levels below can bypass intervening managers and transmit information directly to the intended receivers. Time and the necessity for clarity in the message often warrant this action. But on the receiving end, subordinates may be frustrated by receiving information—or orders—which may conflict with what they have received from the manager directly over them. In addition, the bypassed managers are almost always resentful, and will be in the dark concerning some vital information. The problems engendered by this direct communication, which is only superficially efficient, are great enough to cause most senior managers to observe the protocol of at least telling the bypassed managers that they are going to communicate directly, and often having them present when they transmit the messages.

Communicating with upper-level managers. Going in the other direction, subordinates may feel the need to bypass the manager to whom they normally report, and perhaps several levels of managers, and communicate with someone higher up. Sometimes the message is work-related, but more often is of a personal nature. And while many senior managers publicize their "open-door" policy, subordinates are wise to observe precautions in bypassing managers in the communication process. One way is to obtain their permission to contact a higher-level manager; another way, required by some organizations, is to submit a memo to the immediate superior explaining the nature of the contact with a higher-level manager; and a third way is the military's "information copy" system. Here, a subordinate puts information to be transmitted in a memo to the immediate superior, with a copy to a higher authority. This is a bureaucratic method of letting the cat out of the bag, and assures that the higher-ups know what is going on.

Lateral communication.   Communication between individuals laterally related in the organization structure (see Sections 23–25) is a different subject altogether. If the formal hierarchy were observed, the only way a design engineer could communicate with a production planner, for example, would be for their respective messages to travel all the way to the top of their own department, and then all the way to the bottom of the other department. This would, of course, be impossibly cumbersome, and some circumvention of such a restrictive policy is legitimate in all organizations. In fact, the trend seems to be toward more permissive interorganization communication. It is, however, not uncommon within departments to find formal specifications as to who may communicate with whom in other departments, and on what matters. The more prevalent policy seems to be for managers to request to be kept informed of what transpires in communications between their subordinates and members of other departments.

In messages between people in different departments, an obstacle to communication is the pre-eminence that the respective communicators will place on the relative role and status of the departments they represent. As mentioned before, organizational subsystems are in rivalry with each other, and this causes biases in the construction and interpretation of messages.

Additional Factors

A few other factors influencing the efficiency of communication have to do with the status of communicators' roles and the quality of communication skills.

Status of sender vs. receiver.   A sender of information is perceived as having more status than a receiver. People who are predominantly on the receiving end of messages become aware that in the informal organization they are cast as responders rather than initiators. Therefore, their tendency is to change roles, that is, put into motion enough messages to become recognized as senders. This is not a theoretical ploy, but one that is commonly practiced in organizations. And the senders get out of it more than just increasing their perceived informal status; formal performance appraisals are often influenced by how often people are on the sending end of messages. The result is that the magnitude of written communications within most organizations is excessively large, and there are few group meetings where the efficiency is not obstructed because most of the participants want to be senders of some oral messages, however unnecessary they are.

The tendency for people to want to become senders is itself potentially inefficient, but in addition it has an inefficient consequence. Communications generate further communications; in fact, a cycle can develop in which a receiver responds to a message and confirms the fact, thus providing himself with an opportunity to initiate a new message. And so on, with the result that most modern organizations could save large sums if they could only find a way to curtail unnecessary communications.

Impairment of communication ability. Two major impairments of effective communication are poor listening and poor reading. The rapt attention displayed by people when others are speaking is often a cover-up; they may be thinking of something not specifically related to what is being said or deciding what to say when the speaker is finished. In neither case can the efficiency of the communication be very high.

Receiving efficiency is limited in poor readers as well as poor listeners. Many people, including top-level managers, are slow readers and retain very little of what they read. Individuals often do not realize that they have this handicap, because they lack a standard with which to measure their ability. Speedreading courses can remove this barrier to communication for people who are motivated to improve their communication ability in this way.

On the opposite side of the coin, poor speaking and poor writing are significant criteria in the weeding out of individuals not destined to move up in an organization, and are much more easily detected than inadequate listening or reading ability.

Communication will be dealt with again in Section 65, relevant to the managerial function of controlling; in that treatment, it will be analyzed through the use of simple cybernetic (feedback) models.

Discussion Questions

1. Idioms and contemporary slang are communication barriers, particularly if senders and receivers are from different cultures or age groups. What are some differences between your vocabulary, your instructor's, and some of the words used in this book, that may present communication problems?

2. What means of communication would a senior manager use in transmitting information down through the organization hierarchy?

3. How will the subordinates' understanding of company politics influence the content of messages that they send upward?

4. How does project management facilitate interorganization communication? (See Section 19.)

5. What significant costs are associated with unnecessary communication?

54. Accomplishing Change

For the purpose of this discussion, the modern business organization can be compared to a hollow core ceaselessly bombarded from within and without by forces demanding change. Internally, the forces are all kinds of indications that the system is out of equilibrium, such as rising costs, slipped schedules, quality rejects, and personnel grievances. External forces demanding change include technological advances, competitors' strategies, evolving social values, union demands, and government controls. Formerly, in the tradition of *laissez-faire* economics, adjustment to change was assumed to be a function of the price system, with adjustments coming about automatically and efficiently. But the contemporary notion on change is that it must be planned.

Present-day managers must be constantly alert to the necessity for change, must determine the adapting measures that will enable them to cope with change, and finally, must implement the measures in such a way that change is effective. The first two of these steps are part of the managerial function of planning, and assessing the effectiveness of the adapting measures is part of controlling. It is the part of the third step—concerned with the way that the measures are implemented—that is part of the directing function, because here the manager will be requiring a behavioral change from subordinates in conformance with the systems change being introduced.

The Perceptor of Change Signals

A popular term in the literature on change is *change agent*. This term applies to anyone within the organization, or outside of it, who is professionally qualified to diagnose a need for change, to prescribe the way of accomplishing it, and to assist in making it effective. In a business organization, a change agent could be—in addition to a manager—a computer expert, an engineer, or a psychologist (as discussed in Section 6). However, the view is taken in this book that these latter specialists act as an extension of some manager, who either tacitly or explicitly commissions and endorses their activities.

Alternative Methods for Inducing Change

Assume that a need for change is indicated. Further assume that there will be two parties to the change, the manager and the subordinates who will be affected by the change. And finally, assume that the two parties will contemplate the change with different values. The manager will perceive the change as being for the good of the organization, and will favor it. The subordinates will look at the change as a threat to their security and will resist it. *Threat* is used here in the relative sense; for example, the perception of the consequence of change can vary from mildly annoying to traumatic.

Unilateral prescription.   One extreme alternative for introducing change is for the manager to unilaterally prescribe changes of behavior for subordinates, or changes in working conditions. This action is consistent with the classical image of the authoritarian manager (Section 45). The subordinates will conform to the change to the degree necessary to avoid the penalties for nonconformance, but their resistance to the change will persist and their performance will suffer. There are possibly two causes of resistance when change is introduced in this manner. One is the threat of the change itself, and the other is the subordinates' resentment that their feelings in the matter have been completely ignored.

Explanation of the change.   The manager can, without really much effort, make an important improvement in the above change procedure by simply informing subordinates ahead of time why a change is necessary. If the explanation is honest and made with the proper timing, some of the resistance to the change will probably be reduced. With this alternative, after giving the reasons for the change, the manager proceeds to establish the specific steps whereby the change will be accomplished.

Manipulation of subordinates' suggestions.   A third alternative for introducing change is for the manager to carefully explain the reasons for it. Then—although the best way to make the change effective may already be decided—subordinates' suggestions are invited regarding ways of accomplishing the change. Their contributions are guided until they come around to the manager's way of thinking. A clever and adroit manager may be able to use this technique to reduce resistance to changes, and at the same time conceal from subordinates that they are being manipulated. It may be supposed, however, that eventually most subordinates would realize that they had been duped, and would resist change all the more because of this knowledge.

Involvement of employees in deliberations. Most managers these days have enough understanding of human behavior to know that true involvement of subordinates in change procedures will improve the possibility that the change will be effective. As has been mentioned, management by objectives—a whole new philosophy in directing people—is based on this concept (see Section 46). Therefore, a fourth alternative becomes apparent, which is, after the reasons for the change have been fully explained to all subordinates, to have them select representatives who will deliberate with the manager over methods of implementation. In these meetings the manager avoids any indication of dictating to subordinates, and welcomes recommendations for effecting the change in the manner most acceptable to them. A drawback to this procedure is that the subordinates' recommendations may be less efficient, from the standpoint of meeting the organization's goals, than methods unilaterally initiated by the manager; or at least, many managers will think so.

Achievement of consensus. The other extreme alternative is to involve all individuals who will be affected by the change in choosing the ways to accomplish it. What this amounts to in pure industrial democracy is for the manager to identify the fact that change is necessary, and then to leave it entirely to the consensus of the affected subordinates as to how it will be accomplished. It is easy to see in theory that change totally implemented by the people who have to work with it should meet with minimum resistance.

Time to Accomplish Change

Time is the practical consideration that so often is in conflict with the democratic process in all social systems, and perhaps this is particularly true in business organizations. Figure 54-1 depicts how the time required to accomplish change may vary inversely with the reduction in resistance to change as the direction procedures vary from unilateral to full participation.

The apparent implication in Figure 54-1 is that although the ideal way to introduce change may be through full participation by the people who will be affected by it, time pressures will often preclude managers from doing much more than openly explaining to their subordinates why the change is necessary and the reasons for the

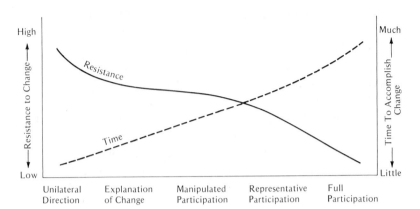

Figure 54–1. Resistance to Change Vs. Time to Accomplish Change.

choice of the prescribed change procedures. While this reasoning would probably be endorsed by many managers, its flaw lies in the assignment of equal, or greater, weight to the cost of time as compared to the cost of resistance to change. Such weighting is understandable, because the costs of time are tangible. Costs of resistance to change are much more difficult to estimate; in fact, by managers who are inclined to do so, it can easily be rationalized that they are comparatively insignificant.

The findings of the behavioral scientists suggest that resistance to change is a serious impairment to the effectiveness of the change. Even though the costs of resistance may not stand out as starkly as the costs of time, they are nevertheless highly important, and will become increasingly so with the advancing education levels of the working population. The well-educated workers will tend to be more resentful of unilateral change procedures, and because they are paid higher salaries, their apathetic conformance to the change will be more costly to the organization. An additional factor to be considered is that highly educated individuals have the potential of making worthwhile contributions when they are permitted to participate in choosing change procedures.

The challenge to managers who are to accomplish change is twofold. First, they will have to overcome personal tendencies to unilaterally prescribed change procedures. Second, they will have to develop the skills and techniques for involving subordinates in change without a destructive increase in time. This challenge can be met only by changes in the attitudes and modes of interaction on the part of managers now developing. One way of accomplishing this objective is through sensitivity training, the subject of Section 55.

Discussion Questions

1. Explain the view that specialists brought into an organization to effect change merely act as an extension of the manager.
2. Explain by example how subordinates' perceptions of the consequence of change can vary from mildly annoying to traumatic.
3. Do you think that, in most cases, resistance to an imposed change will persist indefinitely?
4. Is there any substance to the argument by many managers that their subordinates do not know when and how a change should be effected as well as the managers do?
5. What kinds of change decisions in business must be made so quickly that there is no time for subordinates' participation?

55. Sensitivity Training

The use of sensitivity training goes back to about 1949, when it was originated at the National Training Laboratory in Bethel, Maine; and in approximately a quarter century the technique has gained enthusiastic supporters and vehement detractors, seemingly in equal proportions. Moreover, reports concerning the extent to which business organizations have experimented with the technique are conflicting, some claiming widespread adoption by industry and others, widespread rejection. In any event, sensitivity training, or the related concepts of T groups and group dynamics, seems important enough as a technique for behavior change to merit an explanation and discussion.

The Sensitivity Concept

The basic thesis of sensitivity training is that people are unaware of the way others perceive them. Each individual perceives himself as behaving in a certain way and in conformance with certain values. He is, however, perceived quite differently by other people, and they ascribe other motivations to his behavior than the values he professes. The objectives of sensitivity training are

- to induce an awareness in individuals of their impact on other persons.
- to help them understand and correct unconsciously cultivated mechanisms that obstruct free interaction.
- to help them experience what can be accomplished through nonstructured group processes.

Application to the Business Organization

The premise on which sensitivity training is used in industry is that on-the-job interpersonal conflicts derive primarily from misunderstandings between people. Individuals attribute faults to others but are insensitive to the faults that others see in them. The conflicts that result divert energy from productive effort. Therefore, the sensitivity technique is applied in business organizations with the goal of improving group performance, whereas in other groups or clubs sensitivity training focuses more on effecting a change in the individual as a goal in itself.

The foremost rule, and one that probably is not followed as strictly as it should be, is that the formal leader should be competent. There is an explosive potential in sensitivity training for causing personality damage to the participants, and the leader must have the skill to prevent this. When the training is done with people from the same work organization, it should be conducted at a site away from the job environment. Supervisors should not be in the same training group as subordinates. The ideal size for training groups is between twelve and eighteen participants. The program should last long enough for the participants to go through a full cycle of stages, which would probably take at least thirty hours spread over several weeks.

Conduct of a Training Program

Typically, a program evolves through five stages.

1. The embarrassment stage.   At the beginning session, the formal leader will open with this kind of statement: "I presume that we are all here to learn something about the impact that we have on other people." After that, he says absolutely nothing. When the silence becomes unbearable, some member, or members, will begin to volunteer topics to talk about, such as personal introductions by participants, or statements as to their understanding of sensitivity training. After the first session, some participants feel so frustrated at the awkward silences that they may drop out of the program. The embarrassment stage may extend into the third session. During this stage informal group leaders will begin to emerge.

2. The hostility stage.   Predictably, during the third or fourth session some behavior by a participant will precipitate a hostile remark by someone else. Often the hostility will be directed toward one of the informal leaders who emerged during the embarrassment stage. Sometimes it will be directed to a member who has withdrawn from participation. In this stage, people will begin to tell other people frankly, and sometimes brutally, what is annoying about them. Often the formal leader must break his self-imposed silence to prevent excessive and destructive conflict.

3. The revelation stage.   People who are being attacked, or who are attacking, will suddenly change their behavior, and a new stage begins. At this point people will begin to confide to the group what they perceive to be the cause for their behavior in the previous two stages, and in other social interactions as well. Individuals will be motivated to enunciate inner feelings that they have never expressed before, even to themselves. The formal leader's intervention to prevent these catharses from going too far is essential, because the group will encourage the revealers to tell more and more.

4. The incipient cohesion stage.   At a later session the revelations will begin to taper off, and hostility will appear only occasionally. Now the group begins to think of problems that it can solve. In an industrial training group, this stage may actually begin concurrently with earlier stages, but at some point the problem-solving process begins to show indications of effectiveness. Interpersonal barriers begin to dissolve, and communication becomes easier and less inhibited.

5. The full cohesion stage.   Eventually, the members will come to consider that their group is the best that was ever assembled. The group will have confidence in itself to be able to solve any problem effectively and efficiently. And by this time it will have a high level of problem-solving ability. Moreover, the individual members will feel, even if only temporarily, closer to each other than they have ever felt to almost anyone else. If things go this way, this is the end of a successful sensitivity program.

Effectiveness of the Technique

To the question of how effective sensitivity training is, two answers must be given. The first is that within the training group the behavior of most people unquestionably changes, because the pressures of the group simply force individuals to drop their defenses, and thereby free the way to effective interaction.

Evidence as to whether the changed behavior persists when people get back to their jobs is inconclusive. The conventional validating technique is to ask their peers and subordinates over varying time periods whether there has been a noticeable change in their behavior. Some surveys indicate that there has, even over enduring periods of time. Other surveys suggest that there are changes at the beginning, but that these gradually disappear. Finally, some reports suggest that people revert to their old behavior immediately upon leaving the sensitivity training environment.

An explanation of why changes in behavior might not continue is that the sensitivity training is conducted in an artificial environment conducive to change, and all members of the group are undergoing a common experience. Back on the job, the individual is exposed to entirely different stimuli, and readopts familiar behavioral mechanisms to cope with them. A way to get around this tendency for a person to revert to previous behavior is to have an entire work group go through sensitivity training at about the same time.

Negative Factors

A company might be deterred from trying sensitivity training for several reasons. For one thing, it is expensive. The direct costs of engaging a qualified leader and setting up a program are high, not to mention the loss of productivity while trainees are away from their jobs. Second, there is no assurance that sensitivity training really accomplishes any results that can be positively identified. And third, there may be negative results. If the program does not last long enough to get past the hostility stage, damaging antagonisms can become ingrained. Also, if the leader lets revelations get out of control, serious psychological problems can occur for some people. The most important factor for business firms to realize is that the two- or three-day "quickie" programs that are frequently being promoted can offer nothing good, and most likely will produce harmful results.

Discussion Questions

Reference Case A. The Case of the Leopard That Couldn't Change Its Spots (Section 45)

1. Do you think that most people really want to know how they are perceived by others?
2. What reason might there be for not including supervisors and subordinates in the same full-scale sensitivity program?
3. In Reference Case A, Al Kirschman attended a week's sensitivity

training session. What do you think the long-term effects of the experience will be on him?

4. Explain why a sensitivity training group might develop high cohesiveness. (See Section 50.)

5. As a future manager, what might make you consider sponsoring sensitivity training with company funds?

56. Directing Engineering and Scientific Personnel

Only recently have managers in the United States begun to realize that a strong case can be made for the position that all employees should not receive equal treatment. A new caste is growing in American business, comprised of people possessing professional degrees. A comfortable approach would be to assume that a firm's general policies are suitable for handling this type of employee, thereby avoiding the complications associated with multiple standards; but the rising body of specialists has the potential power to require differentiation in all aspects of the treatment it receives from an organization. Some companies have already instituted special policies for engineers and scientists, and it is possible that all firms dependent on technical personnel will have to make similar concessions.

Uniqueness of Professional Employees

Professional employees are unique because of two factors. One has do with what they represent to the organization, and the other with the characteristics of the people themselves.

Meaning to the organization. To the organization, its pool of engineers and scientists represents an extremely valuable asset that is often in very short supply. The value derives from the dependence of business organizations on the continuous generation of new ideas that can be incorporated into future products or services. The ideas, and the development of them, in most cases come from the professional employees. These people represent a considerable investment by the organization. Including salary, training costs, and fringe benefits, an engineer's or scientist's anticipated forty years with a company can be interpreted as an investment in excess of $800,000.

Professional employees have another implication for the organization in the increasing authority they exercise over high-level decision making. This informal authority derives from the professional employees' specialized knowledge. As there are so many subject areas in which only specialists in the fields are at all informed, often senior managers must defer to the judgments of specialists on issues without having any effective way of knowing whether they are right or wrong.

Personal characteristics.   The personal characteristics of engineers and scientists set them apart from other nonmanagers in an organization, such as salesmen, production workers, and clerks, whom they resemble only on the basis of being productive through individual effort. That is, they are differentiated from these other nonmanagers by:

- the implication from their investment in themselves that they want more than the ordinary things in life.
- an unusual power of choice in employer selection.
- a stronger identification with their profession than to their employing organization.
- needs for recognition, deep involvement in their work, and self-actualization.

Their Preferences

Probably engineers and scientists place number one priority on work assignments that are challenging and stimulating enough to provide them with a sense of achievement. They want to receive recognition for outstanding performance from the organization and from their colleagues. They rate highly the ability to exercise considerable personal discretion in carrying out their work. They want to be treated like other professionals, such as physicians or professors, in being accorded good working conditions, unstructured hours of work, and assistants to perform routine tasks. And, as they have indicated by choosing industry instead of the academic life, they are interested in high salaries and commensurate fringe benefits.

What Can Be Done

The most important consideration in satisfying employees of this type lies in choosing the right manager to put over them. Such a manager must possess an unusual combination of talents. Business organizations have learned from experience that people who are not technically trained can rarely be successful in managing engineers and scientists, regardless of their managerial qualifications. The manager must be able to communicate with these subordinates in the language of their disciplines, and, in order to have their respect, must have some personal professional competence.

The manager must have an understanding of human motivation

as well. The work assignments should be geared to the personalities, abilities, and interests of each subordinate, while at the same time be consistent with the goals of the organization. The work environment should be open and permissive in order not to stifle creativity, and the subordinates should be able to have confidence in the way the manager represents them to higher management.

In addition, organizational policies can be aligned with the interests of professional employees. A system should be set up, enabling them to advance in salary and privileges on the sole basis of technical competence. Graduations of technical job titles also should be set up so that status can be recognized. The company should subsidize professional development, encourage such things as attendance at professional meetings, and provide recognition to individuals who present research papers. Top management should make special efforts to communicate organization objectives and prospects directly to engineers and scientists and should encourage their return communication.

Current Policies

Some business organizations have moved in the above direction in the treatment of their professional employees. However, interview data from over three hundred engineers in four companies indicates that many firms are seriously neglecting this important asset.

The work assigned to professionals tends to be repetitive, because from doing the same kind of work over and over again they become so proficient that they are not given different assignments. Over time, the skill in which they are specialized often becomes obsolete, and as they have not had an opportunity to keep up with the state of the art, they find their skills and knowledge outdated.

Starting salaries for engineers and scientists are high, but are very close to the top salaries. Therefore, the only way these people may advance is to move into managerial jobs, which is often in conflict with both their interests and their qualifications.

The managers placed over engineers and scientists tend to be given very narrow spans of control. As a result, there are many management levels, which effectively insulates professionals from top management. Another effect of placing few professional subordinates under each manager is that the managers tend to exercise close supervision.

Argument for Change

The difference in productivity between professional people who are treated in the apparently usual way and those treated in the way they feel is warranted has implications for management. Predictably, senior managers will become increasingly aware of the potential increase in productivity within their organization which can be activated by more enlightened management of its engineers and scientists.

Discussion Questions

Reference Case A. The Case of Why Some Engineers May Join Unions (Section 48)

1. What other specialists, in addition to engineers and scientists, can claim professional status and the privileges that this status implies?
2. What checks may managers use when relying on the decision-making authority of individuals possessing specialized scientific knowledge?
3. What should be the criteria for selecting managers who will direct highly technical workers?
4. In Reference Case A, how could Amalgamated Aircraft get more productivity out of its engineers? Suggest some ways.
5. What implications does the setting up of separate personnel policies for engineers and scientists have upon employee relations in other departments of the organization?

Summary

The effectiveness with which the directing function is performed depends on the leadership ability of the manager. It may be true that some individuals are natural leaders and are able to capitalize on this asset in a business organization; but in any case, an individual can develop the essential characteristics of leadership. These characteristics include the manager's ability to influence subordinates' acceptance of objectives and their response to prescribed methods for achieving these objectives, together with inspiring their confidence as a person who can help them achieve their personal goals.

A view of leadership styles has been constructed in management theory which has authoritarian and production-centered managers at one pole, and democratic and employee-centered managers at the opposite pole. There is a tendency to consider these types as mutually exclusive, rather than ends of a continuum on which real people fit somewhere toward the center. In theory, there are persuasive reasons favoring the democratic and employee-centered style, but in practice, managers will be forced to adopt modified versions of both polar styles alternately in conforming with varying conditions.

An outgrowth of the interest in democratic leadership is management by objectives, or objective-centered management, the central feature of which is that subordinates determine for themselves what their short-term objectives will be, as well as the criteria by which their accomplishment will be measured. With their supervisor's concurrence, subordinates pursue their objectives, and at the end of the agreed-upon time, the subordinates and the supervisor review the performance together. In addition to being a new directing technique, management by objectives also has the potential of being a performance-appraisal device.

In a business organization, leadership ability is measured by the degree to which the manager is able to motivate subordinates to extend their productive efforts. Various incentives may be employed as motivators. These may be positive or negative. Positive incentives include recognition, financial rewards, promotions, competition, job-related security, participation opportunities, and emulative personal conduct by the manager. A negative incentive may be demotion or discharge. A problem in choosing incentives is that people differ in what motivates them; to be effective, incentives must be specific to the individual.

A theory of motivation, developed by Abraham Maslow, is that

all humans have fundamental needs, and that these needs are perceived in a sequence of ascending order. On the lowest level is the
need for physiological factors which sustain life. Upon satisfaction
of this need, the person will desire satisfaction of the need for safety.
Next in theoretical sequence is the need for love, or social belongingness, and following it in the need hierarchy is the need for self-esteem
and the respect of others. Finally, a person aspires to satisfy the need
for self-actualization. A significant feature of need theory is that a
satisfied need ceases to be a motivator; upon even partial satisfaction
of one need, the human aspires for satisfaction of a higher-order need.

In a different view of needs as motivational drives, the psychologist David C. McClelland differentiates people with a compelling need
to achieve (n Ach types) from those whose primary need is for affiliation (n Aff types). The former will succeed because they are
preoccupied with improving their performance and they tend to set
goals that, though difficult, are achievable and have a high predictability of success. Family and cultural influences can strengthen the
n Ach characteristic in people, but McClelland also believes that it
can be acquired. Results of his training programs to increase n
Ach in people suggest that n Ach is useful in predicting business success, and that it can be stimulated or acquired through training.

The norms of the work group can be a significant influence in
shaping employees' behavior, especially if they derive certain need
satisfactions from being accepted by the group. The problem to managers is that the group norms can be in conflict with the organizational
norms. A way to deal with this problem is to direct the motivating
power of group cohesiveness toward positive ends. The Scanlon
Plan is one attempt to use what is known about group behavior to
motivate individuals to higher productivity.

A natural assumption is that if people derive satisfaction from
their jobs, their productivity should increase. However, research has
not found this to be true, possibly because researchers were ascribing
the wrong factors to job satisfaction. Such factors as adequate working
conditions and fringe benefits are not motivators, but people are dissatisfied if they are taken away. Real motivators are achievement,
recognition, and the job itself; therefore, if needs of the highest order
are satisfied, productivity will probably improve.

Human motivation is too complex to be fully explained by any
single theory. Nonrational influences on behavior, for example, can
be very powerful. Some writers, like Charles Darwin, say that instincts
inherited from animal ancestors influence human behavior. Ethics

teaches that some behavior is right, and other behavior wrong, and conscience tends to act as a governor over an individual's acts. Moreover, Freudian psychology holds that the unconscious mind is a significant motivating force.

The directing function of managers requires effective communication. Complicating the process are these factors: (1) the bias of the sender, whose personal values are reflected in the message; (2) the effect of the organization hierarchy in distorting messages for reasons associated with the time of transmission and the possibility of amplification and filtering; and (3) the bias of the receiver in interpreting and responding to the message. Relaxing of rules restricting communication in the formal hierarchical structure will alleviate some of the obstacles.

Change is a characteristic of the modern organization. As far as the directing function is concerned, coping with external change requires that the manager accomplish a responsive behavior change in subordinates. This can be done in various ways, ranging from authoritarian to democratic: (1) unilaterally prescribing change procedures; (2) explaining the reason for change before specifying the method; (3) manipulating subordinates into thinking that the predetermined choice of change methods is theirs; (4) inviting subordinates' representatives to confer on the change; or (5) involving the full participation of all subordinates who will be affected by the change to choose the method of its accomplishment.

Sensitivity training is a group-process technique for making individuals aware of ways in which their personal behavior may obstruct effective interaction with other people, and of ways for correcting such behavior. In addition, sensitivity training gives participants the chance to observe the power of informal group action.

Engineers and scientists differ in several respects from other nonmanagerial personnel, and should be given different and preferential treatment. Representing an important asset to the business organization, they require unusual directing methods and working conditions if a firm is to realize their full potential. Many companies have been tardy in recognizing that routine treatment of professional employees may be working to their disadvantage.

Selected Bibliography

Ardrey, Robert, *African Genesis*. Delta, 1963.

Argyris, Chris, "A Brief Description of Laboratory Education." *Training Director's Journal,* Vol. 17, No. 10, October 1963.

Bayfield, Arthur H., and Walter H. Crockett, "Employee Attitudes and Employee Performance," *Psychological Bulletin,* Vol. 52, No. 5, 1955.

Bennis, Warren G., Kenneth D. Benne, and Robert Chin (eds.), *The Planning of Change*. Holt, 1961.

Cartwright, Dorwin, and Alvin Zander, *Group Dynamics*. Row, Peterson, 1960.

Chruden, Herbert J., and Arthur W. Sherman, Jr., *Personnel Management*. South-Western, 1968.

Freud, Sigmund, *A General Introduction to Psycho-Analysis*. Washington Square, 1952.

Gerth, H. H., and C. Wright Mills (trans.), *From Max Weber: Essays in Sociology*. Oxford, 1946.

Herzberg, Frederick, *Work and the Nature of Man*. World, 1966.

Katz, D., "Morale and Motivation in Industry." In W. Dennis (ed.), *Current Trends in Industrial Psychology,* University of Pittsburgh, 1949.

Katz, Fred E., "Explaining Informal Work Groups in Complex Organizations: The Case for Autonomy in Structure." *Administrative Science Quarterly,* Vol. 10, No. 2, September 1965.

Likert, Rensis, "Motivation: The Core of Management." Personnel Series No. 155, American Management Association, 1953.

McClelland, David C. "Business Drive and National Achievement." *Harvard Business Review,* July-August 1962, pp. 99–112.

McClelland, David C., "That Urge to Achieve." *Think* Magazine, IBM, 1966.

McClelland, David C., and David G. Winter, *Motivating Economic Achievement*. The Free Press, 1969.

McGregor, Douglas, "An Uneasy Look at Performance Appraisal." *Harvard Business Review,* May-June 1957.

McGregor, Douglas, *The Human Side of Enterprise*. McGraw-Hill, 1960.

Maslow, A. H., "A Theory of Human Motivation." *Psychological Review,* Vol. 50, 1943.

Newman, William H., Charles E. Summer, and E. Kirby Warren, *The Process of Management*. Prentice-Hall, 1967.

Odiorne, George S., "The Trouble with Sensitivity Training." *Training Director's Journal,* Vol. 17, No. 10, October 1963.

Raudsepp, Eugene, *Managing Creative Scientists and Engineers.* Macmillan, 1963.

Reeser, Clayton, "Some Potential Human Problems of the Project Form of Organization." *Academy of Management Journal,* 1969.

Rosow, Jerome M., "The Growing Role of Professional and Scientific Personnel." National Industrial Conference Board, *Management Record,* Vol. 24, No. 2, February 1962.

Shannon, Claude E., and Warren Weaver, *The Mathematical Theory of Communication.* University of Illinois, 1949.

Tannenbaum, Robert, and Warren H. Schmidt, "How to Choose a Leadership Pattern." *Harvard Business Review,* Vol. 36, No. 2, March-April 1958.

Tannenbaum, Robert, Irving Weschler, and Fred Massarik, *Leadership and Organization.* McGraw-Hill, 1961.

Tead, Ordway, and Henry C. Metcalf, *Personnel Administration.* McGraw-Hill, 1920.

Vroom, Victor H., *Work and Motivation.* Wiley, 1964.

Weber, Max (translated by Talcott Parsons), *The Protestant Ethic and the Spirit of Capitalism.* Scribner's, 1958.

Wickstrom, Walter S., "Management by Objectives, or, Appraisal by Results." *The Conference Board Record,* July 1966.

CONTROLLING

Controlling is the terminal function of management, in the sense that its purpose is to validate the functions of planning, organizing, staffing, and directing that precede it, or, in other words, to confirm that efforts are commensurate with results. Control is most intimately associated with planning, but is pervasively present in the performance of the other functions as well.

Control is found to be a descriptive task in all organized groupings of operational activities, such as the departments of finance, engineering, production, and marketing. Thus, in addition to assuring the effectiveness of the managerial functions, control also implies validation of the ways that operations are performed.

Vital to the controlling function is the feedback process. After goals are formed for business operations and resources committed to achieving them, it is essential to have effective feedback of results. The most successful control systems employ feedback of probable *future* results, rather than of past outcomes. Modern forecasting techniques and computerization of data is making this ideal achievable in an increasing number of control applications. The primary medium for feedback is the written report (in numerical or narrative terms); but common supplements are oral review and personal observation.

Of all the managerial functions, controlling has become the most mechanistic and indifferent to human concerns. Whereas (1) directing is concerned entirely with human behavior; (2) the values involved in staffing are primarily humanistic rather than quantitative; (3) the modern emphasis in organizing is on consideration of individuals and human needs; and (4) planning (though moving toward quantitative approaches in most areas) still indicates a fresh awareness of human needs, controlling is almost completely objective, with quantitative methods assuming ever increasing dominance. In the process, human behavior, resistance, and attitudes seem to be overlooked, and the effectiveness of the function appears to be suffering as a result.

57. The General Nature of Control

The essential prerequisite to the performance of the managerial function of controlling is the existence of comprehensive, dynamic plans covering all areas of a company's operations. Just as planning is the attempt to set the courses of future events, controlling is the assurance that the courses are followed, and that actual events are in phase with planned events. Thus, controlling is the corollary of planning; without plans, control would be impossible. And, conversely, without control mechanisms, planning would be a meaningless exercise. Controlling is necessary to bring the plans to fruition.

Description of the Controlling Function

Control is used in various contexts. It is sometimes offered as a synonym for *authority;* for example, managers are said to have certain subordinates under their control. On other occasions *controlling* is interchanged with *directing;* thus, statements are found to the effect that a managerial function is controlling the actions of subordinates. There is a considerable amount of accuracy in both of these uses. However, it is suggested that to ascribe the term *controlling* to a specific and differentiated managerial function, a narrower description is required. To provide it, we might say that the controlling function entails

- the establishment of standards by which the achievement of plans can be measured.
- the comparison of performance results with these standards, and the seeking out of deviations.
- the initiation of actions to correct continuance of the deviations or to modify the plans.

Standards of Measurement

Standards relate to the characteristics of the events that are desired to be accomplished; therefore, they must be specific to the individual plans. All standards have one requirement in common: as far as possible, they should be expressed in numerical terms. This requirement is critical because quantitative standards minimize the necessity for human judgment. If there is one number that expresses desired performance, and another that reflects what has actually been achieved, the two can be compared and an objective conclusion reached. Qualitative standards, on the other hand, are open to interpretation, which means that assessment of the achievement of plans may be distorted by personal biases.

One way of setting standards is according to the input-output concept; in other words, the standards apply to input factors to an activity and output factors from the activity. Input factors are the resources committed to an activity, and primarily include labor, raw materials, and capital. A common unit of measurement for these factors is dollars, although labor hours and material weights may also be used. It should be plain that input factors are the costs of performing an activity. Output factors are the final products, services, or other results generated by an activity. These also may be expressed in dollars, but, in addition, are often identified by such values as units of production or sales.

Standards may also be set according to the criterion of time; that is, dates may be established for the completion of sequential mileposts, or subevents necessary for the accomplishment of a plan.

Stemming from the input-output concept of standards is the expression of outputs in relative terms. Thus, it is common to conceive of profitability as a ratio of sales or capital investment. Share of the market is also a commonly applied standard. Additionally, proportional increases in scale of operations, among many others, constitute a popular measurement of achievement.

Bases for Constructing Standards

In setting standards, managers often tend to base them on past performance or even on high hopes—neither of which can compare in effectiveness to objective analyses.

Past performance.   Extrapolation from historical data is one usual method of constructing performance standards, the apparent theory being that even though past performance may not have been perfect, future performance certainly should not be worse. In using this method, standards expressed as ratios are often projected from past accomplishments and become minimum measurements of performance. For example, a firm that has never operated at less than 85 percent of capacity, has always earned at least 15 percent on invested capital, and has traditionally had more than 25 percent of the available market, will tend to project these ratios as cutoff points, so that problems will be indicated if they are not at least equalled. Some disadvantages of projecting past achievements as standards are the possibilities that inefficiencies will be perpetuated and changes (actual or predicted) will be overlooked.

High hopes.   Aspiration is another basis for setting standards. Managers often subjectively establish standards higher than have been achieved through previous performance in the hope that the striving for them will result in some improvement, even though it is not likely. There is a danger in this approach, because people tend to be discouraged from even trying to meet standards which they perceive to be unrealistic.

Objective analyses.   A final method for setting standards, and the one that is by far the most effective, is to employ objective analyses to determine the theoretical optimum in achievement. Frederick Taylor (Section 2) is often said to have started the movement toward objective analysis with time and motion study for setting labor standards; and in recent years the quantitative methods for decision making (Section 16 and the appendixes) have come to be applied in many areas of a company's operation to determine theoretically possible standards.

Comparison of Plans and Events

The reports which permit comparison of plans and actual events are necessarily of many varieties. Traditionally, a large proportion of these reports has always been generated by a firm's accounting department, but a modern trend, caused by the increasing use of the computer, appears to be centralized reporting in a data-processing department. However, regardless of the source of reports, certain elements must be observed in measuring performance.

Pinpointing strategic factors.   Because of the hosts of data that can be spewed out of a reporting system, it is crucial that the strategic factors relevant to the achievement of each individual plan be identified. Factors are strategic if they make a significant difference between the success or failure of a plan, whereas nonstrategic factors may vary widely from plans, but have little effect on the final outcome. Reports should be designed to focus on the strategic factors. (See the sections on the planning function for discussions of the factors that are strategic to plans.)

Predicting deviations.   The most meaningful reports are those that indicate deviations from plans before they occur. Such prescience is possible through sophisticated trend analysis, and enables managers to do something about potentially unfavorable conditions. If deviations cannot be predicted, the next best thing is to report them right after they have happened. In this way, corrective action may be taken to prevent a dangerous situation from getting out of control. It should be obvious that reports that tend to be ancient history are relatively useless. A manager can make little effective response to a report that tells him that plans are completely awry because of an event that went undetected three months before.

Using valid units of measurement.   Events should be reported in valid units of measurement. For example, in reporting engineering accomplishments, it is far more meaningful to report mileposts achieved, as related to those that were scheduled, than to report the current status of expended engineering labor hours. Again, actual production as of a certain date is a more useful statistic than percent of plant capacity that was worked in the time period. It is so easy for events to appear favorable when they are reported in one fashion, when, if they are reported in a way that more appropriately represents the condition, they will be seen to be completely out of line.

Distributing the report.   A key imperative in reporting performance is to transmit the information in each case to the manager who can do something about it, and to the higher-level manager who assesses whether appropriate action has been taken. In addition, reports should be sent to other managers whose own operations might be affected by the events. This probably is as far as the distribution of reports should go. A common tendency in business firms is for the reporting source to try to blanket the entire organization with reports, while frequently omitting the manager who is most directly responsible for the cause of deviations.

Corrective Action

Depending on the severity of the deviations, corrective actions taken by a company will take the form of either short-term or long-term adjustments.

Short-term adjustments. Some deviations of actual events from planned events can be remedied by "fire-fighting" tactics, or short-term adjustments. Perhaps, for example, the responsible manager foresees that a deviation from plans is about to happen, and because this deviation was a contingency that was considered in the original planning effort, an alternative course was developed that can be adopted now that the contingency turns out to be a real fact. Or the deviations may be less easily correctable, but still within the manager's ability to remedy, such as malperformance by individuals, underallocation of input resources, or inefficient use of resources. Some specific action is appropriate to deal with each of these possible causes of deviations, and once the manager has isolated the cause and applied the action, the short-term crises should be resolved. The same tactics can be used, although with somewhat less effectiveness, to handle deviations of the immediate past that have been brought to the manager's attention.

Long-term adjustments. Deviations necessitating long-term adjustments have causes that are built into the system itself. In such cases, the plans are theoretically possible to be realized, but when deviations occur and short-term adjustments are applied to them, improvement does not take place. The presumably responsible managers are frustrated by their ineffectiveness, their efforts are criticized by higher-level managers, and the chasm between plans and events becomes wider. The only solution lies in making significant, and probably long-term, adjustments in the total system.

Kinds of adjustments that may be necessary include change of the method of organization, for instance, from functional to project, the dropping or adding of product lines, revamping of the firm's capital structure, or vertical or horizontal merger. Often the basic cause for deviations that cannot be corrected readily is the incompetence of the management team. For example, a large wholesale grocery company in Los Angeles just after World War II was forced to finally liquidate its assets because its management was comprised of elderly men who were no longer capable of operating the company

in a highly competitive environment, and who could not be satisfactorily replaced because of the then national shortage of qualified
managers.

The following sections are concerned with specific control techniques.

"I warned you six months ago that you were going to get into trouble because of Brooks and his high-pressure selling tactics," exclaimed Dominic Bianco, attorney for B and J Building Materials, Inc., and who was also on the firm's board of directors.

"What's the matter now?" nervously asked Joe Bradley, manager and part owner of the company.

"A group of the homeowners to whom Brooks and those crooks that he calls salesmen sold aluminum siding have hired an attorney, Tom Davis, to contest their contracts. Davis just called me about it," replied Bianco.

In an effort to bolster B and J's somewhat sagging earnings record with an allied product, Bradley had taken on a line of aluminum siding about a year previously. The product was made by a reputable manufacturer, and although expensive by the standards of the average homeowner, did improve the exterior of a house when installed over the original frame construction. Bradley hired an installation crew, and invested in an inventory of the siding. He advertised on television and in the newspaper, and when inquiries came in, two salesmen who had formerly worked in the hardware department of B and J for many years called on the homeowners and submitted price estimates. Sales were, however, extremely disappointing. In the first six months, only five installations had been sold.

While thinking about writing off the siding venture as a bad investment, Bradley received an impressive letter from a Mr. Mal Brooks. Brooks described himself as a highly successful developer of direct sales, cited the firms that he had worked for, his titles, and the dramatic increases in sales that he had effected. He said he now wanted the challenge of developing the aluminum siding market, and would like to meet with Mr. Bradley at 2:00 P.M. on the coming Friday.

The proposition that Brooks made was as follows: He would assume the management of a division to be created—the Aluminum Siding Division of B and J Building Materials, Inc., with the title of Vice-

358

President. In the first month he would be on probation while he proved that he could sell ten installations. After that it would be considered a permanent arrangement, as long as sales increased 50 percent each month until they leveled off at thirty to thirty-five per month. His compensation would be a draw against a 10-percent commission on all installations. He would build a sales crew of about five salesmen, each of whom would have a draw against a 10-percent commission on every installation that they personally sold. A bank account would be set up for the division, and he would manage it. He would deposit the homeowners' down payments in it, and pay the salesmen's advances out of it. Bradley was to open the account with $5000. Bradley was to leave all of the details of the aluminum siding business to him, and judge him by his sales performance. To protect Bradley, Brooks adamantly insisted that he become bonded.

Sales went as promised, and Bradley was delighted. The only sour notes were those sounded by Bianco at the monthly board meetings. Bianco called Bradley's attention to the scandalous "suede shoe gangs" who had exploited the aluminum siding market in other states. Through the local police department, he found that four of the five salesmen that Brooks had hired were ex-convicts, and that Brooks had been charged twice for extortion, although he had never been convicted. He said that he was sure that Brooks was not using the contract and warranty forms that he had prepared, but was employing forms of his own design. He prophesied that an indelible stain would be put on B and J's name, and now the action taken by the dissident homeowners confirmed his worst suspicions.

There was nothing for Bianco and Bradley to do but meet with Tom Davis, the homeowners' attorney. The following discussion took place in Davis' office:

"What are these people complaining about?" exploded Bradley. "They bought an aluminum siding installation, and they got it."

"Although this is far from the whole of it," Davis began, "even this statement isn't true. Don't you know that your own installation crew is so far behind that people who made down payments three months ago haven't had work started on their houses yet? And, don't you also know that your Mal Brooks lined up a fly-by-night construction

outfit to make installations that were so badly done that the siding is falling off the houses?"

"No, I didn't," admitted Bradley.

"Their next step, after getting a homeowner to agree to buy an installation, was to clinch the financing arrangement," Davis went on. "Brooks had made a deal with a shady finance company to take the paper for 75 percent of the installation price. Although you have to look carefully to find it in the contract, interest is at 24 percent compounded on the original balance. Another interesting obscure clause in the contract is that the homeowner assigns a second mortgage on his property to the finance company. Then, to get the 25-percent cash down payment, the sales pressure must have been awesome to behold. People borrowed on their life insurance, took their children's education funds, and mortgaged their cars and furniture. You might say that they're adults and should know what they're doing, but if this goes to court I'm going to say that they are victims of unscrupulous and systematized chicanery."

"I had no idea that Brooks was using tactics like that," confessed Bradley.

"Mr. Bradley," Davis said sharply, "I know some judges who would say to you that you are either a liar or a fool."

When Bianco and Bradley got back to the company office, Bradley said, "I sure let it get out of control, didn't I?"

Bianco replied, "I'm not sure we know everything yet. Let's try to get Brooks in here."

About ten minutes after the request to locate Mal Brooks, Edna Wilson, Bradley's secretary and office manager, informed them that Brooks had checked out of his motel.

"We do have him bonded, don't we?" Bradley asked her.

"No, we don't," she replied. "On the first day that he was here he made a big show about getting an application form from the bonding company, but he never filled it out."

"Mrs. Wilson," said Bianco, "please find out what the balance is in the bank account of Aluminum Siding Division."

A few minutes later the phone rang. It was the bank manager. "I was going to call you anyway," he said. "The balance is now $15.83. Mr. Brooks made a withdrawal of close to $10,000 yesterday."

Discussion Questions

1. Why are standards essential to the controlling function?
2. How does a student perform the controlling function while proceeding through a college course?
3. What long-term adjustments may students have to make when they assess the grade that they get in a course, as measured against the standard that they have set?
4. In the Case of the Slippery Siding Salesman, what standards did Joe Bradley have for control over Mal Brooks?
5. In what ways was Joe Bradley derelict in performing the controlling function?

58. Budgetary Financial Control

The dependence of the controlling function on plans is clearly evident when the technique known as budgeting is examined. The first step in budgeting is to decide on the forms to be used in expressing the results of the company's operations. It will be desired to present in an organized fashion such factors as revenues aligned with expenses, the fluctuations of cash, and the allocations of capital funds. The second step is to enter on the appropriate forms the company's expectations with respect to revenue, expenses, cash flow, etc.; and these should be entered in numerical terms. So far, budgeting is purely planning. Finally, when actual results are obtained, they are entered opposite the expected results, the differences are analyzed, and conclusions are reached regarding indicated actions. At this point the budget becomes a control device.

The typical firm will develop many types of budgets. Moreover, each type of budget will vary in the amount of detail it includes, depending on which organizational level it is prepared for. In other words, budgets prepared for top-level management tend to be summaries; but the closer budgets get to the organizational level at which performance takes place, the more detailed they will be.

An Example of the Budgeting Process

The process of budgeting can be explained with reference to Figure 58-1, a simple operating statement (revenue and expense budget), plus a few supporting expense budgets—Figures 58-2 to 58-5.

Sales performance. The first response of the general manager of a hypothetical company to Figure 58-1 would be elation. To provide for a quarterly budget review, which he regards as an adequate means of control, he had the operating statement prepared immediately following March 31, and it confirms the sales manager's reports that gross sales for the quarter exceeded expectations by 19 percent. The major criterion of success or failure to managers of most small companies is sales performance, and an excess of this magnitude is usually regarded as a good omen. However, since this particular budget has been prepared with all elements represented as proportions of gross sales, as well as in absolute values, when the manager proceeds to the next two lines of the operating statement his initial ela-

Figure 58–1. Operating Statement, Quarter Ending March 31, 1973.

	Actual		Budget		Variance (Unfavorable variances in parentheses)	
	($000)	Percent of Gross Sales	($000)	Percent of Gross Sales	($000)	Percent
Gross Sales	284.0	—	238.0	—	46.0	19
Less:						
Freight Out	14.2	5	4.8	2	(9.4)	(3.0)
Net Sales	269.8	95	233.2	98	36.6	(3.0)
Cost of Goods Sold:						
Direct Labor	83.2	29.3	64.3	27	(18.9)	(2.3)
Direct Materials	34.5	12.0	30.9	13	(3.6)	1.0
Overhead	58.5	21.0	52.4	22	(6.1)	1.0
Cost of Goods Sold	176.2	62.3	147.6	62	(28.6)	(0.3)
Gross Profit	93.6	32.7	85.6	36	8.0	(3.3)
Sales & Administrative:						
Sales Expense	68.2	24.0	38.1	16	(30.1)	(8.0)
Administrative Expense	24.0	8.5	23.8	10	(0.2)	1.5
Sales & Administrative	92.2	32.5	61.9	26	(30.3)	(6.5)
Net Profit	1.4	0.2	23.7	10	(22.3)	(9.8)

Figure 58–2.   Direct Labor Analysis, Quarter Ending March 31, 1973.

	Actual Hours	Budget Hours	Variance	Actual ($000)	Actual % GS	Budget ($000)	Budget % GS	Variance ($000)	Variance %
Foundry (Straight Time)	6400	6270	(130)	19.3		18.8	8	(5.3)	(0.5)
" (Overtime)	1070	–	(1070)	4.8	8.5	–			
Machine Shop (ST)	7300	7180	(120)	22.0		21.5	9	(6.0)	(0.7)
" (OT)	1220	–	(1220)	5.5	9.7	–			
Finishing Shop (ST)	3350	3200	(150)	10.0		9.6	4	(2.9)	(0.4)
" (OT)	545	–	(545)	2.5	4.4	–			
Assembly (ST)	5100	4800	(300)	15.4		14.4	6	(4.7)	(0.7)
" (OT)	815	–	(815)	3.7	6.7	–			
Total Direct Labor	25,800	21,450	(4350)	83.2	29.3	64.3	27	(18.9)	(2.3)

Figure 58–3. Direct Materials Analysis, Quarter Ending March 31, 1973.

	Actual		Budget		Variance	
	($000)	% GS	($000)	% GS	($000)	%
Raw Materials	17.5	6	16.5	7	(1.0)	1.0
Subcontracted Components	8.5	3	7.2	3	(1.3)	–
Purchased Parts	8.5	3	7.2	3	(1.3)	–
Total Direct Materials	34.5	12	30.9	13	(3.6)	1.0

Figure 58–4. Overhead Analysis, Quarter Ending March 31, 1973.

	Actual		Budget		Variance	
	($000)	% GS	($000)	% GS	($000)	%
Indirect Labor	22.8	8	16.7	7	(6.1)	(1.0)
Salaries	11.9	4	11.9	5	–	1.0
Supplies	4.8	2	4.8	2	–	–
Depreciation	14.2	5	14.2	6	–	1.0
Power	2.4	1	2.4	1	–	–
Other	2.4	1	2.4	1	–	–
Total Overhead	58.5	21	52.4	22	(6.1)	1.0

tion may somewhat dampen. The expense of shipping the firm's product to its customers has gone sufficiently over the budget to lower the ratio of net sales to gross sales by 3 percent. Even at that, actual net sales exceeded the budgeted figure by $36,600, so things continue to look good.

Cost of goods sold. It would be expected that it would cost more to produce $284,000 worth of product than $238,000 worth. Therefore, higher amounts for labor, materials, and overhead are not surprising. A disturbing item is the 2.3-percent higher ratio of direct labor to gross sales. This will have to be looked into later. Offsetting this higher ratio, however, are lower ratios of materials and overhead to gross sales; moreover, the ratio of cost of goods sold to gross sales is only 0.3 percent above budget, which does not appear too alarming. Then, too, actual gross profit is $8000 higher than the budget figure, even though this amount represents a less favorable ratio to gross sales—32.7 percent, as compared with the 36-percent ratio that was budgeted.

Figure 58–5. Sales Analysis, Quarter Ending March 31, 1973.

	Total						Territory 1						Territory 2					
	Actual		Budget		Variance		Actual		Budget		Variance		Actual		Budget		Variance	
	$	%GS	$	%GS	$	%	$	%GS	$	%GS	$	%	$	%GS	$	%GS	$	%
Gross Sales	284.0	–	238.0	–	46.0	–	145.0	–	143.0	–	2	–	139.0	–	95.0	–	44.0	–
Less:																		
Freight Out	14.2	5	4.8	2	(9.4)	(3.0)	2.9	2	2.9	2	–	–	11.3	8.1	1.9	2	(9.4)	(6.1)
Net Sales	269.8	95	233.2	98	36.6	(3.0)	142.1	98	140.1	98	2	–	127.7	91.9	93.1	98	34.6	(6.1)
Sales Expense:																		
Salaries	22.7	8	19.1	8	(3.6)	–	11.6	8	11.5	8	(0.1)	–	11.1	8.0	7.6	8	(3.5)	–
Travel	25.6	9	9.5	4	(16.1)	(5.0)	5.8	4	5.7	4	(0.1)	–	19.8	14.2	3.8	4	(16.0)	(10.2)
Entertainment	19.9	7	9.5	4	(10.4)	(3.0)	5.8	4	5.7	4	(0.1)	–	14.1	10.2	3.8	4	(10.3)	(6.2)
Total Sales Expense	68.2	24	38.1	16	(30.1)	(8.0)	23.2	16	22.9	16	(0.3)	–	45.0	32.4	15.2	16	(29.8)	(16.4)

Sales expenses.   When the manager's analysis reaches the sales expense entries, his optimism will undoubtedly disappear. It has cost $30,100 to generate the additional $46,000 in gross sales, and sales expense as a proportion of gross sales has gone 8 percent over budget. Even though administrative expense has held constant in absolute value, and is actually below the budget in relative amount, the ratio to gross sales of sales and administrative expense combined is over budget by 6.5 percent. The final blow is that profit only amounts to $1400, in comparison with a budgeted $23,700, and its ratio to gross sales is below the budget by 9.8 percent.

Investigating Deviations

The cost of freight out was an early clue that the additional sales were inordinately costly, which is conclusively borne out by the high sales expense. In the face of these figures, the manager would turn first to the sales analysis schedule to get to the root of the problem. The total columns in Figure 58-5 indicate that travel and entertainment expenses, in addition to shipping cost, are sources of the trouble. Total travel relative to gross sales is 5 percent higher than budgeted, and entertainment, 3 percent. Now, have both sales territories generated excessive travel and entertainment increases?

A look at the figures for Territory 1 discloses that nothing out of line has occurred. The actual sales produced in the territory were consistent with the volume that was planned, it cost no more to ship the product than the budgeted 2 percent, and the elements of salaries, travel, and entertainment were each satisfactorily within $100 of the budgets.

Territory 2 has a different story, however. It is in this territory that the sales increase has been bought at a high price. The 6.1-percent excess in freight and the 10.2-percent excess in travel, as ratios of gross sales, indicate that the salesmen must be ranging far afield to find customers for their wares. In addition, the buyers must be receiving lavish entertainment in return for their purchasing favors, as is revealed by the 6.2-percent higher ratio for that element.

Taking Corrective Action

Reform must start with the responsible manager. In this case it is obvious that the manager of Territory 2 is the guilty party. Either he encouraged his salesmen to buy sales in order to make an impressive sales record, or completely lost control of how they conducted their personal selling activities. The courses of action open to the general manager vary from discharging the sales manager to getting him straightened out and giving him another chance. The specific action in real life would be dictated by careful investigation of all of the circumstances.

Further Tracking

Now that the increase in sales has been disclosed to be a serious problem rather than a blessing, what effect has it had on other phases of the company's operations? The operating statement showed that direct labor costs were in trouble, so Figure 58–2 warrants attention. What stands out immediately is that the manufacturing operation was budgeted for straight-time activity only, but that the increase in sales required the plant to be worked overtime. Other than the 50-percent higher labor cost for overtime hours, the manufacturing departments consistently stayed within their budgets. Figure 58–3 reveals that absolute cost of materials went over budget, as would be anticipated because more materials were needed for the increased goods produced. It is shown, however, that quantity discounts for raw materials apparently caused the ratio of this element to gross sales to go below budget by 1 percent.

Overhead elements, which tend to be fixed costs, are shown in Figure 58–4. These generally have remained constant with the budget in absolute terms, with salaries and depreciation under the budget in relative terms. The one element, indirect labor, is above budget, both in dollars and percentage. An investigation would probably disclose that the unexpected increase in sales necessitated crash measures in scheduling, expediting, and shipping activities, with the resultant need for additional people.

What Comes Next?

Despite the fact that a serious problem was uncovered by budget analysis and can be corrected in the future, it should be apparent to the manager that quarterly reviews are insufficient. He must sophisticate his budgeting system so that potential variances can be detected before problems develop. In addition to remedying the budgeting defect, the unfortunate sales splurge probably developed other problems that can be isolated by nonbudgetary financial controls.

Discussion Questions

1. Why should budgets be prepared in greater detail the closer they get to the actual performance level in the organization?
2. What is the advantage in presenting budget data both in absolute dollars and as a percentage of some variable?
3. How is the principle of the strategic factor brought out in the budget analysis example?
4. When the general manager takes corrective action with the manager of Territory 2, what possible defect in the firm's reporting system should he investigate before censuring him too much?
5. What kind of control should have brought the increase in direct labor costs to the general manager's attention?

59. Nonbudgetary Financial Control

The control techniques in most business organizations employ dollars, or relationships between dollars, as the units of measurement, because dollars focus on the ultimate objective, which is profit. The controlling of revenues and expenses by budgets, as described in Section 58, is one form of financial control; in addition, budgets will be developed for product lines, organizational departments, and many other aspects of a firm's operations. The convenience of using dollars as units of measurement leads to methods of financial control that are not strictly budgets, although the distinction may be somewhat shadowy. Three popular methods are balance sheet analysis, break-even analysis, and capital investment evaluation.

Balance Sheet Analysis

The budgeting process was explained in Section 58 by the example of the company whose operations got out of control. The same example will be continued in the following explanation of balance sheet analysis.

The balance sheet.   The conventional accounting device for expressing a firm's financial position at a given moment in time is the balance sheet. Assume that Figure 59–1 represents actual financial positions of the company discussed in Section 58 for the past two time periods, and a projected position for the next time period. The firm is in trouble because of uncontrolled sales, but may not yet realize the full consequences.

Ratio analysis.   Much can be learned about a firm's financial position by deriving the relationships between the various elements of the balance sheet. Ratios can be compared with accepted standards, or to past records or projected plans, in order to ascertain the state of the company's financial health. In Figure 59-2, the manager assesses the firm's position as of the end of March 1973 in comparison with the end of the preceding quarter, and finds that the runaway sales and the optimism they generated seriously hurt the company. With consideration of the corrective action he plans, he projects a balance sheet as of the end of the next quarter.

Figure 59–1. Balance Sheet as of March 31, 1973.

	Quarter Ending 12/31/72 ($000)	Quarter Ending 3/31/73 ($000)	Plan Quarter Ending 6/30/73 ($000)
Current Assets:			
Cash	65	15	50
Accounts Receivable	110	156	115
Inventories	80	115	95
Total Current Assets	255	286	260
Fixed Assets			
Net Plant and Equipment	263	319	305
Total Assets	518	605	565
Current Liabilities			
Notes Payable	61	115	65
Accounts Payable	82	90	90
Total Current Liabilities	143	205	155
Long-Term Debt	150	200	200
Total Liabilities	293	405	355
Stockholders' Equity			
Common Stock	150	150	150
Net Retained Earnings	75	50	60
Total Stockholders' Equity	225	200	210
Total Liabilities and Equity	518	605	565

Figure 59–2. Ratio Analysis.

	Balance Sheets		
	12/31/72	3/31/73	6/30/73
Current Ratio	1.8:1	1.4:1	1.7:1
Quick Ratio	0.5:1	0.1:1	0.3:1
Equity/Debt Ratio	0.8:1	0.5:1	0.6:1

Current ratio. As indication of a firm's ability to pay its short-term debts, current ratio is derived by dividing current assets by current liabilities. Since banks usually favor a current ratio of 2:1 when considering a loan application, it can be seen that the firm's current ratio of 1.4:1 is very unpromising. Its unusual sales activity drained cash and forced short-term borrowing to create working capital. The plan for the next quarter includes aggressive collection efforts to generate cash from receivables, and the working down of the inventory. The short-term debt reduction will take a substantial part of the cash flow.

Quick ratio.   Derived by dividing cash by current liabilities, a quick ratio of 1:1 indicates a good cash position. Thus, with a ratio of 0.1:1, this firm is critically short of cash and will have difficulty surviving.

Equity/debt ratio.   This ratio, derived by dividing equity by total liabilities, indicates where the real ownership of a firm lies. A 1:1 ratio is considered to be a safe one, yet in the example, where the ratio is 0.5:1, the creditors own more of the company than the stockholders. What happened was that the optimistic sales reports offered encouragement to borrow on long-term mortgages to buy new equipment, and, in addition, to pay dividends out of retained earnings. Now the company is stuck with the higher debt, and must slowly increase equity through profitable operations.

The moral of this example is that the information contained in a reporting system may be adequate to permit control, but if it is out of date when it is received, effective control is impossible.

Breakeven Analysis

The term *breakeven* means that at some quantity of goods sold a company's fixed costs will be covered, and from that point on, the difference between variable costs and sales revenue will be profit. Owners of small businesses are keenly sensitive to the breakeven point in their operations, perhaps because it can be calculated when conditions are simple. When a firm's operations become more complex, the breakeven point becomes more of a theoretical concept than a practical one.

Example.   Breakeven analysis can be explained by a simple graphic model (see Figure 59–3). Assume that a firm's fixed costs—that is, those costs such as rent, depreciation, and managers' salaries, which go on at a constant amount regardless of sales volume—are $100,000 per year. Assume that costs which vary with sales volume, such as labor and materials, are $1.50 per unit sold. The firm's total costs for any number of units sold would be $1.50 times the units sold (x) plus $100,000:

$$TC = 1.50\,x + \$100,000.$$

Assume that the selling price for each unit is $2.00. Sales revenue would then be $2.00 times the number of units sold:

$$S = \$2.00\,x.$$

The breakeven point is where sales revenue and total costs are equal, or where

$$\$2.00\,x = \$1.50\,x + \$100,000.$$

This point would be 200,000 units. Sales volume in excess of 200,000 units would produce a profit, as shown in the shaded portion of Figure 59–3.

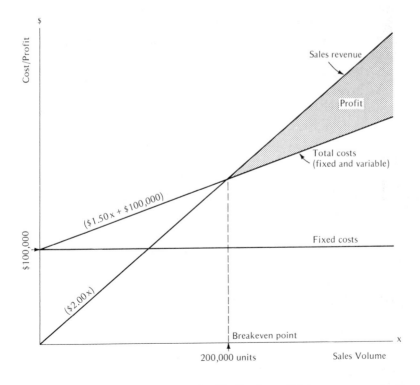

Figure 59–3.   The Breakeven Point.

Problem.   Implicit in the concept of breakeven analysis is that fixed costs are really constant, and that variable costs are directly proportional to quantity. Unfortunately, some so-called fixed costs tend to change when quantity changes, and the so-called variable costs do not vary in direct proportion to sales volume. In the budgeting example that was developed in Section 58, more indirect workers had to be hired to cope with the disorder caused by unexpected sales, and it cost more both to produce and sell the additional units. The fact that these conditions are generally typical does not invalidate breakeven analysis; it simply means that it is difficult to apply with accuracy. Changes in fixed costs and variable costs must be calculated for each change in volume.

Capital Investment Evaluation

Most business firms are confronted by the problem that each year there are more demands for funds for equipment of various kinds than there is capital available. Therefore it becomes necessary to discriminate between the investment opportunities in such a way that the firm's available capital is rationed to the most promising investments. In addition, it must be assured that any investment into which capital is placed must earn enough over its economic life to both pay for itself and generate a return consistent with some minimum standard. A conventional standard is the expected rate of return on the total of the firm's debt and equity capital, or in other words, how much interest is earned on the total investment.

Variables.   Usually the investment opportunities will vary in several respects. They will require different amounts of capital, produce different amounts of absolute earnings, and have different economic lives. Hence, it is essential that some common denominator be derived by means of which all investment opportunities can be compared.

Discounted rate of return.   One popular method for evaluating investment opportunities is the discounted rate of return. As mentioned in Section 12, the discounted rate of return is the interest rate at which the cost (negative value) of an investment, plus the present (positive) value of the estimated future flow of earnings from the investment, equal zero. This method takes into consideration the time value of money, or the fact that the sooner a promised sum of money is received, the greater its value.

Figure 59-4 illustrates the procedure for deriving this statistic. An investment opportunity has been carefully analyzed, and it has been determined that its cost will be $500,000. This is the negative value of the capital invested, or the money that flows out. The analysis shows that there will be a net flow of earnings of $125,000 for each year of its estimated five-year life. These are the positive values, before discounting, or the money that flows in. These data by themselves provide no clue to whether the investment should be undertaken, but the discounted rate of return does provide an index with which to evaluate the investment.

To explain the figure, 0 years from now, which is the present time, a dollar is worth a dollar at any interest rate, so the $500,000 that is paid out is at full value. A dollar that would be earned next year is worth $.94 now at an interest cost of 6 percent, and $.91 now at an interest cost of 10 percent. Therefore, the $125,000 that would be earned next year is only worth $118,000 now at 6 percent, and $114,000 now at 10 percent. The farther into the future money is received, the less value does that money have now, so the $125,000 annual earnings will have decreasing values as the times at which they will be received become more distant.

By adding the −$500,000 and the positive flow of earnings discounted at 6 percent, the net sum is $27,000. The net summation of −$500,000 and the positive flow of earnings discounted at 10 percent is −$25,000. Therefore, the effective rate of return is between 6 percent and 10 percent, and by interpolation it is found to be 8 percent:

$$6\% + (4\% \times 27/52) = 8\%$$

Figure 59–4. Discounted Rate of Return.

Year	Absolute Flow of Earnings ($000)	PVSP * 6%	Discounted Flow of Earnings @ 6% ($000)	PVSP * 10%	Discounted Flow of Earnings @ 10% ($000)
0	−500	1.00	−500	1.00	−500
1	125	0.94	118	0.91	114
2	125	0.89	111	0.83	104
3	125	0.84	105	0.75	94
4	125	0.79	99	0.68	85
5	125	0.75	94	0.62	78
		Totals	27		−25

* Present value of a single payment.

How it is used.   If a company had a hundred investment opportunities, the discounted rates of return could be calculated for each of them. Then the investments could be arrayed, with that one yielding the highest discounted rate of return at the top of the list, then the next highest, and so on down to the lowest. Available capital could then be rationed to the opportunities high on the list until it was exhausted. Another use is to preclude capital from ever being placed in low-return investments. If a firm has an objective of 15-percent return on its total capital, the above invesment promising 8 percent, or any return less than 15 percent, would not be considered.

*The Bayou Land Company owned something over 400,000 acres
of land in southern Louisiana. For a long time nothing much was
done with the property except to collect royalties from the oil production on the extreme western sections, but starting in the 1950's
the company began clearing and leveling the land for agricultural
development. BLC, as the firm was known on the stock exchange,
maintained a large fleet of earthmoving equipment for getting its
land into productive condition, and performed all of its own repairs
to the equipment in extensive shop facilities.*

*Bill Paton was the shop superintendent, as well as acting purchasing
agent for new equipment. "I don't act as purchasing agent as often
as the equipment salesmen would like me to," he often quipped, "because I believe in getting the last hour of life out of a tractor, or a
blade, or a scraper. That's the way that I control the company's
costs."*

*It was true that the equipment dealers and their salesmen in the
area would like to see BLC replace its fleet at a faster rate. Paton
had worked out a schedule whereby he annually submitted a capital
expenditure request to BLC's directors for the replacement of one
eighth of the equipment in terms of its original market value. Expressed differently, he expected to get eight years of life out of every
piece of equipment. When equipment salesmen reminded him that
construction companies using the same kind of equipment usually
figured on a four- or five-year life, his response would be: "That's
because they can't do their repairs as well, or as cheaply, as I can in
this shop." The fact was that Paton's mechanics were good, and the
equipment did last for eight years. As a result, the salesmen tried to
content themselves with their share of BLC's equipment that was
bought each year. The dealers made money on the spare parts business, which did not reach BLC's top management attention but was
a substantial yearly cost.*

*Kelley Grant was a young salesman for Delta Tractor Company,
which was owned and managed by his father. Kelley had been a
business major at college, and seriously tried to apply some of the
things that he had learned to improving his father's company. Getting*

BLC to change its equipment replacement policy, and assuring that Delta would gain a large share of the increased business, would certainly improve the firm's sales and profits. This Kelley set about to do.

While entertaining Bill Paton at lunch one day, Kelley made the comment: "Your company's annual report shows that most of the profits still come from oil royalties, and that the agricultural operation is only returning about 5 percent on its investment. Is this right?"

"Yes, it is," said Paton, who liked Kelley and respected his father. "Top management is trying every way possible to improve the return from agriculture, but nothing has worked so far."

"Your own department is part of the agriculture division, isn't it?" asked Kelley.

"Yes, I report to the division manager," replied Paton.

"Mr. Paton, I have an idea that might help you pick up some points with your company. I know that you keep excellent equipment records. Will you give me permission to work at night on these records, and see what I can come up with? Your night watchman will be there, so that part of it will be all right, and I really think that I can help you bring your operation under better control."

Paton saw no reason for rejecting this request, and told Kelley to get started whenever he wanted to.

As crawler tractors represented two thirds of the number of pieces of equipment in BLC's fleet, Kelley began a detailed analysis of the records for every tractor that had ever been owned. He calculated the repair cost—parts and labor—for each year in each tractor's life, and the hours that the tractor was out of service because of repairs. As crawler tractors rented for $15.00 per hour, he used this figure to estimate the cost of down time. He then developed an average cost per year for repairs and down time. The rise in yearly costs as a tractor got older was impressive, especially the cost in the fifth year, which was the time when Paton always scheduled a complete major overhaul. However, there was an additional variable that Kelley wanted to include, which was the periodic operating improvements which the tractor manufacturers built into their products.

Kelley made an appointment with Bill Paton for the purpose of making another proposition. "Mr. Paton," he said, "I am almost through with my analysis, but there is one more thing I want to do. Let Delta lend you two brand-new crawler tractors, with the increased horsepower and all of the other improvements, for thirty days. Let's match how much dirt they move against the average dirt moved by all of your tractors over four years old."

Paton said, "I have a suspicion of what you are trying to prove, but go ahead, I haven't anything to lose."

At the end of the thirty-day period, Kelley worked up his comparative figures. Paton was obviously impressed. He said, "I guess I will have to concede that the old tractors have what you call an annual operating inferiority of $5000 in comparison with a new piece of equipment."

Kelley prepared his formal report, and took Paton to lunch to show it to him. "First," he said, "let's look at the average annual costs for a crawler tractor until it is four years old:

FIRST 4 YEARS
OF A TRACTOR'S LIFE

Year	Repairs	Down Time	Total
1	$100	$45	$145
2	400	180	580
3	750	375	1125
4	1000	450	1450

"Next," Kelley said, "let's see how much a tractor costs, on the average, for its ages five through eight."

SECOND 4 YEARS
OF A TRACTOR'S LIFE

Year	Repairs	Down Time	Operating Inferiority	Total
5	$15,000	$2400	$5000	$22,400
6	2,000	900	5000	7,900
7	4,000	1000	5000	10,000
8	6,000	1500	5000	12,500

"Now," Kelley went on, "let's say that the difference between the cost of a tractor one year old and a tractor five years old is the

savings of a one-year-old tractor, and the same with the difference between a two-year-old and a six-year-old, and so on. A new tractor costs $45,000, but you would get a $10,000 trade-in allowance for a four-year-old tractor, so the net cash outlay is $35,000. Suppose we find the discounted rate of return over four years for a new tractor that you buy instead of keeping an old one until it is eight years old."

Year	Net Flow of Savings	PVSP 4%	Discounted Savings @ 4%	PVSP 20%	Discounted Savings @ 20%
0	−$35,000	1.00	−$35,000	1.00	−$35,000
1	22,255	.96	21,400	.83	18,470
2	7,320	.93	6,800	.69	5,050
3	8,875	.89	7,900	.58	5,150
4	11,050	.86	9,500	.48	5,300
			10,600		−1,030

Discounted rate of return $= 4\% + (16\% \times 10,600/11,630) = 18.6\%$

"Mr. Paton," said Kelley quietly, "I suggest that your company's management will be pretty impressed when you show them how they can make over 18 percent on an investment."

"Young man, you have certainly taught an old dog some new tricks," said Paton, "and I promise that you won't regret the time that you have spent doing this study."

Discussion Questions

1. In the balance sheet shown in the text (Figure 59-1), the company's assets increased from $518,000 to $605,000 in a three-month period. Why could not this increase be interpreted to mean that things were going well?
2. In the breakeven point example, what would happen if the firm's sales volume were less than 200,000 units?
3. Why should the time value of money be incorporated in a model for evaluating investment opportunities?
4. In the Case of the Salesman Who Did His Homework, what theory is behind the assumption of an operating inferiority for productive equipment as it ages? What parallel might there be with an old automobile?

5. Also in the case presented, what implications do you see for personnel if BLC changes to a four-year life span for its earth-moving equipment? Are there other implications besides those affecting personnel?

60. Production Control

A production system is a complex of major plans and derivative plans, and control devices for implementing them. The effectiveness with which the system is controlled is measured by two standards, one having to do with the quantity and quality of the units produced (output), and the other with the employment of the resources committed to the operation (input). Control efforts to meet these standards must be balanced, because as much loss can be suffered by the inefficient use of a resource, such as labor, as can be incurred by failure to deliver the specified quality of goods in the required quantity at the proper time. Therefore, production control amounts to a descending order of parallel control procedures—there being at each level controls over output factors and input factors. In the descent, controls become increasingly detailed.

Aggregate Control

Few business firms produce only one product. The number of products that must be controlled in a typical company may range from a dozen to several hundred or more. However, looking at production control from the top, the first concern is with overall activity. And, because stable production effort is more efficient and less costly than fluctuating effort, aggregate control focuses on avoiding—to the extent possible—violent peaks and valleys in both inputs and outputs.

Figure 60-1 represents a company's forecast of the demand for the aggregate of its products and its production plan for meeting this demand, both having been converted to direct labor hours. Of course, a host of plans must precede this graphic model. The timing of actual unit sales for each of the firm's products must be forecasted, then scheduled for production. The detailed plans for making the parts and assemblies for the various products must be integrated into the aggregate production plan, then smoothed to conform with the implied policy of a gradual buildup in production activity, a leveling-off period, and then a controlled decline. The implication is that for the first 190 days, excess production effort will be reflected in a moderate rise in inventories, followed by a period during which excess demand will be satisfied from inventory, and finally, another stage of slight inventory accumulation. The obvious objective of the plan is avoidance of cyclical swings in employment, since total em-

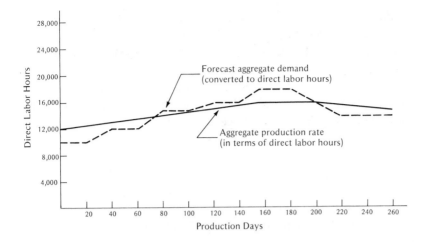

Figure 60–1. Forecast Demand and Aggregate Production Plan.

ployment of all workers tends to be in proportion to direct labor hours.

Differences in Demand

Unfortunately, the future can never be predicted with precision, although the incidence of such radical deviations of actual demand from forecasted demand, as shown in Figure 60-2, may be out of the

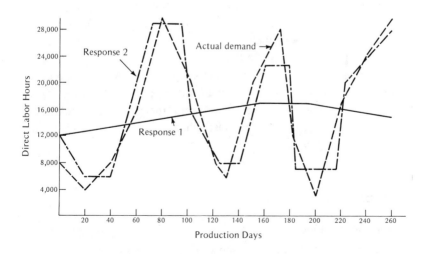

Figure 60–2. Actual Demand and Alternative Production Responses.

ordinary. However, the model in the figure is designed to make the point that the central problem of production control is deciding what production changes, if any, will be made in response to differences between actual and forecasted demand. In the face of such differences, the choice of responses lies between two extremes. A firm may stay with its original plan and not adjust its production rate at all. The opposite extreme is to respond with 1 to 1 adjustments.

Costs of Alternative Actions

Regardless of the action a company takes in responding to differences in demand, the action will entail significant costs.

Production changes.   Since production changes imply the hiring and laying off of workers, costs incurred include loss of investment in training, lower employee morale, poor community relations, investment in retraining, and so on. Another costly result comes in either overtime pay or pay to direct workers for indirect work, such as maintenance, when they are retained despite a reduced production rate; and additional costs accrue simply from the disorder that accompanies a change in the rate of production.

Holding to a stable production rate.   The costs of holding to a stable production rate result from conditions associated with having high inventories when demand is appreciably lower than production, or a high volume of back orders (those for which customers have to wait for delivery) when demand is substantially higher than production. Large inventories tie up capital, increase storage costs, entail higher taxes and insurance rates, and represent losses through obsolescence and deterioration. Back orders mean lost sales and the forfeiting of the profit that would have come from them, because customers usually will buy from someone else when they cannot get what they want when they want it.

Optimal Response Rate

Figure 60-3 represents a manner of evaluating the above two sets of costs, which run counter to each other: cost of production changes vs. costs of inventory or back orders. The objective of charting these so-called counter costs against *response rate* (the percentage of pro-

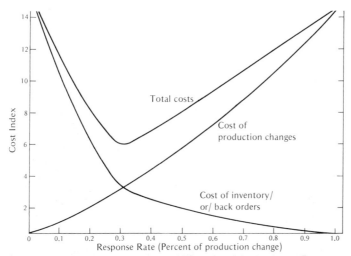

Figure 60–3. Counter Costs Affected by Response Rate.

duction change required for responding to the alternative demands)
is to ascertain the optimal response rate—the point where the combination of the two sets of costs is minimal. A firm can develop a
model like the one shown in Figure 60-3 from empirical data.

On the horizontal axis, degrees of production change in response to altered demand are in a scale ranging from zero to 100
percent. On the vertical axis are arrayed calculated costs for each
degree of production change. Thus, it can be seen that at a 70-per-
cent production change, the cost index is 8. Now, the costs of inventory or back orders will vary in an inverse proportion to the cost
of production changes (being less than 20 percent in this example).
As the response rate of production approaches 100 percent, therefore, the costs of inventory or back orders approach zero. At some
response rate, the combination of the two sets of costs will be at its
lowest value. In Figure 60-3 the optimal response rate is a 30-percent
adjustment of production to either a positive or a negative difference
between planned sales and actual sales. In other words, if planned
sales were 100 units and actual sales turned out to be 150 units, then
production would be increased to a rate of 115 units.

Intermediate Level of Control

At the intermediate control level, on the output factor side, schedules
of finished good production will have to be developed for each item

in the firm's product line, and corrective measures instituted either when schedules are not met or demand changes require adjustments in the schedule.

A major problem with intermediate-level control of input factors is maintaining balanced employment in all of the specialized labor skill areas. Foundrymen cannot do assembly work, machinists are not competent to do electroplating, and spray painters are not usually qualified to operate a punch press. Yet the application of diverse labor skills in a production operation tends to be sequential; that is, in the making of a product, some are applied at the beginning, some in the middle, and some at the end. Control of schedules to prevent the layoff of some people when people with other skills are being hired is essential. Another input factor necessitating tight conrtol is machinery. Schedules must be developed so that demand for specific machines is balanced; a clue to poor machine control is when some tools are standing idle while others are swamped with work.

Control at the Basic Performance Level

A key feature of production control at the basic performance level is the breaking down of each work task into indivisible units, setting normal performance times for each unit, then totalling the unit times into a standard time for the task. The standard times provide the basis for controlling the efficiency of the labor resource.

Gantt Charts

A traditional technique for controlling the output of a production operation is the Gantt chart. There are innumerable variations of this control device, but Figure 60-4 illustrates one of them. In the figure, some quantity of an unmade part is scheduled for assembly in twenty working days. There is a sequence of operations that must be performed in making the part. Standard times are assumed to exist for each operation, so, working back from plating, the last operation, it can be determined when each preceding operation must begin and end in order to have the part completed by the scheduled date. An allowance of one day for inspection and transportation is scheduled between each operation.

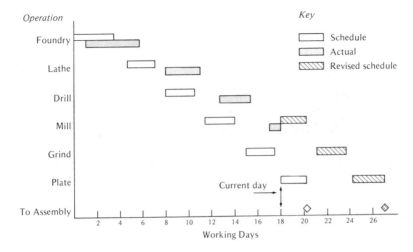

Figure 60–4. Gantt Chart—Part Process Flow.

As a study of the chart reveals, the operation is running late. Whatever kind of internal feedback system is in use at the plant— oral or written progress reports by the shop foremen, tracing and reporting on the movement of work by expediters, or transmission of shop infomation to the control center by computer—none of the three is really efficient. In any event, the part was a day late getting started in the foundry, and required a day longer than was planned for the casting operation. When it arrived in the machine shop, the scheduled lathe had been put on another job, and another delay resulted. Some other problems occurred, and finally it was realized that the part would have to be rescheduled. An incident of this kind can have an impact on a whole series of subsequent events, but the control system has given a somewhat belated, and unfortunately typical, warning that corrective action may have to be initiated.

Inventory conrtol, which is a corollary of production control, is treated in the following section.

Discussion Questions

1. In addition to labor, what are some input factors, or resources, that a firm commits to its production operation?
2. Why will the actual demand for the aggregrate of a firm's products usually vary considerably from the planned production rate? (See Section 10.)

3. Explain, by referring to time periods charted in Figure 60-1, what effect the production plan would have on production rate and inventory buildup and leveling off if the demand proved to be as forecasted. Now explain what would happen if the plan were adhered to despite the wide differences in actual demand that are charted in Figure 60-2. In the latter case, what would be the response rate? (Refer to Figure 60-3.)

4. How can a firm cope with the problem that a production operation requires different labor skills sequentially?

5. Why may shop information systems be less efficient than desired?

61. Inventory Control

Few efforts are more crucial to the viability of a business organization than the effective control of inventories. Its accounting statements may show profitable operations, but if profits are inflexibly tied up in the inventory account, the managers may find one day that they are headed for bankruptcy court. Creditors are singularly uncooperative in accepting pieces of steel, semifinished parts, or gear boxes in lieu of cash when it is time to be paid. And an under-inventory position can be equally damaging. If operations are continually shut down or otherwise impaired by material shortages, costs can rise to the point where a company becomes unable to compete.

Inventory Responsibility

Because many aspects of inventory control can be routinized, it is often assumed that responsibility for the entire process can be relegated to personnel on a lower management level. It is true that procedures can be developed that will minimize the attention that top managers must direct to their firm's inventories. However, the policies for inventory control that the routine procedures are intended to implement must come from the managers with the most mature judgment. And, in fact, the few highly critical inventory items may even be directed by the personal decisions of top-level individuals in the organization structure.

A B C Analysis

The prospect of exercising control over the thousands, or even tens of thousands, of individual items that comprise the total of a typical company's raw materials, in-process, finished goods, and supplies inventories would indeed be formidable were it not for A B C analysis. The essence of this method is that inventory items vary markedly in significant value, and that with any inventory—regardless of the firm or industry—a particular phenomenon will be at work. As shown in Figure 61-1, this phenomenon is that approximately 10 percent of all the items in inventory (the A items) will be worth about 75 percent of the investment in inventory; 25 percent of all items (A + B) will be worth about 90 percent of the investment; and the

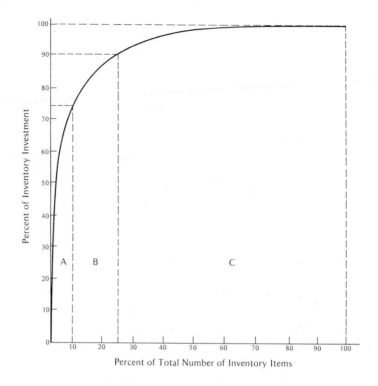

Figure 61–1.   A B C Inventory Categories.

bulk of the inventory items, or about 75 percent (C), will be worth about 10 percent of the investment. It should be plain that the focus of inventory control should be on money, rather than numbers of items. Therefore, if extremely close control is exercised over the highly important A items, and as careful attention as is consistent with cost is directed to the B items, it can be said that the inventory is under control. Relatively speaking, what happens to the C items is not so important; thus, mechanical systems can be applied to them with a minimum of management decision making.

Inventory Control Systems

Inventory control systems generally are of two types, *fixed-reorder cycle* and *fixed-order quantity,* although combinations and variations of them are often designed for specific cases.

Fixed-reorder cycle. Under the fixed-reorder cycle system, the first step is to calculate usages for each inventory item for some minimum period of time, usually about one month. Periodically, such as every month, the balance on hand of each item is reviewed. Policies relative to some determined coverage in each classification of items for a future interval of time are guides in the replenishment of the various items. These policies normally originate with top management and reflect management's attitudes regarding consumer demand, availability of funds for inventory purposes, future prices and supply, and such forces as strike possibilities in vendor plants, war, or economic recession.

The stipulated coverage in the various inventory classifications will vary, depending on the factors mentioned. For example, the possibility of a strike in the steel industry might dictate a policy of a nine-month coverage for all raw steel items, while the prospect of a decline in copper prices might suggest a thirty-day inventory for copper-based items. Obviously, the fixed-reorder cycle system is most appropriate for the A and B inventory items, where the proportional size of dollar investment is large enough to warrant careful management attention to fluctuating coverage. Because the fixed-reorder cycle system is so much based on the subjective judgments of individual managers, details of its workings are difficult to describe. It is also not too amenable for use of mathematical models. For these reasons, it is not treated extensively in management literature.

Fixed-order quantity. Fixed-order quantity is a relatively mechanical inventory control system highly adaptable to operation through mathematical models, and now, by the computer. It is especially appropriate for C items.

Figure 61-2 graphically describes the theory of inventory control by fixed-order quantity. For each inventory item, the average rate of disbursement and the average time needed to replenish the stock—or the *lead time*—are determined. Then the maximum quantity that should ever be on hand at any time is calculated. These data make it possible to determine what size of inventory balance necessitates a replenishing order, and what size the order should be. No matter how much time has elapsed, an order is always placed when the balance reaches the order point. A safety stock is provided to compensate for inaccuracies in calculating disbursement rates and lead times.

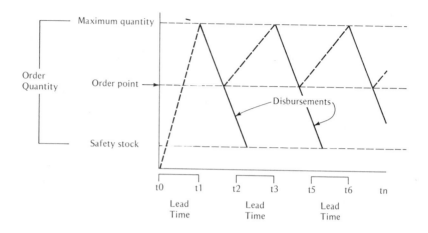

Figure 61–2.   Basic Concept of the Fixed-Order Quantity System.
(Lead time designations of t0, t1, etc., are notations for time intervals.)

The order quantity. The quantity ordered for any inventory item will obviously be a determinant of the amount of inventory carried for that item. When the order quantity is large, few orders will have to be placed annually in order to have a sufficient stock on hand to meet a year's requirements, but the costs of carrying the inventory will be high. As mentioned in Section 60, these costs include the cost of capital tied up in inventory, warehouse rent and warehousemen's salaries, taxes, insurance, obsolescence, and deterioration. On the other hand, when the order quantity is small, inventory carrying costs will be commensurately reduced, but many orders must be placed each year to assure that stock on hand is adequate to avoid shortages. Ordering costs primarily include wages and salaries necessitated by placing and handling transactions, such as those involving purchasing, recording, follow-up, receiving, and inspection. In addition, the cost of supplies will be proportional to the number of orders placed. Thus, the most economic order quantity (EOQ) becomes a function of balancing the carrying costs (CC) against the ordering costs (OC).

In Figure 61-3, it is shown graphically how carrying costs tend to rise as the size of the order increases, and the way that ordering costs generally decrease when the ordering quantity becomes larger. The economic order quantity for any inventory item is the point at

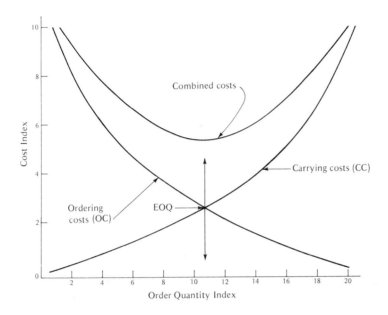

Figure 61–3. The Economic Order Quantity.

which the curve for the combined costs is at its minimum point, or the point at which carrying costs and ordering costs have equal values.

It would be possible to calculate EOQ for all inventory items graphically, but it would be cumbersome and time-consuming. Instead, a mathematical model can be constructed that will greatly simplify the calculation and which, when programmed into a computer, makes the determination of EOQ virtually an instantaneous process.

It has been said that EOQ is at the order quantity point where CC = OC. Let us introduce some notation so that a mathematical model can be formulated. Let

Q = quantity,
U = annual usage of an inventory item,
A = total cost of placing an order,
I = interest rate (time value of all carrying costs),
and
C = total unit cost of an inventory item.

Then average carrying costs equal interest, times quantity, times unit cost, divided by 2:

$$CC = IQC/2.$$

And ordering costs equal annual usage, times the cost of placing an order, divided by the quantity ordered:

$$OC = UA/Q.$$

Now, if EOQ is at the point where $CC = OC$, then by substitution it is at the point where

$$IQC/2 = UA/Q$$

or, by cross multiplying the denominators, where

$$IQ^2C = 2UA,$$

and, by dividing both sides by IC, where

$$Q^2 = 2UA/IC.$$

Then, by deriving the square root of both sides, it is at the point where

$$Q = \sqrt{2UA/IC},$$

which is EOQ.

Practical application of EOQ.   The model

$$Q = \sqrt{2UA/IC}$$

is oversimplified, because it assumes linear disbursement rates, requires an exact knowledge of the interest rate of carrying costs, omits the possibility of quantity discounts, and assumes constant lead times. These defects are partially compensated for by the flatness of the combined cost curve in the area of the EOQ, which means that a mistake could be made in calculating Q, but that it would not be too important. In addition, it is possible mathematically to make the model more sophisticated by including some of the variables that have been omitted in this simple version.

The appeal of the fixed-order quantity inventory control system employing the EOQ concept is that it reduces the incidence of subjective decision making. The facility with which the system can be adopted to the computer is making it increasingly popular with all sizes and kinds of business firms as a method for controlling inventories on an objective basis.

Discussion Questions

1. How can a company be making profits, yet be threatened by bankruptcy at the same time? (See Section 11.)
2. How would you find the A inventory items—that is, the 10 percent which represent 75 percent of the inventory investment? (Refer to Figure 61-1.)
3. What are two obvious assumptions in the fixed-order quantity model (Figure 61-2) that weaken its practical use?
4. Using the figure of $10.00 as the cost of placing an order and 100 units as the firm's expected usage of some item over a year's time, show how ordering costs decrease as the ordering quantity becomes larger.
5. Explain by example the assumption that average carrying costs equal interest times quantity times unit cost divided by 2, or:

$$CC = IQC/2.$$

62. Statistical Quality Control

Quality control has to do with the assurance that goods produced or services rendered by a business firm measure up to some specified quality standard. Basically, there are two ways to control quality— by inspection of all units of output (100-percent inspection) and by inspection of samples. Statistical quality control is a way of determining the probability that a sample is representative of the whole lot.

Alternatives for Quality Control

When there is 100-percent inspection of the units of output produced by a work activity, all units that do not conform to the established quality standards are rejected. In many cases, nothing less than 100-percent inspection is acceptable because of the enormous costs in money—or even human lives—that would result if a defective unit were passed on to its ultimate use. However, in less extreme cases the advantages of having theoretically perfect quality must be balanced against the cost of such thoroughgoing inspection. In addition, some inspection methods are necessarily destructive, which precludes inspection of more than a determined number of samples.

In the second alternative—inspection of samples drawn from the total of the units, or the *lot* as it will be called—characteristics of the lot are inferred from the characteristics of the sample. Sampling inspection is an intuitive human impulse, and is used in virtually every instance where judgment must be exercised concerning an unknown total condition. Quality is controlled to some extent when the characteristics of a sample of random size dictate the acceptance or rejection of the lot.

Terms Used in Statistical Quality Control

Certain key terms are identified with statistical quality control. One set deals with the characteristics to be examined. If the inspection discriminates between units that are either good or bad, or that are accepted or rejected according to some single quality standard, it is said that the units are *examined for attributes*. On the other hand, if measured differences between inspected units are recorded and inferences drawn from them, the technique is called *control by variables*. Inasmuch as this book can present only a general discussion of statistical quality control, and especially as the difference in handling attributes and variables is mainly a matter of the details, the focus of this discussion will be directed to attributes.

Another set of terms deals with the methods of control. *Acceptance sampling* is one of these, and involves the basing of acceptance or rejection of a population on the characteristics of a sample or, in this treatment, the attributes. As the units involved have already been produced, acceptance sampling is after-the-fact control.

Acceptance Sampling

When basing inferences about a population on the attributes of a sample, the possibility always exists that the sample is not representative of the population. Assume a simple transaction between a buyer and seller of ping-pong balls. The buyer wishes all of the balls to be white, and to the best of his ability the seller makes only white balls. However, sometimes in the process gray, or defective, balls are produced. To avoid the high cost of 100-percent inspection, the buyer and seller agree to basing a decision about each lot of 1000 balls on a sample of 50 balls. Again to avoid 100-percent inspection, the buyer concedes to accepting a maximum of 2 percent of gray balls in any lot (in other words, one gray ball in each sample). Two extreme possibilities could occur with the samples of 50. Suppose that in a lot of 1000 balls, 500 might be gray but none of the gray balls would appear in the sample. A bad lot would be accepted. Or suppose that there might be only 10 gray balls in the lot but all would appear in the sample. A good lot would be rejected. The first instance exemplifies the buyer's risk that is always present when sampling is used, and the second, the seller's risk.

The operating characteristic curve. To apply statistical quality control to acceptance sampling, the buyer and seller must agree on certain factors which will permit the development of a sampling plan. One factor is the acceptable quality level, and the plan must provide for a high probability that lots with this level of quality will be accepted. (In the example above, the acceptable quality level is 2 percent of defective balls.) A second factor is the risk the seller is willing to take that even very good lots will be rejected; for example,

the seller might agree to a 5-percent probability that lots with 1 percent or less of defectives will not be accepted. A third factor is the
quality level at which the lot will be considered very bad, and will
have a high probability of being rejected. For example, 4 percent of
defectives might be considered to be very bad, and a 60-percent
probability would be established that such lots would be rejected. A
final factor is the risk the buyer is willing to accept that extremely
bad lots will be accepted; for example, the buyer might agree to a
10-percent chance that lots with more than 7 percent of defectives
will not be detected by samples. With these factors agreed upon, the
buyer and seller can determine either by formulas or from statistical
tables the appropriate size of the sample and the number of rejects
in the sample which will cause the lot to be rejected.

Figure 62-1 shows an operating characteristics curve which con-
forms to the agreed-upon factors mentioned in the ping-pong example. Reading from the left of the figure, it can be seen that with
1 percent of defectives in the lot, there is a 95-percent chance that
there will be no defectives in the sample; with 2 percent of defectives,
a 73-percent chance; and so on; that means, of course, that there is
a 27-percent probability of rejecting lots with 2 percent of defectives.
The curve falls off rapidly when there are more than 2 percent of

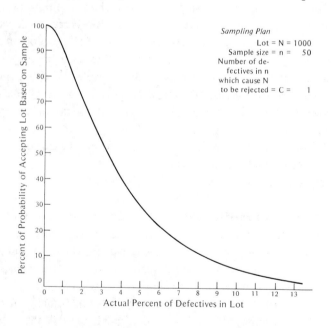

Figure 62–1.   Operating Characteristic Curve.

defectives in the lot, resulting in increasingly greater probabilities of rejecting the lot based on the sample.

Average outgoing quality.   When lots are rejected on the basis of acceptance sampling, there is still the probability that the rejected lots contain some acceptable units—maybe even a high proportion of them. Therefore, a common practice is to conduct 100-percent inspection of rejected lots to extract the acceptable units, with the result that the outgoing quality of combined lots will be an average of the quality of some lots that have been accepted by sampling, even though they contain some defectives, and the theoretically perfect quality of other lots that have been 100-percent accepted. It can be seen in Figure 62-1 that a lot containing 1 percent of defective units (or 10 bad pieces out of 1000) will have a 95-percent chance of being accepted by sampling, and thus a 5-percent chance of being rejected. In other words, 5 times out of 100 the lot will be 100-percent inspected, which will remove the bad pieces. The average outgoing quality of such a lot will be slightly better than 1-percent defective, and can be found by the formula

$$AOQ = Pa(PD)(N-n)/100N$$

in which Pa = the probability of acceptance, PD = the actual percent of defectives in the incoming lot, N = the number of units in the lot, and n = the number of units in the sample.

Figure 62-2 shows the result of applying the formula to percentages used in Figure 62-1. The average outgoing quality has been calculated for each percent of actual defectives in a lot, and the curve that is developed exhibits an interesting phenomenon. Since,

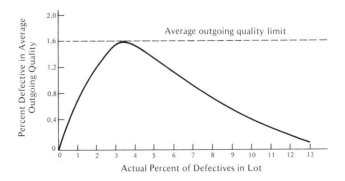

Figure 62-2.   Average Outgoing Quality.

with any actual percent of defectives in the incoming lot there is a rejection probability and the consequent 100-percent inspection, the percent of defectives in the combined lots will rise at first, but then decline sharply. The reason for it is that the worse the incoming lots, the greater the probability of 100-percent inspection.

Discussion Questions

1. Explain by example that sampling inspection is an intuitive human impulse.
2. What is the primary requisite of a good acceptance sampling plan?
3. What justification is there for 100-percent inspection of lots that have been rejected on the basis of acceptance sampling?
4. What is the outstanding advantage of statistical quality control?
5. As a buyer, why might you agree to some percent of defectives in the goods you get from a supplier?

63. Marketing Control

Profitability is the significant unit of measurement in the control of the marketing effort. Other common measurements, such as sales volume and market penetration, are useful supplements to profitability, but by themselves serve to conceal rather than reveal what is really happening as a result of committing resources to marketing operations.

Moreover, effective marketing control is achieved through detailed examinations of profitability, rather than aggregate measurements. It is necessary to fractionalize marketing into microsegments, and apply specific profitability standards to each of them. As a beginning, marketing might be divided into the following discrete areas for control: product line, selling effort per customer, marketing territories, and advertising.

Control of the Product Line

Decisions that bear on control of the product line have to do with assessing what stage in its life cycle a product has reached, detecting maldistributions of profits and effort, and eliminating unprofitable products.

Assessing a product's progression. Products generally can be subdivided into three categories:

- the approximately 80 percent of the new products introduced in the United States that never generate profitability.
- a large proportion of the remainder that have only temporary or spasmodic success.
- the small percentage of extremely profitable items that must cover the costs of the unsuccessful ones and, in addition, produce the profits that enable business firms to survive.

Few of even the most successful products enjoy unlimited life spans. Like the humans who conceive them, they have their struggling periods of infancy and adolescence, then an advancement into productive maturity, and finally, a decline toward inevitable demise. Unsuccessful products die after often unbelievably long lives as infants.

Figure 63-1 depicts the typical life cycle of a successful product, but the beginnings of all products are fundamentally the same. Re-

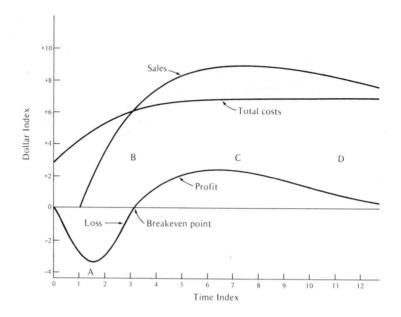

Figure 63–1. Typical Life Cycle of a Successful Product.

sources of all kinds are committed to getting initial market acceptance, and there is an outpouring of funds without receiving anything in return. A critical control point for a new product is at A in the figure. Some products will never reach point A, and control is effective to the extent that this fact is realized before further losses are incurred. A second point of control is at B, where sales cover fixed costs, and the difference between variable costs and sales is profit.

Many products that pass point A find point B unattainable, and it is crucial that this prospect becomes known and the product "scrubbed" early in its life cycle. At point C, signs begin to suggest that the market's appetite for the product is becoming jaded and that returns are diminishing relative to the costs of generating sales. Finally, at point D the end is in sight. The control decision here is what to do with the venerable product that is coming to the close of its profitable life.

Detecting maldistributions of profits and effort. An analysis of the product lines of most companies will disclose that relatively few items are sustaining the firm's profits, often with a disproportionate share of the total marketing effort. An essential marketing control is the determination of the regression between effort and profitability for each item in the product line. For some items there may be a direct cause-and-effect relationship, and profitable items may be made more profitable by increasing the effort directed to them. Other items may be inelastic to effort, and their profitability may be held constant with a reduction in effort. (For example, a firm may have a patent-protected product for which demand is consistent but limited, and it might be just as well to reduce the effort expended in promoting it.) Still other items may have a diminishing profit potential, regardless of the magnitude of resources committed to them. What this kind of analysis amounts to for the managers of the marketing operation is a thorough effort to understand the true nature of their business.

Eliminating unprofitable products. Sentiment may have some place in the business world, but the attachment that many firms apparently feel for products that have outlived their usefulness is extremely wasteful. One explanation why clearly unprofitable items are retained in a company's product line may be that the company is preoccupied with total sales and market share—rather than profitability—as criteria for control. There seems to be an attitude with many managers that it is somehow immoral to reduce the scale of their firm's operations, even though the reduction may mean an increase in profitability. Another explanation may be that certain products are associated with a company's image, and it might suffer damage if the products are dropped. If this is true, then the products are indirectly profitable despite what the records show, and should be retained. However, in many cases myths grow up about a company's image which have no objective foundation.

Probably the main reason for the retention of unprofitable products, however, is that their unprofitability is not clearly recognized. In any event, a firm's marketing operation is out of control—aggregate profitability notwithstanding—if items are retained in the product line for reasons other than direct or indirect profitability.

Control of Selling Effort per Customer

An important analysis for marketing control is the differentiation between profitable and unprofitable customers. Basically, they are classified according to the volume of their orders in relationship to the costs of generating those orders. Small-volume customers may be profitable if they require minimum sales effort. Conversely, large-volume customers may be unprofitable if the sales depend on unusual service, high transportation costs, special competitive allowances, or exorbitant entertainment expense.

Reducing the selling effort.   One obvious course of action in dealing with unprofitable customers is to reduce the sales effort to a level at which the sales become profitable. At the same time, the released effort can be concentrated on existing or potential profitable accounts. Whenever a firm must buy its sales, its future is in jeopardy. Although a tapering off of the attractions that have induced sales from an unprofitable customer may lose the account, this loss would actually be a blessing.

Increasing the gross return.   Instead of reducing the sales effort, an alternative would be to hold this factor constant, but increase the gross billings to unprofitable customers. This can be accomplished by giving those customers a lower discount, which has the effect of increasing prices, or by adding a service charge to all invoices sufficient to cover the detailed items calling for extra cost.

Changing the distribution channel.   It often can be discerned from customer analysis that some accounts simply do not have the buying volume to justify a direct distribution channel. A manufacturer might profitably turn such accounts over to a wholesaler, or a wholesaler might direct small-volume customers to a retail outlet.

Cancelling unprofitable accounts.   Probably all business firms have some customers who are simply not worth retaining. Feelings might be hurt and resentments aroused, but over the long run a company will be better off by a control policy of periodically pruning its customer lists of those accounts that have no potential of being anything but a drain on profitability.

Control of Marketing Territories

Analysis of profit contribution by various sales territories will, in most companies, reveal that a relatively small proportion of the territories are yielding the bulk of the profits. Moreover, products that are sold profitably in some territories will be found to be markedly unsuccessful in other territories. Assuming that the first step of comparing the personal qualifications of the regional managers and salesmen has been performed and has not been determined to be a variable, then several marketing control actions are possible.

Evaluating the market potential. The real market potential for the firm's products in the unprofitable territories should be evaluated. It can easily happen that a company will extend itself into market areas where it really does not belong. If this appears to be the cause of low profits, alternatives include increasing sales effort to create a demand for the products, turning the territories over to secondary distributors—such as wholesalers or jobbers—to handle, or pulling out of the barren lands altogether.

Adjusting to varying demand. Another possibility is that demand exists in the territories for part of the firm's product line, but not for all of it, and that sales effort is being wasted. Here the course of action would be to curtail efforts in selling the unwanted products and concentrate on the ones where profit can be realized.

Diverting efforts to profitable territories. Analysis might also suggest that part of the sales effort in the unprofitable territories be abandoned and the effort diverted to the territories where profits are being generated. In these successful territories, profits may be elastic to sales efforts and the increased effort will be rewarded, while in the unprofitable territories a reduction in costs of sales efforts may make the operation profitable.

Control of Advertising Effort

Two important control decisions hinge on the effectiveness of the media employed to get a firm's advertising messages across to consumers, and the point to which spending for advertising should go.

Analyzing the effectiveness of the media. The effectiveness of the various forms of advertising media employed, such as television, radio, newspapers, magazines, and outdoor displays, varies with the product, the market, and consumer saturation. (It is assumed that the advertising concept is appropriate, and that the only object of inquiry is the media employed to convey it.) A firm's managers can analyze the media and bring the costs allocated to them under control by alternately emphasizing or reducing one form and holding the others constant. The effects of the change on sales, vs. the relative costs associated with the change, can be measured and conclusions drawn. Another tactic is to use different media in different territories in an effort to isolate the most effective forms.

Determining the point of diminishing returns.   Typically, if the demand for a product is at all responsive to advertising, increased advertising will cause increased sales, up to a point. Beyond this point, the cost of further advertising to generate additional sales will be greater than the profit realized by the marginal sales. This is a crucial control point, and one that is not easy to determine. Carefully designed market experiments offer the best solution to determining the point of diminishing returns. An example of such an experiment would be where a soap company would select a town in which to systematically increase its advertising, and would carefully measure the effects of each increase on sales. Knowing when to stop expanding advertising, or when to reduce it, are among the most important decisions of marketing control.

When George Simmons, owner of Apex Tire & Recapping Company, hired young Bill Thompson as a tire salesman, he told him that the one thing he wanted him to do more than anything was to get back the California Construction Company's account.

Apex had enjoyed California's new tire and recapping business for many years, but approximately six months before the hiring of Thompson, California's new purchasing agent, Dan Delaney, had abruptly switched the bulk of his tire purchases to Apex's main competitor. As the volume of the account amounted to over $250,000 annually, its loss was a bitter blow to Simmons. Not only did Apex lose the fair profit that had always been earned on California's business, but the loss of the volume put the company in a lower discount bracket with the manufacturer that it represented, Goodwell Tire & Tire Rubber Company.

Bill Thompson began calling regularly on Dan Delaney, and quickly learned that he was quite amenable to being taken out to lunch at the most expensive places. These occasions worried Bill because he still was not getting any appreciable tire business from Delaney, although his expense account began to look excessive even to him.

One day he voiced these concerns to George Simmons, who listened attentively, then asked, "Do you think that you are making headway as far as getting back California's account?"

Bill answered, "Delaney told me yesterday that he was going to put a huge tire order out to bid, and that he hoped we would get it. He hinted that 40 percent off list was being talked about by our competitor."

"Wow! To go lower than that I would have to get help from the manufacturer," said Simmons. "However, let me see what I can do."

Goodwell wanted the business back as badly as Simmons did, and extended an additional discount. Apex bid 45 percent off list, and got California's order. George Simmons was happy about the order, but uneasy about the extremely slim profit margin. Bill Thompson was not nearly as jubilant as he thought he would be, because the cost of *acceding to Delaney's thinly veiled demand for a dinner celebrating the order was close to $75.*

Any thought that Apex had California's tire business back on a permanent basis was dispelled three months later when the competitor was given another order. Delaney's smug answer when Bill asked him why Apex lost the order was, "I guess your pencil needs sharpening. Another 5 percent makes a lot of difference."

Toward the end of that month, California Construction Company was awarded the contract to build a seven-mile stretch of freeway through the Sierras. It was to be a two-year job, and the order for heavy equipment tires that would have to be replaced during that period would probably run close to $300,000. Every tire dealer in the state hoped to be the exclusive supplier, and Delaney shrewdly played each one against the others.

Simmons, Thompson, and the Goodwell representative, Evan Peterson, discussed what strategy could be used to get the business for Apex. "It's a cinch to go for as low as 50 percent off list," said Simmons, "unless Delaney is lying to Bill, which I wouldn't put past him."

"In addition to price, Delaney is now hinting about having an inventory of tires consigned to the construction site, but not to be paid for until they are mounted on equipment," Bill said.

"The company might be willing to go for something like that if we were guaranteed to get the total business," Evan Peterson responded. "What we could do is handle the paper work through the main office and compensate Apex with a selling commission. I suggest that the three of us talk to Delaney."

Delaney sat quietly while George Simmons explained the proposition. "What we are doing is offering you a blanket deal, which is better than anything that you can get by asking for bids," was George's final remark.

"I'll have to admit that I am interested," Delaney responded. "Suppose I think about it, and I'll let Bill here know tomorrow at lunch."

"Do you know what he's asking for now?" said Bill to Simmons and

Peterson the next afternoon. "He wants us to furnish a tire-changing truck on the construction site at no cost, in addition to what we have already offered him."

"That's too much," said Simmons. "There is no way that we could supply a truck and break even."

"Now wait," Peterson said. "You figure the cost of a truck at $5.00 per hour. At 200 hours per month, that would be 2400 hours per year, or $12,000. Two years would be $24,000. Suppose Goodwell would pay half. Would you pay the other half to get the business?"

"Let's see how we would come out on the total account. We will never get all of California's local tire purchases, so assume that we will get half, or $125,000 per year. At the prices Delaney has driven us down to, we only net about 5 percent, not including Bill's expense account, so that is $6,250 per year, or $12,500 for two years. Our 2 percent commission on the freeway business would give us $6,000, or $18,500 total profit. Take out $12,000 for the truck, and the $1,000 a year that it looks like Bill is going to have to spend entertaining Delaney, and that leaves us $4,500 profit for two year's work. That's not much, but see if you can get it on this basis, Bill."

The next afternoon Bill phoned Simmons. "I just took Delaney to his office," Bill said. "What he wants now is for us to furnish a driver for the truck."

"Let's cross California Construction Company off our list," responded George Simmons wearily.

Discussion Questions

1. If product profitability is such an important factor, how can you explain the tactic employed by supermarkets of deliberately selling some items at a loss?
2. What are some possible reasons for a product selling well in some territories yet being unsuccessful in others?
3. What would be some controls that a hardware store owner could use to determine whether people were reading his newspaper advertisements?

4. In the Case of the Greedy Tire Customer, why didn't George Simmons instruct Bill Thompson to recapture the large account on the basis of product and service quality, rather than price-cutting and entertainment?

5. What implications might Dan Delaney's tactics of playing competitors against each other in getting price and service concessions have for his own firm's long-term financial health, not to mention that of companies like Apex who vied for his orders?

64. Control of Research and Development

The environment of business operations of all kinds is now so dynamic that most companies of medium size and above, and even very small firms whose products are of a technical nature, must prepare in some way for the future. One thing that is almost certain is that whatever product or service a company is offering in the present, that offering must undergo substantial change within the next decade if the firm is to stay alive. The financial ability to get ready for the future is becoming one of the most powerful advantages that a large company has over a small one. But no matter how large it is, no company has the financial stamina to withstand for long the enormous drain of uncontrolled research and development projects. The first decision that must be made by a company looking to the future is what the scope of its R & D program will be.

The Nature and Extent of R & D

It is common to use the terms *research* and *development* together, as though they were a single activity. Sometimes they are, with *development* referring to the activity of getting a product which was discovered by the company's own research team ready for the commercial market. *Research* may, however, be an independent objective, without any intention by the firm of developing its own productive ideas. Where this is the case, a firm will sell the products of its research effort to other companies for development—companies that deliberately avoid the expense and frustration of research and look for likely ideas that can be acquired and commercially developed.

If a company is going to do research, another decision is whether its efforts will be directed toward pure research, out of which commercial applications may possibly come, or toward research with determined commercial applications. With most companies, the decision will be for the latter, which then prompts the need for deciding in fairly specific terms what the objectives of its applied research are to be. Companies that buy their research ideas must have similar objectives when they evaluate promising research discoveries.

411

Budgeting the R & D Program

Having determined its R & D goals, the firm next must carefully assess the costs of achieving those goals over some future series of years. In most cases, these goals will not be attainable either cheaply or quickly. Often the firm will have to moderate its R & D ambitions in light of its ability to finance the effort, and achieve a balance between available money and the magnitude of its R & D program. When this is done, total annual budgets for R & D, projected over at least the next three to five years, should be prepared. The top managers should establish a strict policy that these budgets are not to be invaded even if business conditions should take a downturn. Managers are sometimes tempted to reallocate funds earmarked for R & D, but the practice has suicidal implications. When a firm's operations begin to turn sour, often the only rejuvenating factor will be some newly developed products.

The total budget for the R & D program, when established, should then have allocations made from it to specific projects that have been approved and are ready to get under way. This step entails some of the most careful decision making, because relatively few of these projects will ever pay off. The trick is to decide which are the most likely ones, and start them off with the most generous budgets. Some part of each year's total budget for R & D must be withheld, both to provide for the contingency of overruns of allocated budgets and for allocations to promising new projects that might come along in the interim. Control techniques applicable to an R & D budget are discussed on the facing page.

Staffing the R & D Effort

An effective director of an R & D program is a singular individual— combining the attributes of a business manager and a scientist or research-oriented engineer. Simply having the general attributes of a good manager is not enough, because, as was mentioned in Section 56, professionally trained subordinates require technical competence in the person they work under. Other reasons that the director must be professionally qualified, and possibly more compelling ones, are the abilities required to discriminate potentially productive research opportunities from those that are not, evaluate ongoing research and development projects, and select and train a professional staff. At the same time, the R & D director must demonstrate managerial ability in assuring that the program is under control and moving in a positive direction, in motivating scientists and engineers to put forth their maximum efforts, and in representing the program to senior managers in such a way as to sustain their confidence in it.

Criteria for selecting the professional staff should include diverse but complementary technical skills, a high tolerance for frustration, dedication to professional achievement, and a preference for the research environment over alternative working conditions. In addition to these personal characteristics, some recruits to the research staff should have incipient feelings that they might like being managers, because potential managers of the individual projects must be identified and provided with the development opportunities that they need.

R & D Facilities

Some companies try to economize by mixing their R & D activities with their regular operations. This approach is only partially successful. Most often it causes confusion and disorder in the departmental areas concerned with engineering, testing, and manufacturing the firm's existing product line, and it also thwarts the creative processes so essential to the formulation of future product lines.

An R & D budget ideally should provide for working areas and experimental apparatus completely separate from the facilities devoted to regular operations. Many firms go so far as to establish their R & D programs in a different geographical area from where current products are engineered and manufactured. An R & D program should be looked upon as an independent operation, with everything provided to induce a climate where creative productivity will flourish.

Specific Control Techniques

The R & D program director is faced with the dilemma of having to be innovative in providing new products upon which the firm's future business will be based, but doing it while under both monetary and time limitations, and while exerting subtle and nonoppressive control.

The primary R & D control objectives are to

- identify the projects that have no marketable potential while they are still in their early stages, so that they can be eliminated

before further funds are wasted on them.
- assure that time, money, and manpower resources committed to promising projects are commensurate with their ultimate market worth.

One big problem with meeting these objectives is forecasting what flow of earnings might be realized from a product when the project is still in the embryonic stage. Another equally formidable problem is determining exactly where any project is at a given point in time, in terms of percent completed, and what additional resources will be required to have its end product ready for the market when the market is ready for it. The task of solving this latter problem is fraught with frustration, because a project may appear to be progressing beautifully up until its final testing, when it may utterly fail. Now the decision has to be made whether to scrub it or go back to the beginning and start again.

Essentially, R & D programs are controlled by means of periodic reports of progress relative to budgetary and scheduled milepost standards. The control process is upward flowing, with the individual project managers reporting their performance to the R & D director, who in turn summarizes the project reports in reviews to top management. Ascertainment of the current status of funds actually committed to a project is, of course, easy, especially with computers available to collect and transmit cost data.

In Figure 64-1, a budgeted cumulative cost curve is shown, plus a curve depicting the actual cumulative expenditure of funds committed to the project's work order number. In the example, on the 50th day the project is approximately $8000 overrun. For the determination of the project's accomplishment, mileposts which presumably separate the project's mission into discrete stages are conventionally used. These reveal that the project is apparently 10 days behind schedule on the 50th day.

In reporting to the R & D director, the project manager in the case represented by the figure would explain the reasons for the negative budget and performance variances, and outline plans for corrective action. Often the variances will be due to the impossibility of estimating R & D effort with precision. But sometimes budgetary or schedule variances (or both as in the example), may be attributable to technical obstacles, which may or may not have ready solutions. In situations where obstacles are great and a project is very important, all of the technical wisdom and managerial acumen that the firm can muster must be directed to the decision of whether to continue or abandon the ailing project.

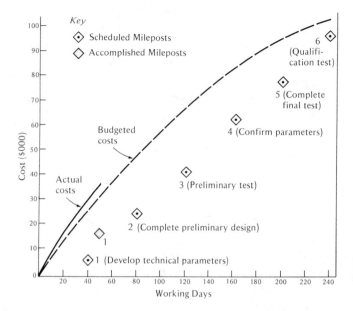

Figure 64–1.   R & D Project Costs Vs. Accomplishment.

Applied Computer Information, Inc. (ACI) had been formed in 1963
by Dave Whittlesey, Bill Coplen, and Don Jackson, three former programmers of the largest computer hardware and software company
in the industry. (Software is programming, of which the routines and
subroutines for inventory control are an example.)

On the first day of their new venture, Dave said, "One thing that I
think we have going for us is our similar backgrounds—all mathemati-
cians, and with a combined experience of almost thirty years in developing software programs."

Their aggregate capital when they started, made up of their personal
savings and what they could individually borrow, came to about
$50,000. The initial project on which their venture was based was a
data bank program for storing real estate listings. Such information
was in demand by real estate agencies all over the country, and by
using time sharing on leased computers once the program was developed, ACI had the prospect of furnishing data to its customers for a
profitable monthly fee.

At the end of six months, the program was still not developed, and
ACI's owners realized that they had grossly underestimated the amount
of money it would take to complete it. However, they were able to
interest a private investment firm in ACI's exciting growth potential,
and received new financing in the amount of $500,000 funded by con-
vertible debentures. The new capital gave ACI the strength needed to
develop and market its program, and by the beginning of 1965 the
firm was operating well in the black, and showed prospects of a sky-
rocket growth.

In the following year, ACI developed two additional storage bank programs. One was for motor vehicle registrations, and the other, for consumer credit ratings. Both were within the capacity of ACI to handle
the computer logic, and although there was growing competition in
the software industry, ACI's good start gave it a marketing edge. The
company continued to grow.

Upon the advice, and in fact, pressure, of the private investment firm *that had come to ACI's rescue, ownership of the firm went public in 1966. Stock with a par value of $10 shot up to $80 as a result of the continued success of ACI's programs, plus speculation that computer software companies' brightest future still lay ahead. The investment firm sold out in 1967 and took its capital gain, and in that year ACI's sales were over $25 million.*

Dave, Bill, and Don had three new programs in the embryonic development stage in 1967. The objective of one was to provide daily information to entertainment ticket dealers regarding the availability of tickets to shows, concerts, athletic events, etc. The three founders of ACI, who by this time were sharing managerial responsibilities without any clear delineation of duties, envisaged this program as materializing into a steady "bread and butter" business, something like the ones to which the firm owed its present success. They estimated that the program could be developed for less than a million dollars. A more ambitious program was to provide on-line information concerning room reservations in hotels and major motels nationwide. A number of competitors were already trying to crack this nut, and the talk in the trade was that the potential annual revenues from a successful program would be upwards of $120 million. The third program on which ACI had started to incur development costs was of even broader dimensions. It involved computerizing supermarket check-out systems. Strong, rational arguments could be mustered for having a computer price the customer's grocery selection, receive payment and give change, including stamps, delete the purchases from the inventory balances, and prepare purchase orders to replenish the stock as it was reduced. Getting the first such system successfully on the market had such staggering growth possibilities according to the way that Dave, Bill, and Don looked at things that they began envisaging their firm in the billion-dollar-a-year class.

The year of 1968 was one of tremendous outpourings of cash to get the new programs developed and get market acceptance for the promises that ACI's managers were making to potential customers. In addition, competition was beginning to dilute the firm's established revenues, and Dave, Bill, and Don were so immersed in trying to broaden their product line that they lost sight of the need to diligently manage what they already had. The first major shock came when they realized that close to $5 million had been spent in starting the entertainment ticket program, and a market analyst whom they had tardily *engaged to study the actual potential revenue informed them that it would take at least ten years to recoup the investment. "You were simply shooting for too narrow a market," was the essence of his report.*

The success of commercial airlines with computerized on-line systems for ticket reservations goaded ACI to continue dumping money into the hotel reservation program. The big hotel chains were all interested, but the technical problems of developing an integrated system appeared formidable. However, it was the competition of giant competitors that finally made it necessary for ACI to scrub this venture. When one big software company announced to a meeting of security analysts that it had budgeted $100 million for developing a program, and that it did not expect to break even for five years, Dave and his associates elected to take their loss of about $10 million.

The general business decline in 1969, plus the news of ACI's vicissitudes, resulted in a precipitous fall in the price of the company's stock. Moreover, its remaining development program, the supermarket system, ate up money as fast as it was poured in. Dave, Bill, and Don frantically worked on the program while pioneering in the market, but the prospects that their efforts would result in any kind of an immediate payoff became increasingly dim. Finally, news that a competitor had installed a successful pilot system, but anticipated three or four more years of developing costs before it could be marketed successfully, made ACI decide to abandon this ship as well.

In June of 1971, with the company's stock at $2 per share, Dave and his unhappy associates met to discuss an impending creditor's action against ACI's assets. "Fellows, I guess the big mistake that we made was trying to take too big a bite," was Dave's postmortem remark.

Discussion Questions

1. What major decision must precede a firm's determination of objectives for applied research and development? (See Section 9.)
2. What inferences can you draw concerning a given firm's R & D objectives and the allocation of funds to its R & D budget if its managers manifest a tendency to invade the R & D budget when business conditions take a downturn?

3. What would you think of having an experienced business manager and a scientist jointly head an R & D program? Under such an arrangement, which one should have final decision-making authority over disputed policies?
4. In the Case of Taking Too Big a Bite, what were the glaring weaknesses of ACI's R & D planning and control?
5. As of June 1971, what could Whittlesey and his associates do to save ACI?

65. The Systems Approach to Control

Systems theory has long provided models for explaining relationships between interacting elements in the physical sciences, and for more than a decade it has been imaginatively applied to management processes. Fundamentally, it provides a conceptual framework for bringing natural combinations of dependent elements into sharper focus. The development of management applications of systems theory, however, has been shrouded in some cases with an aura of profundity, and the concepts have been expressed in an obscure fashion. Perhaps this is because of the presumed necessity to explain systems theory by analogies to the physical sciences, or possibly it is because of the specialized vocabulary associated with it. Whatever the case, systems theory is more correctly perceived as offering an orderly way of looking at things, rather than representing a new theory of management.

Systems theory is particularly adapted to explaining the control function (giving us still another way of expressing what has been said in the preceding sections); and it is also useful in making it possible to go further in the analysis of the communication process.

Control Characteristics

In Section 57 it was stated that the controlling function entails (1) the establishment of standards by which the achievement of plans can be measured; (2) the comparison of performance results with these standards, and the seeking out of deviations; and (3) the initiation of actions to correct continuance of the deviations or to modify the plans. The characteristics of control, which may be inferred from that statement, are four in number: the normative output, together with three devices which are identified as the sensor, comparator, and corrector, respectively.

Figure 65-1 puts these four characteristics into graphic perspective, and it also shows the pervasiveness of the system's mechanics, that is, the information forms and the channels of communication. The system accommodates acceptance of the first control characteristic, normative output, or the desired performance standards. The

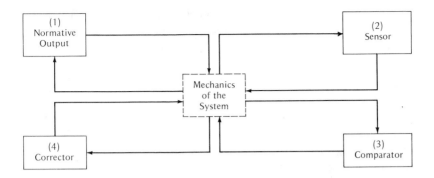

Figure 65–1.   The Characteristics of a Control System.

sensor, which is the second characteristic, measures actual units of output and, like the subsequent characteristics, may be a person, a machine, or a process. An imperative at this stage of the system is that measurements be in the same terms as the standards. The comparator—the third characteristic—balances the measurements of the actual output against those of the normative output. In the process, variations between the measurements are analyzed for assignable causes, and corrective action is determined. Finally, the corrector—the fourth characteristic—implements the corrective action throughout the system and, by appropriate follow-up, assures that the action is effective.

The practical advantage of looking at control within the framework of this model is that a manager can employ the model as a checklist for all types of control systems, whether they are for expenses, production, inventory, or whatever else is being controlled. In any case, provision should be made for each of the four characteristics to be present in sequence in the system. Then the designation of organizational responsibility, places and times of performance, identification of information forms, and routings of information flow can all be named at each characteristic point to assure that the system has the potential of control.

The Feedback Loop

Control, in the management sense, fundamentally involves making adjustments in response to stimuli that are built into the system and that maintain it in a desired state of goal accomplishment. A feedback loop is a natural phenomenon in any system that strives for goals, because in some way an assessment of whether the goals have been achieved or not is always made. *Feedback* is a highly descriptive term, and refers to the happening that makes control systems or communication processes complete—namely, the transmission of the output's characteristics or of responses to messages back to the point of origin. This transmission of response is accomplished via a circuit of some kind.

In Figure 65-2 a feedback loop (control process) in a system is represented by the dotted lines, whereas the operational process of the system is depicted at the top of the diagram by solid lines connecting the sequential stages. The characteristics of the particular system under study establishes what actually takes place at each point in the total circuit. An activating agent (top left) may be a manager, a process, or an authorized plan, such as a production program. Inputs (at the right of the activating agents) include messages, resources, policies, and so on. Standards (lower center) may be as diverse as balance-sheet ratios, units of production, or dimension tolerances. Operations (top center) may be the transformation of raw materials, the transmittal of a directive, the marketing of a product line, and so on. Completing the operational process, typical outputs (top right) are profits, attributes in a sample, or the behavior of subordinates in response to a change order.

In the feedback loop, output characteristics are transmitted by

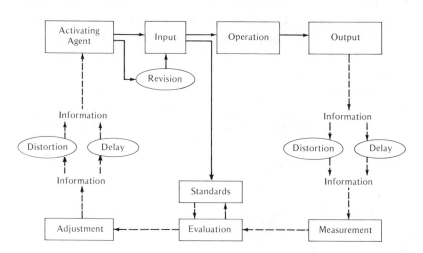

Figure 65–2.   Control Via a Feedback Loop.

reports of all kinds or are interpreted from observation. At the sensor stage, measurements may be in numerical terms, such as how many units were produced in a period and what proportion of defectives were found in a lot; or they may be subjective, such as how the morale in a work group is perceived. Evaluation of output measurements may also take objective or subjective forms; for instance, a comparison may be made between a department's actual and budgeted expenses, while at the same time an evaluation may be made of the department manager's personal conduct in relation to company norms. Based on the evaluation, adjustments may include eliminating an unprofitable product, replacing a worn-out machine tool, or instituting a management development program. Implementation of the adjustments are fed to the activating agent via confirming messages, change orders, or personal behavior.

Problems in a Feedback Loop

Distortions and delays impair the communication process, as explained in Section 53. Thus, control, which depends on effective communication, will be impaired to the extent that distortions and delays occur in the feedback loop.

Delays between the generation of output and the measurement of the data or behavior associated with the output result in what might be called "postmortem examinations." These are of limited value because, as has been mentioned several times, it is impossible to control past events. Under certain conditions—that is, when the purpose of a postmortem is to spot trends and apply remedies—the measurement of recent output provides a useful analytical base. However, the knowledge of a particular unfavorable event that happened some time previously is of minimum value.

Output information is often distorted at the sensor stage—a major cause being the ambiguity of output data. This ambiguity may result from a number of causes:

- The data may not have discrete meanings, in which case various and diverse measurements may appear to have equal applicability. For example, the statistic that the manufacturing plant is operating at 100-percent capacity can be interpreted to mean that it is producing all possible output under conditions ranging from straight-time, single shift, to maximum overtime, triple shift.

- The output data, though discrete, may be transmitted in different units of measurement than the standards with which they are to be compared. Distortion of numerical data is a special hazard when inferences are drawn from them in predicting trends. An extreme example might involve the assumption that a trend is linear, when in fact it has a point where a decline will start to show.
- The data may be qualitative, or subjective, and therefore difficult to verify.

The effectiveness of corrective adjustments is also obstructed by distortions and delays. For example, cyclical fluctuations will reveal themselves as negative trends which, if given time, will correct themselves; but delays in detecting corrective tendencies at the sensor stage often result in adjustments being made to the system after it is back in equilibrium. A concrete example is afforded by a situation in which a quarterly balance sheet, examined at the sensor stage, showed accounts receivable to be unusually large—double the amount of the average collection period. The corrective action decided upon was to initiate aggressive collection policies, but by the time this action was carried out, the delinquent customers had long since paid their bills and were offended to the point of changing suppliers.

Overreaction to stimuli often causes distortion through amplification in the adjustment process. For example, it might be determined in the feedback loop that the cause for a negative variance in engineering performance is a shortage of engineers; and the corrective action that appears to be indicated might call for intensive recruiting efforts. In the early 1960's, recruitment of engineers reached almost panic proportions among the aerospace companies, so this is not just a theoretical example. By the time the additional engineers had been hired, it was found that the requirement had been greatly overestimated, and an excess number of engineers were on hand at many companies.

Self-correcting tendencies in a system and the hazards of overreacting suggest that the effective approach to control is through frequent and timely reviews of output data, augmented by minor adjustments. In other words, the response rate to a difference between actual and normative outputs would be on the low side of a scale ranging from 0 to 1. A further implication for control is that the decisions involved are of a patient and plodding nature, rather than heroic ones.

"What we professors of management must do is communicate systems theory to operating managers in industry and convince them that they should begin applying it," said Dr. Ernest Talcott, chairman, to the other members of the management department of the College of Business Administration at Midwest State University. "The perfect opportunity will come at the forthcoming management seminar. I'm certainly going to stress it at the sessions I conduct."

The seminar that Dr. Talcott referred to was held annually at the college, and was directed to the upper-middle-level managers in the industrial firms of the area. The managers lived for a week in a dormitory, and attended morning, afternoon, and evening classes. The purpose of the seminar was to update the managers' formal business educations and stimulate them to apply the new management concepts.

True to his promise, Dr. Talcott focused entirely on systems theory in his part of the seminar. "And so," he went on in his third session, "you can see that the deliberate construction of a feedback loop in every operational process will permit a refinement of control not possible when output analysis is performed randomly. There isn't a single function that managers perform that can't be elevated to a higher standard through the application of systems theory."

"Are you open for questions, Dr. Talcott?" asked Lyle Peterson, the marketing manager for Elco Products, and a highly motivated student in the seminar.

"Of course, Mr. Peterson," said Dr. Talcott. "I want to know what you think about systems theory."

"How is systems theory being applied by educational institutions?" Lyle asked. "Or specifically, how are the schools of business administration using feedback loops to control the quality of their outputs—that is, the students who have graduated from them?"

"Perhaps you can explain a little more fully what you mean," said Dr. Talcott.

"Well, looking at the feedback model," said Lyle, "it would appear that the activating agent would be comprised of the professors. Input would be the various course contents, and the operation would be course requirements, schedules, instruction, examinations, and finally graduation. As I have suggested, output is young men and women entering business life. What standards do business schools have to measure the outputs of their system?"

"By standards, I suppose that my answer is that the grading system discriminates between various performance levels as students proceed through their educational programs," said Dr. Talcott.

"I think what Lyle is getting at is, what roles do you expect your outputs to perform during their business careers, and at what success levels, rather than what they do while, as students, they are still part of the operational process," volunteered Doug Lehman, credit manager of Litco Industries.

"We can point to many successful managers in this area who are graduates of Midwest's business school," answered Dr. Talcott.

"Yes, but do you have any systematic way of getting back information on all of your graduates?" Doug pressed. "Do you know what strengths may have been built into your outputs as a result of the inputs and the operation, and what weaknesses may exist in your outputs as a result of omissions or defects in the operation?"

"No, we don't have information of that kind," Dr. Talcott admitted.

"But if you did set up mechanisms to provide it," Lyle interjected, "wouldn't you benefit the educational program by permitting a comparison of the data relative to your graduate students with the standards expected of them? That is assuming, of course, that you have established standards."

"Yes, that would be quite useful," conceded Dr. Talcott.

"And if you found variances between what your students accomplish, or do, in business life, and what is expected of them, you could seek out means of correcting the differences, couldn't you?" Doug asked.

"Yes," answered **Dr.** *Talcott, now obviously very cautious of his ground.*

"This information could then be fed back to the professors, with recognition of the delays and distortions explicit in the model," said *Lyle, as he resumed the questioning. "The professors could make the indicated revisions to the input, and to the standards, and the operation would presumably start producing improved outputs. Isn't this analogous to what you have been telling us that business managers should do with their processes?"*

"Yes, the analogy is accurate," said Dr. Talcott.

"Then if there is an apparent potential application of the feedback loop model to educational systems, do you know of any business school that is seriously using it?" Lyle queried.

"No, I don't," Dr. Talcott answered.

"With due respect, sir," said Lyle, "aren't you advising business managers to do as professors preach, not as they practice?"

Discussion Questions

1. While designing new control systems, or evaluating existing ones, what would a manager gain by keeping a systems model in mind?
2. Explain why a feedback loop is essential in any effective control system.
3. What are the advantages of frequent and timely processing of output data through the feedback loop?
4. In the Case of the Double Standards, what do you think of the feedback loop system proposed by Lyle Peterson for evaluating schools of business administration?
5. How many of Dr. Talcott's seminar students do you think may be impressed with the potential value of feedback loops built into control systems? How many do you think will diligently try to apply feedback control on their jobs?

66. Behavioral Criticism
of Control Systems

Although the broad objective of the control function is to effectively employ all the resources committed to an organization's operations, the fact that the nonhuman resources depend on human effort for their utilization makes control ultimately the regulation of human performance. According to behavioral scientists, the trouble with the conventional control processes that have been described in the preceding sections is that they are based on rational, impersonal assumptions about human behavior. The same defect is advanced as applying to the planning and organizing functions, and thus the grievance may be perceived to be lodged against all systematic methods of management. Although the behavioralists represent only one point of view, their diagnosis of the faults of systematic methods, and specifically here of control devices, suggests why control is rarely as effective as it is meant to be.

Natural Resistance to Control

Probably most people are ambivalent toward control; that is, while conceding that it is necessary, they do not like having it applied to them. The threatening aspect of having one's performance subjected to searching scrutiny is commonly felt by people on all occupational levels, no matter how high or low. The inventory clerk who is called on to explain how seventeen years' supply of paper clips have accumulated is probably no more uncomfortable than the organization's president who must explain a 300-percent overrun on a government contract. Some relief from subjection to control comes to individuals who get to the upper levels in organizations, in the sense that the number of people who can exercise control over them becomes smaller. At the lower levels of an organization, the control devices and control agents are multitudinous, and the view upward is oppressive.

The natural dislike of being under the threat of personal controls is not normally alleviated by the manner in which employee performances are reviewed against standards, particularly if a performance shows negative variances. A person can know few lonelier and more humbling experiences than trying to defend a budget or a schedule that has gotten out of control. A remedy would be to em-

428

phasize the constructiveness of controls and minimize their punitive possibilities.

Many individuals show a tendency to adapt to controls—not necessarily because their performance is any better than those who do not, nor because they come to like being controlled, but rather because they learn "how to play the game." There are ways to "beat" controls, and perhaps the reason that some persons are successful in organizations is that they have learned to use them. For example, as is frequently done, they may pad budgets to give the impression of an efficiently run operation when costs show up to be under the planned figure.

Inhibitive Standards

Standards quite often have the effect of making people who are expected to measure up to them feel resigned to failure rather than stimulated to extend their efforts. A number of causes can be seen: the setting of arbitrary and unrealistic standards, as well as the tactic of continually shifting standards upward.

When standards are set arbitrarily, the effect on employee morale will be poor. A typical example of an arbitrary standard is an order specifying that each department shall reduce its operating costs by 10 percent. Lower-level managers receiving such an order will accurately perceive it as evidence of laziness on the part of the senior managers; it certainly takes far less effort to issue a blanket edict of this kind than to diligently search out and correct the operations where serious cost excesses are occurring. Its most dampening impact will be on the efficient managers whose costs are already pared to the bone; they can cut them no further, they know that they will suffer in comparison with their peers who deliberately maintain "fat" in their organizations, and they will become resentful as a result.

Perception of standards as barriers rather than stimuli to extended effort also results from the setting of unrealistic standards. Individuals who are expected to accomplish the impossible frequently will just set their own standards at an attainable level and prepare to suffer the consequences. Their attitude is something like that of a golfer who cannot shoot par on par-4 holes longer than 400 yards. Since only a lucky fluke would enable him to make par, he responds by establishing 5 as his own acceptable score for the hole.

Standards that are continually shifted upward represent a third reason for people to become resigned to failure. Periodically adjusting higher the criteria for a normal day's work was a favorite tactic of the old-time efficiency experts in their attempts to set production records. It is commonly used to goad salesmen to greater and greater efforts, and has its analogy in the tactic of the farm boy who, aspiring to greater strength, picked up the same calf each day as it grew to be a cow. People who have a high inner motivation often achieve unbelievable goals by shifting their own standards upward, but usually the tactic is met with bitterness when it is applied by control agents.

Participation as a management concept has been dealt with several times in this book (see especially Sections 46 and 47). Its proponents urge that the performance of individuals may greatly improve if they are involved in decisions which affect them, such as setting the standards by which their efforts will be measured. Surprisingly, people often set higher standards for themselves than would be set by control agents. However, management by objectives is a situational matter; the nature of the job can affect how well this technique will work.

Problems Associated With Measurement

Previous control sections have stressed the efficiency of expressing measurements in numerical terms. With respect to human performance, however, not all variables can be expressed quantitatively nor measured objectively, with often discouraging effects on individuals during performance reviews. Qualitative variables, or those that cannot be expressed quantitatively, include such elements as the patient development of subordinates' skills or the cultivation of customers' good will. A control system that focuses solely on unit cost of production or net profitability completely overlooks the importance of these elements. As rewards in most companies are bestowed on individuals who perform well when measured quantitatively, those who build for the future without numerically measurable short-term results may frequently be criticized in performance reviews and bypassed for raises and promotions. As a result, they might feel a resigned conformity to the system or antipathy toward the company, or maybe even sufficient indignation to quit outright—none of which would be in the best interests of the organization.

Another problem related to measurement has to do with the frustrations employees can experience when important numerical data are omitted from a control system. An example of how such omissions can occur might be related to the preoccupation of engineers with measurements of technical excellence. Although these are unquestionably significant criteria in control systems, they must be weighed against such other data as time to develop a product, cost of production, and potential saleability. When the latter factors are omitted, real frustration and discouragement for the work force will result.

Damaging Evaluations

The myopic concern of managers with variances per se can obscure the fact that the variances could have been far worse than they actually are. Sometimes more credit is due an individual whose record shows negative variances, but whose outstanding performance kept them from being considerably worse, than more fortunate peers who were faced with easy challenges.

The impersonal objectivity with which control evaluations are frequently made also can be extremely damaging to the motivation of individuals. Standards are rarely inviolate, and variances often mean that the standards are wrong, rather than the performance. People punished for not performing up to par—when no real effort has been extended by the monitor to ferret out the cause—may sometimes defend themselves, but in many instances will simply adopt a contemptuous attitude toward the entire control system.

Another practice that embitters people is being evaluated for elements over which they have no control. Allocated costs to budgets afford one example. A manager whose budget is continually overrun because of costs that are outside his jurisdiction soon loses interest in even trying to meet target costs. Also, people will think that they have been judged unfairly when failure in another person's area of responsibility prevents them from meeting the standards set for their own performance. This is a common occurrence because of the interdependence between successive stages in an organization's total activity. A typical case would be a slipped production schedule, with blame laid on the production manager, when actually the cause was a combination of delay in receiving raw materials, a mandatory reduction in allowable manpower, and unanticipated engineering changes.

Ineffective Adjustments

Individuals often fail to respond to prescribed corrective action because they do not agree that the remedies are appropriate. It must be remembered that corrections usually do not represent one person's decisions, but result from a pooling of judgments. Since there frequently are dissenters to the outcome of group deliberation, the persons who have been outnumbered may hope that events prove them right, rather than work to support the majority position. When the unwelcome corrective action is designated by an individual's supervisor, the latter might, rightly or wrongly, be perceived as lacking the authority to decide such matters, and the subordinate may comply with enough lack of enthusiasm to make the remedy ineffective.

Another reason why adjustments intended to bring a system back into control are frequently ineffective is that the responsibility for implementing the correction is not clear-cut, and apparently no single person will assume the obligation, with the chance of failing and becoming discredited. This situation is comparable to one in football where several defensive backs wait for one of the others to tackle an elusive open field runner. People instinctively seek to protect themselves, and when a prescribed action is only minimally assured of success, a natural instinct is to avoid being directly associated with it.

Multiplicity of Controls

The typical middle manager in a modern organization, such as a machine-shop superintendent, is governed by a maze of controls, the objectives of which are often in conflict with one another. To name but a few, there are production schedules, cost budgets, quality rejection reports, manpower ceilings, wage minimums and maximums, safety codes, overtime limitations, the union contract, and machine utilization standards. Individuals in all of the company's operations face similar controls.

The result is that people perceive that they cannot possibly win in terms of all of the standards by which they are measured. Typically, they will choose the control which they think will result in the best impression if they comply with it, and take the chance that success along this line will sustain them through failures along others. The frustration and demoralization attendant upon such a course are not difficult to imagine.

Preceived Illegitimacy of Control Agents

Staff relationships (which in this book refer to advisory and service relationships; see Section 23) bring controls to bear on individuals by persons other than their direct line supervisors. People may tolerate having their performances regulated by line supervisors, especially since the latter usually have the power to punish or reward. But having controls established over their activities by persons outside their own department is often more than their patience will bear. *Illegitimate* is often the label applied to control exerted by outsiders, and such control is a central source of conflict between members of different departments.

A good subject for behavioral research is the formulation of control designs which would motivate human effort, as opposed to the kinds of control which are primarily inhibitive. There is a great deal of discussion about the human problems of control, but aside from those proposed in the management by objectives concept (Section 46), not many solutions are being offered.

Jim Blakewell, a star lineman in college football, suffered a knee injury in his first year of pro ball. He then got a job in the production control department of Pilgrim Container Corporation, a large manufacturer of corrugated containers in the Midwest. Within a few years he rose to production control manager.

Under Jim's careful control of production schedules, Pilgrim gained a reputation among container buyers of always keeping its delivery promises. To accomplish this, Jim had developed standard lead times (intervals between receipt and delivery of orders) with built-in safety allowances for each item in the product line. For example, carload lots of one-color regular slotted containers (RSC's) had a lead time of six weeks. A week was added for two colors, for waxing, and for specialty boxes. Less-than-carload orders carried an extra week lead time because of the problem of economically fitting them into a production run. Pilgrim's salesmen were generally happy with the support that they got from production control, but sometimes tried to persuade Jim to let them offer customers shorter lead times in order to capture desirable orders. This Jim adamantly refused to do, because, as he said, once he started making exceptions his whole control system would break down.

One such instance occurred when a salesman, Ollie Babcock, was convinced that he could get an initial order for containers from a major paint company. Jim had cooperated with Ollie in rushing the production of six sample boxes that had been used in the sales presentation, but turned deaf ears to Ollie's plea for four weeks' delivery of a carload trial order of one-color RCS's.

"Jim, you know you have an allowance built into your lead times," Ollie argued. "Most of my orders sit in the warehouse for a week before they are due to be delivered. And I am sure you could squeeze another week out for this order if you tried."

"That's right, I probably could," said Jim, "but if I did, within a day half of the other salesmen would be asking for four-week lead times. The plant can't work consistently to that kind of scheduling, and we would very soon start breaking our delivery commitments."

"I'm going to see Jones about it," said Ollie heatedly. "I don't think that you have the authority to control this tightly."

Art Jones was Pilgrim's sales manager, and was at the same organizational level in the company as Jim's boss, Bob Skinner, production manager. As Jim expected, he received a call from Skinner the morning following his dispute with Babcock.

"Jones is pretty upset at the possibility of losing that new order," Skinner said. "Is there anything that we should do to help him?"

Jim explained the position that he had taken regarding any relaxation of standard lead times.

"I am going to support you, of course," responded Skinner. "As far as I am concerned, you have complete control over production scheduling."

The first dampening of Jim's elation at having his decision upheld was the receipt of a memo from the personnel manager denying his request for a salary increase for his assistant. The explanation for the denial was that the individual was already at the top salary bracket for his job classification, and that if an exception was made in this case it could cause such a clamor for other exceptions that the entire salary structure would be threatened. Jim was honest enough to see the validity of the argument, and to also perceive the analogy to his own stand on not relaxing lead times, but it did irk him to realize how little control he had over conditions affecting his subordinates.

Pilgrim's paper mill was independent of the container manufacturing plant, but supplied the plant with its requirements for liner and corrugating medium materials. A source of conflict between mill personnel and plant personnel was the wide variation in the quality of the materials that the mill furnished. Some batches were so bad that the customers began to complain, and Lee Wing, the container plant quality control engineer, decided to take action. With Skinner's authorization, Wing set a control policy whereby he would stop further conversion of board that did not exceed the industry standard bursting strengths by at least 5 percent.

The impact of this policy hit Jim Blakewell on the same day that he received the memo from the personnel manager. The press foreman came to his office to tell him that Wing had condemned all of the 200-lb. bursting strength board then in the plant. Jim was horrified, because the action meant at least a two weeks' slippage of all of his production schedules. He immediately called Skinner and asked him to rescind Wing's order.

"I'm sorry, Jim, because I am as proud as you are of our scheduling performance," Skinner said. "However, the mill has to get the message that we won't accept shoddy materials, and getting the labor invested in that bad board charged back to them is one way of doing it."

"Yes, but the board almost comes up to the 200-lb. standard. Why don't we go ahead and use it, but warn the mill that we will reject the next bad batch?"

"No, now is the time to show them that we mean business," Skinner replied. "I am afraid that this is something that is outside your control."

Jim resignedly asked his secretary for some of the yellow pads that he used to block out schedule changes. In the place of the pads that he was accustomed to, she handed him some that were a dirty gray in color, and of a rough, abrasive texture.

"I knew you wouldn't like these, Mr. Blakewell," his secretary said, "so I called purchasing to see what caused the change from yellow ones. They are on a campaign to cut unnecessary costs, and they save 7¢ each on the gray pads."

Discussion Questions

1. Suppose that you are a salesman for a company that awards vacation trips and bonuses to individuals whose annual sales most greatly exceed quotas. The sales manager partially sets territory quotas, basing them on forecasts prepared by the salesmen themselves. What would be your objective in preparing your forecast? What would be the sales manager's objective in setting quotas? Knowing that objective, what strategy would you use in preparing your forecast?

2. Should the same standards be applied to all individuals performing the same type of work?
3. What are the advantages and disadvantages of appointing a committee to correct a situation that has gotten out of control?
4. In the Case of the Controlled Controller, what do you think of Jim Blakewell's policy of making no exceptions to his six-week delivery policy?
5. How would you describe Jim Blakewell's general attitude toward control systems? Is it different from yours?

Summary

Controlling may be defined as the function of assuring that plans are achieved. The first step in control is the setting of standards, or the desired characteristics of future events; the second is the measurement of actual events; the third is the comparison of events with standards; and the last is the introduction of changes to correct tendencies for actual events to deviate from standards.

A budget is both a plan and a control device. Budgets are of many kinds, some of the more important ones being revenue and expense budgets, cash budgets, departmental operating budgets, and project budgets. The process of budgeting starts with the identification, in numerical terms, of the desired results of future events. This is the planning phase. The control phase is entered when the results are posted, variances are calculated, causes for the variances are investigated, and corrective action is determined.

Since dollars are a convenient unit of measurement, they facilitate the use of various kinds of financial controls in addition to budgets. The balance sheet, being essentially a firm's scorecard at a given point in time, can be analyzed by deriving the ratios between accounts, and comparing the results with conventional or planned standards. Breakeven analysis is a technique for determining the point in the flow of revenue at which fixed costs will be covered. It is important that a firm's capital be channeled into the most profitable internal investment opportunities. The discounted rate of return method for evaluating alternative investments offers a way of accomplishing this control.

Aggregate control of a company's production operations centers on the problem of determining the least costly way of accommodating production rate to consumer demand. That is, in adjusting planned production rates to fluctuating demands, the company must ascertain the optimal response rate between two sets of costs—those incurred by changing production rates and those incurred by holding the production rates constant. Production rate changes result in the costs of hiring and discharging workers, overtime and undertime charges, and general disruptions. Holding the production rate constant costs the company, too, in terms of high inventories and lost sales. The optimal response is that point where the sum of the two sets of costs is lowest. As production control moves from the aggregate to lower levels of production, the system becomes a complex of increasingly more detailed control devices.

In effective inventory control, a key prerequisite is the discrimination between high-value items that require careful attention at all times and the much more numerous, relatively low-value items that can be controlled by routine procedures. The fixed-reorder-cycle system has control characteristics that make it appropriate for handling high-value or strategic items, whereas the fixed-order-quantity system, which mechanically controls inventories to levels determined to be optimal, is adaptable to the bulk of the items in a normal inventory. The latter system is now facilitated by the use of computers.

In quality control, the inspection of samples drawn from a lot to infer characteristics of the lot is improved by the use of statistics, in that the probability of any sample being representative of the lot can be determined. Statistical quality control deals with attributes, which means either a completely acceptable characteristic or a completely rejectable characteristic, and with variables, where the measured characteristic falls somewhere on a scale of possible values. Processes used in statistical quality control include acceptance sampling, on the basis of which it will be determined whether a lot will be accepted or rejected.

Profitability is the most significant unit of measurement in the control of marketing operations, having application to products, customers, sales territories, and advertising. (1) Profitability must be applied continually to all items in the product line to assess their stage in their life cycle, their contribution to aggregate profits, and the time when they should be eliminated; (2) customers should be differentiated according to their profitability, and action taken to reverse unprofitable accounts; (3) profitability comparisons provide the clearest perspective of the relative performance of sales territories; and (4) the key to the control of advertising effort is the relationship between the cost of generating sales by the various media, and the net return derived from increments in sales.

The incidence of change, which is characteristic of most markets and product lines, dictates that business firms expend efforts in the present to prepare for future conditions. These efforts take some form of research and development; and, because they are a drain on working capital with only promises of eventual return, they require extremely careful control. An overall R & D program must be decided, and funds budgeted for it; then a budget must be developed for each project in the program. In addition to cost control by means of budgets, periodic reviews must be made of the progress of each project in relation to milepost schedules, and the decision must be regularly faced of whether to continue or abandon the project.

Systems theory gives us an orderly way of viewing the relationships between dependent elements in a system. In a control system there are four essential characteristics: (1) the normative output; (2) the sensor, or measuring device; (3) the comparator, or device for balancing measurements and normative output; and (4) the corrector, or adjusting mechanism. In any control system of a goal-oriented organization, such as a business firm, there must be provision for feedback in order to assure the effectiveness of the operating system. Feedback is provided through the sequential steps of (1) measuring output information; (2) evaluating the output relative to standards; (3) determining what corrective adjustments are needed; and (4) communicating needed adjustments back to the activating agent.

The paradox of the control function is that while its main objective is to regulate the performance of the human resource of organizations, it must be accomplished through the efforts of these same people. The theory underlying control mechanisms is sound, except that it does not take into consideration human emotions and other variables. The connotation of being controlled is distasteful to people and foreign to their natural instincts, and the systematic control models in current use appear to aggravate the conflict between rational and personal objectives more than they relieve it.

Selected Bibliography

Blau, Peter M., and W. Richard Scott, *Formal Organizations*. Chandler, 1962.

Buffa, Elwood S., *Modern Production Management*. Wiley, 1969.

Dale, Ernest, *Management Theory and Practice*. McGraw-Hill, 1969.

Etzioni, Amitai, *Modern Organizations*. Prentice-Hall, 1964.

Fetter, Robert B., *The Quality Control System*. Irwin, 1967.

Johnson, Richard A., Fremont E. Kast, and James E. Rosenzweig, *The Theory and Management of Systems*. McGraw-Hill, 1967.

Miles, Raymond E., and Roger C. Vergin, "Behavioral Properties of Variance Controls." *California Management Review*, Vol. 8, No. 3, Spring 1966.

Newman, William H., Charles E. Summer, and E. Kirby Warren, *The Process of Management*. Prentice-Hall, 1967.

Ridgway, V. F., "Dysfunctional Consequences of Performance Measurements." *Administrative Science Quarterly*, Vol. 1, No. 2, September 1956.

Sayles, Leonard, *Managerial Behavior*. McGraw-Hill, 1964.

Sevin, Charles H., *Marketing Productivity Analysis*. McGraw-Hill, 1965.

SIGNIFICANT FACTORS
IN THE FUTURE
OF MANAGEMENT

Managers of the future will undoubtedly face many of the same problems that preceding generations of managers have had to face. Wars, or the threat of wars, will continue to cause temporary but complete reversals in goal values. Cyclical fluctuations in the nation's economy can be expected to continue, but probably not reaching the extremes that they have in the past. No abatement can be foreseen in labor's demands for a larger share of earnings, nor of the struggle to prevent a decline in labor productivity. Obsolescence of products and processes will continue, perhaps at an even faster rate, and preparation for change will continue as a necessary managerial behavior.

The rising educational level of the work force will require modifications in the managerial function of directing. Managers will be challenged to design motivational elements into the content of jobs. Moreover, the changing composition of the work force, which will include a larger proportion of women and members of minority ethnic groups, will necessitate managerial adjustments with respect to norms, attitudes, and personnel practices generally.

There will be a trend away from strictly localized operations, with business firms tending to widen the markets for their products and services. Multinational companies will become more common, with the whole world being the scene for the deployment of resources. Managers will be required to adapt to diverse cultures, in which values may be conflicting.

However, of all the factors that will bear on management of the future, two stand out. One is the computer, with the crucial question it poses: will managers use it or be used by it? The other is the relationship between managers and the rest of society.

67. The Impact of the Computer

People thinking about management generally agree that the computer will be a highly influential factor in the future, but they are sharply divided in their predictions concerning the kind of influence it will exert. The extreme view is that computer technology will eventually take over managerial functions, and render managers, as they are now known, obsolete. An opposite view is that human managerial capability will expand to proportions not now imagined through the use of the computer.

A way of projecting what impact the computer may have on management of the future is to examine its characteristics and applications, assess what it may do to job content and employment, consider some human consequences, and identify the implications for organizing and decision making.

Characteristics of the Computer

Two unique sets of characteristics have made the computer the powerful, although limited, tool it is. One set consists of mechanical attributes—speed, accuracy, and memory—and the other, its suitability for programming so that it can choose from among alternatives.

Mechanical attributes. The computer's incredible speed at making calculations—at least a million times faster than human skill—is its most distinctive characteristic. This capability permits data of unlimited variety to be collected, sorted, analyzed, and reported with a detail and immediacy completely impossible by any other means. In addition to improvements in data processing, the speed of the computer makes possible the ready solution of problems involving complex formulas, which otherwise, if achievable at all, might literally require thousands of man-years.

The extreme accuracy of the computer is another singular characteristic. Unless people make mistakes in feeding data into the computer and telling it what to do with them, the output will be accurate. However, the computer will compound input errors, often with horrendous results.

A third mechanical attribute of the computer is its ability to store information in its memory cells. Thus, unlimited data can be put away for future use, then called upon and applied under appropriate conditions.

Discriminatory attributes. Conditional transfer processes can be programmed into the computer, which permit it to discriminate between alternatives in a way somewhat like human thinking. The computer can learn a vast array of instructions, and then apply the proper instruction to a given situation. It can be taught to retrieve the right information from its memory cells. It can reach a decision point in its operation, and make the correct choice from among numerous possibilities. The computer learns to verify the results of its manipulation of data, and to know when one problem is finished and when to go to the next assignment.

On the other hand, the computer cannot make intuitive discriminations in the way that humans get a "feel" for a situation. It has no values other than those put into it. There are no means for the computer to reach outside its programming to get additional information with which to refine its interpretations.

Applications of the Computer

The characteristics of the computer make it appropriate for use in data processing, real-time computation, automation, forecasting, simulation, and data storage and retrieval.

Data processing. Manual handling of data has been almost entirely supplanted by computer in all but the smallest business firms in every type of industry. The processing of accounting, inventory, production, and marketing data has undergone marked changes.

The computer has completely altered the detail with which cost accounting records can be maintained and reported. A business organization's payroll calculations, record keeping, and check preparations are now almost entirely done by the computer; so also are invoicing and payment transactions.

Inventory control is another major usage. The computer assesses inventory balances, calculates requirements, writes requisitions, often selects suppliers and prepares purchase orders, calculates unit prices, and reports classified and aggregate totals as routine operations.

In production, lot sizes are determined, schedules prepared, and daily, or even hourly, progress is reported.

Marketing usages include cutting out of sales information by every conceivable classification, figuring prices and discounts, calculating commissions, and so on. The voluminous cost proposals required for bidding on government contracts are only possible by use of the computer.

Real-time computation.   A rapidly growing application of the computer is in posting data up to real time, or recording and reporting events the instant they occur. Often the reporting is done via a television screen. A nonbusiness example is seen in the way election results are compiled and posted as vote subtotals are reported. Sales information in a department store or supermarket according to item, classification, dollar value, and many other breakdowns can be similarly transmitted. Another fairly well-known example of real-time computation is afforded by the way that airlines book and report passenger reservations. And the nation's defense system is largely dependent on the computer's ability to interpret, analyze, report, and even initiate action on events as they take place.

Automation: process applications.   Numerical-controlled machining of tools has been a technical advancement of immense proportions. Before the introduction of the computer, the process of cutting metal began with the development of engineering sketches. From these, detailed engineering drawings were prepared. Next came the making of the tooling, such as jigs, dies, and fixtures. Then the drawings and tooling were delivered to a machine tool, where a machinist would index the feed and speed mechanisms and guide the cutting tools to their work location. When the operation was completed, the machinist would inspect his work and then start the next piece.

With numerical-controlled machining, a tape program is created from engineering design computations, bypassing all the intermediate stages described above. The tape contains detailed commands to the computer for running the machine tool. The tape is fed into the computer console of the machine tool, raw material is clamped on the bed of the machine, and the computer directs the machining of the part. The work is done faster and more accurately, and the costs of engineering drawings, tooling, and machinists' time are avoided. New costs, however, are imposed in the form of programming time and the investment in the computer.

In addition to numerical-controlled machining, the computer is having an increasing number of other process applications—indeed, in some instances, actually running complete plants. Plants having continuous processing, such as those in the paper, steel, glass, and cement industries, have computers start the operations, check quality, make adjustments, change product mix, and report results.

Forecasting. The characteristics of future conditions can be forecast by determining the functions of the related variables, establishing their coefficients, arranging the related sets in equation form, and solving the equations simultaneously. The complexity of this task would make it impossible by manual means. However, econometric models operated by the computer, such as the Wharton model at the University of Pennsylvania, are forecasting future economic conditions with improved precision each year. On an individual basis, too, more and more companies are using the computer to forecast sales, changes in consumer buying habits, manpower needs, prices, and other conditions.

Simulation. The computer makes it possible to simulate inputs and outputs for unlimited alternatives and conclude from the reports that one decision is potentially the most effective. Then the costs of implementing the decision may be undertaken, with considerably improved confidence that the best possible course of action is under way. Without the computer, managers attempt to estimate which of the alternatives available for any decision is likely to produce the most desirable results and then go ahead with that one. They never know what would really have happened if they had tried the others.

Data banks. As indicated earlier in this section, the computer's memory capability makes it possible to continually feed it information that can be used for some future purpose. An example of such use is in the development of a manpower inventory, in which all pertinent data on each employee are stored. The magnitude of this information can be realized when it is related to a firm employing 50,000 people. In the future, whenever any data relating to personal characteristics or combinations of characteristics are required—such as, for example, the names of all unmarried cryogenics engineers in their thirties who speak Russian—the computer can instantly search its memory and print out the answer. Other uses for data banks include the storing of technical information, indexes of possible suppliers, court decisions, and applicable patents granted or applied for.

Effect of Automation on Employment and Job Content

Since the 1940's, when the widespread applications of the computer began to be recognized, grave concern has been voiced in the United States over the possibility that the computer will make millions of people jobless. Some dire predictions have been made to the effect that the computer will lead to a national depression far more disastrous than the Great Depression of the 1930's. However, the record shows that in 1949, unemployment was running at a level of about 7 percent of the population available for work. By October 1972, with an expanded work force and computer applications in magnitudes not even imagined twenty years before, unemployment was approximately 5.6 percent. There is, of course, no suggestion that the computer has reduced unemployment (the incidence of wars and inflation must be considered), but only that the grim prognostications of widespread worker layoffs have not come to pass.

Localized problems.   Although there has been no widespread unemployment as a consequence of computerization, the computer indisputably has rendered many job skills obsolete. Significant numbers of people who have been displaced have acquired other skills, sometimes to their advantage. Conversely, some individuals, particularly older workers, have had their job careers terminated prematurely. To these people, national statistics do not mean much. Their lives have been directly affected, and for them the computer is the source of a serious social problem.

Paradox.   Clerical workers, who would seem particularly vulnerable to being displaced, have actually become more numerous in many firms after the introduction of the computer. In most instances the increase was not intended, because firms investing in computers thought the cost would be more than offset by a decrease in the clerical payroll. Paradoxically, however, what seems to happen in such cases is that the computer generates so much more data than ever was produced before that additional people are required to handle, file, digest, and respond to the volume of paper work.

Job content.   Jobs that are subject to programming, and thus to elimination, are those that are routine—requiring limited skill and little initiative. Disappearing jobs include those at the supervisory and managerial level as well as the operating level. The new jobs that are necessitated by the computer—such as those of programmer or systems analyst—are in some way related to it, and they generally demand greater education and initiative than those that are displaced.

Even jobs not directly related to the computer, in the way that those of programmer or systems analyst are, usually require a knowledge of it. In fact, some knowledge of the computer is becoming essential for practically all occupations, up to and including the professions. In many fields, such as accounting and engineering, high-level computer competence is becoming a required additional specialization. And, as implied in the discussion of the computer's applications, jobs in areas like inventory control, production control, market analysis, and credit and collection have become so oriented to the computer that the traditional ways of performing them have almost vanished.

Human Consequences

Changes as widespread as those attributable to the computer cannot fail to have profound human consequences. For members of business organizations who must adapt to the computer era, the changes have often induced tension and fear. Some of that fear is legitimate, as it relates to the depersonalization of performance standards. However, fears arising from the need to learn computer-related skills are less well founded and can be conquered by individuals willing to face the challenges the computer represents.

Tension.   People in a range of occupations—in education, business, and the government—have evidenced tension attributable to the computer. For the most part, they are persons who, having learned their job skills before the era of the computer, fear and resist it. Rather than adjusting to the computer, many appear to adopt an ostrich-like attitude, attempting to ignore it and work around it as long as possible. This explains why the already impressive role of the computer is not even more dominant—many logical applications for it are still only being tried in a minimal way. In business, for example, trial and error is often being called on where simulation (Section 16 and Appendix C) could yield better answers; in government, files of paper work are maintained instead of the data being stored in computer memories; and in education, professors often still require manually derived answers to problems appropriate to computer solution.

Alongside people in their twenties and thirties who have had exposure to the computer in school and can readily adapt to jobs of which it is an integral part, those in the older age group are apt to feel insecure and left out of things, perceiving themselves as old and obsolete before their chronological age indicates that they should. They are very conscious of the competition of youth, because young people with computer competence are being promoted into jobs at the middle-management level and above in increasing numbers.

Dispelling the threat. Although many people have viewed the changes introduced by the computer as threatening, others have been more receptive toward it. There is no reason why they should not take a positive attitude toward the computer, for it is not so mysterious that people of normal intelligence cannot learn to live with it. Managers, in particular, can successfully learn to cope with the computer if they master the following essentials:

- Develop the ability to communicate with computer specialists, and learn enough about their systems approach to analyzing problems to be able to digest their reports. Understanding a computer language, such as FORTRAN, is not important.
- Learn what information can be obtained from the computer. If managers would simply put down all of the information that they would like to have in order to do their jobs better, they might be surprised to find out how much of it the computer can readily provide.
- Determine the computer's practical limitations, and do not put insatiable demands on it. Reach a balance between what the computer can produce and the costs of obtaining it.
- Capitalize on the added capability that the computer offers; that is, learn to view it as a highly competent assistant.

Legitimate fear. For individuals in subordinate roles, the potential of the computer to depersonalize organizations is a basis for legitimate fear. In integrating job performance by computer and humans into a total system, the computer has reduced managers' reliance on subordinates' judgment and has caused jobs to be rigidly and impersonally defined. These aspects have been discussed in previous sections, especially 8, 41, and 66.

Those contemplating the consequences of the computer in this light may fear that companies that are so systems-oriented might go the way of further mechanization as a means of forcing apathetic and frustrated employees into working for company goals.

As indicated in earlier sections of this book, however, companies might well consider an alternative approach to motivating employees, namely, accommodating their organizations to human needs and using the computer to improve the probability of satisfying those needs. An encouraging sign of accommodation of organizations to human needs is the trend for business firms to experiment with "organization development," in which behavioral scientists help managers remove from the organizational environment the causes for employee tensions, frustrations, and anxieties. The computer can help in this effort by freeing managerial time from routine details so that more attention can be directed to "people" problems.

Implications for Organizing and Decision Making

The computer's implications for organizing and decision making center chiefly upon the level in the organization at which decisions are to be made, the authority of computer specialists in contributing to decisions, and the type of decision factors for which the computer is best suited.

Decentralization or centralization of decision making?   A continuing debate over the influence of the computer is on the issue of whether it will lead to decentralization or further centralization of decision making.

Arguments that the computer will foster centralization are based on the communication facility of the computer; the timely feedback to top management of complete and accurate information will enable relatively few individuals to make all the decisions necessary to maintain the system in a state of equilibrium. Consequently, it is felt that many middle-management levels will disappear, with charts of organization structure taking on a much flatter look. In other words, the key levels are envisioned to be those of top managers and operators, with some functional specialists in between.

Although there does seem to be a trend back toward centralization, after all the popularity the decentralization concept had in the 1950's and early 1960's, the computer is only one cause. When decision-making authority is withdrawn from middle management, it often is because decentralization has resulted in an organization's getting out of control, or because interactions with big government and big labor have required tighter interpretations of policies by business firms.

Despite the apparent trend back to more centralized decision making in business firms in the United States, it is possible that some decentralization may result from the computer. Through real-time computation, as mentioned earlier in this section, senior managers have the capability of knowing precisely what is going on in their organizations at any time, and thus should be able to remedy situations that have gotten out of control. Therefore, it may be that the computer will permit the advantages of decentralization, but without the disadvantage of loss of control, which has been a plaguing problem in the past.

Reckoning with a new kind of specialist.   As explained in Section 23, the evolution of business organizations since 1900 has largely been characterized by the increase of specialists in so-called staff functions, such as personnel, purchasing, quality control, industrial engineering, and traffic. Obviously, computer technology has introduced another kind of specialist.

Individuals who are trained in working with the computer are being placed either in centralized computer processing departments, or are being added to the staffs of central and supporting departments as technical advisers. Central computer processing departments have become major service organizations. Although in some cases they are part of the accounting operation, the trend seems for them to be independent of the accounting department, but with authority over many of the traditional accounting activities in modern guise, such as the development of specialized reports to managers. Computer technical advisers in operating departments quickly acquire prescriptive authority and become persons to reckon with in organizational power struggles.

Whether authority is delegated down from the top or rises by acceptance from the bottom has been discussed earlier in this book (see especially Sections 1 and 5). However, the computer is contributing to another view of the source of authority; it is now wondered whether a great deal of authority may not be inherent in a specialized function, with computer expertise being an outstanding example. In other words, senior managers in an organization may understand enough about the computer to use its capabilities and base a decision on its printout, but unless they have unusual background they must rely on specialists for the programming of the decision model, with its equations and weighting of variables. Such a reliance cannot fail to place the specialists in an authoritative role, because they can, in effect, limit the choice of the managers for whom they render service.

Differentiating between decision factors. Inasmuch as the computer permits mechanization of decision making when factors can have numerical values assigned to them, it becomes necessary to differentiate between the kinds of factors involved in a decision. Some decisions will involve only quantitative factors, and others only nonquantitative ones, while a third kind will involve factors of both kinds.

Previous sections, especially those dealing with planning, have stressed the value of quantitative analysis in facilitating decisions where all of the related factors have numerical values assigned to them, such as whether optimal profit can be realized by making Products A, B, and C in equal amounts or in varying proportions. The typical organization will have hosts of operational decisions of this kind to make at all management levels. Where in the past they required a great deal of management time, the computer now permits them to be made routinely. And because they are completely objective, the location at which they are made can safely be delegated to secondary levels in the organization.

On the other hand, the difficulty of making sound managerial decisions in which none of the factors can be quantified has also been discussed in previous sections, especially those pertaining to the staffing and directing functions. Major decisions of this nature are the ones involving people, and are also necessitated at all management levels. When a foreman tries to decide whether to promote Paul or Jim to lead man, the factors are the same as when the president deliberates over two candidates for a vice-president's spot. While the computer cannot assist directly in making these qualitative decisions, it can release managerial time for doing so through its capacity for handling the purely quantitative ones.

Certain decisions, which involve both quantitative and non-quantitative factors, must be based on computer evaluation and managerial judgment combined. For example, a computer can evaluate many alternate uses for funds available for capital investments, but it cannot objectively assess whether the funds should be put into a company cafeteria, whose only justification would be a possible improvement in employee morale because of convenience and low-cost, nourishing meals. Thus, in deciding a capital budget, the firm's senior managers would have to balance the quantitative weights provided by the computer, and the subjective weight that they would have to assign to the cafeteria, and come to a partially objective—partially reasoned—rationing of funds.

If managers become so preoccupied with the computer's apparent efficiency that they attempt to mechanize all decision making, it will not be the fault of the computer, which provides time for managers to humanize their organizations. The reason will be the difficulty of providing a motivational climate suited to each employee's requirements, and the present scarcity of information on how to carry out that objective.

From this overall discussion of the ways in which the computer is affecting management, a view emerges that managers will continue to plan, to organize, to staff, and to control, but their skill in performing these functions can be greatly enhanced through computerization of data. And, because the computer will release managerial time from the present routine of these functions and thus permit a greater focus on the directing function, it has the potential of contributing to the solution of human problems in organizations.

"What I want to know is, when am I going to see the cost savings you promised when I let you talk me into that new-fangled computer system," demanded Janis Micovitch, semiretired but still domineering principal stockholder of Four Counties Machinery Company. "I want all of the facts brought out before this meeting adjourns today," was his ultimatum. The occasion was the monthly meeting of the Operating Management Committee.

Four Counties Machinery Company was the franchised dealer for a number of leading lines of industrial and construction machinery. It also operated a thriving used-machinery business. In addition, it depended for a large part of its annual revenue on the sale of spare parts, which required the carrying of an inventory of close to 100,000 items. Besides its central operation in Los Angeles, it had 13 branch outlets in four Southern California counties. The number of employees in all job classifications ran around 750.

About three and one-half years earlier, a joint proposal was made to the Operating Management Committee by Bill Craig, inventory control manager, and John Simpson, accounting manager, that a feasibility study be made of computerizing the firm's perpetual inventory, payroll, and accounts payable systems. Craig thought that a computerized inventory control system might substantially reduce the firm's inventory investment, while at the same time increase the efficiency with which parts orders were filled from stock. Efficiency at that time was about 75 percent. Simpson thought a study would show that a computerized accounting system would result in a marked improvement in accuracy and timeliness of paper-work processing. Both managers said that computer company salesmen and articles in trade and business journals implied that the salaries of the clerical workers whose jobs would be done away with would pay for the cost of a computerized system. They felt that there was no moral issue involved in displacing workers, because new workers would simply not be hired to take the place of those lost by normal attrition.

When the proposal for a feasibility study was made, Micovitch, who still ran the company even though he had made his son-in-law, Tom Geiger, president, was against it. "We don't need anything like a computer in this business," he said. Finally, after about three months of patient selling by Craig and Simpson, he agreed to authorize an investigation. "However, it's going to be arranged by a sharp-pencil man like me," he stated, as he authorized the purchasing agent, Tom Downey, to have a study done. (Downey, who had been both his employee and close friend for forty years, was about the only one in the company whom Micovitch trusted.)

Downey talked with representatives of several of the computer manufacturers, and although each of them agreed to conduct a simple feasibility study at no cost to Four Counties Machinery Company, he was resentful of the similarity in their estimates of how much a "bundle" (hardware, software, and training) would cost. In order to get competition in price estimates, he called in a consulting firm, EDP Systems, Inc. EDP also agreed to do a no-cost study, but proposed that for a fee it would assist Downey in separately contracting for the computer equipment itself, the programming, and the training. Even with EDP's fee, the price estimate was considerably lower than those submitted by the computer manufacturers. As a result, Downey let EDP do the study.

EDP's study focused on the cost savings that would be effected by computerized systems. An abstract of the analysis is as follows:

Estimated Cost/Savings Comparison.

Computer System Costs:		
Hardware lease cost ($4500 per month, 36 months)	$162,000	
Programming	29,000	
Training	18,000	
Salaries of personnel to run the system (36 months)	387,000	$596,000
Computer System Savings:		
15 inventory clerks ($600 per month, 36 months)	$324,000	
18 accounting clerks ($500 per month, 36 months)	315,000	639,000
Saving over first 36 months		$ 43,000

After making the cost savings pitch, the EDP representative pointed out that the programming and training costs would be nonrecurring, so that the annual savings after the first three years would be even larger. Therefore, as the proposal went, Four Counties Machinery Company could have the efficiency of computerized systems, and save money besides.

On Tom Downey's assurance that the comparative costs were figured *accurately, Micovitch let the computerized system be installed. Soon after that, Downey died.*

After almost three years, each month's profit and loss statement showed increasing costs, prompting Micovitch's heated demand at the Operating Management Committee meeting.

"Let's first see how much this whole computer thing has cost," Micovitch *stated. With obvious lack of enthusiasm for being the one who had to do it, Simpson showed him the following figures:*

```
Computer System Actual Costs:
  Hardware lease cost ($5700 per month, 34 months)   $193,800
  Programming                                           92,300
  Training                                              33,000
  Salaries of computer personnel (34 months)          469,000
  EDP consulting fee (27 months)                        81,000
  Systems Control consulting fee (7 months)             28,000  $897,100
```

"What in blue blazes has happened?" Micovitch exclaimed.

As calmly as he could, Simpson made his explanation: "EDP badly underestimated the lease cost of the peripheral equipment. Then the company that EDP subcontracted the programming to couldn't make it work on the computer that had been leased. In addition, our sales department wanted computerized market analysis, which required programming that hadn't been planned for. EDP also underestimated the various technicians that we would have to hire. EDP's estimate didn't include its own consulting fee which Mr. Downey had agreed to, and when we fired EDP seven months ago, we simply had to take on another consulting firm."

"Isn't that all just dandy?" Micovitch said. "Now where are those fabulous savings in clerical costs that I was told about?"

"We have eliminated all of the manual inventory posting," Craig reported, "but the additional work of analyzing the data that the computer puts out has meant that we have created a lot of new jobs. Actually, we have about the same number of people in inventory control as we had before. I do want to say this, however. We have had a lot of trouble getting the computerized system to function as it should, but it finally is and we are going to have some very positive results to show at the end of next year."

"*The story is about the same in accounting as it is in Bill's operation,*" Simpson said. "*It seems that, now the branch managers know that we have the computer, there is no end to the number and varieties of new reports that they want us to do for them. Like Bill, I have cut out most of the old manual posting jobs, but the new jobs that have been made are in higher salary brackets. I can show some net saving, but it would be less than $50,000 since we started the computer systems.*"

"*Well, that just about does it,*" Micovitch exploded.

"*I wish it did, sir,*" said Simpson. "*Our office space is so crowded because of the amount of room that the computer equipment and the technicians occupy that we can't avoid adding on to the building. The architect estimates that it will cost about $250,000.*"

Discussion Questions

1. Of the various applications of the computer that are listed in the text, which one seems to have potentially the most important use by the top managers of a business organization? For what reasons?
2. What are the implications of the computer for students who contemplate a business career?
3. Do you think the computer will reduce, or increase, the importance of middle managers in business organizations? Explain your views.
4. At the top management level in business organizations, do the decisions that have to be made primarily involve factors that can be quantified, or are they more concerned with human factors?
5. How could other medium-sized companies benefit from the experience that Four Counties Machinery Company had in the Case of the Elusive Cost Savings?

68. Corporate Bigness
and Social Responsibility

There are two issues of deep public concern on the business scene in the United States. One has to do with the growing concentration of wealth among a relatively few industrial and financial corporations and what should be done about it. The other has to do with the concept that business firms, through the personal efforts of their top managers, should make more positive contributions to the solution of the country's social ills.

The issues will be examined by considering the power that business managers possess—together with available means for controlling this power—and by assessing the implications for managers of the social responsibility concept.

The Power of Corporate Managers

This country's form of government was deliberately constructed to preclude bigness and the unbridled power that is feared to be associated with it; and the same philosophy has been applied to its institutions. More than any other nation in history, the United States favors the distribution of economic power and opposes the concentration of it. Yet, despite legislative and judicial precautions, business firms in the United States have grown to astonishing size. An examination of the characteristics of today's corporate system will help define the power of corporate managers.

Diffusion of ownership. A characteristic of the corporate system is that it permits business organizations to grow to extraordinary size from the accumulation of capital raised from many investors. The past six decades of American business history have witnessed a change in the ownership of companies from founder, or at most founder family, to hundreds of thousands of shareholders. In theory, this would appear to be consistent with the objective of preventing concentrated power. What could be more ideal than that the millions of owners of common stock in American corporations pool their rights in deciding how the business firms should be run?

The answer is that the exercise of corporate power just does not —and probably could not—happen that way. For one thing, the average owner of common stock is chiefly interested in the increasing value of the stock and the dividends it pays. Besides, the mechanics of running a business subject to stockholders' decisions are impossibly cumbersome. Therefore, most stockholders abrogate their right to a voice in the firm's operations if they are at all satisfied with the stock's behavior.

Corporate size.   To the degree that the ownership of corporations has become more diffuse, the corporations have become more gigantic and their share in the national wealth more awesome. In 1933, two hundred corporations controlled one fifth of the national wealth. In the early 1940's, the Temporary National Economic Committee conducted a detailed study of the composition of asset ownership in the United States, and found an even greater concentration of corporate power. In each succeeding decade, the leading corporations have expanded the extent of their holdings as a share of the total economy. Those holdings mushroomed in the 1960's, when firms saw a way to expand horizontally by means of merging with noncompetitors. As a result of these "conglomerate mergers," the wealth of the United States that is controlled by the top five hundred corporations must be of tremendous proportions.

But asset size alone does not tell the complete story of the power concentration of the huge corporations. Expanding that power are the financing capability that is commensurate with their size, intercorporate stockholdings, administered price structures, and reciprocal trade agreements. Reciprocal trade agreements provide that two or more firms buy from each other, regardless of objective purchasing criteria. For example, Company A wants to sell to Company B. B makes something that A uses. Therefore, A agrees to buy from B if B buys from A.

To a very large degree, the effective power in the United States resides in its fabled business corporations.

Transfer of power to corporate managers.   In theory, nominal control of corporations is in the hands of stockholders, and the latter exercise their property rights by electing boards of directors to oversee the affairs of the corporation, particularly in the selection of top managers and the monitoring of their performance.

In electing directors, stockholders have one vote for each share of stock owned. Thus, a single stockholder owning a large block of shares, or a coalition of many small stockholders pooling their votes, could influence the composition of a board. However, there are not many corporations in which one individual owns sufficient shares to have an important voice in electing directors, and it is difficult to organize enough small stockholders to present a united front. The tendency, therefore, is for individual stockholders to sign over their voting proxies to be exercised by the existing board of directors—so long as they are not dissatisfied with the stock's performance.

The board of directors of a large corporation may either be an "inside board"—that is, a board whose membership is composed primarily of the top managers of the firm—or a board composed partly of managers and partly of outside directors, with most of the latter representing fiduciary institutions. An inside board is paradoxical, in that when managers act as directors their function is to pass judgment on their own performance. Fiduciary institutions, which include pension trusts, mutual funds, and insurance companies, own enormous amounts of common stock bought with funds from small investors, but the representatives of fiduciary institutions who sit on corporate boards are essentially salaried managers themselves.

Numerous surveys, including the one by the Temporary National Economic Committee previously mentioned, have indicated that only in exceptional cases do directors of large corporations personally own any significant number of common stock shares. (A significant number of shares would be enough to provide some voting control over the selection of directors.)

From this description of the typical formation of a corporate board, it is apparent that what is happening is the separation of ownership from management. Professional managers run the giant corporations, which in turn own the bulk of the nation's wealth, with mainly only theoretical interference from the stockholders. Exceptions, of course, exist in the few remaining family-owned business firms.

Traditionally, professional managers have been expected to act as trustees for the absentee stockholders and to conduct the affairs of the corporation with the single objective of protecting and improving the interests of these anonymous owners, but that view is undergoing reevaluation. For one thing, it is argued that stockholders have surrendered effective control of their property to management, and are therefore not realistically entitled to unswerving fidelity. For another thing, as will be discussed shortly, it is argued that the power of business corporations requires that their affairs be conducted in such a way as to serve all of society.

A third interest wanting to be served is that of the corporate managers themselves. Primarily, they want to continue in office, with all of the attendant benefits. If they can manage corporations in a way that will cause an increase in the value of the common stocks, and thus satisfy the stockholders, they are not likely to be replaced. Therefore, the tendency is for managers to behave like owners and accord high priority to growth and earnings as objectives.

It is not at all clear that the public interest is subverted by corporate bigness and the consequent power invested in managers of corporations, although it is customary by some people in the United States to assume that it is. Further, it is a national principle that power in any form must be controlled by appropriate checks and balances.

Means for Controlling Business Power

Checks and balances to which corporate power is subject are of several kinds. Our market system and limiting legislation account for two of them, and public opinion for another.

Free enterprise and the market system.   According to the theoretical concept of free enterprise, which fundamentally assumes unlimited freedom of entry of new firms into a potentially profitable market, the market system is supposed to automatically regulate the power of business firms through competition. Free enterprise is thus diametrically opposite to state-sponsored restrictions on the number of firms permitted in a market, which are customary in most countries other than the United States.

In theory, the market system works this way: A firm creates a market for a product and sets a price high enough to yield a maximum profit. Other firms see the profitability and enter the market, which causes a larger supply of the product and forces the price down. Additional entrants continue to increase the supply and reduce the price until the point of marginal revenue is reached. The market at this point is stabilized; no new firms will enter because any more of the product would lower the price to a loss, and no firm in the market could independently raise its price because customers would not pay it. The firms in the market share in it equally, and none can move to a position of greater power.

This theory contains such unrealistic assumptions that the actual results of the market system are not as envisaged. Differences related to such factors as management ability, financial resources, product innovation, and consumer taste for the product preclude any possibility that all firms wanting to enter a market would do so and compete on an equal basis. Moreover, competition in the real world does not lead to an equilibrium of power but to the concentration of it. Whenever there is competition, someone, or at most a few, of the entrants will succeed and the rest will fail. Since the invention of the automobile, for example, hundreds of firms have tried to manufacture automobiles in the United States, but after seventy years only four have survived. The result is called *oligopoly,* which is considered to be in conflict with the public interest. However, it has been reached through the most intense business competition that it is possible to generate.

In short, despite the fact that prescribed behavior for business managers in the United States appears to be "compete but don't win," the competitive market system does not prevent big winners. Therefore the checks and balances the system provides have had to be supplemented by government regulation.

Antitrust laws. National aversion to concentrated business power, and the belief that it could be prevented by regulated competition, led in 1890 to the Sherman Act, and in 1914 to the Clayton Act.

The Sherman Act contains two main prohibitions:
Sec. 1. "Every contract, combination, or conspiracy in restraint of trade is illegal."
Sec. 2. "Every person who shall monopolize . . . any part of the trade or commerce among the several states, or with foreign nations . . . shall be guilty of a misdemeanor."

The Clayton Act specifies four types of illegal restrictive or monopolistic practices:

Sec. 1. Price discrimination.
Sec. 3. Exclusive dealing and tying contracts.
Sec. 7. Acquisition of competing companies.
Sec. 8. Interlocking directorates.

Although the antitrust laws were supposed to foster competition, their language exclusively prohibits achievements reached by following competitive instincts. People who compete strive to come out ahead, not to tie their opponents—whether it be in an athletic contest, a poker game, or a business operation—and given that tendency, a position described as "dominant" or "monopolistic" may result. It has not been proven that the public suffers economic harm when firms grow to large size as a result of competition, but that does not exonerate the victors.

It is bigness itself that is constantly on trial, and the attitude of the interpreters of the public will is exemplified by Supreme Court Justice Learned Hand's opinion in a famous antitrust case: "Congress did not condone 'good trusts' and condemn 'bad' ones; it forbade them all. Moreover, in doing so it was not necessarily actuated by economic motives alone. It is possible, because of the indirect social or moral effect, to prefer a system of small producers, each dependent for his success upon his own skill and character, to one in which the great mass of those engaged must accept the direction of a few."

Social and moral objectives and antitrust laws notwithstanding, big business has become increasingly bigger. However, the concentration of business power would probably be greater without the Sherman and Clayton Acts.

Desire for growth, and imaginative ways of finding loopholes in the antitrust laws, have led to managers employing a new way for corporations to become bigger, namely, through conglomerate mergers. There is nothing specific in either the Sherman or Clayton Acts which prohibits firms from acquiring noncompeting companies. Hence, since the 1960's there have been massive concentrations of power through the technique of horizontally expanding a firm's markets through such acquisitions. The Justice Department has taken strong action to stop the wholesale practice, but so far none of the suits have reached the Supreme Court. Whatever is accomplished through legal action, the effective diminishing of managers' appetites for horizontal expansion may come principally from the stock market, because the stocks of most of the corporations resulting from big-name mergers have not performed according to expectations.

Other government controls.   In addition to antitrust laws, the federal government possesses an arsenal of controls, such as price controls, to wield against the abuse of power by big business. Any or all of them can be put into effect whenever the President and Congress feel they are warranted. In addition to price controls, they include punitive taxation, entrance by the government into a market as a competitor (or as sponsor of competitors, as happened in the aluminum industry), withdrawal of contracts from offenders, and so on. Once again, however, it must be noted that corporate power has steadily increased, regardless of the potentiality or actuality of these controls being exercised.

Possibility of public action.   The American voters, if aroused over the concentration of corporate power, could demand the imposition of severe limitations on business firms. These moves might range from stronger antitrust legislation to the extreme one of forcing the dissolution of corporate giants. Perhaps the threat of what an angry public could do has been one of the most restrictive influences on the abuse of power by corporate managers.

Business' counteractions.   It is illegal for corporations to make donations to the campaigns of politicians running for office, but there is nothing in the law forbidding business managers from personally giving money to campaign funds. The high cost of campaigning for even minor offices would rule out candidates who were not personally wealthy, except for the contributions people make to campaign coffers; and such contributions come to a large extent from industrialists and business executives. Donations to President Nixon's campaign in 1972 totaled many millions of dollars from business leaders, with lesser amounts going to Republican candidates for other offices. Democratic candidates have not fared so well in recent campaigns, but over the long run they probably get their fair share. Without suggesting chicanery, it is reasonable to assume that politicians elected to office on funds provided by business managers will not aggressively favor legislation that would be viewed as harmful by those same managers.

All large corporations, as well as the industry associations to which they belong, employ lobbyists to represent their interests in Washington. Lobbying is very influential, and corporations are able to exert influence against the passage of legislation that would be detrimental to them—such as tax revisions, product reliability requirements, and really stringent antipollution requirements—by the skilled strategies of the lobbyists that they have working for them.

The Social Responsibility Concept

A concept being advanced by many businessmen and academic theorists is that of the manager's social responsibility. It calls for the manager of the future to identify personal interests with the social system as a whole, rather than the subsystem of a particular firm. Because every business decision has an effect on other institutions in society, the concept implies that the manager must be conscious of these effects and give them equitable weight in the decision process.

Not all corporation managers recognize, or admit to, the power that they collectively hold. The social responsibility concept requires that they sensibly assess the extent of this power and consider what might be accomplished if it were used in the interests of all of society. Moreover, it suggests that they consider what might result from abuse of their collective power and the inevitable public pressure for reformation of the national business structure.

Thus the social responsibility concept implies the urgent need for self-control by managers in the use of the power that they hold. But there is far more to it than that. Political theorists urge that the intervention of business leaders in the social arena is necessary to curb the increasing power of the federal government. A highly practical argument is that the demonstrated competence of business managers is what is needed to achieve effective social reforms.

The dual emphases of self-control by managers and managerial participation in social reforms have led proponents of the social responsibility concept to delineate several areas of management responsibility: economic, social, cultural, civic, and environmental.

Economic responsibilities. Of the various areas of managerial responsibility, one of the more obvious ones is in reducing economic problems, both by seeking them out and finding solutions, and by doing nothing to aggravate them. For example, managers can combat inflation both by increasing productivity through worker training and motivation, and by not raising prices. Other ways in which managers can contribute to overall economic welfare include anticipating displacement of workers by machines and providing job retraining, building maximum quality into their firm's product or service, passing on cost reductions to the consumer, avoiding misleading advertising claims, fostering small businesses through orders, subsidies, and managerial assistance, and planning their operations to prevent cyclical unemployment.

Responsibilities to underprivileged groups. Another managerial behavior that is being emphasized is responding appropriately to the needs of people whose standard of living is below the minimum.

Within the scope of things that socially motivated managers can do is sponsoring programs to design jobs that the undereducated, physically handicapped, and culturally different members of society can perform. In part, these programs would involve the financing of job training and the providing of continuing employment at living wages.

Assistance to education and the arts. The proposal is being made that through the acts of managers business corporations can establish scholarships to finance the education of young people, and can also subsidize the educational institutions so that they can keep up with modern advances.

Responsibilities to the community. Another proposal is that managers bring their personal competence to community affairs by taking active roles in local governments, school systems, planning commissions, and other community organizations. In addition, corporations could contribute funds to the building of hospitals, recreational programs, relief agencies, and similar objectives.

Responsibilities of citizenship. Another action proposed to be taken by social-minded corporations is helping defray political campaign costs by giving equal sums to contending political parties rather than on a partisan basis. They could also encourage a climate of political awareness among employees and community residents by providing opportunities for political contenders to make mass addresses to employees on company property, such as in the cafeteria. Some firms have exchange programs where some of their employees trade jobs with government employees for six months to a year. And there are instances where senior business managers accept key government posts; for example, David Packard of Hewlett-Packard was recently Deputy Secretary of Defense.

Environmental responsibilities. By far the most powerful pressure being exerted on corporations, by government agencies and the public alike, is for more responsible action in correcting environmental problems, chiefly that of pollution. The processes and products of industrial corporations are under heavy fire as the major contributors to the ever increasing pollution of waterways, air, and landscapes; and corporations have been warned to either take the initiative in correcting these detriments, or they will be forced to do so.

Part of the existing pollution is traceable to the processes employed by corporations in the manufacturing and extractive industries. These processes spew wastes into streams and lakes, belch noxious fumes from furnaces into the atmosphere, and deface land areas with unusable by-products. Whereas the attitude of corporate managers in the past has been that they are entitled to the free use of water, air, and nearby land to dispose of industrial wastes, they are now coming, willingly or unwillingly, to accept the responsibility for preventing pollution caused by wastes. The cost to corporations for correcting this situation will run into the trillions of dollars.

A Conflicting Viewpoint

Despite the persuasiveness of some of the arguments favoring the social responsibility concept, there is no general agreement among managers on the subject. Those taking an opposing stand have three main arguments. The first questions the criteria that managers could follow in allocating their efforts, since the social responsibility concept provides multiple claims for managerial attention but no apparent means for assigning priorities to them. The traditional view of managerial behavior, on the other hand, which charges managers to act solely in the best interests of the stockholders of the corporation, provides a straightforward single goal and a standard for appraising managerial performance.

A second argument against the social responsibility concept is that it compromises the profit-making motive and implies that business management can be made more "respectable" if the profit goal is subordinated to more idealistic pursuits. Losing sight of the profit objective, goes the argument, would put the fate of business organizations in jeopardy.

Third, it is argued that the power of corporate managers is held in balance by the countervailing powers of the government, trade unions, and segments of the general public. Moreover, this equilibrium would be destroyed by adding to the present power of any one of the major subsystems, which would happen if business managers were assigned responsibility for solving the nation's social problems. Thus, as the argument runs, if there is concern now over the influence that a relatively few giant corporations may exercise, how much more concern would there be if these corporations directed the sociocultural aspects of people's lives?

Evaluating the Managerial Role

Perhaps in shouldering their social responsibilities, managers should first evaluate each claim for their attention individually according to its moral imperatives, consistency with the firm's objectives, and realistic implications for social betterment. First of all, then, this means that there are public areas in which business managers can appropriately, and should rightfully, operate. One of these areas obviously is ecological; correction of pollution caused by industrial wastes would appear to have the strongest claim for priority as an imperative responsibilitiy.

Many suggested managerial responsibilities fall in the economic category and are consistent with traditional management behavior, in that they contribute over the long run to the companies' profit and growth objectives. For example, programs to make underprivileged groups employable can result in identifiable benefits to the firms by providing skilled, and frequently very loyal, workers, taking people off relief and thereby reducing tax burdens, and increasing the consumer market.

Certain of the other areas suggested for managers' attention, however, may be beyond their proper domain. Some critics argue that if the arts, education, and community affairs are subsidized by business corporations, they will take on the form desired by the corporate managers. Often the point is made that there used to be many company towns in this country, and that although the employees and their families who lived in these towns were relatively well taken care of, their lives were shaped by company policy. The question is then raised whether it would be socially desirable for business managers, with their propensity for control, to take an active part with time and corporate funds in public areas that could become analogous in dependence to company towns.

The Case of
Who Gets the Slice of Pie

It had been the policy of Grayson Cast Steel Foundry, Inc., since the days when Henry Grayson, the founder, had put the company on a consistent profit-making basis, to annually donate 10 percent of the net profits to some socially worthwhile outside activity. The policy had lasted as something of a tradition, even after the Grayson heirs had sold most of their interest in the firm to a conglomerate, National Holdings, Inc., which operated Grayson as a semiautonomous subsidiary. At the board of directors' meeting held one month prior to the stockholders' meeting, when the distribution of the donation was always announced, John Pigot, chairman, asked for recommendations from the directors for recipients of the 1972 donation. It had been a good year for Grayson, and the fund available for donation, if the firm adhered to its past policy, amounted to $100,000. The matter of the donation was the last item on the agenda.

"Gentlemen," he began, "although some of you are new directors, I think you are all familiar with the company's policy of donating 10 percent of the annual net profits to some desirable community effort. As an officer and director of National Holdings, I can tell you that the parent company will not do anything to disturb the policy so long as the balance of the earnings is at a satisfactory level, and this board continues to endorse it. The subject at issue is the disposition of $100,000. Let us hear the recommendatons, and when they have all been voiced we will vote, either for or against, each one on the slate. Mr. Carstairs, as the senior member of the board, what is your recommendation?"

"I know what Mr. Henry Grayson, Jr., would say if he were alive. This town is trying to raise funds to build a new hospital, and a $100,000 donation from us would give the campaign just the boost that it needs. If we donate this much, the other firms in town will also get back of the drive. I urge that Grayson contribute the entire amount to the new hospital."

"Very well, Mr. Carstairs," said Pigot, "your recommendation that the full donation go to the hospital is acknowledged. Gentlemen, let us withhold discussion of the recommendations until they have all

been made, and just before we vote. Mr. Prentice, as another old-time director, what are your thoughts?"

"The colleges and universities in this country have never had a harder time meeting operating expenses, let alone getting any new building programs started, than they are having now. When the two Graysons were running this company the annual donation quite regularly went to either of their alma maters. I propose that we split the $100,000 this year between the two schools."

"I am completely against that," said Bruce Bergdorff, a new director, quite heatedly. "Universities these days are a disgrace, what with the riots and strikes that are going on. The stockholders wouldn't stand for us giving anything to a university."

"Please hold your comments until all of the recommendations have been made, Mr. Bergdorff, and then you may say what you like," said John Pigot. "Mr. Allen, you were here in the old days. What do you think we should do with the money?"

"The last conversation that I had with Mr. Henry Grayson, Jr., was on this subject, and I have repeatedly brought it up prior to the annual stockholders' meeting for the past four years. I think we should do something lasting for the arts—specifically, set up a Grayson Fellowship in Music. The $100,000 would provide a fellowship of about $5000 per year to a gifted student. We could have an annual competition in the local schools for the fellowship, and it would do more to help our community image than anything I know."

"All right. Mr. Allen has spoken for a Grayson Fellowship in Music. Now let's hear for the newer members of this board. Mr. Kelley, you are a labor relations attorney, and your background may give us a new slant on the most productive use for $100,000," invited Pigot.

"I can't criticize any of the recommendations that have been made," replied Kenneth T. Kelley, "but what I have in mind would be both socially beneficial and at the same time help the company. As everybody knows, this town has a hard core of unemployed people, particularly among the young blacks. Paradoxically, Grayson is having difficulty in getting good foundry workers. Now, what I am suggesting goes beyond a normal training program, because in that kind of

a setup a company picks trainees who have all of the attributes to be successful. I propose that we select fifteen or twenty young men who appear untrainable, and who are therefore unemployable for any kind of a decent job. We would have to start with the very basics of work environment behavior. In many cases we would even have to teach the trainees to read. The content of jobs might have to be redesigned. Despite our care, some of the trainees would quit the program and we would lose our investment. It would take all of $100,000 to even get ten of the kind of young men I am talking about headed toward a useful life, but I hold that it would be worth it."

"That is an innovative thought, Mr. Kelley," answered Pigot. "Mr. Bergdorff, what is your reommendation?"

"I think that it is time to examine the policy itself. Let's remember that the Graysons were wealthy people, and making a donation of 10 percent of the net profits every year meant little to them person-ally. Now we have the stockholders of National Holdings to think about. Their interests should be our prime concern. They want growth or payout, or both, and if we continue to give away their money to the kinds of things that have been recommended here today we may find ourselves off the board. I propose that we use this $100,000 for an acquisition; for example, it would buy a controlling interest in the new die casting company in town that seems to have everything it needs for success except capital."

"I knew the policy was bound to be questioned sometime," John Pigot replied. "As a matter of fact, I am receiving letters and phone calls from stockholders complaining about it. I am confident that if this board agrees to continue it that I can sell it next month to most of the stockholders, but if Mr. Bergdorff is voicing a consensus, then we will have to make a change. Mr. McHenry, as our new president, perhaps your views should have been the first heard. However, I thought it would be better to hold you until last so that you can put all that has been said in perspective. What is your recommendation?"

"Because of the importance of our payroll to this town, the most valuable community contribution that Grayson can make is to stay viable. My assessment of our plant and equipment is that it is rapidly approaching obsolescence. In addition, our smokestacks for our oil

furnaces are major causes of air pollution, and we should immediately start converting to all-electric furnaces. I can see substantial demands for capital improvements over the next five years, and it is to our own operations that our money should go, which indirectly fulfills our social responsibilties."

"Well, gentlemen, you have heard the recommendations," said Pigot. "Let us have a discussion of them before taking a vote."

Discussion Questions

1. Why are the precepts of the United States' form of government so opposed to concentrations of power?
2. How does the principle of competition behind antitrust laws tend to defeat its own purpose?
3. Do you suppose that labor union leaders would endorse any move toward government-forced dissolution of corporate giants in the United States? Why (or why not)?
4. Would you support the idea that business leaders should assume a greater role in social reform? Why?
5. In the Case of Who Gets the Slice of Pie, the Grayson directors must make an important decision. How would you make it? What would be the consequences of your decision if it were the one adopted?

Summary

One thing that is certain is that future generations of managers will not face a scarcity of conditions demanding the best of their talents. Rapidly changing factors will bring challenges that now can only be speculated upon.

The computer has the potential of being the most powerful tool ever made available to us. Its capacity for doing routine work will revolutionize both the collection and use of data, and the kinds of jobs that workers do. Moreover, the actual use of the computer has not nearly caught up with its latent capabilities. Some day people will learn how to capitalize on what the computer can do to predict and control factors that will contribute to a better way of life. While learning to use it to control, managers will also have to learn to control it, because its potentials include some that are humanistically threatening.

The apparent power of business managers is awesome, and the characteristics of the corporate form of organization generates the increase of this power. The market system, government regulation, stockholder monitoring, and the possibility of public action all combine to curb the power, and keep its use headed in a socially desirable direction. Now there is a clamor for business managers to not just act indirectly for the public's good, but to make their efforts for society their top priority action. It is wondered if what now amounts to a demand for managers to extend the area of their responsibility beyond serving the stockholders is really as much in the public interest as it is made out to be.

Selected Bibliography

Berg, Ivar (ed.), *The Business of America.* Harcourt, 1968.

Berle, Adolf A., Jr., *Power Without Property.* Harcourt, 1959.

Bowen, Howard R., *Social Responsibilities of the Businessman.* Harper, 1953.

Brady, Rodney H., "Computers in Top-Level Decision Making." *Harvard Business Review,* Vol. 45, No. 5, September–October 1967.

Burck, Gilbert, *The Computer Age.* Harper, 1965.

Dean, Neal J., "The Computer Comes of Age." *Harvard Business Review,* Vol. 46, No. 1, January–February 1968.

Glaser, George, "Plain Talk about Computers." *Business Horizons,* Vol. 10, No. 3, Fall 1967.

Mitchell, W. N., *The Business Executive in a Changing World.* American Management Association, 1965.

APPENDIXES

Appendix A.   Critical-Path Scheduling

Appendix B.   Linear Programming

Appendix C.   Monte Carlo Simulation

Appendix D.   Probability Decision Theory

Critical-Path Scheduling

The planning technique known as critical-path scheduling can be explained simply by the example of a house-building project. Figure A–1 contains a list of events that must be done and the sequence

Letter Designation for Event	Description of Event	Immediately Preceding Event	Estimated Time for Event (Days)
a	Start		0
b	Excavate and rough grade	a	2
c	Pour foundation	b	3
d	Erect frame and rough roof	c	5
e	Put on siding	d	5
f	Install sewer drains	c	1
g	Install rough plumbing	f	3
h	Install rough wiring	d	3
i	Install heating and ventilating	e	5
j	Erect interior walls and ceilings	g, h, i	8
k	Lay finish flooring	j	3
l	Install finish plumbing	k	3
m	Pour garage floor	c	2
n	Install fixtures	k, m	2
o	Install cabinet work	k	4
p	Finish roofing	e	3
q	Install gutters and downspouts	p	1
r	Paint	e, l, n, o	5
s	Finish electrical work	r	2
t	Lay carpet	r	3
u	Finish grading	q	2
v	Pour sidewalks and driveway	u	2
w	Finish	s, t, v	0

Figure A–1. **The Sequence of Events and Estimated Times To Build a House.**

for doing them. In addition, it gives the estimated time in days to complete each event, from the start of the event to the finish.

After the basic data are obtained for the required events, the sequence of their performance, and their estimated times—and this is probably the most difficult task the planner has to do—the next step is to develop a network analysis. Figure A–2 shows the network of events for the house-building project, with the circles representing the activities, and the connecting arrows representing the sequence in which they must be performed.

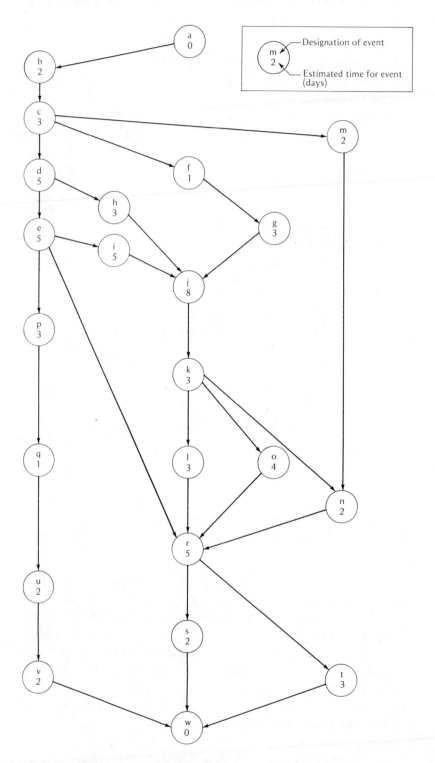

Figure A–2.   The Network of Events to Build a House.

The next step in critical-path scheduling is to calculate the earliest start (ES) and the earliest finish (EF) for each event. The ES for any event is the latest EF of the immediately preceding events; and the EF for any event is its ES plus the estimated time for it to be completed. ES is conventionally entered to the left of the circle representing the event, and EF to the right of the circle. Figure A–3 shows the ES and EF for the events in the house-building project. Note that the process of calculating ES and EF is additive, beginning with the start event and ending with the finish event. [Refer to event (j) for an example of the calculation of ES and EF. Since event (j) is preceded by event (g) with an EF of 9 days, event (h) with an EF of 13 days, and event (i) with an EF of 20 days, the latest EF of any event immediately preceding event (j) is 20 days, which becomes the ES of event (j). The estimated time to complete event (j) is 8 days. Thus the EF for event (j) is 20 days plus 8 days, or 28 days.]

Calculation of the latest start (LS) and latest finish (LF) for each event in the network is subtractive, or, in other words, the opposite of the calculation of the ES and EF. The LF for any event is the earliest LS of the immediately succeeding events; and the LS for any event is the LF for the event, minus the estimated time to complete it. LF is conventionally entered just to the right of the EF for the event, and LS just to the right of the ES. The LF for the total network is either some scheduled target time for completing the project, or, if there is no target time, the accumulated time at EF at the finish event.

Figure A–4 shows the LS and LF for the events in the project of building a house. It is emphasized again that the process of calculating LS and LF is subtractive, beginning with the finish event and ending with the start event. [Refer to event (k) for an example of the calculation of LS and LF. Since event (k) is succeeded by event (l) with an LS of 32 days, event (n) with an LS of 33 days, and event (o) with an LS of 31 days, the earliest LS of events immediately succeeding event (k) is 31 days, which becomes the LF of event (k). The estimated time to complete event (k) is 3 days. Thus, the LS for event (k) is 31 days minus 3 days, or 28 days.]

After the ES, LS, EF, and LF for each event have been calculated, it is possible to calculate the total slack (TS) and free slack (FS) for each event. TS is the maximum amount of time that an event can be delayed beyond its ES without delaying the completion time of the project; it is calculated by subtracting the event's ES from its LS. Since each event that has the same TS as the difference between the EF and LF in the finish event cannot be delayed without

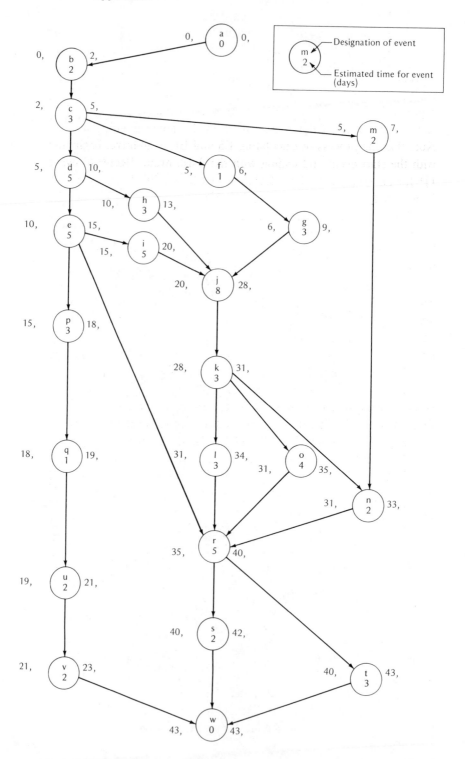

Figure A–3. The Development of Earliest Starts (ES) and Earliest Finishes (EF).

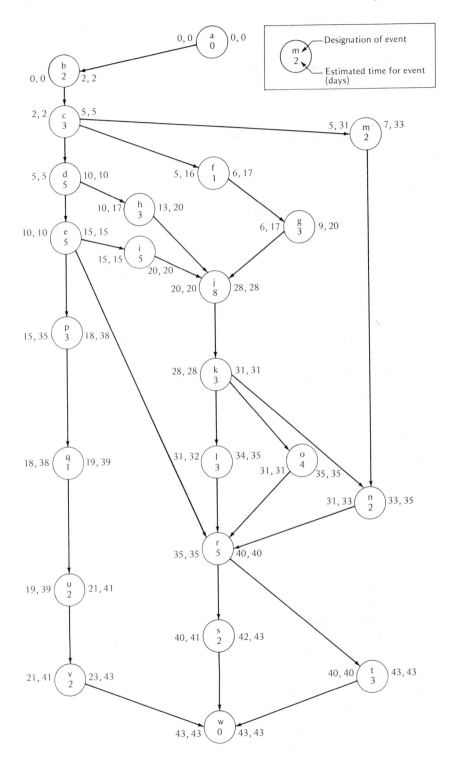

Figure A–4.   The Development of Latest Starts (LS) and Latest Finishes (LF).

delaying the completion time of the project by the same amount, all events of which this is true constitute the critical path of the network. FS is the maximum amount of time that an event can be delayed without delaying the ES of any other event in the network, and is calculated by subtracting an event's EF from the earliest ES of the event's immediate successors.

Figure A–5, which shows the TS and FS for each event in the

Event	Total Slack in Event	Free Slack in Event
a		
b	0	0
c	0	0
d	0	0
e	0	0
f	11	0
g	11	11
h	7	7
i	0	0
j	0	0
k	0	0
l	1	1
m	26	24
n	2	2
o	0	0
p	20	0
q	20	0
r	0	0
s	1	1
t	0	0
u	20	0
v	20	20
w	0	0

Figure A–5.   Total Slack and Free Slack in Each Event.

house-building project, indicates that the TS in the finish event (w) is 0. Therefore 0 is the TS in the project—every event that has a TS of 0 is in the critical path. In Figure A–6, the heavy line connecting events with TS's of 0 traces the critical path through this particular network.

(See page 486 for a problem in critical-path scheduling.)

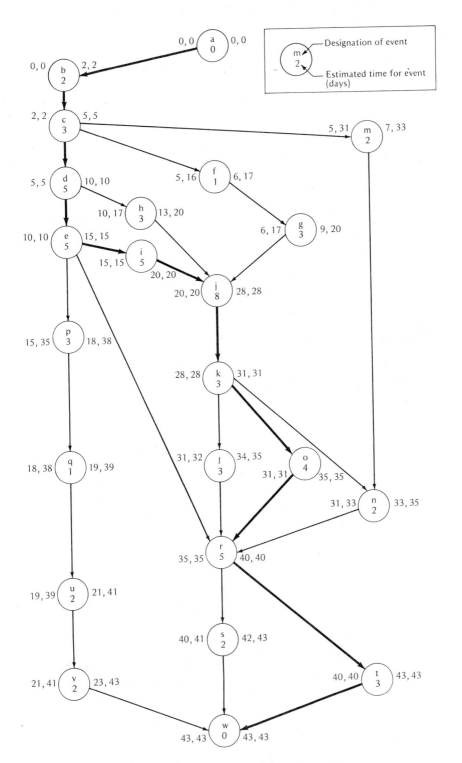

Figure A–6. The Critical Path Through the Network of Events to Build a House.

Problem

Listed below is a set of events, sequence requirements, and estimated event times for a construction project.

   a. Prepare a network diagram.

   b. Compute ES, EF, LS, and LF for each of the events.

   c. Calculate TS and FS for each event.

   d. Determine the critical path for the construction project.

Letter Designation for Event	Immediately Preceding Event	Estimated Time for Event (Days)
a	—	5
b	a	6
c	b	8
d	b	30
e	a	85
f	a	120
g	d	42
h	e,f,g	38
i	h	8
j	h	35
k	j,v	8
l	c	29
m	n,o	14
n	l	34
o	l	9
p	m	11
q	p,w	12
r	q	15
s	r	42
t	r	3
u	r	19
v	i,y	35
w	m	3
x	c	12
y	x	15
z	v	9
aa	a	15
bb	aa	8
cc	k	5
dd	s,t,u,z,bb	3
ee	cc,dd	5

Linear Programming

The planning technique of linear programming may be illustrated by a company that has a labor resource of 100 hours and an equipment resource of 80 hours. It has two products, A and B. Product A requires 1 hour of labor and 1 hour of equipment time to produce 100 units, and Product B requires 2 hours of labor and 1 hour of equipment time to produce 100 units. The profits made from Products A and B are \$20.00 per 100 units, and \$30.00 per 100 units, respectively.

The problem is how to allocate the limited resources of labor and equipment hours to the two products in a way to secure the highest possible combined profits.

Since the objective is to maximize profits, the objective function is said to be a maximizing one. It is expressed in mathematical form as:

$$f(\max) = \$20(A) + \$30(B).$$

To find the amounts of A and B that can be substituted into the above equation to produce the highest profit, equations should be set up for labor and equipment and solved for the optimal values of A and B. However, there are constraints that must first be considered:

$$1(A) + 2(B) \leq 100 \text{ hours of labor.}$$
$$1(A) + 1(B) \leq 80 \text{ hours of equipment.}$$

That is, the combined total number of units of Product A (using 1 hour of labor per 100 units) and Product B (using 2 hours of labor per 100 units) cannot exceed 100 hours of labor. Nor can the total combined number of units of A and B (both using 1 hour of equipment time per 100 units) exceed 80 hours of equipment time.

Note that the above constraints are, so far, not equations but inequalities. They can be made into equations by adding another variable to each one of them. These variables are called "slack" variables. In symbolic form, slack variable C can be put in the first inequality, and slack variable D in the second. Because a rule of linear programming is that any variable that appears in one equation must appear in all equations in the same program, $0(D)$ will be put into the first equation, and $0(C)$ in the second. In the final solution of a linear program, slack variables may have positive values if some part of the resources are unused, or will equal zero if the resources can be allocated to the real variables with no remainder. After adding the slack variables, the constraining equations now appear as:

$$A + 2B + C + 0(D) = 100.$$
$$A + B + 0(C) + D = 80.$$

The slack variables must also appear in the objective function, and as no profit is realized from these variables, the profit coefficients are zero. The objective function is now expressed as

$$f(\max) = \$20(A) + \$30(B) + \$0(C) + \$0(D).$$

Now we are ready to solve for the optimal values of A and B. To do this, a form of algebra called Simplex has been developed. Simplex merely requires that some fundamental rules be followed, and if they are, any number of equations can be solved simultaneously. The process that Simplex follows is to start with a minimum feasible solution, and then to continue to improve the solution until an optimal solution is reached.

To begin, the constraining equations are put in a matrix form. Each row is an equation. A minimum feasible solution would be to allocate the constants to the slack variables. A conventional form for proceeding with the solution is shown in Table B–1(a). (Note: the c_j values are obtained from the objective function.)

Variable	Profit	Quantity	A (cj) $20	B (cj) $30	C (cj) $0	D (cj) $0
C	$0	100	1	2	1	0
D	$0	80	1	1	0	1

Table B–1(a). First Simplex Table.

The next step is to calculate what is called the z_j row, which is derived by multiplying the profit for the variable in an equation times the values in each column for that equation, and adding the resulting product to the product obtained by multiplying the profit for the variable in the next equation times the values in each column for that equation.

To demonstrate, C has a profit of $0. $0 times 100 = $0. D has a profit of $0. $0 times 80 = $0. And, $0 plus $0 = $0, which is the z_j value for the Profit column. Perform the same step for the A, B,

C, D columns. When the slack variables are in the equation, zero is
the sum in each case.

zj row $0   0   0   0   0

Now subtract the zj values for A, B, C, and D from the cj values.

cj–zj row $20 $30   0   0

The complete beginning solution is shown in Table B–1(b).

| | | | A | B | C | D |
| | | | *(cj) $20* | *(cj) $30* | *(cj) $0* | *(cj) $0* |
Variable	*Profit*	*Quantity*				
C	$0	100	1	2	1	0
D	$0	80	1	1	0	1
zj	$0		0	0	0	0
cj–zj			$20	$30	0	0

Table B–1(b).   First Simplex Table Completed.

What we want to do now is force a real variable, either A or B,
into the solution, which in turn will drive a slack variable, either C or
D, out of the solution. A Simplex rule is that if the objective function
is a maximizing one, and in this case it is, then the variable to enter
the solution is the one with the highest positive value in the cj–zj row.
$30 is the highest positive value, so B will enter the solution. The
variable leaving the solution will be the one with the lowest quotient
obtained by dividing the number in the column of the variable entering the solution into the value in the Quantity column in the row. In
the above case:

$$C = 100/2 = 50,$$
$$D = 80/1 = 80.$$

C has the lowest quotient, and will therefore leave the solution.

The next step is to find the values in the new row for which B
is the variable. The way to do this is to divide the values in the old
row for which C was the variable by what is called the "key number."
The key number is the number at the intersection of the column
headed by the variable entering the solution and the row headed by
the variable leaving the solution. In this case, the key number is 2.
An exception will be the value in the Profit column, which will be the
cj value for B.

Old row: C　$ 0　100　　1　　　2　　1　　0
New row: B　$30　 50　　½　　　1　　½　　0

As the entrance of B into the solution will affect the values in the row for which D is the variable, these values must be scaled down. Do this by subtracting from the old D row the values in the old C row, multiplied by a fraction composed of the number in the D row and B column as numerator and the key number as denominator.

Old D Row		*New D Row*
80	− (100 × ½) =	30
1	− (1 × ½) =	½
1	− (2 × ½) =	0
0	− (1 × ½) =	−½
1	− (0 × ½) =	1

It is now possible to take another step in the solution; refer to Table B–2 for the demonstration of how the new rows for B and D are entered into the equation.

Find the zj row as in the first table, except now one of the multipliers is $30 instead of $0.

zj　　　　$1500　　　　　$15　　$30　　$15　　0
cj–zj　　　　　　　　　　$ 5　　　0　　−$15　　0

This second trial solution in complete form is contained in Table B–2.

			A	B	C	D
Variable	*Profit*	*Quantity*	*(cj) $20*	*(cj) $30*	*(cj) $0*	*(cj) $0*
B	$ 30	50	½	1	½	0
D	$ 0	30	½	0	−½	1
zj	$1500		$15	$30	$15	0
cj–zj			$ 5	0	–$15	0

Table B–2.　Second Simplex Table.

With this second solution, the company would make a profit of $1500 by producing 5000 units of Product B. (Remember that in the original statement of the problem, the values were for 100 units. Thus, 50 × 100 = 5000 units.) However, a Simplex rule is that if the objective function is a maximizing one, an optimal solution has not been obtained until all positive values are driven out of the cj–zj row.

One positive value, $5, remains, which means that A will enter the solution. Find the variable that will leave the solution as before:

$$B = 50/\tfrac{1}{2} = 100,$$
$$D = 30/\tfrac{1}{2} = \ \ 60.$$

D has the lowest quotient, and will therefore leave the solution.

Find the values in the new row for which A is the variable. Divide the values in the old D row by the new key number, which is $\tfrac{1}{2}$ — except for the interjection of A's cj value.

Old row: D	$ 0	30	$\tfrac{1}{2}$	0	$-\tfrac{1}{2}$	1
New row: A	$20	60	1	0	-1	2

The introduction of A into the solution necessarily means that not as many units of B can be made. Therefore, the values in the row for which B is the variable must be scaled down. Do this by subtracting from the old B row the values in the old D row, multiplied by a fraction composed of the number in the B row and A column as numerator and the key number as denominator. This fraction is $\tfrac{1}{2}/\tfrac{1}{2}$, which equals 1.

Old B Row		New B Row
50	$- (\ \ 30 \times 1) =$	20
$\tfrac{1}{2}$	$- (\ \ \tfrac{1}{2} \times 1) =$	0
1	$- (\ \ 0 \times 1) =$	1
$\tfrac{1}{2}$	$- (-\tfrac{1}{2} \times 1) =$	1
0	$- (\ \ 1 \times 1) =$	-1

Having obtained the values for the A and B rows, another step toward a solution may be made. Refer to Table B–3, which contains the new values.

Find the zj row as in the first and second tables, except now one multiplier is $30 and the other multiplier is $20. To demonstrate, $30 times 20 plus $20 times 60 = $1800.

zj	$1800	$20	$30	$10	$10
cj–zj		0	0	$-$10	$-$10

The complete final solution is shown in Table B–3.

As the objective function is a maximizing one, and as a Simplex rule is that an optimal solution in such a case is obtained when all positive values are driven out of the cj–zj row, the optimal solution has now been reached.

The company should produce 6000 units of Product A (60 ×

Variable	Profit	Quantity	A (cj) $20	B (cj) $30	C (cj) $0	D (cj) $0
B	$ 30	20	0	1	1	−1
A	$ 20	60	1	0	−1	2
zj	$1800		$20	$30	$10	$10
cj–zj			0	0	−$10	−$10

Table B–3.   Third Simplex Table.

100) and 2000 units of Product B (20 × 100) with the labor and
equipment resources available, and as a result will generate a profit
of $1800, which is the maximum possible under the resource con-
straints that exist.

Problem

A widow has two recipes for making candy that have been passed
down in her family. She wishes to supplement her small income by
making and selling candy. She has obtained 150 pounds of sugar and
120 pounds of chocolate, which are the main ingredients for both
recipes. Recipe A requires 1 pound of sugar and 1 pound of chocolate per gross pieces of candy. Recipe B requires 5 pounds of sugar
and 3 pounds of chocolate per gross pieces. She estimates that she
can make $7.00 profit per gross of the Recipe A candy, and $15.00
profit per gross of Recipe B.

    How can she ration her sugar and chocolate to the two recipes
and make the greatest profit?

Monte Carlo Simulation

Monte Carlo simulation can be illustrated by the case of a manufacturer's representative who sells a line of novelty items to department stores. A characteristic of the items is that they have a limited period of market popularity, ranging from six to twenty-four months. Wanting to maintain a line of ten active novelty items at all times, the representative has kept careful records of the market lives of his items over the past fifteen years. The records show that the specific life spans, and the percentage of items in the line corresponding to each one, have been as follows:

Market Life Spans	Percent of Items
6 months	5
9 months	15
12 months	20
15 months	25
18 months	20
21 months	10
24 months	5

At this point, he wants to determine how many new novelty items he will have to add to his line over the next three years in order to maintain an active line of ten items. His starting line is composed of all brand new items.

The first step is to develop, from the past records, a cumulative frequency distribution curve of the novelty items. Figure C–1 shows the construction of the complete cumulative frequency distribution.

The second step is to obtain, from the cumulative distributions, numbers that will designate specific lives of items for the simulation of thirty-six months of market experience. This is done by randomly selecting numbers between 0 and 100. There are many ways of generating random numbers, but the use of a city telephone directory can serve the purposes of this illustration. The directory can be opened to any page, and a number randomly pointed to. Its last two digits provide the first random number. Subsequent random numbers are obtained in the same manner.

Assume that the first number the manufacturer's representative has drawn is 31. As shown in Figure C–2, he would inscribe a horizontal line starting at 31 in the cumulative percentage column

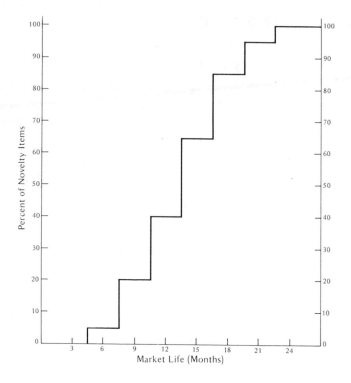

**Figure C–1.   Cumulative Frequency Distribution,
Lives of Novelty Items (Months).**

and extending to the point where it intersects the cumulative frequency distribution curve. He would then go back to the center of the interval bounded by the cumulative frequency distribution curve and inscribe a vertical line downward to the point where it intersects a possible life of a novelty item. The possible life so intersected is twelve months, which is the probable life of the first item in the starting line. Assume that the next random number he obtains is 81. He would follow the same procedure to find that the probable life of the second item in the starting line is eighteen months.

As shown in Figure C–3, he would continue this process until the probable lives of all ten of the novelty items in the starting line were calculated; then he would calculate the probable lives of the items that would replace the items in the starting line. For example, the random number 16 indicates that the probable life of the replacement for the first item in the starting line is nine months. Nine months, plus the probable life of twelve months for the first item, equals

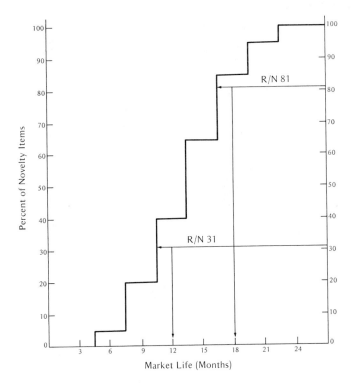

Figure C–2.   Calculating Lives of Novelty Items.
(R/N = random number.)

twenty-one months, which is the probable combined life of the two items. The calculations are continued until all items in the starting line, plus their replacements, have a combined life of at least thirty-six months.

From Figure C–3, it can be seen that the manufacturer's representative can predict that over the next thirty-six months he will have to make one complete replacement of the ten novelty items that he wants to carry in his line, and, in addition, will have to find second replacements for the four items marked x.

(A problem for the use of the simulation method is given on page 497.)

Item Number	Random Number	Probable Lives of Items in the Starting Line	Random Number	Combined Life of Items in Starting Line & First Replacements	Random Number	Combined Life of Items in Starting Line & First & Second Replacements
1	31	12	16	21 x	41	36 x
2	81	18	75	36	66	54
3	97	24	74	42	2	48
4	57	15	89	36	37	48
5	89	21	99	45	14	54
6	87	21	55	36	6	45
7	72	18	10	27 x	98	51 x
8	7	9	82	27 x	35	39 x
9	23	12	94	33	12	42
10	28	15	1	21 x	43	36 x

Figure C–3. Simulated Combined Lives of Ten Original Novelty Items and Their Replacements.

Problem

Assume that a construction company has just purchased ten crawler tractors for a total cost of close to $1 million. The firm's top managers want to know approximately how many additional tractors will have to be bought over the next ten years to maintain a constant scale of operations. An analysis of equipment records shows that 10% of the crawler tractors bought by the firm in the past have worn out in three years; 20% have had to be replaced after four years; another 20%, after five years; 30%, six years; 15%, seven years; and 5%, eight years.

Approximately how many replacement tractors will have to be purchased over the next ten-year period?

Probability Decision Theory

A company that manufactures a line of mobile homes can be used to illustrate probability decision theory. To gain the advantages of mass production, it manufactures the homes in lots of varying sizes before receiving firm orders from dealers, and must hold the finished units in inventory until it sells them. The selling price to dealers is $7500 per unit, and if the homes can be moved out of inventory within 30 days of completion, the full expected profit of $750 per unit is realized. However, if the inventory period is extended, the combined cost of money tied up in inventory, storage, insurance, and taxes begins to erode the profit margin. A critical factor determining how long the finished mobile homes will remain in inventory is the prevailing interest rate on mortgages that ultimate buyers will secure to finance the purchase of the mobile homes from dealers.

The company's manager is trying to decide the best lot size for the next manufacturing order from alternative lot sizes of 100, 80, or 60 units. These alternatives will be called his *strategies*. He is concerned with what the prevailing rate of interest will be when the mobile homes are completed, and although he cannot be sure what will happen, his judgment tells him that the interest rate can go down .5 percent; it can remain the same as it is now; it can go up .5 percent; or it can even go up 1 percent. These possibilities will be called the *possible future states of nature*. Through his reading and business contacts, the manager knows that there is not the same chance for each state of nature to occur. After careful consideration, he decides that there is only a 10-percent probability that the interest rate will go down, and only a 25-percent probability that it will stay the same. He decides that there is a 50-percent probability that it will go up .5 percent, and a 15-percent probability that it will go up 1 percent.

Analyzing the probable outcome of each of his alternative strategies relative to each of the possible future states of nature, the manager decides that if the interest rate goes down .5 percent, enough potential buyers will be attracted to the market to encourage dealers to stock up on mobile homes, and his own production will move out of inventory rapidly enough to enable him to make his full profit with any of his three strategies. However, he detects buyer resistance to a long-term commitment at even the present interest rate, and he knows that the larger the lot of mobile homes that he puts into inventory, the slower will be the turnover, and hence the lower will be the average profit. When he projects his alternative strategies into states of nature of interest rate increases, it becomes clear to him that if he manufactures 100 mobile homes, some of them will remain in inventory so long that he will actually lose money on them, and his average profit will be substantially reduced.

Figure D–1 illustrates in matrix form how the manager can perform his analysis by considering a given state of nature momentarily to be certain, and then determining the outcome of each of his strategies under that condition. The outcome of each strategy/state of nature combination can be measured in terms of the probable profit payoff.

The final step that the manager must perform in order to make his decision consists of calculating the expected payoff for each of his alternative strategies (S1, S2, and S3 in the equations), weighted by the probabilities of each of the alternative states of nature. These calculations are as follows:

$$S1 = 75,000(.10) + 56,250(.25) + 37,500(.50) + 18,750(.15)$$
$$= \$43,125.$$

$$S2 = 60,000(.10) + 51,000(.25) + 39,000(.50) + 33,000(.15)$$
$$= \$43,200.$$

$$S3 = 45,000(.10) + 42,750(.25) + 33,750(.50) + 29,250(.15)$$
$$= \$36,450.$$

The manager's decision now becomes straightforward. There is no apparent reason to manufacture 100 or 60 mobile homes in preference to a lot of 80, after considering everything that can be predicted about the future. Although there is still the possibility that the interest rate will decrease by .5 percent, and a profit of $15,000 will be lost because of not having manufactured 100 mobile homes, the decision to manufacture 80 units appears to be the best one on the basis of present facts and estimates.

(See page 501 for a problem requiring the application of probability decision theory.)

Alternative State of Nature \ Alternative Strategies	N1: Interest rate decreases .5% (P) = 10%	N2: Interest rate remains constant (P) = 25%	N3: Interest rate increases .5% (P) = 50%	N4: Interest rate increases 1% (P) = 15%
S1: Manufacture 100 mobile homes	OUTCOME: Sell 100% of mobile homes at full profit. Payoff: $75,000	OUTCOME: Sell 50% at full profit, 50% at half profit. Payoff: $56,250	OUTCOME: Average one-half profit on all mobile homes sold. Payoff: $37,500	OUTCOME: Average one-quarter profit on all mobile homes sold. Payoff: $18,750
S2: Manufacture 80 mobile homes	OUTCOME: Sell 100% of mobile homes at full profit. Payoff: $60,000	OUTCOME: Sell 70% at full profit, 30% at half profit. Payoff: $51,000	OUTCOME: Sell 30% at full profit, 70% at half profit. Payoff: $39,000	OUTCOME: Sell 10% at full profit, 90% at half profit. Payoff: $33,000
S3: Manufacture 60 mobile homes	OUTCOME: Sell 100% of mobile homes at full profit. Payoff: $45,000	OUTCOME: Sell 90% at full profit, 10% at half profit. Payoff: $42,750	OUTCOME: Sell 50% at full profit, 50% at half profit. Payoff: $33,750	OUTCOME: Sell 30% at full profit, 70% at half profit. Payoff: $29,250

Figure D-1. A Payoff Matrix of Various Strategy/State of Nature Combinations.

Problem

Jim Lowe, a senior business student, won a $1000 first prize for a paper submitted in a contest sponsored by a national trade association. He wanted to maximize the value of the $1000 over the next year but recognized that there were certain risks involved with any investment he decided upon. Business conditions in the country could improve, and he thought that there was a 15-percent probability of that happening. If he invested in common stocks, improved conditions would result in an expected growth of his $1000 to $1300. Bond investment would yield a more modest growth to $1100. The $1000 invested in a combination of stocks and bonds should grow to $1200 under improved conditions.

If business conditions remained unchanged, which Jim thought was 35-percent probable, a stock investment should grow to $1100, bonds to $1050, and a combination investment to $1075.

However, Jim was pessimistic, and thought that there was a 40-percent chance of a recession. In such a case, $1000 in stocks would drop in value to $800, and in bonds, to $950; and an investment half in stocks and half in bonds would be worth $875.

If a depression occurred, which Jim thought was only 10-percent probable, $1000 invested in stocks would be worth only $500 at the end of the year, a bond investment would fall to $900 in value, and a combination investment would depreciate to $700.

What was the end-of-year expected value for each of Jim's strategies? What should he have done with his $1000?

GLOSSARY

A B C analysis In inventory control, differentiation between the 10 percent of the items that are worth about 75% of the investment (the A items); the 25% of the items that are worth about 90% of the investment (A and B items together) and the 75% of the items that are worth about 10% of the investment (the C items)

Acceptance sampling In statistical quality control, basing the acceptance or rejection of a lot on the characteristics of a sample

Acceptance theory of authority From Chester Barnard, the view that authority is accorded to superiors by their subordinates

Achievement need The chief motivator of persons who succeed, according to David C. McClelland, who classifies achievers as "n Ach" types

Activities Broad elements of work that are done by the members of an organization in carrying out their jobs

Advisory relationships Interactions characterized by the extending of advice on work-related matters by a member of one department to a member of another department

Aggregate control Overall control of a firm's production operations, centered on determining the least costly way of accommodating production rate to consumer demand

Alternatives Various means by which objectives may be achieved

Amplification Distortion of communication through overreaction to stimuli

Authoritarian manager One who relies heavily on formal authority, who is an "order giver," and who mistrusts subordinates' ability to make decisions

Authority The right of a manager to make decisions within certain limitations, to assign duties to subordinates, and to require conformance by subordinates to what is expected of them

Back order An order for which the customer has to wait for delivery

Balance sheet Accounting statement of a firm's financial position at a given point in time

Ball of work concept A fear ascribed to workers (by Frederick W. Taylor) that available work is of a fixed amount and that it should be done slowly to make it last

Behavioral approach The use of the scientific method by psychologists, sociologists, and anthropologists in attempts to understand, explain, predict, and change human behavior in organizations

The black box In systems theory, the place where inputs are transformed into outputs

Breakeven point The point in the quantity of goods sold at which sales revenue and fixed costs are equal, and beyond which sales effort produces a profit

Budget A plan, expressed in numerical terms, which becomes a control device when actual results are analyzed and conclusions reached concerning indicated actions

Bureaucracy An impersonal, rational management system commonly associated with Max Weber and "red tape"

Central activities Broad elements of work associated with a firm's main income-producing operations

Centralization   The reserving of decision-making authority for top managers

Change agent   In organization development, a person professionally qualified to diagnose a need for change, prescribe the way to accomplish it, and assist in making it effective

Charismatic leadership   A natural, inspired form of leadership

Chief executive officer   The top manager of an organization, in business often called the president or chairman of the board

Cohesiveness   The close-knit character of a group that has attraction for its members

Collection period   The length of time that it takes for a firm to be paid by its customers for the goods it has sold

Committee   A formal group charged with either specific or general responsibilities associated with organizational goals

Communication   The process whereby a message transmitted by a sender has some impact on the behavior of a receiver

Comparator   In a control system, the person, machine, or process that balances the measurements of the actual output against some standard

Competition   The striving, on an individual or organizational basis, for rewards that are in limited supply

Conflict, organizational   A behavior of rivalry and hostility between members of different departments in an organization

Conformity   Obedience to organizational procedures and norms of conduct

Conglomerate mergers   Horizontal expansion of business firms by acquisition of noncompetitors

Control by variables   In statistical quality control, the recording of measured differences between inspected units, and the drawing of inferences from them

Controlling   Assuring that actual results conform to plans

Coordinating   Assuring that the contributions of individuals and departments in an organization are made as required, and that they are effectively linked together; or, the composite of the functions performed by all managers at all levels

Corrector   In a control system, the person, machine, or process that implements corrective action throughout the system

Critical incident   A technique for performance appraisal based on a record of significant impressions—good and bad—made by subordinates

Critical-path scheduling   A program type of plan that uses networks of events for planning and controlling the performance of activities

Current ratio   An indicator of a firm's ability to pay its short-term debts, derived by dividing current assets by current liabilities

Data bank   Computerized storage of information that can be used for some future purpose

Data processing   The rapid and discriminatory handling of data and performing of processes by a computer in accord with instructions programmed into it

Decentralization   The forcing of decision-making authority down into lower levels of management

Decision making   Choosing the means of achieving an objective from possible alternatives

Democratic manager   One who relies on the consensus of subordinates, who trusts them, who delegates decision making to them, and who exercises loose supervision

Departments   Organizational units formed by grouping activities; also, activity groupings at a particular level

Development   Provision of successive management experiences whereby candidates may grow to be managers

Directing   Activating subordinates to perform their work tasks

Discharge   Termination of employment for violation of rules or incompetence

Discounted rate of return   The interest rate at which the cost of an investment, and the present value of the estimated future flow of earnings from the investment, equal zero

Diversification   Making and selling products in unrelated industries

Division of work   The principle that large tasks should be divided into small ones, with people specializing in performing them

Down time   Time that equipment is out of service for repairs or maintenance

Econometric model   A series of complex simultaneous equations which simulate the operation of the total national economy or some segment of it—used in forecasting

Economic life   The period throughout which the advantages of operating a piece of equipment outweigh the disadvantages

Economic order quantity   The quantity ordered for an inventory item that is determined by balancing carrying costs against ordering costs

Empirical data   Objective data from testing and observation, on which hypotheses or conclusions can be based

Employee-centered manager   One who consistently represents the best interests of subordinates

Equity/debt ratio   An indicator of the real ownership of a firm, derived by dividing equity by total liabilities

Esteem need   The need that people have for self-respect and the respect of other people

Evaluative relationships   Interactions between peers in different departments, characterized by informal performance evaluations

Examining for attributes   In statistical quality control, discriminating between units that are good or bad according to some single quality standard

Feedback   In a control system, information concerning output that is communicated to the input source for the purpose of regulating performance

Feedback loop   The circuit in an operational process which transmits feedback and permits control of output

Fire-fighting tactics   Short-term adjustments for attacking problems as they arise, rather than systematic long-term plans

Fixed costs   Costs, such as rent, depreciation, and managers' salaries, that go on at a constant amount regardless of sales volume

Forced-choice method   A performance appraisal technique entailing the checking of statements on a review form that are most appropriate, and least appropriate, to the person being evaluated

Forecasting   Attempting to predict future events, such as demand for a firm's products or services

Frequency distribution   Tabulated occurrence of certain events in some past time period—used in projecting the number of times such events may occur in the future

Fringe benefits Nonfinancial supplements to direct wages or salaries

Frustration Conscious recognition that certain needs are not being satisfied

Functional authority The right of members of one department to prescribe certain behavior for members of other departments

Functional boundary lines Sharp distinctions between activities and authority in different departments

Functional organization The grouping of activities by the kind of work done

Functional-sequence relationships Interactions between members of different departments whose work is done in series to result in a product or service

Functions of managers The things that managers do when acting solely as managers

Geographical organization The grouping of activities by the territorial location at which they are performed

Grapevine An unofficial, unauthorized channel of communication

Graphic rating scale In performance appraisal, a technique for measuring an individual's traits or performance characteristics

Grass roots inputs Feedback from lower levels in the organization

Hierarchy of authority The pyramid formed by management levels, in which authority increases and the number of positions decreases as ascent is made from bottom to top

Hierarchy of needs Abraham Maslow's arrangement of five basic needs into a sequence of ascending order, from physiological to self-actualization

Human engineering Designing jobs and equipment to fit people's physiological, psychological, and sociocultural characteristics

Human relations A management approach preoccupied with assuring the contentment of workers with their jobs

Incentives Payoffs gained by taking some specific action (positive incentives), or punishments avoided by not taking some action (negative incentives)

Inducement-contribution balance In Chester Barnard's view, the equilibrium between the inducements that a member of an organization gets from the organization, and the contributions he makes in return

Illegitimate control Control brought to bear on employees by someone other than their direct line supervisor

Informal organizations Instinctive groupings of people, without conscious purpose, within a formal organization

Information-copy system A method of putting information the sender wants higher-ups to see into a memo to an immediate superior, and sending a copy to the higher official

Input Resources committed to a production operation

Interview, nondirective The use of broad, general questions that permit interviewees to talk freely

Interview, patterned The technique of asking standard questions of all interviewees

Interview, stress An interview method designed to find out an interviewee's tolerance for stressful situations

Inventory   A stock of goods in excess of immediate demand

Job   The smallest subsystem or grouping of activities within an organization

Job description   Statement identifying and describing the content and duties of a job

Job enlargement   Broadening the scope of jobs, and making them richer in terms of variety, interest, and significance

Job evaluation   Determination of the relative worth of jobs within an organization

Job grade   The level occupied by different jobs having the same relative worth to the organization

Job rank   In a simple form of job evaluation, the place of a job in the order of perceived importance

Job satisfaction   A state of mind that varies in a favorable degree with the worker's positive impressions of the total job environment

Job specifications   Statements of the personal qualifications required to properly perform jobs

Justice, corrective   The system for remedying inequities in the administration of distributive justice

Justice, distributive   The fair distribution to individuals of the good and bad things of life according to the way they are deserved

Lateral relationships   Work-related interactions between members of different departments

Layoff   Termination of employment because of lack of work, usually with the idea that the employee will be called back if business condition improve

Lead time   In inventory control, the scheduled interval between the placing and receipt of an order; in production control, the interval between receipt and delivery of an order

Leadership   The ability of a manager to influence subordinates to accept his interpretations of objectives, to follow his ways of doing things, and to see that their personal goals can be achieved by consenting to his authority over them

Leading indicators   Factors in the total economy, such as the gross national product or housing starts, that point to the direction that the economy may go

Life cycle   The evolution of a successful product, from its development to market maturity and on into obsolescence

Line/staff concept   The traditional distinction between line people (those who command) and staff people (those who advise them)

Linear programming   A mathematical system for allocating resources to alternate uses to get best results

Long-term plan   A set of alternative courses of action that, depending on external conditions, could lead a firm to achieve its basic objectives over an extended time period

Love or belongingness need   The human need for affection and affiliation

Management   The utilization of physical and human resources through coordinative efforts

Management by objectives   A technique in which subordinates are encouraged to set their own objectives, plus the means whereby achievement of those objectives can be measured

Management principles   General guides that have been abstracted from managerial experiences and deduction, such as those enunciated by Henri Fayol

Manpower inventory   A detailed appraisal of the human resource of an organization

Manpower plan   A systematic attempt to ensure the future availability of a firm's human resource in the proper quality and quantity

Market system   The process in free enterprise in which price is considered the key factor in regulating supply and demand, with competition assuring equilibrium of power among firms in the market

Marketing control   Techniques primarily concerned with applying specific profitability standards to discrete areas of control, such as product line, selling effort per customer, marketing territories, and advertising

Maximizing function   An optimal decision that generates the greatest possible profit, the highest output, and the highest return on investment

Merit   The appraised value of an employee's performance on the job

Minimizing function   An optimal decision that produces the desired result at the lowest possible cost

Model   A description or representation of a thing or a process, useful in decision making for predicting results obtainable from alternative solutions

Motivation   The inducement of employees to extend their efforts for the good of the organization

Norms   Standards of behavior

Objectives   Goals toward which plans are directed

One best way   The most efficient way to do a job, used as the basis for setting minimum production rates

Open-door policy   Provision for dissatisfied employees to bypass their immediate superior and present their case to a higher-level manager

Optimization   Selection, from available alternatives, of the solution to a problem that is most effective in terms of the total system

Organization development   The efforts of behavioralists, employing various educational strategies, to diagnose human problems that obstruct organization goals and to point to their correction

Organizations   Cooperative systems comprised of members consciously striving for a common purpose, the achievement of which is made possible by communication (from Chester Barnard)

Organizing   Grouping activities into departments, assigning authority, and providing for coordination

Output   Units produced in an operation

Participative management   Involvement of people in decisions affecting them

Peer rating   A performance appraisal method in which all members of a group with equal status evaluate each other

Performance appraisal   The assessment of the way employees perform their assigned job duties

Physiological need   The human requirement for elements, such as air, water, and food, that are essential to life

Piecework   Work paid for by the unit, thus implying a financial incentive for workers to earn more by producing more

Planning   Establishing an organization's objectives and determining the means for achieving them

Plural relationships   Interactions between individuals in group meetings

Policies   Reflections of a firm's attitude on various issues, which set the course for actions on all organizational levels

Position   One of the slots authorized for a job classification

Power politics   The informal struggle for power within an organization

Primary level of management   The level of managers in an organization who report directly to the chief executive officer

Probability decision theory   A quantitative technique for making decisions under assumptions of what probably will happen

Procedures   Step-by-step methods for performing specific actions

Product organization   The grouping of activities required to turn out specific products or product lines

Production-centered manager   One who focuses attention on output of work and is indifferent to subordinates' needs

Production control   A complex of procedures for measuring input and output factors against standards, and for determining what adjustment to make if actual demand varies from forecasted demand

Productivity   The ratio of output to the input of labor hours

Profit   The surplus in excess of costs that a business firm realizes from its operations

Programmed instruction   A classroom training method in which material to be learned is arranged into a sequence of steps, or frames, through which trainees proceed individually at a rate determined by their ability to correctly answer a question accompanying each frame

Programs (projects)   Detailed long-term plans for accomplishing specific objectives

Project organization   The team or task-force approach to getting a particular job done, involving the temporary grouping of activities according to the requirements of the project or program

Psychological tests   Supplemental selection devices used to assess skills, interests, and personality traits of job applicants

Quality control   Assurance that goods produced or services rendered by a firm measure up to some specified quality standard

Quantitative techniques   Methods for making decisions that employ mathematical forms—such methods including critical-path scheduling, linear programming, simulation, and probability decision theory

Quick ratio   An indicator of a firm's cash position, derived by dividing cash by current liabilities

Rank order   A method of performance appraisal in which relative values are applied to the performance characteristics of the people in the same job classification, thus placing them in the order of perceived merit

Rate of return   The surplus that a firm receives from an investment after the investment is recovered

Real-time computation   The recording and reporting of events by a computer the instant they occur

Reciprocal trade agreements   Arrangements by two or more firms to buy from each other, regardless of objective purchasing criteria

Recruitment   The search for potential employees to fill job openings

Reliability of tests   The capability of generating consistent test results over time

Research and development   Two activities—often but not always combined in particular organizations—which include the testing of product ideas and the getting of likely products ready for the commercial market, respectively

Responsibility The obligation of a manager to properly execute authority

Retraining Teaching new skills to employees whose former jobs have become obsolete

Reward system A particular company's system of distributing raises, bonuses, and promotions for reasons of merit or seniority

Rules Stipulations concerning the personal conduct of employees in such matters as care of company property, times for starting and quitting, safety precautions, etc.

Safety need The compulsion that people have to feel secure from physical, social, and economic threats

Salary Compensation paid to a jobholder on a weekly, monthly, or yearly basis

Satisficing Selecting, from a limited number of alternative solutions, one that is satisfactory, though not necessarily optimal

Scalar chain The ladder-like chain of command linking superiors and subordinates from the top to the bottom of organizations

Scanlon Plan A group incentive system in which management and labor work together to improve productivity

Scientific management A philosophy, commonly associated with Frederick W. Taylor, dedicated to improving efficiency through the elimination of wasted effort

Self-actualization need The need people have to attain their full potential

Semantics Meanings that people attach to words

Seniority An employee's length of service—with the company, in a department, or in a particular job classification

Sensitivity training A group process in which individuals learn of their impact on other people and of ways to correct negative behavior

Sensor In a control system, a person, machine, or process that measures actual units of output

Service relationships Interactions characterized by the rendering of specialized service by one department to other departments, such as recruiting and screening of job applicants by the personnel department

Short-term plan Implementation of the long-term plan for the immediate period ahead—prepared in detail and intended to be carried out exactly as stated

Simulation Imitation of real conditions so that the outcome can be predicted

Single-purpose plan A plan applied to a single and probably nonrecurring series of future decisions, often called a program or project

Slipped schedules Missed deadlines, causing postponement of planned events

Social responsibilities All responsibilities charged to a manager that are external to the obligations to the company's stockholders

Software Computer programming, rather than the equipment itself (hardware)

Span of control The number of subordinates that report directly to a manager

Speedup practices Techniques for getting employees to produce more, such as periodically adjusting higher the criteria for a normal day's work

Staffing   Developing and maintaining the human resource of an organization

Standing plans   Policies, procedures, and rules intended as guides to decisions made regularly

Statistical quality control   Use of sampling inspection for determining the probability that any sample is representative of the lot

Stockholders   Owners of shares of stock in a corporation

Strategic factors   Factors that most critically stand in the way of objectives and thus make a significant difference between the success or failure of a plan

Strategies   Complex long-term plans focused on broad goals

Supporting activities   Broad elements of work that back up, or assist, a firm's central activities

Systems theory   A way of looking at every organization as part of a larger whole, in constant interaction with all other subsystems

Tactics   Detailed short-term plans focused on specific goals

Task force   A team comprising people with different skills, assembled to work on a specific problem or project

Technical functions   Things that people do on their jobs that are specific to a task and are nonmanagerial

Termination   The action—either discharge or layoff—taken by a company to remove an employee from the payroll

Theory X/Theory Y   Diametrically opposite views of worker motivation, pointed out by Douglas McGregor. In Theory X, workers are viewed as naturally lazy and resistant to work and must be strictly controlled by management; in Theory Y, workers are perceived as avidly seeking responsibility and capable of accomplishing great things on their own if given the opportunity

Training   Teaching workers how to do some technical task

Trait theory of leadership   The view that leadership could be predicted on the basis of the possession of certain traits

Unequal-status relationships (nonvertical)   Interactions between members of different departments who are at different status levels

Unity of command   The traditional principle that no subordinate should receive directions from more than one boss

Validity   Accuracy of screening devices for selecting applicants—ascertainable by the subsequent performance on the job of those hired

Variable costs   Costs, such as those for labor and material, that vary in proportion to a firm's sales volume

Vertical relationships   Interactions between managers and the subordinates who report directly to them

Wage range   The spread between the minimum and maximum compensation for a job grade

Wages   Compensation paid to jobholders on an hourly or daily basis

Zone of indifference   A term Chester Barnard used to designate the area occupied by the type of supervisory orders that workers regard as acceptable

NAME INDEX

Page references in roman type are to mentions of given individuals within the text; those in italic type are to citations of their works in the bibliographies.

Ardrey, Robert, 318, *348*
Argyris, Chris, 27, *40, 184, 348*
Aristotle, 258

Barnard, Chester I., 23–25, 38, *40, 133, 184,* 502, 505, 507, 510
Baumgartner, John Stanley, *184*
Baumol, William J., *40*
Bayfield, Arthur H., *348*
Belcher, David W., *265*
Bendix, Reinhard, *40*
Benne, Kenneth D., *348*
Bennis, Warren G., 28, *40, 348*
Berg, Ivar, *475*
Berle, Adolf A., Jr., *475*
Blau, Peter M., *441*
Boddewyn, J., *40*
Bowen, Howard R., *475*
Bower, M., *265*
Brady, Rodney H., *475*
Buffa, Elwood S., *265, 441*
Burck, Gilbert, *475*

Calvin, John, 318
Carlson, Phillip G., *97*
Cartwright, Dorwin, *348*
Chapple, Eliot D., *265*
Chin, Robert, *348*
Chruden, Herbert J., *348*
Cordiner, R. J., *184*
Crockett, Walter H., *348*

Dale, Ernest, *40, 184, 441*
Dalton, Melville, *184*
Dantzig, G. B., 31
Darwin, Charles, 318, 346
Dauten, Paul M., Jr., *40*
Davis, R. C., *40*
Dean, Neal J., *475*
Dennis, W., *348*
Dickson, W. J., *40*
Drucker, P. F., *97*

Emerson, Harrington, 10
Etzioni, Amitai, *184, 441*
Fayol, Henri, 15–18, 38, *40,* 68, 507

Fetter, Robert B., *441*
Filley, A. C., *40*
Franklin, Benjamin, 319
French, Wendell, *265*
Freud, Sigmund, 319, 322, 347, *348*

Gantt, Henry, 10, 13, 386–387
Gellerman, Saul W., *265*
Gerth, H. H., *348*
Gilbreth, Frank, 10
Gilbreth, Lillian, 10, 13
Glaser, George, *475*
Goetz, B. E., *40*
Gross, Martin L., *265*

Haire, Mason, *265*
Hand, Learned, 464
Harper, Shirley F., *265*
Henning, D. A., *97*
Herzberg, Frederick, *265,* 316–317, *348*

Jacques, E., *184*
James, Virgil A., *265*
Janger, Allen R., *184*
Johnson, Richard A., *40, 441*

Kast, Fremont E., *40, 441*
Katz, D., *184, 348*
Katz, Fred E., *184, 348*
Knight, F. H., 31
Koontz, Harold, *40, 97, 184*

Lawrence, Paul R., *184*
LeBreton, P. P., *97*
Leontief, Wassily W., 31
Likert, Rensis, *348*
Litterer, Joseph A., *184*
Littlefield, C. L., *265*
Lorsch, Jay W., *184*

Machiavelli, Niccolò, 163, 165–166
March, James G., *184*
Martin, Norman, 164–165
Maslow, Abraham H., 27, *40,* 159, 291, 296–298, 345–346, *348,* 505

Massarik, Fred, *349*
Mausner, Bernard, *285*
Mayo, Elton, 19, 23, 26, *40*
McClelland, David C., 291, 303–306, 346, *348,* 502
McCormick, Ernest J., *265*
McGregor, Douglas M., 27–28, *40, 184,* 271–272, *348,* 510
Mechanic, David, *184*
Metcalf, Henry C., *349*
Miles, Raymond E., *441*
Miller, D. W., *97*
Mills, C. Wright, *348*
Mitchell, W. N., *475*
Morgenstern, Oscar, 31

Neumann, John von, 31
Newman, William H., *40, 97, 348, 441*

Odiorne, George S., *349*
O'Donnell, Cyril, *40, 97, 184*

Packard, David, 467
Parsons, Talcott, *349*
Patton, John A., *265*
Petersen, E., *40*
Plowman, E. G., *40*

Raudsepp, Eugene, *349*
Reeser, Clayton, *349*
Ridgway, V. F., *441*
Roethlisberger, F. J., 19, *40*
Rosenzweig, James E., *40, 441*
Rosow, Jerome M., *349*

Sayles, Leonard R., *184, 265, 441*
Scanlon, Joseph, 309, 509
Schlender, William E., *40*
Schmidt, Warren H., *349*

Scott, W. G., *40*
Scott, W. Richard, *441*
Self, Stanley Allen, *265*
Sevin, Charles H., *441*
Shannon, Claude E., *349*
Sherman, Arthur W., Jr., *348*
Simon, Herbert A., 32, *40, 184*
Sloan, Alfred P., Jr., *40, 184*
Snyderman, Barbara, *265*
Spriegel, William R., *265*
Starr, M. K., *97*
Steiner, G. A., *97*
Summer, Charles E., *97, 348, 441*
Suojanen, W. W., *184*
Sweet, Franklin H., *97*

Tannenbaum, Robert, *349*
Taylor, Frederick W., 10–14, 17, 18, 23, 34, 38, *40,* 40, 76, 207, 292, 354, 502, 509
Tead, Ordway, *349*
Tiffin, Joseph, *265*

Vergin, Roger C., *441*
Vroom, Victor H., *349*

Walras, Leon, 31
Warren, E. Kirby, *97, 348, 441*
Weaver, Warren, *349*
Weber, Max, 6–9, 23, 24, 38, 40, 76, 269, 305, 319, *348, 349,* 502
Weschler, Irving, *349*
Whisler, Thomas L., *265*
Whitehead, T. N., 19
Wickstrom, Walter S., *349*
Winter, David G., *348*

Zander, Alvin, *348*

SUBJECT INDEX

A B C inventory analysis, 389–390, 502

Absenteeism, 211

Acceptance, by subordinates, of objectives, 270, 345; of prescribed methods, 24–25, 270, 345

Acceptance sampling, 397–400, 439, 502

Acceptance theory of authority, 25, 133

Accountability, 7, 461

Achievement need, 272, 291, 303–306, 342, 346, 502

Activating agent, 422–423, 440

Activities, central, 101–102, 107–109, 143–144, 150–152, 181, 502; supporting, 101–102, 109, 111, 143–144, 150–152, 181, 510; work, 100–102, 181, 187–188

Adjustments to corrective actions, 432

Advertising effectiveness, control of, 405–406, 439

Advisory relationships, 143–149, 182, 433, 502; change of role in, 144; how established, 143; impact of, on authority, 145; and line-staff concept, 143; reactions to, 145, 433; reasons for, 143–144

Aerojet-General, 69

Aggregate control, 382–383, 438, 502

Allocated costs, 362, 405, 412, 431

Alternatives, 88, 502; computer's ability to discriminate between, 445; for decision making, 31, 41, 88; for inducing change, 331–333; for production control, 384–385; for quality control, 396; for taking effective action, 356

Amplification, of a message, 325–326, 347, 424, 502

Analytical techniques. See Quantitative techniques

Antitrust laws, 463–464, 478

Applicants, job, selection of, 222–226, 263; sources of, 218–221, 263; testing of, 231–234, 263

Appraisal, performance. See Performance appraisal

Aptitude tests, 231–232

Army, psychological testing in, 231

"Assistant to" positions, 240–241

Attributes, examine for, 396–397, 439, 504

Attrition, of manpower resource, 211

Authoritarian leadership, 271, 276–279, 345, 347, 502

Authority, acceptance theory of, 25, 133; as "cement" of an organization, 23; centralization of, 136–138, 182, 451–452; chain of, 327–328; computer's impact on, 452–454; concentration of, 7; control as synonym for, 352; definitions of, 132, 502; hierarchy of, 6–8, 505; how much assigned, 7; levels, 6; for a project, 119; responsibility for using, 16, 133–134; source of, 132–133, 452–453; specialists' impact on, 145, 452–453; structure of, 7; unilateral exercise of, 133, 277, 332, 334, 347; vertical, 132–135

Automation, 212–213, 446–449. See also Computer

Average outgoing quality, 399–400

Back order, 384, 502

Balance sheet, 370, 422, 424, 502

Balance sheet analysis, 370–372, 438; current ratio, 371–372; equity/debt ratio, 372; quick ratio, 372; ratio analysis, 370

Ball of work concept, 10, 13, 502

Behavioral approach, 26–29, 38, 502

Behavioralists. See Behavioral scientists

Behavioral research, 179, 433

Behavioral scientists, basic assumptions of, 26–28; contributions of, 179, 268, 292; criticism of control systems, 428–433, 440; findings concerning resistance to change, 334; methods of, 28; role of, in effecting change, 26

Bill of Rights, 258

Black box, 35–37, 502

Boards of directors, 460–461

Boeing, 69

Breakeven analysis, 372–374, 402, 438

Budgetary financial control, 362–369, 438; corrective action in, 367–368, 438, 414; example of, 362–367; investigating deviations in, 367, 414

Budgets, kinds of, 438; overruns, 431; for research and development, 412, 414, 439; sales, 56, 362–369; padding of, 429

Bureaucracy, 6–9, 38, 502; assumptions of behavioralists about, 28; principles of, 6–9; as related to scientific management, 13; similarity to systems theory, 36

Capital, budgeting, 362–369, 454; as a resource, 65–66, 90–91, 185, 353, 438

Capital investment plan, 64–66, 374–376, 438

Carrying costs, of inventory, 392–395

Cash forecast, 213

Central activities, 101–102, 107–109, 143–144, 150–152, 181, 502

Centralization, of authority, 17, 136–138, 182, 451–452, 502

Change, accomplishing of, 29, 330–335, 347, 443; *by change agent*, 29, 331, 335, 503; *by consensus*, 333, 347; *by explanation*, 332, 347; *by involvement*, 333, 347; *by manipulation*, 332, 347; of a firm's objectives, 44; *time needed to accomplish*, 333–335; *unilateral*, 332, 347; control of, 297; plan for, 29, 212, 443; resistance to, 331–335; threat of, 297, 332, 450

Change of status, by demotions, 252, 264; by discharges, 252, 264; by job transfers, 253; by lateral changes, 253, 264; by layoffs, 252, 264; managing of, 250–253; by promotions, 251–252, 258, 264; by terminations, 252, 264

Charismatic leadership, 269, 503

Chief executive officer, 119, 132, 503; setting salary of, 196, 203

Clayton Act, 463–464

Cliques, avoidance of, 219; in informal organizations, 160–161; as power resources, 164

Cohesiveness, of sensitivity training group, 338–340; of work group, 307–308, 346, 503

Collection period, 56–57, 424, 503

Colonial Insurance Company, 188

Commanding, Fayol's definition of, 15–16

Commercial employment agencies, 219

Committees, 156, 178, 180, 437, 503

Communication, barriers to, 328–330, 338; as "cement" of organizations, 23; channels of, 81, 323–328; distortion in, 82–83, 128, 324–329, 423; by grapevine, 155, 161, 183; process of, 24, 323–330, 347, 503; *in bypassing authority chain*, 327–328; *with manager as sender*, 324–325; *model of*, 323–324; *receivers' role in*, 324–329, 347; *senders' role in*, 324–329, 347; *with subordinates as senders*, 325–327, 330

Comparator, 421, 440, 503

Compensation. *See* Financial compensation; Indirect compensation

Competition, and conflict, 169; definition of, 503; in free enterprise, 462–464; as incentive to workers, 163, 293, 295, 345; negative aspects of, 293–294

Computer, 9, 138, 354, 444–454, 473; applications of, 445–447; *automation*, 212–213, 446–449; *data storage*, 447; *data processing*, 354, 445–446; *forecasting*, 447; *real-time computation*, 446, 508; *simulation*, 447, 449; characteristics of, 444–445; *discriminatory*, 445; *mechanical*, 444; human consequences of, 212–213, 238, 449–451; language of, 450; latent capabilities of, 449, 474; organizational implications of, 138, 212–213, 451–454; as related to bureaucracy, 9; Wharton model of, 447

Conflict, organizational, 167–170, 183; definition of, 503; development of, 167; effects of, 169; goal, 83; locations for, 168; reduction of, 170, 336–338; source of, 433, 440

Conformity, 133, 503; in informal groups, 308, 311–314; pressures for, 173, 176, 322; resigned, 430

Conglomerate mergers, 460, 464, 503

Constitution, U.S., 258

Control, behavioral criticism of, 428–433, 440; budgetary financial, 362–369, 438; inventory, 388–394, 439; marketing, 400–406, 439; nature of, 352–357, 438; *via corrective action,* 356; *via reports,* 354–355; *standards for,* 352–354; *strategic factors in,* 354–355; nonbudgetary financial, 370–376, 438; in product organization, 109; production, 382–387; 438; research and development, 410–415, 439; statistical quality, 396–400, 439; systems approach to, 420–424; by variables, 397, 503

Control agents, 28, 430, 433

Control systems, behavioral criticism of, 428–433, 440; damaging evaluations, 431; illegitimacy of control agents, 433; inhibitive standards, 429–430; multiplicity of controls, 422; problems of adjustment, 432; problems of measurement, 430–431; resistance to, 428–429

Controlling, 351–440, 503; definition of, Fayol's, 16; description of, 352; need for. in decentralization, 136

Coordination, 177–179, 183; achieving of, 178–179; definition of, Fayol's, 16; of functional departments, 108; as managerial function, 1, 323; means for, 99; what it is, 177

Corporate bigness, 459–465; and diffusion of ownership, 459–460; means for controlling, 462–465; *antitrust laws,* 463–464; *free enterprise,* 462–463; *other government controls,* 464–465; *public action,* 465; and power of corporate managers, 459–465

Corrective action, 355–356, 367–368, 432, 438

Corrective justice, 258, 260–261

Corrector, 421, 440, 503

Critical incident appraisal method, 247, 264, 503

Critical-path scheduling, example of, 479–485; network analysis in, 89; in Polaris program, 90; problem, 486; uses of, 89–90, 94, 96

Current ratio, 371–372, 503

Customers, profitability of, 403–404, 439

Cybernetics. *See* Feedback; Systems management

Data banks, 447, 503

Data processing, 445–446, 503

Decentralization, of authority, 134–138, 182, 451–452; advantages of, 137–138; definition of, 134–135, 136, 503; extent of, 137; factors in, 136; present trend in, 138

Decision factors, 88, 453

Decision making, 39; as choosing, 88, 503; in committees, 178; the computer in, 138, 451–454; delegation of, 137, 277–278, 283; location of, 135, 278; as a mathematical process, 31–34, 88–94, 96, 354–355; models for, 32–33; nonprogrammed, 69, 74; optimizing as, 31–32; policies to guide, 144; programmed, 70; satisfying as, 32. *See also* Planning; Plans

Decision theory, 31, 92–94, 96

Deductive method, 269

Delays, in communication, 423–424

Delegation, of decision making, 137, 277–278, 283

Demand, for a firm's products, 382–388

Democratic leadership, 272, 276–279, 345, 347, 503

Demotions, 252, 257, 259, 264, 345

Departmental levels, 126–128

Departmentation, 1, 107–121, 181; act of, 132; conventional, 107–111, 181; functional, 107–108, 117, 167, 181; geographical, 110, 117, 181;. product, 107–109, 117, 181; project, 116–121, 181

Development. *See* Management development

Directing, 267–349, 351, 504; of engineering and scientific personnel, 341–344, 347; future changes in, 443; span of control for, 126–131; as synonym for controlling, 352

Directors, 460–462

Disability Insurance, 208

Discharges, 252, 257, 264, 504

Disciplinary action, 258–261, 291

Discounted rate of return, 65, 374–376, 380, 438, 504

Distortion, of communication, 324–329, 423–424
Distributive justice, 258–260
Diversification, of product lines, 42, 504
Division of work, 16, 172, 187, 317, 386, 504
Down time, 378, 384, 504
Drives, 291
Du Pont, 108

Econometric models, 51, 504
Economic life, 375, 504
Economic order quantity, 392–395, 504
Educational institutions, assistance to, 467; as sources of job applicants, 219
Efficiency, as end objective, 6; indifference to, 171; logistic, 110; systems designed for, 99
Efficiency experts, 430. *See also* Scientific management
Empirical data, 33, 504
Employee-centered management, 272, 276–279, 345, 504
Employment application forms, 222–223, 231
Engineers, directing of, 341–344, 347. *See also* Professional employees
Entropy, of manpower resource, 211
Equilibrium, of business power, 463, 468; of a system, 39, 331, 424, 451
Equity/debt ratio, 372, 504
Esteem need, 297, 316–317, 346, 504
Ethical teachings, as motivators, 319
Evaluations, resentment toward, 431. *See also* Performance appraisal
Evaluative relationships, 155–156, 182, 504
Evolution theory, 318, 346

Fair Labor Standards Act, 206, 260
Federal Reserve Bank, 51
Federal Reserve Board Industrial Production Index, 50
Feedback, 422–424, 504; adjusting to, 178, 183; as feature of systems theory, 36; of possible future results, 351; loop, 421–424, 431, 504; in project organization, 119; provision for, 440; requirement of, in n Ach people, 303

Fiduciary institutions, 461
Financial compensation, 185, 204–207, 213, 262; in commissions, 207; legislated minimum of, 206–207, 262; for overtime work, 260; for piecework, 207; range, 204, 510; through profit sharing, 207; in salary, 196, 204; in wages, 204, 206–207, 259
Financial incentives, 11–12, 207, 292, 345
Fire-fighting tactics, 180, 356, 504
Fixed costs, 372–374, 504
Fixed-order quantity, 391, 439
Fixed-reorder cycle, 391, 439
Forced-choice method, 247, 264, 504
Forecasting, 48–51, 55, 62, 95, 504; of aggregate demand, 382–383; by computer, 447; of flow of earnings, 414; of future job openings, 185; pioneered by Fayol, 15; as related to future results, 351
Fortran, 480
40 plus associations, 221
Free enterprise, 462–463
Frequency distribution, 92, 493, 504–505
Freudian psychology, 319, 322
Fringe benefits. *See* Indirect compensation
Frustrations, 172–173, 183, 187, 414, 431, 505
Functional authority, 144–145, 505
Functional boundary lines, 167–168, 505
Functional organization, 107–108, 117, 167, 181, 505; subsystems, 34
Functional-sequence relationships, 154–155, 182, 505
Functions, commonality of managerial, 2, 15; emphasis on, 108; of managers, 1–3, 36, 454, 505; maximizing and minimizing, 31, 91; objective, 91; types of managerial, *controlling,* 351–440; *directing,* 267–349; *organizing,* 99–183; *planning,* 41–96; *staffing,* 185–265

Game theory, 31
Gantt charts, 386–387
General Electric, 108
General equilibrium theory, 31
General Motors, 108

Geographical organization, 110, 117, 181, 505
Goals, 42-44; conflicting, 82–83, 173, 183; divergent, effects of, 173, 183; feedback essential for achieving, 178–179, 183, 351, 421–422; personal, 173, 183, 270, 370, 345; short-term, 284. *See also* Objectives
Gordon Personal Profile and Inventory, 232
Government controls, 464–465
Grapevine, 155, 161–162, 183, 505
Graphic rating scale, 246, 264, 505
Grass roots forecasting, 50
Grievance procedure, 260–261, 264
Gross National Product (GNP), 50
Group behavior, 307–310, 346; in Hawthorne studies, 21
Group dynamics. *See* Sensitivity training

Handicapped, jobs for, 467
Hawthorne studies, 19–22, 28
Hewlett-Packard, 467
Hierarchy, of authority levels, 6–8, 505; of human needs, 296–298, 346, 505
Human engineering, 188, 505
Human needs, 296–298, 346; esteem, 297, 316–317, 346, 504; hierarchical arrangement of, 296, 346, 505; for love, 297, 346, 506; physiological, 296, 346, 507; for safety, 296–297, 346, 509; for self-actualization, 272, 297–298, 317, 342, 346, 509
Human relations approach, 13, 19–22, 505

Incentives, 291–295; achievement as, 303–306, 346; competition as, 293–294, 345; definition of, 291, 505; example of, 294, 345; money as, 11–13, 207, 237, 292–293, 345; motivation through, 291–295; as need satisfiers, 296; negative, 11, 270, 291, 345; participation as, 83, 294, 345, 430; positive, 271, 291, 345; promotion as, 237, 293, 345; recognition as, 292, 345; security as, 294, 297, 345; success as, 237
Indirect compensation, 208–210, 213, 262; classifications of, 208–209; control of, 210, 262; definition of,

Indirect compensation (*cont.*)
505; importance of, 208, 262; paternalism of, 21; returns to firm from, 209
Inducement-contribution balance, 24, 505
Induction method, 269
Inflation, combatting, 466
Informal organization, 158–161, 171, 182, 308–309, 505; from Barnard, 24; distinguishing features of, 158; grapevine in, 161–162, 183; inner workings of, 160, 336–339, 347; roots of, 160
Information copy system, 327–328
Information systems, efficiency of, 386–388
Input, 35–37, 353, 382, 386–387, 422, 447; definition of, 25, 505
Input/output analysis, 31, 353–355
Inspection, for quality control, 396–400
Intelligence tests, 231–232
Interviews, methods of, 223–224; *nondirective*, 224, 505; *patterned*, 224, 505; *stress*, 224, 230, 505; mistakes of, 225–230, 263; performance, 247–248; preliminary, 223, 263; subsequent, 223, 263
Inventory, definition of, 506
Inventory control, 388–394, 439, 445; A B C analysis for, 389–390, 502; of order quantity, 392–394; responsibility for, 388; systems of, 390–391
Inventory of manpower, 211. *See also* Manpower planning

Job, 177, 187, 506; composition, 187–188; descriptions, 189–190, 194–195, 506; design, 172, 187–190, 194, 262, 443; elements, 198; enlargement, 187–188, 262, 506; financial compensation for, 185, 204–207, 213, 262; grade, 223; monotony, 172; and position, 187; reasons for creating, 187; regimentation, 172–173; satisfaction, 82; *criteria for assessing*, 315–316; *definition of*, 315, 506; *dilution of*, 128; *as distinct from morale*, 315; *extrinsic*, 317; *Herzberg's studies concerning*, 316–317; *instruments for measuring*,

Job (*cont.*)
315–316; *intrinsic,* 13, 317; *motivation through,* 314–317, 346; *removed from work,* 13, 172–173; as smallest subsystem, 177, 187; specifications, 189–190, 506; transfers, 253

Job evaluation, methods of, *factor comparison,* 197, 199, 262; *grade or classification,* 197; *point,* 197–199, 262; *ranking,* 197, 262, 506; problems in, 198–199, 203; of top-level jobs, 196

Jobs, 185, 211, 443; for experienced managers, 220–221; for the handicapped and underprivileged, 466–467, 469; for management trainees and professional employees, 220; relative worth of, 185, 196–199, 204, 258, 262; subject to programming, 448–449; wage and commission type, 218–220

Justice, assurance of, 17, 258–261, 264; corrective, 258, 260–261, 506; distributive, 258–260, 506; meanings of, 258

Justice Department, 464

Labor, costs, 368, 373, 382–386; supply, 206, 208, 211–213, 219. *See also* Unions, labor; Workers; Work force

Laissez-faire economics, 331

Lateral changes, 253, 264

Lateral relationships, 143–157, 182, 506; advisory, 143–145, 182; evaluative, 155–156, 182; functional-sequence, 154–155, 182; nonvertical unequal-status, 156–157, 182; service, 150–152, 182; significance of, 154, 182

Layoffs, 252, 259, 264, 506

Leadership, 268–272, 290, 345; as an acquired ability, 271; characteristics of, 345; charismatic, 268; effective, 270, 345; natural, 268, 345; trait theory of, 269

Leadership styles, 276–279, 345; authoritarian, 276–279, 345; democratic, 276–279, 345; employee-centered, 276–279, 345; production-centered, 276–279, 345

Lead time, 506; in production control, 57; in inventory control, 391–392

Leading indicators, 50, 506

Life cycle of a product, 44, 401–403, 439, 506

Line-staff relationship, 143, 154, 168, 433, 506

Linear programming, 30, 90–91, 96, 487–492, 506

Long-term adjustments, 356

Long-term plans, 68–77, 506; priority of, 68; current emphasis on, 68; length of, 68–69; nature of, 69–70

Love need, 297, 346, 506

Management, definition of, 1, 506; definition of, Fayol's, 15; employee-centered, 272, 276–279, 345, 504; mathematical approach to, 30–33, 39; principles, 267; production-centered, 271, 276–279, 345, 508; of a project, 37; scientific, 10–14, 509; systems, 34–37, 39; theorists, 267; theory, evolution of, 3, 5

Management by objectives, 249, 264, 284, 290, 294, 333, 345, 430, 433, 506; advantages of, 284–285; as appraisal method, 286, 290; motivational value of, 294; preparation for, 285, 290; results of, 285, 430; significant feature of, 284

Management development, 238–241, 263, 504; criteria for validating, 241; on middle-management level, 240; mistaken belief concerning, 238; plan, 64–65, 67; on supervisory level, 240; on top-management level, 241; vs. training, 239

Managerial, function, 1, 505; functions, from Fayol, 15–16; position, duties of, 7; role, 185, 278, 469

Managers, as communicators of messages, 324–325; computer's impact on, 444–454, 473; conflict between, 168; corporate, power of, 459–465; of the future, 443–473; as inducers of change, 332–335, 347; professional, 8, 461; project, 119; purpose of, 1; of research and development, 412–413; roles in vertical structure, 134; social responsibilities of, 465–469; span of control, 126–128, 181, 267, 283, 509

Manpower planning, 64, 66–67, 211–217, 262

Marketing control, 400–406, 439, 507; of advertising effort, 405–406, 439; of product line, 401–403, 439; profitability as measurement in, 400–406, 439; of selling effort per customer, 403–404, 439; of territory, 404–405, 439

Market system, 462–463, 507

Mathematical approach, 31–33, 39

Maximizing function, 31, 507

Measurement, problems related to, 430–431. *See also* Numerical terms; Quantitative techniques

Media, advertising, 405–406; of organizational communication, 324, 326

Merit, as basis for change in status, 251–253, 257–259, 264; as determined by performance appraisal, 246–250; increases, 260

Mileposts, 355, 414, 439

Minimizing function, 31, 507

Models, for decision making, 32–33, 51, 507

Money, as an incentive, 11–13, 207, 237, 292–293, 345

Monopolism, 463

Monte Carlo simulation. *See* Simulation

Morale, 315

Motivation, coordination through, 179; definition of, 291, 507; in future, 443; and human needs, 296–298; through incentives, 290–294, 345; through job satisfaction, 314–317, 346; and need for achievement, 303–306, 346; nonrational influences on, 318–319, 346–347; *animal ancestry,* 318; *ethical teachings,* 318–319; *Freudian psychology,* 319, 346; process of, 27; Taylor's principles of, 11–13; through work group, 307–309, 346

Motivators: *See* Incentives; Motivation

Multinational companies, 443

National Research Council, 19

National Training Laboratory, 336

Natural leaders, 268, 346

Navy, psychological testing in, 231

Need for achievement, 291, 303–306, 346

Need hierarchy, 27, 291, 296–298, 345–346

Network analysis. *See* Critical-path scheduling

New Jersey Bell Telephone Company, 23

Newspaper classified advertising, 219

Nonbudgetary financial control, 370–376, 438; balance sheet analysis, 370–372, 438; breakeven analysis, 372–374, 438; capital investment evaluation, 374–376, 438

Nonunion employees, redress of grievances, 261, 264

Nonvertical unequal-status relationships, 156–157, 182

Norms, defined, 507; of work group, 21, 307, 346

North American Rockwell, 69

Numerical terms, 43, 88–89, 430–431, 438, 453

Objectives, 42–44, 95, 270, 345, 440, 507; of a bureaucracy, 7; of Hawthorne studies, 19; of manpower planning, 212; in numerical terms, 43; in the planning function, 41; as prerequisites to planning, 23; primary, 42; supporting, 44. *See also* Goals; Management by objectives

Objectivity, of controls, 431

Obsolescence, of inventory, 392; of managerial functions, 444; of products and processes, 212–213, 443; of skills, 212–213, 237–238, 448–451, 466

Old Age Insurance, 208

Oligopoly, 463

One best way, 11, 38, 76, 507

Open door policy, 261

Operations, scale of, 212

Optimization, 31–33, 507

Ordering costs, 392–395

Organization, development, 28–29, 451, 507; functional, 107–108, 117, 167, 181, 505; geographical, 110, 117, 181, 505; need deprivation in, 159; plan, 64; product, 107–109, 117, 181, 508; project, 116–121,

Organization (*cont.*)
181, 508; in rigid, structural sense, 23
Organizational levels, 117, 126–128
Organizations, complexity of, 144, 154; as cooperative systems, 23; conflict in, 167–170; definition of, 507; evolution of, 99, 150–151; formal, 171–173, 183; frustrations in, 171–173, 183; informal, 21, 24, 308–309; power politics in, 163–166
Organizing, 99–183, 267, 351, 507; a continual process, 100; definition of, Fayol's, 15; deliberate and conscious, 158
Output, 35–37, 353, 382, 420–427, 447, 502, 507. *See also* Input/output analysis
Overhead, analysis of, 365; costs of, 368

Participation, in Hawthorne studies, 19–20; as an incentive, 83, 294, 345, 430; in job design, 188; in setting objectives, 249, 284–286, 345, 430; standards set by, 430
Peer rating, 156, 248, 507
Pension plans, 208–210
Perception, of arbitrary standards, 429; differences in, 81; of illegitimacy of control, 433; of managers by subordinates, 270–271
Performance appraisal, 185, 246–249, 259, 264, 507; new methods of, 248–249; results of, 248; subjectivity of, 232–233, 248; techniques of, 246–247, 264; use of, 247–248
Personnel department, 185, 218, 222
Physical examination, of job applicants, 223
Physiological need, 296, 346, 507
Piecework, 12, 207, 507
Planning, 41–96, 267, 479–499, 507; analytical techniques for, 88–94, 479–499; associated with control, 351; definition of, 507; definition of, Fayol's, 15; human factors in, 81–83, 95; manpower, 211–213, 262; pervasiveness of, 41; separation of, from performance, 12; at various organizational levels, 2

Plans, 56–77; budgets as, 362, 438; capital investment, 65; dependence of controlling on, 362; financial, 58, 95; long-term and short-term, 68–70; 95, 102, 137, 213, 506, 509; major, 56–58; management development, 64–65, 67; manpower, 64, 66–67, 211–217, 235, 262, 507; manufacturing, 57–58; organization, 64; production, 57–58, 95; program type of, 77; purchase, 57; research and development, 66, 410–414; sales, 56, 95; standing and single-purpose, 74–77, 95; supporting, 64–66
Plural relationships, 156, 182, 508
Point of diminishing returns, 406
Polaris program, 77, 90
Policies, 74–76, 508; as guides to decision making, 144; as related to rules, 6
Political campaigns, donations to, 465–467
Politics in organizations, 162–166, 183
Pollution, correction of, 467–469
Poor Richard's Almanack, 319
Positions, in organization structure, 7; as related to jobs, 187, 508
Postmortem examinations, 423
Power, of corporate managers, 459–465; definitions of, 162–163; Machiavelli's views on, 163, 165–166; and organizational politics, 162–166, 183, 508; steps in achieving, 164; will for, 162
Price controls, 464
Primary level of management, 107, 508
Principles, of bureaucracy, 6; of management, Fayol's, 15–17; of scientific management, 10–13; systematization of, 267
Probability, in quality control, 397–400, 439
Probability decision theory, 92–94, 96, 497–499, 508
Procedures, 6, 76, 508
Product life cycle, 44, 401–403, 439, 506
Product line, 401–403, 422, 439; diversification of, 42, 504
Product organization, 107–109, 117, 181, 508

Production-centered management, 271, 276–279, 345, 508
Production control, 382–387, 438, 445, 508; aggregate, 382–385, 438; basic, 386–387, 438; intermediate, 385–386, 438; response rate as factor in, 384–385, 438
Production schedule, 431. *See also* Schedules
Productivity, adverse effect of change on, 297; as affected by fringe benefits, 11–12, 21–22, 209–210, 262, 294; as affected by group norms, 307–314; decline in, 443; definition of, 508; Hawthorne studies of, 19–22; and job satisfaction, 296–306, 315–317, 346; incentives for, 291–295, 309–310, 346; and need satisfaction, 296–306, 314–317; quotas for, 293, 430, 436; and scientific management, 10
Professional employees, 341–344, 347; current policies toward, 341; uniqueness of, 341
Profit, definition of, 42; goals, 43–44
Profitability, controls to assure, 400, 430, 439
Profit-sharing systems, 207
Program, 77, 508
Program director, R & D, 412–414, 439
Programmed instruction, 236–237, 508
Project organization, 116–121, 181, 508; advantages of, 118; authority for, 119; criteria for applying, 121; differences from other forms, 117; management, 37; personnel, 116; problems in, 119–120, 194–195; similarities to other forms, 117; as task-force approach, 116
Promotions, 211, 251–252, 257, 259, 264, 293, 345
Protestant ethic, 305–306, 319
Psychological testing, 223, 231–234, 263, 508; attitudes toward, 233; characteristics measured by, 231–232; main purpose of, 230; problems in the use of, 222–223; reliability of, 233, 263, 508; requirements for, 234; secondary uses of, 230; supplemental value of, 230; validity of, 232

Public employment agencies, 218
Punishments, 258–261, 291. *See also* Incentives, negative
Purpose, of book, 1; of managers, 1; of organizations, 181; of rules, 6

Qualitative variables, for measurement, 430
Quality control, definition of, 508; statistical, 396–400, 439; acceptance sampling, 397–400, 439; *examining for attributes*, 396, 439; *average outgoing quality*, 399–400; *inspection*, 396–400; *operating characteristic curve*, 397–400; *probability*, 397–400; *variables in*, 397, 439
Quantitative techniques, for decision making, 31–34, 88–94, 96, 354–355, 508. *See also* Numerical terms
Quick ratio, 372, 508

Rank-order method, 246–247, 264, 508
Rate of return, 374–375, 508
Ratio analysis, 370
Real-time computation, 446, 508
Receivers, of communication, 324–329
Reciprocal trade agreements, 460
Recognition, as incentive, 292
Recruiting, of personnel, 185, 218–221, 263, 508; as centralized service, 218, 221; pirating in, 221; sources of applicants in, 218–221
Reference checking, 223, 225–226, 230
Referrals, by present employees, 219; from former employers, 225–226
Relationships, in organizations, advisory, 143–149, 182, 433, 502; evaluative, 155–156, 182, 504; functional-sequence, 154–155, 182, 505; other lateral, 154–157, 182; line-staff, 143, 154, 168, 433, 506; non-vertical unequal-status, 156–157, 182, 510; plural, 156, 182, 508; service, 150–152, 182, 433, 509; vertical, 132–135, 181, 510
Relative worth of jobs, 185, 196–199, 204, 258, 262
Reliability, of tests, 233, 263, 508

Reports, distribution of, 355; of output characterics, 422–423; sources of, 354

Research and development, control of, 213, 410–415, 439; *budgeting for,* 412, 439; *extent of,* 411; *facilities for,* 413; *staffing for,* 412–413; *techniques of,* 413; definition of, 411, 508–509; plan, 64, 66–67

Resistance, to change, 331–335; to control systems, 428–429; to job evaluation, 199

Resources, capital, 65–66, 90–91, 185, 353, 438; committed, 6; how well developed, 185; human, 1, 185–186, 211–213, 262–263; physical, 1, 3, 186

Response rate, of production, 384–385, 438

Responsibility, managerial, definition of, 133, 509; designation of, 421; effect of specialists on, 145; lack of clear-cut, 432; in project organization, 120; profit-making, 137, 460–461; social, 465–469

Retraining, 237–238, 466, 509

Rewards, 326–327, 430, 509. *See also* Incentives

Reward system, 271, 277, 282, 509

Rules, 76–77, 259, 509; purpose of, 6; stipulated, 6–7

Safety need, 296–297, 346, 509

Salary, 196, 204, 509. *See also* Financial compensation

Sales forecasting, 48–51, 55, 62, 95, 447

Sampling, 396–400, 439, 502

Satisficing, 32, 509

Scalar chain, 17, 509

Scanlon plan, 309–310, 313–314, 346, 509

Scatter diagram, 204–205

Schedules, facilitated by computer, 445; production, 57, 386–387, 431, 445; research and development, 413, 439; slipped, 331, 386–387, 431, 509

Scientific management, 10–14, 317, 509; and bureaucratic approach, 13; effects of, 12–13; and human relations approach, 13; and separation

Scientific management (*cont.*)
of planning from performance, 12; and worker motivation, 11–12, 317; and worker selection and training, 11

Scientists, directing of, 341–344, 347. *See also* Professional employees

Screening, of job applicants, 222–225, 230–234, 263; by interviews, 222–225; preliminary, 222; by psychological testing, 233, 230–234

Sears, 91

Security, as a need, 294, 345; willingness to risk, 302

Selection of new personnel, 185, 222–226, 230–234, 263; by interviews, 222–225; by physical examination, 223; by preliminary screening, 222; by psychological testing, 223; by reference checking, 225–226; Taylor's principle of, 11; validity of, 222

Self-actualization need, 272, 297–298, 317, 342, 346, 509

Self-esteem, lowering of, 172; need for, 297, 316–317, 346, 504

Semantics, 324

Senders, of communication, 324–329

Seniority, 250–253, 257–258, 264, 509

Sensitivity training, 335–339, 347, 509; application of, 336–337; concept of, 336; conduct of, 337–338; effectiveness of, 338–340; group cohesiveness in, 338; negative factors in, 339; in organization development, 28, 335

Sensor, 421, 423, 440, 509

Service relationships, 150–152, 182, 433, 509; characteristics of, 151; explanation of, 150; problems, resolution of, 152; reasons for, 150

Sherman Act, 463–464

Short-term adjustments, 356

Short-term plans, 70, 509

Simplex, 487–492

Simulation, 92, 96, 447; via computer, 447, 449; Monte Carlo, 92, 493–496

Single-purpose plan, 77

Slipped schedules, 331, 386–387, 431, 509

Social responsibilities, of corporate managers, 465–474; as citizens, 467;

Social responsibilities (*cont.*)
in the community, 467; conflicting viewpoints concerning, 468; economic, 466; for education and arts, 467; environmental, 467–468; for helping underprivileged groups, 466–467; for retraining workers, 237

Software, computer, 445–447, 509

Sources of job applicants, 218–221

Span of control, 126–128, 181, 267, 283; definition of, 509; over engineers and scientists, 343; factors affecting, 126–127, 181; wide, 128

Specialization, 107, 109–110, 144–145, 150–152, 167, 187, 340, 452–453

Speedup practices, 12–14, 430, 509

Staffing, 185–267, 351; definition of, 510; as perceived by Fayol, 15; of R & D effort, 412–413

Standards, definition of, 352; inhibitive, 429–432; milepost, 414; performance, 420–424, 428, 440; for production control, 382; quality, 396–400; ways of setting, 353–354, 438; of work, Taylor's, 11

Standing plans, 74–77, 510

Statistical quality control, 396–400, 510

Status, changes in, 264; discrepancies, 173; hierarchies, in informal groups, 182, 308; as incentive for training, 237; of job vs. position, 187; of scientific and engineering personnel, 341–344, 347; of sender vs. receiver, 328–329

Stimuli, 420–424, 429

Stockholders, 460–462, 475, 510

Strategic factors, 24, 354–355, 510

Strategies, 69, 510. *See also* Long-term plans

Strong Vocational Interest Blank, 232

Supporting activities, 101, 109, 111, 143–144, 150–152, 185

Supreme Court, 464

Survivors Insurance, 208

Systems, approach to control, 420–424, 440; *characteristics of,* 420–424, 440; *comparator,* 421, 440; *corrector,* 421, 440; *feedback loop,* 421–424, 440; *normative output,* 420, 440; *sensor,* 421, 440; manage-

Systems (*cont.*)
ment, 34–37, 39; theory, 420, 440, 510

Tactics, 70, 510

Task force, 118–121, 510. *See also* Project organization

Taylorism, 10, 19. *See also* Scientific management

Technical functions, 2, 510

Technology, advances of, 331; computer, 444; and decision making, 452; impact of, 212

Temporary National Economic Committee, 460–461

Tension, 28, 449–450

Terminations, 252, 264, 510

Territories, controlling profitability of, 404–405, 439

T groups. *See* Sensitivity training

Theory X/Theory Y, 27, 271–272, 510

Time, needed to accomplish change, 333–335

Time and motion study, 10–11

Training, 234–237, 259, 263; essential factor in, 237; vs. management development, 234; methods, 236–237; prerequisites for, 236; as retraining, 237–238, 466, 509; role of, 235; starting place for, 235; Taylor's principle of, 11

Trait theory of leadership, 269

Trend analysis, 355

Trial and error method, 449

Unemployment Compensation, 208

Unequal-status relationships (nonvertical), 156–157, 182, 510

Unions, labor, and ball of work concept, 13; contract, terms of, 76, 253, 259; as curb to business power, 468; demands of, 206, 262, 331, 443; grievance procedures of, 252–253, 260–261, 264; hiring hall as applicant source, 219; need satisfaction in, 173, 299–302; as negotiators of employee benefits, 208–209; policies imposed by, 76–80, 206, 432; position on merit/seniority, 204, 207, 253; pressures exerted by, 138, 443

United Steelworkers of America, 309

Unity of command, 117, 145, 510
University management programs, 241

Validity, of n Ach training, 305–306; of selection process, 222–223, 510; of tests, 232–233, 263; of units of measurement, 355
Variable costs, 372–373, 510
Variables, control by, 397, 439, 503; mathematical, 33, 90–91, 487–492
Variances, 363–366, 414, 438
Vertical relationships, 132–135, 181, 510; communication channel in, 324–327

Wage range, 204, 510
Wages, 204, 206–207, 259. *See also* Financial compensation
Wall Street Journal, 221
Wealth, concentration of, 459–460

Western Electric Company, 19
Women's Liberation Movement, 176
Wonderlic Personnel Test, 231
Work activities, 100–102, 181, 187–188
Workers, behavioralists' views concerning, 26–28, 38–39; Hawthorne studies concerning, 19–22, 38; and scientific management, 10–14, 38. *See also* Incentives; Informal organization; Productivity; Training; Unions, labor
Work force, 443
Work group, 307–310, 346; cohesiveness of, 307–308, 346, 503; collective power of, 308–309; norms of, 21, 307, 346
Working conditions, 259, 296
Workmen's Compensation, 208
Written documents, 6–7

Zone of indifference, 25, 510